One Good Trade

Founded in 1807, John Wiley & Sons is the oldest independent publishing company in the United States. With offices in North America, Europe, Australia and Asia, Wiley is globally committed to developing and marketing print and electronic products and services for our customers' professional and personal knowledge and understanding.

The Wiley Trading series features books by traders who have survived the market's ever changing temperament and have prospered—some by reinventing systems, others by getting back to basics. Whether a novice trader, professional or somewhere in-between, these books will provide the advice and strategies needed to prosper today and well into the future.

For a list of available titles, visit our Web site at www.WileyFinance.com.

One Good Trade

Inside the Highly Competitive
World of Proprietary Trading

MIKE BELLAFIORE

WILEY

John Wiley & Sons, Inc.

To my Mom and Dad for their unconditional love.

Published by John Wiley & Sons, Inc., Hoboken, New Jersey.
Published simultaneously in Canada.

For general information on our other products and services or for technical support, please contact our Customer Care Department within the United States at (800) 762-2974, outside the United States at (317) 572-3993 or fax (317) 572-4002.

Wiley also publishes its books in a variety of electronic formats. Some content that appears in print may not be available in electronic books. For more information about Wiley products, visit our web site at www.wiley.com.

Library of Congress Cataloging-in-Publication Data:

Bellafiore, Mike.
   One good trade : inside the highly competitive world of proprietary trading /
Mike Bellafiore.
       p. cm. – (Wiley trading series)
   Includes bibliographical references and index.
   ISBN 978-0-470-52940-9 (cloth); ISBN 9780470648971 (ebk); ISBN 9780470648988 (ebk);
   ISBN 9780470649008 (ebk)
   1. Speculation.   2. Derivative securities.   3. Investment banking.
4. Competition.   I. Title.
   HG6015.B45 2010
   332.64–dc22

                                                                    2010005945

Printed in the United States of America.

SKY10066825_020724

Contents

Preface

As the U.S. financial system neared the verge of collapse in the fall of 2008, a 23-year-old prop trader I know was about to pocket $30,000 for a day's work. Rewind to 1998 when some twenty-something prop traders, discards from the big banks, were putting away more than $10–25,000 a day without charts, CNBC in the background, a newsfeed, or even air conditioning. So what happened between 1998 and today? The Internet Boom and technical advances caused an explosion in proprietary trading but there was never a book written about it. Now there is.

During the past four years I have been growing a prop trading firm with my childhood friend, Steve Spencer. We started with nothing (not even a phone) and today our firm, SMB Capital, employs more than 60 traders. *One Good Trade* offers all the important lessons the market has taught me over the past 12 years in and around prop trading. I share these market lessons while introducing a cast of characters, some of whom have succeeded, and too many who have failed.

We will start with a look at traders to be emulated like MoneyMaker in Chapter 1, whose previous career as a professional golfer left him with a superior ability to focus, which he now uses daily to chop up the market. You will go inside this previously closed world of prop trading to learn who gets hired (classic Joe Biden story enclosed), how we trade (depends on the market), how we find the stocks we trade (you are only as good as the stocks you trade), our game-changing market fundamentals (One Good Trade), and our superior trading skills (It's called trading!). You will garnish a savoring taste of what is really important to become a successful prop trader.

Trading is about skill development and discipline. Unfortunately, too many people think trading is just about making predictions, loading up, and being "the man" by holding stocks (you will meet Crabby, who predicted the whole run in oil and never made a dime as a trader). Being a consistently profitable trader is about doing the thousand little things every day – like proper preparation – that impact your P&L.

As the partner of a proprietary trading firm, I spend a great deal of my time teaching. While I still trade actively, I am mostly a trading coach. What I teach my students and have learned from my traders I will share with you. Lessons like the importance of adapting which one experienced trader, Point-and-Click, was unable to do; he now sells insurance in New Jersey.

The light I shine on the world of prop trading will include my mistakes and those of other prop traders. A great trader is an elite performer. Elite performers spend every day trying to improve. Every day we trade is an opportunity to learn from the market. My mistakes and those of other prop traders are just gifts from the market for us to improve, and they will be shared so you can learn.

My firm, SMB Capital, will be used throughout this book as an example of how prop firms operate. SMB and its traders have been featured in the TV documentary *Wall Street Warriors*, appear regularly on CNBC, and have four regular spots on StockTwits TV. It's an entertaining place! Many of the learning experiences and anecdotes in this book come from my tenure as partner.

Too many traders do not know the stocks to trade and we will discuss how we find the Stocks In Play. Too many new and developing traders cannot Read the Tape and we will argue how that hinders their results. Most importantly, I will walk you through this P&L-changing skill.

After a speaking engagement, I was approached by Dapper Don to explain the value a prop firm can offer and I spend a chapter answering his question. I will debunk the myth that a new trader should seek out a superstar trader to learn best. Many new and developing traders could improve their P&L if they just understood how to "Score," and we will illuminate the importance of loss limits, ending a trading slump, and keeping excellent trading statistics.

A spot on a prop desk is a dream job for many people, yet they do not know how to succeed once they arrive. Bloomberg, CNBC, and Fox offer endless hours of professionals pontificating their opinions. Still, I know of many new and developing traders overwhelmed with information and empty with ideas to improve. We will use an old teaching technique of the head basketball coach at UCLA, John Wooden, to offer valuable suggestions in Chapter 4 (Pyramid of Success).

Along my trading and teaching journey, market fundamentals have been hammered into me by my boss, Mother Market. A trader with poor fundamentals is a ticking time bomb. That is why each trade for us is One Good Trade. At Duke University, Coach Krzyzewski yells, "Next Play" to his players. At SMB, we think One Good Trade, and then One Good Trade, and then One Good Trade. We judge each of our trades based upon whether we have followed seven fundamentals that compromise One Good Trade.

I have successfully navigated many different markets these past 12 years of trading. I will share my journey with the trading set-ups that worked best for each distinct trading period. Most importantly, I introduce the principle that has allowed me to profit in so many different markets: I adapt.

Welcome to a trading world where you can make your own trading decisions, each day is new, your upside is unlimited, and you likely sit around some funny people. In short, prop trading to me is the very best job in the world.

For the developing traders who are underperforming and for those interested in becoming new traders in the future, this book was written for you. The market has taught me the thousands of little things required to become successful. Many are undervalued by those who have not reached their trading potential. Welcome inside the highly competitive world of proprietary trading. A funny, exciting, enthralling place only for elite performers who master all the skills demanded by Mother Market.

CAST OF CHARACTERS

There are some traders you'll get to know very well through reading this book. Traders are known for using nicknames around the office, and our office is no exception.

Mike Bellafiore, Bella
Steve Spencer
GMan
JToma
Roy Davis
Alexander James
The Enforcer
Franchise
Dr. Momentum
MoneyMaker
The Yipster
Z$ (ZMush, Mush, Mushy, and Z)
G

In addition to their stories, you'll also hear from readers like yourself in the "Traders Ask" sections of the book. There are some questions about prop trading that I receive time and again via e-mail or the SMB Capital blog, and this will help answer some of them.

MIKE BELLAFIORE
June 2010

Acknowledgments

One Good Trade was a collaboration. It could not have been written without extensive contributions from the extraordinary team at Wiley and SMB Capital.

And without all those with whom I have traded, trained, mentored, met, shared emails, conversed via phone, heard of, and read about. To all of you, I offer my deepest gratitude!

Thank you to my ghost writer Chris Gillick for his brilliant writing. You are an extremely talented writer and good friend.

Thank you to my partners GMan, Gilbert Mendez, and Steve Spencer for covering for me all of those days I was sequestered writing this book.

Thank you to my best friend, Steve, for helping transform my idea to build the best equities training desk on the Street into our firm, SMB Capital. What an incredible, exhausting, challenging, and rewarding life experience it has been. I wouldn't have wanted to do this with anyone else.

Thank you to the best trading coach I know, Dr. Brett Steenbarger, for encouraging me to write this book and helping me make it happen. You gifted me the idea for *One Good Trade*, which I may have never contemplated on my own. You have inspired me to become a better teacher, mentor, trader, author and person.

Thank you to all those who have trained and traded with SMB. The best part of SMB will always be you, our traders.

Thank you to Alexander James for your invaluable daily input into this project. Everything you touched always became better.

Thank you to Charles Basner who makes everyday easier for me and a little bit more enjoyable. I hope you enjoy my Seinfeld references.

Thank you to Roy Davis, the best person I know to run SMB Training. When you do great work, you attract remarkable people, which is best demonstrated by your presence at SMB.

Thank you to our interns for your help with research:

Monique Yin
Krysten Sciacca

Bradford Arlington
Grant Yang
Joe Brummitt
Pedro Machado
Kurt Von Weisenstein
Alex Beygelman
Alex Sabharwal
Vishnu Anand
Patrick Traynor
Patrick Daniel
Violet Wang
Ben Klixbull
Brigitte Tugendhaft
Succharita Gaat
Jae Heo
Jay Zalowitz

When you become great traders please remember us.

A special thank you for those who took the time to endorse my book. You are all the best at what you do! I am tremendously grateful for your kind words:

Howard Lindzon, Tim Bourquin, Dr. Brett Steenbarger, Charles Kirk, Jason Gardner, Nadav Sapeika, Brian Shannon, Corey Rosenbloom, Damien Hoffman.

Thank you to Meg Freeborn for your awesome advice on content. Thank you to Melissa Lopez for walking me to the finish line. Thank you to Tiffany Charbonier for assisting on this brilliant cover. Thank you to Kevin Commins for finding me, giving me this opportunity, and steering me through this rewarding experience.

To my mom, your words are in every sentence. To my dad a huge hug and thanks for showing me the value of hard work though never saying a word on the topic.

To my beautiful fiancée, Meghan, the best part of my every day is my time spent with you. My best *One Good Trade* was committing to you.

To all those who have followed SMB on twitter @smbcapital, through our blog at www.smbtraining.com, on CNBC, on StockTwits TV, and reached out to me, thank you. The privilege to meet you and hear your trading war stories is my favorite part of writing.

PART I

Inside a Prop Trading Firm

CHAPTER 1

These Guys
Are Good

I belong to the most exciting part of Wall Street that no one pays attention to. That is, until now.

The kind of trading firm I co-founded, a proprietary trading firm, is not a bailed-out government bank, a broker-dealer, or a hedge fund, though it does run on some of the same core principles as those places.

Proprietary trading firms do somewhere between 50 and 70 percent of all the equity volume on the Street on any given day. Yes you read that correctly: 50–70 percent. Brokers bank hundreds of millions on firms like ours each month in trading commissions. This money flows to the coffers of clearing firms that take no risk but enjoy the rewards of the traders' hard work. The government also makes out nicely, raking in hundreds of millions annually in SEC taxes. (I'm not complaining, just offering facts.)

To offer some background, proprietary trading exploded during the Internet Boom. When I first began trading in the late 1990s, there were only a few firms hiring recent graduates to trade. There are no exact numbers on how many proprietary trading firms exist today, but the general consensus is more than a hundred and less than three hundred. Obviously this number is now much more than the handful that existed when I first began.

Unlike most firms on the Street, proprietary firms have no clients. We do not sell a product or help someone else sell a product. We do not take other people's money and speculate it on their behalf. A proprietary trader's after-hours schedule is not booked with dinners at New York City steakhouses like Sparks, drinks at the trendy Buddakan, or Rangers games (the Knicks are presently unwatchable). We don't need to schmooze.

We eat what we kill. Our profits are generated solely from the bets we make on our traders. When we are wrong, we lose our money. When we are right—and let me say that is a lot more fun—we keep a percentage of our winnings.

WELCOME TO THE WORLD OF PROPRIETARY TRADING

Proprietary trading (or "prop trading" for short) is done for the benefit of the company's partners and employees only, not for the benefit of any client. The firm is the client. A prop firm's traders actively speculate on stocks, bonds, options, commodities, derivatives, or other financial instruments with its own capital as opposed to customers' money.

There is no money made on insider tips at the legitimate prop firms. I wouldn't know an insider unless he walked onto my trading floor and announced, "Hey I am an insider. Get long BNI, Buffett is about to buy a stake in the company." My news comes mainly from Internet sites like briefing.com and Bloomberg.com—sites the whole world can access. Some proprietary firms have an interest in obtaining private research from institutional banks like Goldman Sachs and they can pay for access to it. We have access to some of this data but it does not make a difference. At my firm, SMB Capital, only the floor manager has a phone (his mom calls a lot). We depend on our trading talent. We eat what we kill. I wouldn't have it any other way.

There are some months when a prop trader works 50 hours a week and takes home no money. Heck, there are some months when a trader works even harder and loses money. I spent 2002 unable to make a dime. On the contrary, there have been days that a prop trader is up over $10k by 9:35 AM. He punches a few keys, the stock does what he thinks it will do, and he books these outsized profits faster than most drink a cup of coffee. In fact, there have been some mornings (Black Friday 1999, for example, when I sauntered onto my trading floor, turned on my computer screens, and saw that my account was up over 50k.) Now that is the way to start your morning! This is not one of those jobs where there are guaranteed contracts with a biweekly check that has the same numbers sprawled across the pay stub.

Many of the brightest of the bright leave our industry humbled (perhaps bitter?) by their inability to master the game. The smart ones figure out how to parlay their recent trading education into steady finance jobs. Juxtapose that with prop traders who make seven figures every year walking around in jeans and a t-shirt, sitting right next to overdressed bankers every morning on a downtown subway. I know it sounds unfair. But remember . . . in prop trading, *we* are the client. Would you dress up in a suit to impress yourself?

There is a very real chance that the uber bright-and-talented get sent home packing. It does not do anyone any good pretending to be a prop trader. This is just a lose/lose situation. The would-be trader loses by doing something he wasn't meant to do, and the firm loses time and capital (though other market players may wish for these suckers to stay, like dead money at a poker table). The market demands that a trader follows all of her rules, every day, and every moment. Many just cannot thrive in this unbending universe.

At a proprietary trading firm, the trader makes all of the decisions. Unlike most jobs, there is no supervisor or partner reviewing every decision before it's made. Success, for better or worse, is totally self-dependent. You determine whether a stock is more likely to go up or down and how much capital to risk. If you are correct, then the firm and you make money. Whether a trade works out or not, the results are plastered on a huge scoreboard both on your computer screen and on shared monitors, kind of like standings in the sports pages. Accountability and performance are brutally transparent.

Prop traders are not trying to beat VWAP (Volume-Weighted Average Price, or average intraday price of the stock) or fill orders for some client. For a proprietary trader, beating VWAP is about as difficult as it is for LeBron to put up 30. You are not entering orders as dictated by a portfolio manager, PM, or hedge fund manager. This is hands-on-the-wheel trading— you determine the markets and stocks to trade, the size of the trade, and the entry and exit points. Your future depends upon one thing: *your* trading ability.

If you're just starting out in prop trading, know that very soon you will be given a trading account. You'll probably be asked to complete your firm's training program first, and set some computer keys to buy and sell (hot keys), but then you're off! You won't run errands like an intern might (in which case you are on call at all hours) and you won't fill orders in the Asian markets at 2 AM. A good training program will provide critical feedback concerning your trading but *your* judgment combined with *your* trading skills will determine your future.

At a hedge fund or big bank, most would-be superstars sit on the bench for a few years before being given responsibility with live capital. And oftentimes, one cannot get a job at a hedge fund without having worked at a big bank first. At SMB Capital, traders start with live ammo on Day 26.

Unlike in years past, when "trial by fire" was the preferred form of mentorship, today's better proprietary trading firms have intensive training programs. A firm's partners invest a tremendous amount of capital, time, and teaching to make sure their trainees succeed. If a trader is not successful, the firm has invested a great deal of time, energy, and capital with almost no benefit. Thus, nothing less than an outstanding training program is in the proprietary trading firm's best interest.

Here are the best parts: compensation is practically unlimited, there are no office politics, and no subjective end-of-year performance reviews to determine a promotion or a raise or give constructive feedback like "you need to start asking for more responsibility." Traders take stock of their performance every single day, calculating profits to the cent in real time, and taking home a percentage of the spoils. The only haggling for a "raise" comes in the form of top producers requesting to take home a higher percentage. And at some firms, the partners will invite their best young talent to join them, just like in the old days of the Wall Street investment banking partnerships. Transparency, accountability, and instant feedback . . . where else in the corporate world can you get that?

OK, here's another "best part" of prop trading. Every day is new. Pushing papers around and doing the "same nonsense different day" is the antithesis of our job. As an example, here is how I spent Black Friday of 2009, the day after Thanksgiving, a day I was supposed to spend relaxing, watching an action movie, and eating leftovers: I awoke at 5:15 AM in Albany, New York, and prepared to take a borrowed car to the Amtrak station, then to the subway, then to my office (door to door it took me just under four hours). I was the only one awake on Amtrak from Albany to Penn Station as I was preparing for the day's Open, trying to communicate with my partner and co-founder Steve Spencer, rip through charts, and find patterns from overseas trading that might give us an edge.

Despite my having given the firm the day off, Steve and I contacted all of our traders on the night before because of the news of Dubai defaulting on billions of its debts. (Steve is my business partner, but he's also my best friend since age six.) We reached some of the traders, but not all. We spread word to the StockTwits community, the largest social media finance network, that this Black Friday was not a session to miss. SPY was opening down huge. We might bounce, we might tank, but whatever happens could offer great opportunity. Opportunity is what sustains intraday traders (though one of our traders subsists on Burger King and candy). As I reflected on a Thanksgiving Day–stuffed stomach, I was hard pressed to remember a day that offered more potential intraday trading opportunity than this Black Friday.

As a trader, one never knows when he is going to walk into a market that rains money. Black Friday 2009 could have been that day. I would not risk missing it. So I woke up early, sacrificed time with my family and a day of recharging, and started my travails.

I patched into our firm morning meeting, which was broadcast to the StockTwits community, via a crappy $300 netbook from a spotty wireless region. But I saw and heard Steve from my reclined seat on Amtrak offering me a game plan for this Open. I could have never done this "in the old days." What a super job by Steve and all who helped him prepare for his show running down all the key levels to watch before the Open. But then he said something that mattered most of all. Steve introduced the idea of market psychology.

The news before the Open was not good. Asia had digested the Dubai news and showed signs of food poisoning. The Asian markets got hammered and our markets were poised to open supremely weak. But Steve reminded all of us that market psychology mattered most. The market had shrugged off every piece of negative news since SPY traded at 70 just nine months before. The pattern to "buy the dips" had rewarded traders all during 2009. Steve counseled that if SPY held above 109.10 then this would be a signal that Dubai was just another piece of news the market would likely shrug off. It did.

As I left my office building in downtown Manhattan, I thought "Why did the market have to close early on this Black Friday? Can we fast-forward to Monday?" I just wanted to trade. I felt like Randolph and Mortimer Duke in the classic movie *Trading Places*, yelling in the middle of the trading floor "Turn those machines back on!" The only difference of course was I had just made money, not gotten a margin call for $394 million.

Now if prop firms are essentially their own client, where is the competition? Trust me, there's plenty of that. The market only has so much volume to go around, and every day is like a boxing match, beating all big banks, hedge funds, and automated programs to the punch.

So who are these people? Most were former Division I athletes or Ivy League math whizzes. Some sit around conference tables sipping bottled water, admiring the cufflinks on their French shirts, and stretching their toes in Gucci loafers while enjoying Central Park views from the window. (Not to be outclassed, as one can see the Statute of Liberty from some of my office's windows). Many have more money to play with than we do, and can push us around, not to mention more brain power, experience, and "research" information. They work at firms with names one would easily recognize. NBA superstar Kobe Bryant is known to fans simply as "Kobe" while his worthy counterpart LeBron James is simply "LeBron." Similarly, fans of Wall Street might recognize my competitors with one name as well.

Welcome to my world. Welcome inside the highly competitive world of proprietary trading.

Unlike a big bank that is funded by large shareholders and cheap overnight lending, or a hedge fund backed by wealthy investors and institutions, a proprietary trading firm is generally funded with capital from a few partners like Steve and me. In most cases, prop firm capital is deficient to their better-known Wall Street peers. Certain firms concentrate on trading options and others, arbitrage plays. Some hold for longer time periods. Others, like ours, concentrate on trading US equities intraday. And we seek to do this better than anyone else. We employ our proprietary trading strategies with our money against the rest of the Street.

Steve and I teach our traders to locate important intraday levels and trade off of these levels. We make sure our traders focus on stocks with fresh news (Stocks In Play), and we ask them to make trading decisions based on technical analysis, reading the tape, and intraday fundamentals. If we teach them poorly, then the downside for us personally is significant. It's our money, and our money only, after all. If we choose our traders poorly in the hiring process, then the economic cost is painful. If our firm runs out of money, then we go out of business. And the government will not be there to bail us out, though I secretly like to think we are "Too Small to Fail."

The biggest reward of this job is the challenge to become an elite performer. I seek every day to improve, and I've been at this awhile. I do my best to master the psychology of trading. Traders learn more about themselves in a year of trading than many learn in their entire adult lives. The challenge is so intense it cannot help but force one to find the very best inside of him or her. Embracing the life of an elite performer eventually spills over to every facet of life like friend, brother, and son.

Contrary to what you might think, a prop firm should not be a cult of traders who worship at the altar of its successful firm leader. SMB Capital is not the Mike Bellafiore or Steve Spencer cult; as leaders, we don't purport to be all knowing. We do not have all the answers. Guess how I know that?

I have learned more collectively from the traders I have worked with and trained than I have ever taught anyone. At the time of the publishing of this book, there are over 60 professional traders under my wing, and I am always looking for our next star. Firms exist because of their talented traders. There would be no prop firms, no SMB Capital, certainly not this book, without the traders.

Unlike traditional brick and mortar companies, where things like property, plant, and equipment sit on the balance sheet, the assets of a Wall Street firm walk out the door every night. Steve and I often joke that we hope to build a firm where the worst traders are us. Now that would be some firm!

Cultivating an environment of learning requires stars other than the partners. Having star traders whom new traders can emulate, with whom they can grab lunch or a drink or ask a question, fosters an environment of perpetual learning. And let's be clear: From a business perspective, star traders carry the dozens of mediocre new traders until they are ready to produce.

But enough pontificating about corporate culture and human capital philosophy. Let's move on to my entourage (especially when I am buying lunch). The traders profiled in this chapter are damn good and getting better. You would be hard pressed to find any better in our space. Unlike industries where young talent is groomed to look, act, and dress in a monotonous way, prop traders really come in all shapes and sizes. That alone has kept things fresh throughout my career.

So let's get to this. These are all great guys, and their humorous anecdotes are sprinkled throughout the book to give you a courtside seat at our game, to show you what really goes on inside the prop trading arena. Here's their introduction.

These guys are good.

A FIRM'S GREATEST ASSET: ITS TRADERS

In this chapter, you'll meet Franchise, MoneyMaker, Dr. Momentum, GMan, Z$, The Yipster, and JToma (we'll stick to nicknames for the book—all great traders should have one), and they truly represent all points on the spectrum. They differ physically, ethnically, and possess varying standout talents. Each serves as a lesson on the importance of being competitive, focus, getting better every day, processing information quickly, achieving consistency in trading, perseverance, or a willingness to keep learning despite the number of years on a desk. They possess the characteristics that the market has taught me are most important to become a consistently profitable trader.

Franchise: Good Traders are Competitive

In the spring of 2007, I walked into the conference room at one of our old offices to interview a young man from the University of Connecticut, (my alma mater, yes!) with one of those names as ethnic as my own: let's call him Franchise. Instantly, all these boxes started being checked off in my head: our SMB recruiting matrix was no threat to Franchise!

Franchise was a former college athlete. Check. He had traded before. Check. Check. He had that firm handshake that said *I'm all business but still carry myself with humility*. Check, check, and check.

After a few questions, Franchise oozed elite performer—he understood he would not be good at anything unless he worked hard. I kept thinking to myself, "To what exactly do I owe this privilege? I run a year-old fledgling prop trading firm, and this kid wants to work for me?"

I like to joke with one of our interns, Krysten (soon to be an SMB trader), that as much as I like Franchise personally, he is not exactly the type of person for whom you root. He is not an underdog. (We will meet Dr. Momentum later in this chapter.) Dr. Momentum you root for. Not Franchise.

Franchise was that kid whose father had to build an extension on the house just to store all his trophies. To other guys, he is the one your ex-girlfriend dumped you for, yet to whom you'd gladly defer. To women, Franchise is someone who broke your young heart, but in a nice way.

Did I mention his pedigree? He is 6'4". He is a former Division 1 swimmer who trained to qualify for the 2004 Olympics. His grandfather is an Emmy-and Grammy-winning composer who wrote a musical that still plays on Broadway. He vacations with his family at their compound outside the U.S. He is handsome (I can say that, right?), smart, a natural leader, likable, and talented. I'm sorry, but guys like Franchise always get the girl, make tons of money, and succeed at whatever they do. Simply put, if there were a Wall Street trader draft, and SMB had the number one pick, I'd sign him to a contract a month before I was officially "on the clock."

About 10 minutes into our initial conversation my inner voice shouted, "We need to find a way to make sure this kid does nothing else but trade with us." As I will further discuss in Chapter 3, generally, I un-recruit candidates, but Franchise is the one interviewee whom I actually tried to close. Maybe it was the UConn connection. But somehow we persuaded him. What a find!

There is not a single trader on our desk, including myself, including Steve, including GMan (you'll meet him, too), who is as competitive as Franchise. Not one. In fact, there isn't even a close second. Here's why.

Franchise had a nice run of $1,500–$2,000 days during a period when most on our desk were struggling. Remember, we employ a conservative trading strategy and he was still just beginning. During this run, he asked to talk with me.

Bella: What's up?

Franchise: I feel like I cannot get over this 1,500–2k hump. I just don't
              know how to do it.

These words on their face might seem innocuous. However, his face showed physical pain. His body language communicated disgust in his perceived underperformance. His demeanor shouted that he was ready to do whatever he needed to find the next gear for his trading. He was like a dog that had just broken his leg looking up at you to relieve his pain. And he was doing well!

Being the best of the best on the desk was not a concern to Franchise. The guys are on desk were respectfully all unworthy of comparison as far as he was concerned. He was competing against the market. His goal was to tame this powerful beast. Perhaps it was the naïveté of market youth. No one trader is bigger than the market. But this conversation summarized his thirst for excellence.

First, I offered him some perspective. He was actually doing very well, and I made an argument that supported this conclusion. But then I recommended Franchise work on three short-term goals to improve his trading: (1) Enough with the trading "On Tilt"; (2) Improve your position sizing; (3) Refine your trading on the Open. We could sit in my office all day talking about these weaknesses, but that wouldn't help him improve. So now he had his tasks, and it was up to him to improve.

Franchise now had work to do. There were new goals to focus on. There was a path to get better. This new challenge was like the gift of a first bicycle to a young child. He couldn't wait to leave my office, rid himself of my now useless banter, and get to work.

While most enter trading in Hippocratic Oath mode (For doctors: "First, do no harm," for traders: "First, don't blow up."), Franchise was wacking through the jungle with a thick enough skin to ignore the peripheral prickly brush and swinging a machete to take out every life form in his path, looking for the prize like Indiana Jones. Making money was a given. Being excellent was inevitable in his mind. He continued working, experimenting, studying, pushing, learning until he recognized his potential.

Specifically what did Franchise do? He kept detailed notes in his trading journal on the weaknesses he needed to improve. He watched video of his trading on his laptop as he commuted home. He pulled me aside asking thoughtful trading questions, never wasting a second of my time. He thought about his trading after the Close. He kept up well with the SMB fundamental of sharing ideas with the desk. Slowly but surely, he was improving.

The result? Those middling 1,500–2k days soon became 3–4k days.

I am not sure what the future will hold for Franchise. Nothing would make me happier than for him to run his own desk with us. But I suspect that one day he will leave to go work at a hedge fund (perhaps his own) and trade much bigger positions. If that is what he wants, I will be the first person to thank him for working with us. And if I've made enough for myself by the time he's ready to do that, I'll gladly seed him Julian Robertson–style. But I am interested. I really cannot wait to watch his future unfold. Franchise's story demonstrates how competitiveness, harnessed correctly, can provide the energy the developing trader needs to improve.

TRADERS ASK: "WHY CAN'T I JUST MAKE MONEY?"

An experienced trader, GM, e-mailed me in the summer of 2008 as the Angels were pounding the Yankees again. GM had some very kind words for my previous blog, which I appreciated and made the latest Yankees loss more palatable. In return, I would like to spend some time offering some guidance on his recent struggles. They should not continue.

Sometimes, just like GM, I feel that I just can't make money. And when you are getting beaten up consistently, it is human nature to viscerally conclude that the market is just too hard for you. But a good trader does not succumb to this very human yet initial overreaction. A good trader assumes the mentality that there is always an escape.

There is a wonderful movie, *Red Belt*, written by one of our great playwrights, David Mamet. The protagonist, Mike Terry, played by Chiwetel Ejiofor, is a mixed-martial arts instructor, and the film opens with Mike teaching his best student. This student is in a chokehold that he cannot escape. And Mike is preaching, "There is always an escape. There is no situation you could not escape from. You know the escape." There is always an adjustment that I can make to improve my trading results for a stock. I watch my trading videos to discover what I was doing wrong, my escape. Almost always, I lose money because of my own human error. I fix my errors and move forward. When I do my trading, results immediately improve.

But to improve your results you must review your work and eliminate your mistakes. This experienced trader had conquered the market the past five years. What percent of traders do you think are capable of making that statement? This is undoubtedly enough data to conclude that GM is a very good trader. GM, sit down and identify your mistakes, eliminate them, and you will go right back to making money. You do not slip from trading successfully for five consecutive years to being unable to trade profitably anymore. That is, unless you get in your own way. But your skills are there. Now it's time for you to compete.

I talk about competing a lot to our new traders on our desk. You don't compete by saying, "I really want to see better results." You compete by taking the actions necessary to make your trading more profitable. The reason you are losing money is not because you are a lousy trader. That is not supported by the past five years of trading data. You are struggling because you are making human errors. Your present data is not relevant because it is blanketed with uncommon trading errors. Eliminate these mistakes and your results will mirror your previous years. Make a list of the trades that work best for you. Visualize making successful trades. Then make One Good Trade and then One Good Trade and then One Good Trade.

All good traders have had thoughts that they're at the end, they'll never make money again, or that the market is just too hard. I have sent these very e-mails. We are not Buddhist monks, so these counterproductive thoughts oc-cur. But the good trader moves forward. The good trader finds an escape. The good trader through positive self-talk reminds himself of his past successes and concentrates on the trades that are working presently for him. The good trader competes.

Best of luck with your trading, GM!

Let's meet another talented star trader with an uber-profitable combination of passion and pure, unadulterated trading talent.

MoneyMaker: Stay Focused

"Failing is not an option for me," said MoneyMaker during his interview with me. I didn't make much of this during my first meeting with him be-cause, honestly, a lot of candidates say stuff like this in their first interview. But for some reason I remember in great detail MoneyMaker saying this to me. And recently I asked him if he remembered this. He didn't. But he ex-plained, "Trading is what I want to do, Bella. So failing is not an option." Oh.

Well MoneyMaker, many of us want to play for the New York Yankees, but that isn't happening. So what was it about MoneyMaker wanting to succeed that enabled him to actually succeed? His hunger was genuine. Others claim to love trading but are not willing to pay the price. Dr. Brett Steenbarger wrote on TraderFeed, his psychology trading blog, that many claim to have a passion for trading but few sustain the energy to achieve their goals. And others like MoneyMaker did not have the advantage of trading talent. So what was it with this MoneyMaker?

Ask MoneyMaker what a friend would notice if he visits our trading desk and he answers: "That I just sit in front of my computer the whole day. I could sit all day on my desk and wait for setups to happen to me and I don't get bored."

During a slow August day in 2009, when many traders had convinced themselves that the markets were awful, there was MoneyMaker glued to his seat. He was having a fantastic month. He had put up over $13k the day before. There really was not much going on. The housing number was about to hit in a few minutes. MoneyMaker was watching all the ticks in FAS and FAZ. The number hit, SPY spiked above 102, an important resis-tance level, and MoneyMaker loaded up. FAZ went up a point and slowed, then another point and slowed, then pulled back until it made another up-move. In 15 minutes MoneyMaker made $5k, on a day that many were not on their desk, checking out www.missuniverse.com, or securing tee times. Not MoneyMaker. He was there to trade. He was ready to pounce. And he crushed a simple trading setup.

Like the Franchise, MoneyMaker is a former athlete. In fact, he is a former professional golfer. And I often chuckle at something MoneyMaker said about his ability to focus that plays an integral role in his success as a trader. MoneyMaker explained, "I am used to hitting balls in hundred-degree weather for hours, so sitting in air conditioning in front of my computer for the day is not difficult for me." Makes sense, I guess.

During a one-on-one discussion, I complimented, "I am just amazed at your ability to focus. It is just remarkable." He looked at me quizzically and clarified, "Bella, it is not remarkable. I just love trading. It is not difficult for me to stare at my screens because I love trading."

His focus is not natural. He has developed this skill as a former professional athlete, hitting hundreds of balls, for hours, in hundred-degree weather and worse humidity. A round of golf can last five hours and one must focus on each individual shot. This fact is not lost on him or me.

MoneyMaker made money from Day One (hence the nickname). His first month trading with SMB he received a bonus check. I can count on one hand how many traders out of a hundred do this from Day One. And he has made money in everything, every sector, he traded. First it was the oil stocks. Cha ching! Then it was the financials. Then came the ETFs. Then longer-term trades. MoneyMaker could always just play. He has a "feel" for stocks. He has trading talent.

But MoneyMaker keeps working at his game. A good day used to be $1k, and then it was $3k, and now it's $10k and counting. And again, he is positive 80 percent of all trading days. A horrible day for him might be negative $1k. He has had patches where he has struggled. He traded poorly in June 2009 but then rebounded later that summer for a huge August, a month when most of the Street is on vacation.

MoneyMaker has an uncanny feel for the order flow. As much as I would like to take credit for his tape reading skills, he just got it much faster than most. When talent melds with passion, then you are special. And MoneyMaker is a special trader.

On deck is the most fascinating person ever to walk the halls of SMB Capital. He is Dr. Momentum, the one we all root for.

Dr. Momentum: Be a Sponge

Dr. Momentum started as our first intern. He took a job as an accountant at a Big Four accounting firm but then decided, "You know, this is really not for me. I would rather come back (to SMB). This environment is so much more conducive to growth and learning." Like GMan, the corporate life was not for him. It was like some guardian trading angel was watching over us blessing us with Dr. Momentum.

Dr. Momentum is the smartest person I have ever trained. Dr. Momentum looks and is young, 24. One of his endearing quirks is that he talks incessantly. Well, save the one time Franchise warned, "If you do not stop talking, I am going to come over there and break your (expletive deleted) neck." From one of our traders: "(Dr. Momentum) talks constantly all day long. Seriously, he never stops." This would be annoying from anyone else save Dr. Momentum. Why? Because he is Dr. Momentum.

We all know someone like Dr. Momentum. Brilliant yet modest. Absorbs new information twice as fast as you and remembers twice as much. And someone we all root for. Dr. Momentum is a red-head Jewish kid from Brooklyn, who stands 5'7" (maybe), and yaps all the time with a smile on his face.

I received an e-mail from the location scout for *Wall Street 2*, directed by Oliver Stone. They were looking for a trading floor to shoot some scenes. I offered a few trading floors as ideas (such as the one eventually chosen) and moved on with my day. But if they were to look for more than a trading floor, if they were to scout for traders, Dr. Momentum would not be cast. In fact, anyone who suggested Dr. Momentum for a casting call would be derided.

Why?

Because Dr. Momentum is the anti-Franchise. Dr. Momentum looks like your accountant. He's like that Paul Pfeiffer kid from *The Wonder Years* sitcom. Dr. Momentum sounds like a crazy cousin on speed. Tall, muscular, athletic, he is not. He did not graduate from an Ivy League school only because his allergies are so bad he sought refuge in Colorado. (Remember Paul Pfeiffer's allergies?) Cool and restrained are not what comes to mind. Dr. Momentum will land a girl here and there but I assure you this is all through sheer genius and perhaps some good fortune.

Every conversation is a party to Dr. Momentum, with him as the host. His brain can't stop processing. When I teach he absorbs every piece of wisdom (assuming I share wisdom) that I offer. From Dr. Momentum, "I only have to hear something once and I get it. Same thing in when I would read a textbook. . . . I would just read, go bust out the chapter, boom, and I would be done. I won't have to take any notes. I won't have to highlight anything. I won't even have to review and then go back. I would just run through the chapter, and then it would be done. It would be in my brain." Dr. Momentum is a sponge.

Dr. Steenbarger, expert in trading psychology and prominent author, in a presentation he gave to Kershner Trading Group, commented that a good trader is a combination of conscientiousness and risk taker. You must get your work done so you can identify excellent risk/reward setups but then you must also be willing to put on risk. Dr. Momentum is our poster child for this combination.

When we interview a candidate I ask whether they enjoy new restaurants and travel. Those that travel and sample new restaurants tend to be willing to take risks. Where does Dr. Momentum travel, you ask? Dr. Momentum spent three weeks in Japan, Hong Kong, and China during his vacation in 2009. Before he started with us, he spent a month in Nicaragua learning Spanish and absorbing the culture. From Dr. Momentum, "Most of my friends from Brooklyn are either immigrants or they are sons and daughters of immigrants and when I spend time with their families, whatever accent they have, I would pick up on their accent, and start speaking their accent. When I was in China, I was speaking with a kind of Chinese accent for the two weeks I was there. I think I just like to pick up on things and I absorb them, and they become like part of me very quickly." Dr. Momentum is not afraid to jump into a new stock offering fresh experiences and exceptional opportunity. Given his travels, this fits his personality.

Dr. Momentum is the best young momentum trader on the desk. To trade momentum, you must make lightning-quick decisions. And he can. Back in the fall of 2008, Dr. Momentum crushed Goldman Sachs (GS) short, then flipped and crushed it long, then re-shorted and caught the next downmove, etc. He is not physically imposing like Franchise, but has the fleetest hands around.

He has no fear. I know that fall of 2008 offered many excellent trading opportunities. But it takes guts to trade GS with size when it is moving 70 points intraday. What if you catch the wrong side of the trade? That is a quick $5k out of your pocket. That will make your red hair stand on end.

But he didn't. And he just crushed that fall of 2008 market. In fact, he posted the best results of almost all on the desk after just his first few months of trading. That's impressive! That's because of his extraordinary information-processing ability. He saw the longs and got long. He saw the shorts and hit the bids. He scratched his poor trades when necessary. The young man from Brooklyn, Dr. Momentum, put on a trading master clinic.

Intriguingly enough, Dr. Momentum's best day almost never happened. He managed to score a date with a lovely young lady from the Upper West Side of Manhattan and took her out on the town. That day had been his best, putting up $20k. And according to Dr. Momentum, the day only got better: "Bella, it was a great date!" Dr. Momentum stumbled in just before our morning meeting looking like sleep had not been on the menu the previous night. He was also wearing the very same shirt from the day before and a huge smirk on his face. *Look at you, Dr. Momentum, getting a little something something last night.* But he made it. And this was a good thing for his bank account. On this day, he bested his previous best day by over 50 percent.

What is most hysterical about Dr. Momentum is that during this huge day, he missed the easiest move in GS because he was taking a self-imposed rest. Dr. Momentum has some stamina issues. By 11 AM, he looks like a fighter who needs oxygen. By 4 PM, some CPR might be needed. Add in his night of unrest and he was trading on fumes. GS dropped an important intraday support level of 100 and traded straight down to 86ish. Our desk's P&L spiked like the space shuttle taking off at Andrews Air Force base. Where was Dr. Momentum? Resting.

It was so much fun watching him so happy. As a partner, what could be better than a potential future star like Dr. Momentum, who says things like, "Positivity is a skill," and "It always comes back to the fundamentals: patience, discipline, hard work, a detailed plan." The guy who few would envision as a Wall Street assassin was just that in the fall of 2008.

Dr. Momentum's aggressiveness can cause a stumble here and there. The young trader who is always chattering is also tempted to overtrade. And restraint is a virtue that he has not yet learned but the Street generally values.

But I have my money on Dr. Momentum trading for many years. If not, maybe we can cast him in the next *Wall Street 2* as Gekko's accountant.

Our star of stars is about to enter the room. He is one in a million intraday traders. And it almost all never happened.

GMan: From "I Quit" to Head Trader to Partner

"If you are too comfortable in a trade then you probably do not have enough size."

—GMan, Head Trader, SMB Capital

I still remember the nervousness. It was odd. Why was this young person sitting across from Steve and me so nervous? Was he hiding something?

He, Gilbert Mendez, was a graduate of Columbia University with an engineering degree. His grades were outstanding. This young man had developed a black box for foreign exchange. And now he wanted to intraday trade equities. Or so he said.

We showed him a recent lecture I had written, which impressed him greatly. He asked to take it home. We balked. We do not allow proprietary materials to leave the office.

And we had all these questions.

Steve: What did you think?
Bella: Why was he so nervous?
Steve: He was not that nervous.

Bella: What was with all those questions?

Steve: He is an engineer. They make decisions after gathering as much information as possible.

Bella: I guess.

Steve: He was the best candidate we have ever interviewed.

Well, this last statement was a bit dramatic. We had been in business two months. He might have been the fifth person we had interviewed for our new desk (desk might be a strong word—"Gang of Five" might be more accurate since we had only five traders). But Steve is notorious for over-optimism. I call it being "Spencermistic."

"Spencermism" Never Dies

When we brought in a nice non-English-speaking Fordham graduate for an interview, the conversation went like this:

Steve: We are going to make so much money off of him.

Bella: I hope so.

    The guy was never positive a day trading live. Ever.

When we created some commercial trading products:

Steve: We are going to make so much money off our intraday alerts.

Bella: I hope so.

    We made $500 the first year our intraday alerts were offered.

When we brought in Most Frustrating Trader, whom you will meet later:

Spencer: He is by far the best candidate in his class.

Bella: I hope so.

    He should have been fired before he ever started.

So we had this Spencermistic feeling about this nice young man, obviously much brighter than me, with the hair of a TV soap star, who wanted to trade. It was GMan. GMan, our future head trader and now partner. Give that round to Spencermistic.

And at the start GMan struggled. He did not make a dime for his first six months. In fact, he was decidedly negative. In exchange for us wiping out his negative balance we commissioned him to build our first web site. He did a great job!

GMan was temperamental. He would bang and scream and curse. But he was learning how to fade-trade, which is an excellent way to learn how to expertly Read the Tape. He traded like me, save with a tighter time frame. Before Dr. Momentum, who absorbed everything I said, there was GMan. Like a parrot, he would repeat what I had said a few weeks before about a stock. He still does. It is a great compliment. He was learning. He was like a young Bella but much smarter (and more hair).

Six months into his stint with the ultra-new SMB Capital, GMan infamously walked into our office to quit. That was not going to happen. His argument presented to Steve was like a guard penetrating the lane against Patrick Ewing during his Georgetown years. Rejection. "Get that out of here, GMan," Spencer swatted with sound reasoning as to why he ought to stay and most importantly a few things he needed to improve: tape reading and controlling his emotions.

So back to work GMan went. He crunched his trading numbers. We moved to a trading platform better able to reward GMan for his newfound trading skills. He found some luck with the start of the subprime mess. And finally he started to get it. And when he "got it," "it" came fast. $1k. Then $2k. Then $3k. Then more per day.

Ask GMan about his first year of trading and he responds, "The numbers don't really mean anything for the first year and it's hard to put that aside and stay in the game. But as you progress, you will start to find consistency." Amen.

GMan kept at it. Longer-term intraday trades needed to be conquered. There were new spreadsheets created to track these setups. He created the SMB Chop Tracker from scratch where we break down our trading in a snapshot statistically. There was now less gel in his hair and more money in his bank. GMan had arrived.

How did the SMB Chop Tracker help? "I just started to eliminate a lot of the scalps that are really low-probability plays and I've been starting to work more on the high-probability plays and adding incremental size to them." Also GMan examines the trades from the SMB Chop Tracker when his P&L spikes and concentrates on how to trade these plays even better. At one point, GMan noticed that while he cannot scalp certain stocks like Mastercard, MA, he can position trade them off of key intraday levels. His statistics instructed that he could not trade MA in and out. But GMan found a new way to profit off of MA. Further, GMan's stats tell him not only what sectors he is trading poorly but also the specific setups that are not profitable. So now he can trade all sectors; he just makes adjustments precipitated by his trading statistics. Now that is a chop!

I really do not remember when we named GMan the head trader. He had been with us since Month Two. And one day we looked up and he really was the best trader on our desk. Steve and I had started to handle more firm-related business (recruiting, legal, clearing deals, and so on) and could not focus on trading as much. So we needed someone to run the desk full time who we knew would steward our capital well and lead the desk. Making GMan our head trader was our best personnel decision to date.

How good is GMan? GMan has been stopped out once since he began with us. He's the guy who can beat you in a race giving you a start halfway to the finish line. Let me explain.

GMan missed one Open and an 8-point upmove in AIG because he was working on an SMB training tool. He received a text from a trader on the desk at 12:30 PM informing him of the AIG move. So he flipped open his LightSpeed platform, and spent the rest of day trying to catch our intraday leaders. By 1 PM, he was up $1k. By 2 PM; he was up $1,800 by 3 PM, $2,200 and by 4 PM, $4k. He almost did it. On most days, he is like an ATM. And by the way, AIG moved only three more points that intraday.

GMan enjoys his life as much as any young trader on our desk mixing diligent work with hard playing. If you walk on to our trading floor at 4:01 PM on a Friday, it is quite possible that his SMB coffee mug will be filled with Johnnie Walker Red. It does not go unnoticed on our desk that the trader most likely to be found cozying up to a young female out on the town in NYC is GMan. The indefatigable GMan has been known to make an occasional journey to Atlantic City on weekday night and make it back barely for the Open. The markets are a master challenge for GMan to conquer with his staggering mental acuity, and NYC, with all that it has to offer the young person, is his playground.

GMan will go on to become one of the best intraday traders on the Street. I have it on good authority that he is about to be named to a new best traders under 30 list. GMan recently purchased a partnership with SMB, rounding out his journey from "I Quit" to Head Trader to Partner. The best thing that ever happened to our firm was the day he walked into our trading firm!

Next, let's meet the Joe DiMaggio of trading, the most consistent intraday prop trader on the Street, Z$.

Z$: Make Discipline a Strength

When Z$ (ZMush, Mush, Mushy, and Z are also acceptable nicknames) talks, it is hard to understand what he's saying. It's not that he's speaking a different language. He's just so soft spoken that one has to prompt him several times to speak up. He mixes a low volume voice with an exceedingly quick tempo, only compounding the problem. Imagine a jackhammer without the noise and this is how he shares his words with the world.

Speech recognition patterns aside, Z$ is the most consistent trader on our desk. Not the most profitable, but the most consistent. He was positive for two years straight. How is that even possible? In this regard, he is somewhat of an ungodly phenomenon.

Z came to us from another firm that had stopped making money when Hybrid arrived at the NYSE, so he was searching for a new home. A friend of SMB's, Ray Holland, managing member from Avatar Securities, proposed a sit-down. Mushy wasn't making much money at his other firm (at least that's what I thought he was saying). I found him down to earth and humble, and in the end we were lucky to find him. Thanks, Ray!

We have a bias for traders who have traded elsewhere, are struggling, and want to improve. Once they have bought into our philosophy, they tend to do well with us. First, they appreciate the value that we offer more than the new trader who has no idea how left alone you can be at another firm. Second, they have some built-in trading skills that just need to be utilized most effectively. Hence, their learning curve with us is much shorter.

ZMush was no exception. We got him in the Stocks In Play. We surrounded him with traders who shared valuable information. We stressed the importance of understanding what setups work best for him through statistical analysis. We made sure he was prepared for the day with our SMB AM meeting. Mushy quietly and unassumingly did all the work we asked of him, and he started to make money.

New traders sometimes believe that the path to becoming a big-time trader is paved by the necessary losses of significant money. If I can lose $30k, then I can learn to make $30k, the thinking goes. To me, this makes no sense at all. While losses might teach you good lessons at the beginning of your career, losing too much is irresponsible. The truth is that you must first learn to make $100 before you can make $200, and build on these positive results.

I would label Z the most consistent trader at our firm but that would not be painting the most precise picture. Z is like the Joe DiMaggio of trading, the legendary Yankee great who holds the record for consecutive games with at least one hit, and even that lasted only 56 games. As I write this book, Mush has not had a negative trading day in the last two years. That's 500 or more straight trading days. I guess that is how we derived his nickname Z$. I'm not always sure how these names get started, but this one is par for the course.

Mushy has his setups and he sticks with them. He loves to watch a big offer decrement, pay the offer, and sell the stock when it slows into the upmove. Z$ is so proficient at this scalp trade that we have named it after him, the Mush Trade. This setup offers a high-win rate and little risk. And he just scans the markets for the setups that work for him.

As I've learned, the same setups don't last forever, so GMan pushes Z$ to expand his playbook every once in a while. When GMan finds a Trades2Hold he sends it Mush's way, and prods him to get into this trade.

As traders, we should spend each day stepping outside of our comfort zone so we improve. This is what GMan is offering Z$, and Mushy just keeps getting better. The other day he held the volatile AIG for three points. A trade he would never have made last year.

After the Close of every trading day, you can find Z$ without fail at his desk watching tape of his trading. After the Close, he constantly reviews his trades in his mind. Discipline is his strength. He sticks with what works while expanding his playbook with new trades that work for him. Just like the sun rises every AM, Z$ is positive. The fun is watching him make more and more as he continually improves. Give me a desk full of Z$s and I will show you one grateful trading partner and an extremely profitable firm.

BUILD FROM YOUR POSITIVE BASE

Those who trade professionally wish to make a lot of money. Prop traders are not trying to make $200 a day. They want to make much more. They have rarely failed at anything they have done before. Perhaps they have been told their whole life that they were special. Most are the smartest person in any room. They are uninterested in being ordinary. And they aren't. But all of this can be damaging.

So these special, ambitious people start to do some thinking. On a treacherous, rainy day like the end of 2008 in NYC they might let their minds wander. *I am ready to start making some serious money*, they may think. *I really need to lay into some stocks with more size* certainly will be considered. I would look really cool in that new Benz on the back of the News today. I am better than that Dr. Momentum. Does he ever stop talking by the way? I want to be the Man!

Just some advice. Your risk-adjusted return is more important than your gross P&L. You shouldn't try to make $5k a day by losing $5k. You shouldn't do this after 10 years and you certainly shouldn't do this when you start. Often new traders think their ability to lose a lot symbolizes their potential to make much more. No, it doesn't. You should never lose more than half of your median intraday gains. If you are making $1k a day, and a down day previously for you was −500, then now allowing yourself to lose −$5k doesn't mean you will now be able to make $5k. It means now you can lose $5k. Some new traders just don't understand this.

If you want to make $5k a day you must first be able to make $500 consistently (downside of $250). Then you must show that you can make $750 consistently (downside $375). Then you must demonstrate that you can make $1k consistently (downside $500). Then $1,500 (downside $750). Then $2,000 (downside $1k). You get my point. But for some very strange reason traders think making that jump from $1k to $5k requires them to lose $5k in day. Again no, it doesn't.

You build from a base. You build from your profitable base. The way to make more is to make more while contemporaneously avoiding proportionally greater downside risk. And if you can't make more than $2k in a day with a downside of $1k, then stay at this level for a while. There is nothing wrong with making that kind of money. Keep pushing yourself to get better. But do not force it.

One of the smartest traders on our desk has been making $600 a day. And I know he wants to make more. And one day he will. But he forced it recently. And he didn't make more than $600. He took a huge rip. He took a rip that will set him back weeks.

I was talking with Steve about this the other day. And he became very animated. Steve is ultra calm, so it is amusing to watch him get animated. But it usually means that he is about to make a very good point. And he did. Steve shared that new traders who are making $600 a day can't take these rips for another very important reason. Unlike Steve or myself, they cannot make back $5k. They do not have the skills. If Steve rips up 5k he can make that back in less than an hour. But a new trader cannot. If you are making $600 a day, it will take you weeks to make back a huge rip. And this game is about putting money in your pocket, not throwing away a few weeks' worth of gains.

So build from your positive base. All of the traders presented in this chapter built from a positive base to become successful. Push yourself to get better. But do not force your progression. Losing more means you can lose more. It doesn't mean you can make more.

Let's meet a trader who just crept up on us, became good—damn good, and is still getting better.

The Yipster: Improve Every Day

I can't say I noticed The Yipster's trading for the first six months he was with us. Every once in a while on the subway ride home Steve would brief me that The Yipster's numbers were starting to get better. We preach that you ought to take the beginning slowly, that you ought to get a little bit better every day. In The Yipster, we have found the poster trader for this mantra.

The Yipster wins my award for Most Improved Trader. This is the highest compliment I can offer. After all, this is what trading is all about: embracing the philosophy to get better every day. How many people can accept that they must be self-critical every day and improve? Not many. Many just want to get to a place and rest. Not The Yipster. Not with his trading.

If you ask The Yipster how he improved every day his answer, with a NYC-born twang, is: "Focusing on being consistent, focusing on fundamentals, focusing on doing the right things. . . . Obviously hard work also. . . . You know, working, working, working on everything that I could possibly do to improve on my game." You mean you did not have to visit any Mensa meetings? Oh.

Ask The Yipster how long will it take to realize his full potential and he answers: "I don't think anybody can truly, truly master the markets. . . . I mean, it's just something that you can get better at, but I really don't think it's something that you can master. So, I mean, I'll be working on it. I think my entire career, my entire life." This is how athletes make their respective Halls of Fame, and The Yipster could be headed in that direction.

The Yipster keeps a detailed spreadsheet of all of his work. Every single order, every single trade, since Day One, has been recorded. The Yipster records his tape and watches his trades every other day. The Yipster says, "I just think there are no short cuts." He searches for plays that he could trade better. He looks for ways to add size to his best setups. He does all of this to get better every day.

Do you have this philosophy as a trader? This is a guy who makes serious money regularly now almost every day, with maybe one negative day a month. As I said, he was completely off of our radar for the first six months of his trading. But he just kept working, improving, and now he is one of our best traders. It is not where you start, it is where you are headed that most counts.

At the start of 2010, SMB gravitated toward longer holding periods for our trades, Trades2Hold. Ask The Yipster what he is working on, "I am focusing on my Trades2Hold with bigger size." Every so often I notice a big push from him, indicating progress with this goal. I can't say that this progress jumps off the leader board. But then again, when he started, he took his time getting better. Why would this be any different?

Let's introduce our good-looking TV star, the most optimistic and personable trader on our desk.

JToma: Practice Positive Perseverance

In the spring of 2009, I got a phone call from a woman named Rachel Pine. I had no idea who she was, but my friend and writing partner Chris Gillick had given her my name. Rachel was consulting for CNBC, trying to staff more traders for the network's *Fast Money* program. CNBC loved her since she knew our community well from her time as a marketing executive at *Trader Monthly* magazine. We are not media shy, and her call made my day.

Rachel came to our office to meet us, and liking what she saw, she set up an interview between the *Fast Money* producers, and Steve, JToma, and myself. CNBC sent a car for us, we hopped in and started our trek to a place so far out of the way there had to a be a reward upon arrival, the CNBC campus in Englewood Cliffs across the river. I did a double-take as I noticed Steve did not have any socks on. Typical. Steve couldn't care less about this meeting. Here we were, having built our company from nothing three years ago to our big meeting with the most-watched business network in the world. This was a big moment, and my partner and best friend didn't even bother to wear socks! But Steve was just annoyed to be off the desk in the middle of the trading day to visit a bunch of TV people. Steve doesn't like, get, or do traditional media (Steve later enthusiastically agreed to do three StockTwits TV shows a week, and during the trading day the first Web-native financial television network). Did I mention he also didn't shave?

Of course, I was pretty excited. Exposure on CNBC would only help in our recruiting efforts to attract young talented traders to our firm. And since we are only as good as the players we coach, this was one of the most important business meetings in our firm's young history. Did I mention my partner wasn't wearing socks?

This was a big deal for us, not because people would watch us per se, but rather there would be footage of us on CNBC. Forever. We would display it on our web sites and SMB Blog and there would be no mistaking that this SMB Capital upstart knew intraday trading.

JToma was never supposed to go on CNBC. Steve really was. JToma was a second option I was offering. Some people like a cheeseburger. Steve prefers a veggie burger. And JToma and Steve are as different as a cheese-burger and veggie burger, so CNBC had options.

There was an initial meeting with some bright, very young, energetic, fast talking staffers to vet us. We passed that first test and got sent up to the boss's office. Steve kept growing more annoyed. Another meeting? We need to get back to the office and trade, his body language announced.

And so we start our sit-down with the bosses. I explain who every-one is and why we are there. The producer of *Fast Money* starts making this motion with her hands to speed things up. I have to admit I was a lit-tle taken aback by this. Not to be egotistical, but no one has told me to start talking faster in four years. I am the co-founder of a successful pro-prietary trading firm. I am the one who cuts people off, ends meetings, and shifts the discussion. And often due to my time constraints, I am curt. And here was this producer gesturing at me to talk faster. I actually loved it.

A powerful TV executive, the Boss (I am not going to use her name because honestly . . . I am a little scared of her. She is really tough, but also someone who has a crystal-clear vision of what her programming ought to offer) sat at her desk and scanned the room in our first 15 seconds of this important meeting. She asked Steve, "You don't wear socks?" My worst nightmare was about to come true. Steve blew our chance of being a regular on CNBC because to him this meeting was just a nuisance keeping him from his first love, trading.

And then one of the bright staffers summarized some of what *Fast Money* offered on CNBC. He talked much faster than I did, so apparently this was required in front of the Boss. Steve was inaudible but I knew exactly what he was thinking, "That is a great young TV staffer, but how the hell will that help anyone make money?" And then Steve explained how CNBC should do things differently. He did so in a correcting, almost condescending, fashion. Strike two.

JToma was our last hope (I was not there to audition). Steve wasn't wearing socks, and had clearly communicated his lack of interest for being involved in anything CNBC. As the meeting continued on, I could see him becoming more uninterested. I swear, I thought he was going to ask the Boss to switch seats with him, log on to his LightSpeed account and start trading.

JToma offered his background, but more importantly he fought for a chance. He wanted to be on this leading financial news network. He was positive, complimentary, and likable with his presentation. When he stopped, the producer of *Fast Money* smiled and said, "I like him. He's cute."

And that is how SMB got on CNBC. That is how as JToma likes to describe it, he "became the face of SMB (freaking TV stars)." And this is how JToma has been a successful trader throughout his career.

JToma is off the charts positive and persistent. His wife wouldn't go out with him when they first met so he reoffered a date at Nobu, one of the most delicious and expensive restaurants in the world. She accepted, as this is a dining experience not to be missed no matter who the company.

When we first started prop trading, the goal was to trade your own money. We made 10–30 percent of our P&L and needed to bank about $250k to trade our own account. This was not even enough money, so we had to borrow another $250k at 12 percent interest to sufficiently fund our account. We essentially had to make millions for our firm before we ever had enough of our own personal money to trade our own account. And when we did, we got to keep 100 percent of our profits after paying commissions on our trades (which were as much as 600 percent higher than they are today . . . ouch!)

JToma did whatever he had to do. He was the annoying guy on the floor who talked to anyone about trading at any time, even at the bar and on the weekends, but he was learning. JToma would hop in a car down to the Jersey Shore to talk trading with the best traders at our firm where they relaxed on the weekend. JToma did not have a beach house, or even a summer share. He just went down for the ride hoping to gain nuggets from these successful traders. He would come in early, 7 AM, to rip through charts with the traders versed in technical analysis. He did anything to get better like The Yipster has done a decade later.

Not surprisingly, JToma soon made enough to trade his own account. Not bad for a guy not yet 23 years old. But in his first three months, he lost almost all of his money, more than $200k. He was down to his last $50k. The average trader would become depressed. I might. But JToma shrugged it off. He sought out a prominent performance psychologist and worked to improve some psychological hurdles, which were hindering his trading. JToma had become afraid to trade, and he needed to get his fearlessness back. The shrink worked. More than a decade later, he is still doing what he loves: trading.

This sports psychologist offered training techniques to improve his performance, which he still utilizes today. A daily journal was suggested and implemented. A plan for every trade was discussed and is now followed. Goals were set and surpassed. Favorite setups were identified and exploited.

Ask JToma what has helped him the most in his professional career and you get this response (by the way I had to edit his response by a good five minutes. JToma admittedly loves to talk.): "It's about doing the little things every single day and making yourself better, and that's my goal. My goal in this part of my life is to get better every day. If I do something every day to make myself better, I know eventually my P&L is going to show." Those horrid three months at the beginning of his career were an opportunity to learn and get better. That $200k in losses was parlayed into many millions at a later date.

Before video review there was the JToma Review. And he still does this today. JToma also owns a private equity fund, which requires some travel. After a flight to Texas, JToma sat in his hotel room, stared at the ceiling and reviewed his trading, tick for tick of his trading day. And before video, this was an exercise he did habitually after every Close. He discovered the trades that worked best for him, and made more of them. He identified what did not work for him and eliminated those trades.

Often, behind closed doors, JToma will get frustrated at a trader on our desk that he is mentoring. He will begin, "I just don't get (so and so).... Doesn't he understand this opportunity?" Or JToma will utter, "I just don't get these guys. Don't they want to make money?" JToma believes you work as hard as you have to and do whatever it takes to make it. He did.

And this whole trading thing almost never happened for JToma. He was in DC, waiting to go to law school, and working around the clock to pay the bills. His girlfriend at the time was upset she continually had to wait for him to end one of his late-night jobs. Her brother talked him into a trading job in NYC so the happy couple would have more time together. JToma accepted, put law school aside, and moved to NYC.

The day JToma arrived was April 1, 2006. Before his start date, JToma broke up with his girlfriend. He arrived and someone impolitely met him before he could walk on to the trading floor, "You broke up with the boss's sister, dude. Obviously, you don't have a job here anymore." So JToma, humiliated, turned to walk out of the office. And then everyone exploded into laughter. It was an April Fool's joke.

TRADERS ASK: "I'M RIGHT. RIGHT?"

I received an e-mail from a trader who is a superstar at reviewing his work. Below is an e-mail he sent to me in the spring of 2009:

I need to slow things down and do exactly this:

- Keep doing exactly what I'm doing, in preparation, in hard work, in planning trades, sharing ideas, and reviewing work.
- Have more patience so that you only trade each stock from the best levels—this will result in less volume overall and likely, fewer losing trades. Once you're in a stock, focus on just that one even if it means just waiting on it several minutes.
- Hit the sweep key if your price is .05 or more out of the money and you haven't already got out on offer (bid). Simple. Only way to kick this finally.

This was my response...

You have developed bad habits when it comes to hitting out of stocks that trade against you. You need to form good habits. I would spend 15 minutes every day on the demo working on hitting out of stocks. Pick an active stock, set an exit price, and if the stock hits this price, then get the F out. You must condition your mind to habitually hit out of stocks that exceed your exit price.

Also, you should have a conversation with yourself. Why are you so interested in proving that you are correct with a position? No one cares about your opinion. No one cares that you think a stock will go up or down. No one.

Most importantly, trading is not about being right. Trading is a game of math. It is about finding setups that offer you a good risk/reward and pulling the trigger. Thirty–40 percent of these trades will result in a loss. This is the game. Dr. Steenbarger blogged this a 'narcissistic desire to be correct.'

You are trying to be right. Consistently profitable traders just make good trades. They accept that they cannot control the results. Think about it.

This trader must develop the habit of hitting stocks that trade against him. And he needs to do some drills every day so that he develops this skill. But it is also important for him to understand himself better. Understanding that he has a psychological need to be right will help develop this skill. The reason he is not hitting stocks that trade against him is because he has not developed this habit. The reason he did not develop this habit, though most easily do, is because he has a psychological need to be correct. Understanding this will help him conquer this trading flaw.

We all have flaws. There are things we must all work on. Sometimes having a conversation with yourself can help.

The market has taught me what is important to become successful as a trader. The traders we just met possess characteristics for you to model that will truly impact your trading results. Next, I will share with you a way to measure your trades. Let's go discuss your most important task as a trader—One Good Trade.

CHAPTER 2

One Good Trade

D o not judge a trade based upon its results! A profitable trade may or may not have been a good trade, what I call One Good Trade. A loser may have been One Good Trade. If your fundamentals for a trade are sound, then that is One Good Trade. Consistently profitable traders obsess about making One Good Trade and not money. Your job is to make One Good Trade and then One Good Trade and then One Good trade.

Here are some statements I do not like to hear on my desk:

"Damn, I cut too early. It went up a point after I sold it."
"I was scared to buy XYZ because I thought it would trade lower."
"What a rip! I loaded up and XYZ traded against me. What a stupid trade!"
"I am just long. The stock is going higher."

All of the statements above are about results. Such thinking is your enemy. I am not trying to make money as a trader. My focus is on "doing the right thing." All I can ask for is excellent risk/reward opportunities. And then I execute. Being good at my job requires an obsession to my trading fundamentals. Money is just the by-product of me executing fundamentally solid trades.

But what is an excellent risk/reward setup? And how do I define one?

In this chapter, we'll introduce a good trade, One Good Trade, based on seven fundamentals and then share an example. But let's start by defining the opposite of One Good Trade.

DEFINING A BAD SALE

The most common statement I hear from new prop traders is: "Damn, I sold that stock too early." And without fail, they search for me to discuss this perceived error. Here's how a typical conversation with a new trader usually goes:

Bella: "What was your trading plan?"

Trader: "Thirty was holding the bid so I got long. I was going to sell when the stock traded higher and slowed. I sold the stock when it slowed. But it traded a point higher."

Bella: "Why was that a bad sale? That sounds about right."

Trader: "Well, the stock traded a point higher."

Bella: "So why does that mean you made a bad sale?"

Trader: "I missed out on a whole point of the move."

Most who just read the above will wonder why I am not in agreement. Well, I am not. Or, more accurately, I *might not be*. It depends.

If the new trader followed his detailed exit plan, then he made One Good Trade. This is great! He did his job! Now the new trader may have been slow to reenter to catch the next point upmove, with a new One Good Trade, but his original sale was correct. If we see an opportunity soon after One Good Trade, then we will immediately re-enter. Remember, we make One Good Trade, and then One Good Trade, and then One Good Trade. We do not make One Good Trade and then take a nap.

Perhaps the new trader did a poor job of establishing his exit plan. Perhaps the setup initially called for a longer holding period. Once a new trader realizes this, he should know where and how to fix his problem. We may need a list of all of these longer-holding trades with defined exit plans, distinguishing from shorter-term trades with different exits.

YOU ARE A TRADER, NOT AN INVESTOR

It's important to remember this mantra: I am a trader and not an investor. In fact, new traders ought to put this phrase on a Post-it on their screens when they begin. In an ideal world, traders catch a stock's entire intraday move. Sometimes, you'll get all three points of an anticipated three-point move. On occasion, you'll catch four and a half points of a three-point move. And yes, sometimes you'll sell or cover too early. But the analysis is always the same. Did you make One Good Trade and then One Good Trade? That is all you can do.

If a stock is a sale and I sell, then that stock trades up 10 points, and at no time could I identify One Good Trade, then my initial sale was correct. I do not care where that stock trades after a proper sale nor should the new trader.

"Bella, are you ever scared to buy in front of support because the stock may drop?" a new trader asked once in a Tradecast.

My response? "No."

If I buy in front of support, the stock drops, I exit and take a loss. Assuming I had sound reasoning for doing it and followed my rules, this is still One Good Trade. To borrow phraseology from the Ragin' Cajun James Carville, "It's the process . . . stupid."

Michael Lewis profiled Shane Battier in "The No-Stats All-Star" for the *New York Times* and offers a spot on example of the importance of the process. Shane Battier said about defending Kobe Bryant, "My job is not to keep him from scoring points but to make him as inefficient as possible." With his team, the Houston Rockets, up by two points, Battier forced Bryant to hoist a long jumper that Kobe misses 86.3 percent of his attempts. Kobe buried the three-pointer, winning the contest for his Lakers. Lewis writes as almost a lesson to the intraday trader, "The process had gone just as he (Battier) hoped. The outcome he never could control."

Overvaluing a Rip

Let's talk about taking a rip. GMan was trading HPQ. The resistance level was 35.38. HPQ held above this level, so he got long 7k shares. HPQ quickly dropped to the 35.15, and GMan exited for a loss. He took a rip. I heard, "(expletive deleted) what a rip!"

Who cares? Did he make One Good Trade?

Traders too often overvalue a rip. They find a great setup, it does not work out, and they take a rip. The next time this setup appears, they are hesitant to enter. And then invariably the stock goes up three straight points. Ever happen to you? Of course it has.

How can you judge this specific trading setup if you are sabotaging the results? Your rip must be blended with a potential three-point chop. Then judge that trading setup. But we overvalue the rip and then do not catch the easy trade. That is why we instruct our guys not to care about the results. Again, it's the process . . . stupid.

"I Am Just Long"

Oh, and this is my favorite one: "I am just long. I am not selling." Greeeeat! If you were running a mutual fund or were Warren Buffett directing Berkshire Hathaway, then maybe this phrase would be sound. But remember, our job is to trade. We'll leave the "investing" to those who invest. If you're "just long," you must manage your position.

One Good Trade is not arrogantly concluding that you know best. As 2008 certainly taught us, anything can happen at any time. So if you have a great position, and it is working, you still must manage this position. You can be slow to sell, but you must be looking for clues of when to scale out.

One of our traders pulled this stunt with a position in POT at 100. It was a home run. This idea was first discovered by our desk after watching Dan Fitzgerald of stockmarketmentor.com on CNBC. Like some late 1990s day trading jackass, Stock Holder is long making phone calls in my office two points in the money. Stock Holder, of course, has no idea how to trade this, since he is yapping away in my office (by the way, what the hell is he doing using my office?). Stock Holder comes out of my office and was met with a tongue lashing from me, "What the hell are you doing opening a position and not watching it? Don't you ever do that again! If you want to gamble, I hear the Mohegan Sun is offering discounts this weekend."

I continued to explain what would have happened if POT climbed 3 points, a huge seller appeared, POT went back to 100, all while he was jabbering away on the phone. He would have lost the opportunity to lock in a three-point gain. We would have lost money for the firm and himself. He immediately understood my point.

We meet in our conference room twice per week and traders present their One Good Trade via video. Also, they prepare a Word document embedded in their video that explains how they have followed our seven fundamentals for this trade. Sometimes our more experienced traders chirp that they do not get as much out of the OGT video review sessions as the other Tradecasts. OGT Tradecasts are very basic. That is the point: we reinforce our fundamentals.

Next we'll discuss the seven fundamentals that are important to our firm. Welcome to your front row seat of how a prop firm defines a fundamentally sound trade. How closely we follow these fundamentals is how we judge our trades.

THE FUNDAMENTALS

At SMB, we ask our traders to follow a set of seven fundamentals before entering every trade. Our fundamentals are:

1. Proper preparation
2. Hard work
3. Patience

4. A detailed plan before every trade
5. Discipline
6. Communication
7. Replaying important trades

If they follow all of these tenets in their trading from start to finish, then they have made One Good Trade. And this is what we do. Or certainly try to do. And we do it over and over again. We make One Good Trade, and then One Good Trade, and then One Good Trade.

I created this term based on my following of, no surprise, Coach K at Duke. When his team is up by 30 points, he screams from the sideline, "Next Play." Similarly, if his team is down by 15, which isn't all that often, he still yells, "Next Play." Since I don't run a basketball team, it's hard for me to yell to my traders, "Next Play." Instead, I say, "One Good Trade."

Bear with me on this one, but we stuck to our One Good Trade guns on CNBC, much to their chagrin. In the summer of 2009, Steve and I were preparing JToma for one of his many appearances on CNBC's *Fast Money*. As is the network's protocol, the show's staffers sent over some sample questions before the appearance. One of the questions that host Melissa Lee was to ask JToma was: Do you see the market up or down from here at the end of the year?

JToma's initial response during preparation was "I have no clue." But this is why we prepare. Steve offered an expanded "I have no clue" answer, "I am not Nostradamus. I am not an economist. We only have two quarters of market data. After two more, then I will know. As of right now, I have no idea."

I wasn't crazy about this at all. JToma politicked the answer on our behalf (hey, that's why he's on TV). Instead of offering a year-end projection, he offered levels that were important to us in the short term. He basically didn't answer the question and said what we wanted honoring the principle of One Good Trade.

But this principle that we are not sure where the market is headed in six months is important. We are not certain where the market will trade tomorrow for that matter. We are trained in the short term, and we know what we know. We can't afford to be like some of these bearish economists who joke with reporters after their doomsday forecast is met with, "I'm right once every ten years." If CNBC really wants to know where the market will be in six months, they can ask some rising fund manager who has a 50 percent chance of being proven right down the road. I prefer, in fact I demand, that our win rate is higher! And we do our best to ensure this success by making One Good Trade at a time.

In the fall of 2008, when the banks were getting obliterated and you could hit GS down 10 points and still catch an extra three points, our young traders were making a ton of money. I remember with a huge smile two of our more talented new traders up more than $20k, imploring the other to stay focused.

"Keep going (MoneyMaker)," Dr. Momentum would encourage.

And then during the next hour came these words from MoneyMaker pushing "Keep trading (Dr. Momentum). Don't be satisfied."

The day does not end until the bell rings. These gunners were up some pretty good money for first-year traders. But they embraced the principle of not being satisfied. A decade before, most independent retail traders would have been on the golf course by 2 PM after making five figures going long a tech stock IPO. While IPO mania ended soon after, the crash of 2008 provided similar swings, just in the other direction. In this case, instead of panicking or calling it a day, Dr. Momentum and MoneyMaker stuck to their fundamentals. Like a Buddhist Monk who lives in the moment, their focus was singular. This is One Good Trade in its full essence.

TRADERS ASK: "I'M STILL TRADING POORLY. WHAT NOW?"

I get a ton of e-mails from developing traders who ask me questions about how to improve after a stretch of struggling. These traders, with their confidence low, usually make the blanket statement that their trading has been, well, *poor*. As traders, we need to be more specific about what we are doing poorly. We need a template by which to judge ourselves. And this template should be soaked in trading fundamentals. Is it your stock selection? Is it your entry points? Is it your psychology? "I am doing poorly" doesn't mean anything.

Let me offer an example. Below is an e-mail that I received from an accomplished professional musician. If I told you who this new trader tours with (as a member of his band) you would with 100 percent certainty have listened to his music. I took my sister to hear the singer/songwriter, with whom this trader plays, and she thought I was the coolest brother alive. You cannot obtain a higher level of success in music than the author below. Rock Star wrote to me:

> Hi Mike—I wrote to you last week (the DNDN day) after I'd had a rip after a string of profitable days. I subsequently had four consecutive positive days in the $3–500 range. I was feeling solid.
>
> I mentioned to Roy that since mid-April, when I discovered your blog and came to visit in NYC, I've had an about face in my trading. Not only was I positive 12 of 13 days, I was getting fee rebates because I was adding liquidity to over 80% of my volume. I made graphs in Excel

of my days' trades and they formed (mostly) steady upward trending lines. I looked to find my weak spots in the day.

Then, today, I lost it. My demons took over. I reverted to sloppy bad habits. I got big. I held losers. I was in multiple positions bigger than I should have been. I wanted so badly not to finish in the red that I made things much worse. Today, I did not behave like the trader I have been the last two weeks. It is a disgusting feeling. An overwhelming feeling of shame and waste.

I was just beginning to feel like I could see the light at the end of the tunnel. Not that I had mastered anything, but just by absorbing all I have from your blog, site, and approach to trading, I had made a turn for the better. And I hadn't even started the training program yet.

I have this awful pattern: I work up small profits a few days in a row. I build on that. When I get up a certain amount in my account, I have a day where I lose it. My number one issue is not so much that I can't make money, it's that I can't keep it.

I did so much wrong today, and to add insult to injury, the stock I lost the most in was MGM...and then I read the blog and realized I gave my money to Steve.

I guess if I'm leaning toward a question here, it is this: When you were in your first months trading and were down large, how did you finally turn it around? Did you ever feel like you couldn't do it?

I am very much looking forward to learning from you guys. I feel like I can be great at this. But I was a disaster today and it cost me. My last two weeks said I had promise. Today said get out of the casino. Thanks.

I responded to his e-mail by posting it on the SMB Blog, with his permission, of course. I did not want to be blacklisted from future performances when his band played in NYC. I asked our readers to offer advice to this developing trader in addition to offering my own thoughts. Our online community responded with great enthusiasm. This was indeed a fun exercise.

This e-mail is an example of a talented person who had not yet learned how to judge his trading. And this is very common. He is focusing on his losses as evidence that he traded poorly. We, as prop traders, focus on the process and not our results. Again, this is the essence of One Good Trade.

Rock Star has one issue: he must learn to hit stocks that trade against him. This is covered by one of our fundamentals (Discipline). You must have the discipline to hit a stock that has exceeded your exit price. With One Good Trade he would have recognized this flaw and sought to eliminate this weakness. Rock Star would not have felt lost. There would not have been an e-mail to some trading guy (me, in this case) whom he knew only from the blogosphere. Rock Star would be empowered to make his own adjustments.

But too many traders lack good fundamentals. In fact, most don't have any. And they don't know that they are supposed to have them. So when I respond to any of these types of inquiries (Rock Star is not the only one), I offer a suggestion to think of each trade as One Good Trade.

When new prop traders begin at our firm, we ask that they judge each trade based upon whether they followed our seven fundamentals or not. We are essentially asking developing traders to evaluate their execution, not their P&L. You can make a series of One Good Trades and still be negative for the day. But it is unlikely that if we make a series of One Good Trades over a month-long period that we will be down overall.

PROPER PREPARATION

"By failing to prepare, you are preparing to fail."

—John Wooden

I love this phrase from teacher John Wooden. He was the head coach of UCLA basketball from 1948–1975, and at one point his teams won seven straight NCAA titles, a record to which no other team has come close. The aphorism is so simple, yet it says so much.

There are two parts to proper preparation for us: 1) the preparation necessary before the Bell rings, and 2) the specific trading information you must obtain before you can make a trade. Let's discuss.

Steve and I were invited to speak in early 2009 at Kershner Trading Group, a prop firm in Austin, Texas. Jason Gardner, Head of Trading at Kershner, is an old friend from "back in the day" and invited us to speak with his traders. Kershner holds a Saturday seminar for its traders once a month. The company flies in traders in our business to offer ideas for their traders to consider, and I guess it was our turn. So we hopped on to JetBlue and headed down to Austin. I offered to talk about anything they wanted. They chose "A Trader's Day," which covers how we prepare before the Open.

Admittedly, I had always wanted to visit Austin. And it's an awesome town. They say the only thing wrong with Austin is that it is surrounded by Texas. Great food, great music, clean, and if that isn't enough, there is a city full of University of Texas (UT) women. Also, I was hoping to sneak in a few rounds of golf.

Like great basketball coaches who learn from other coaches, they borrow plays, they learn new defensive schemes. I was interested in learning from Kershner. And we did. Kershner has an amazing facility with

18,000 square feet of trading space dedicated to performance for the developing trader. They do some industry innovative stuff with their filters and advanced statistical analysis of trader performance. Steve and I left with new ideas to consider.

Developing prop traders compete against the brightest of minds, those better capitalized, many with more experience, and sometimes even traders with better information. We know that many fail attempting to become a successful prop trader. As intraday traders, our margin of error is very small. Shouldn't we put ourselves in the best position to compete against our competition by preparing properly? With these kinds of odds against us, failing to prepare properly is preparing to fail.

Below is a checklist of things you can do to put yourself in the best position to compete in the markets. This job is what you make of it. We offer these ideas for your benefit.

☐ Read briefing.com before bed and start thinking about some stocks to trade for the morning. (In an August 2009 *Wall Street Journal* article, Steven Schonfeld, considered by many as the godfather of the prop trading industry, admitted he sleeps only three to four hours a night awaking early to think about trading setups for the next day. We should all be so lucky, as Schonfeld reportedly took home $200 million in 2008 and built himself a nine-hole golf course in his back yard.) Where are they trading in the after-hours? Jot down these prices and compare them to their premarket prices.

☐ Get to the office early. Every once in a while around 8 AM there will be an opportunity to make quick money on a breaking news story. If you live far away from the office, get on that 5-something AM train. It will give you an edge. Also, valuable information can be obtained by watching stocks trade in the premarket. What are the ranges of the stocks you are watching? How much volume are some stocks doing?

Further, the earlier you arrive, the more time you have to leaf through news. Sometimes in those extra minutes you find the stock of the day that you wouldn't have if you had spent less time researching. Moreover, you have extra time to ask members of your desk about a Stock In Play and obtain their feedback.

Most prop traders do not arrive later than 7:30 AM. Certainly experienced traders with a system can stroll in later. And NYSE traders can stroll in later than NASDAQ traders. 8:00 AM is the latest that most serious traders arrive.

☐ Read briefing.com again in the morning and pick a few stocks. Think about your style and determine the best two stocks of the day for you.

☐ Compile statistics such as daily volume, important technical levels, intraday range, and short interest. At SMB, we have developed a SMB Stock Data Sheet for such information.

☐ Set alerts for the stocks that did not make the cut, but are worth some attention. Other pretty good ideas that did not make your two stocks cut should still not be discarded.

☐ Create a road map for your morning. Develop some plans as to when you might take a position in one of your stocks. If you see the xyz scenario, then you will buy at this price. Continue creating "if-then" scenarios for each outcome.

Consider the different ways the stocks you have picked might trade. Will they sell off first and then be bought for the rest of the day? Will the stock quickly climb in the morning trading session and search for a seller? Will you be completely wrong and the stock will just trade lower? Under what scenarios should you aggressively buy the stock?

Are there easier stocks to trade? After you have narrowed your stocks to a few and have gathered all the information necessary, keep asking yourself if there are easier stocks to trade.

☐ Listen carefully during the morning meeting.

☐ Review your index cards (reminders to yourself and the best of the old school techniques) before the Open.

☐ Prepare mentally. Visualize a great trading day. Perform your visualization exercises. Today will be a great day.

☐ Prepare physically. Drink some water to hydrate yourself during the morning stretch. Get comfortable in your seat. Breathe.

☐ Review charts. After the Close, review the charts of top price and volume gainers and losers. Also, check the charts on the stocks that are hot. Find excellent entry points and set your alerts for such prices. Consider developing a basket of stocks, and regularly review the charts of the stocks in your basket.

All these little things make big things happen. Do them consistently, and the profits will follow.

But proper preparation for an intraday prop trader is also possessing specific information. On our desk, we do not make a trade unless we know the average volume, daily range, important technical levels, short interest, and fresh news for our stocks. Only armed with this information can we make One Good Trade.

Proper preparation is not enough to make One Good Trade. Hard work comes next.

HARD WORK

> "Genius is one percent inspiration and ninety-nine percent perspiration."
>
> —Thomas Edison

A prop trader should not work 100 hours a week. We're not investment bankers or corporate lawyers blindly working to make partner. Unlike those other high-paying professions, we actually know the score each day. We don't wait until the end of the year for discretionary bonuses that are often politically tainted. In that regard, this job is the most like being a professional athlete than anything else I can think of, in that one is judged by his or her performance daily. At the same time, great athletes and traders need their rest to recharge. Having said that, we work hard, consistently and productively each day. But for One Good Trade, Hard Work assumes a different context from what you might originally assume. It is about the work you must do beforehand.

Watching your trading screens intently and gathering important information is how we define hard work. We must ask the following questions at a rapid fire pace, just as a batter determines the prospects of an incoming 95 mile-per-hour heater.

- Who is buying?
- Who is selling?
- What levels are most important?
- Is this stock stronger or weaker than the market?
- Is this stock stronger or weaker than its counterparts in its sector?
- Where is most of the volume being done?
- How much volume at a price causes the stock to move up or down?
- What is the spread?
- How quickly does the stock move when it is ready to find another price?
- How is the Specialist treating your orders?
- Are there any big prints?
- Is the stock trading in a particular pattern?

These are the questions that I answer before trading a stock. This information—yes, all of this information—should be gathered before you make One Good Trade. This is what we mean by hard work.

Most successful trades are easy trades. They result from doing the above, seeing an excellent and simple trading opportunity, and then pouncing. Watch, watch, watch, and BAM! Your edge comes into play, and you make your next trade.

If you are trading a stock, and it is not offering excellent risk/reward opportunities, then move on. Type up some other stocks, and watch them intently. Gather all that information from before. And do not make a trade until you have this information, as a new trader. Never. Do not make trades unless the edge you require is present along with the right type of information.

When I first started trading, I got the following advice: "If you are not going to come to work and constantly search for good setups, then don't bother coming to work." These are not exactly the words I would use, but this is still a very important message for developing traders. Those words of wisdom were relayed to me in the late 1990s and they still are meaningful to the new trader today. Spend your trading day searching and watching for excellent risk/reward opportunities.

Furthermore, information gathered yesterday may lead to a good trading opportunity today. When SMB met with the TV executives from CNBC, JToma casually mentioned that he made most of his money on Second Day Plays. One executive decision maker was sold. "Let's have him do a segment on Second Day Plays," came next.

Regarding the Second Day Play, I fondly recall a trade with ADM. The stock sold off from 45 and closed the day not able to break 43.90. The next morning a little after the Open, ADM dipped below 43.90. I immediately shorted ADM because I knew that that level could not be breached the day before. ADM quickly traded lower, and I made a chop based on information I learned from my hard work the previous day.

Woody Allen said: "Ninety percent of life is just showing up." The same idea applies to trading. Showing up every day matters. Searching for support and resistance levels every day will positively impact your trading. Heading home early because a few moves went against you should be saved for special occasions when you really must clear your head.

If you want an example of a person who works hard every day, let me highlight AGA. Picture him intently watching his screens. He hardly ever goes to the bathroom. In fact, AGA delays his lunch at times over an hour if he thinks a stock is about to move. When he once made an easy, quick chop, we congratulated him and he humbly said he was "just lucky." He wasn't lucky. He deserved his gain because he worked hard gathering the information that enabled him to make a quick profit on an easy trade.

Again, most of the money you will earn trading will be easy money. You will see something on your screen that signals a great trading opportunity for you and you will pounce. But these great opportunities present themselves only because you have watched your stock(s) and gathered valuable information.

To make One Good Trade you must prepare properly, work hard, and have patience.

PATIENCE

"In this game, the market has to keep pitching, but you don't have to swing. You can stand there with the bat on your shoulder until you get a fat pitch."

—Warren Buffett

It is not enough to buy a strong stock, or short a weak one. Price matters. Even the legendary Mr. Buffett often says this despite him not being an active trader. You have to open your positions at a price that offers the best risk/reward opportunity.

On our desk you can hear me utter playfully, "Patience, young fella, patience." Successful prop traders are consistently patient. If they see that a stock has strong support at $30, then they develop a plan to buy it at or very near $30. They don't buy the stock at $30.50, or at $30.25, or even at $30.15. $30 is $30!

Patience enables an excellent entry point, which allows a trader to

- Gather a bigger position
- Decrease his chance of being stopped out
- Hold the position for a larger move

Good traders understand that they will not be in every move. They wait for setups with which they are comfortable and confident. A strong stock that has moved well above a good risk/reward entry is left to run without them.

For example, if a stock is trading in a range, breaks out, and you miss the buying opportunity, well, that is one mistake. But if out of frustration you buy that same stock well above the range, you chase it, well, now you have made two mistakes. The first blunder will not cause trading losses (just an opportunity cost), but the second one will. Do not let one mistake cause another.

Mr. Lost Opportunity Cost

Ok, I must share a hilarious story about a trader and his obsession with lost opportunity costs. I sat next to the most disappointed trader on the Street in the late 1990s. Every day was a disaster. Not a ruination that

Mr. Lost Opportunity Cost suffered large losses, but rather he just got frustrated at missed opportunities. Like the guy who comes into work after not hitting the Mega Millions jackpot the night before and saying, "I just lost $163 million in the lottery last night." (I know a guy who actually says this.)

This trader would calculate every missed trade as a loss. YHOO would climb a quick 3 points, he would discover this, and then the banging and screaming would commence.

"I just lost $15k in YHOO. How did I miss that?" he would yawp.

EBAY would climb five points, he would discover this, and then there would be more impressive banging and screaming.

"God Dammit. What a rip! That just cost me $25k."

You can't hit a home run without swinging, and clearly this guy didn't get that.

Price Matters

During a routine video review session, TradeCast, a new trader, bought consistently at poor prices. This Noob was negative trading RIMM, while almost everyone else on our desk was in the green. Let's talk about price some more.

Wharton Junior was trading GS and added to his position after GS broke above its upward channel at 85c. The exact price is not important, hence the reason it is not given. Wharton Junior bought higher, through the figure, at 7c. JToma mocked him until Wharton Junior never wanted to make this error again.

And I agree. If the upward channel is 85c, then the buy is not more than 92c. As an active intraday prop trader, there is a huge difference between your entry of 86c and 7c. And when you review your trades you must ask, *If I buy GS when it breaks the upward channel 1,000 times will I make money with a 7c entry?* And with Wharton Junior's trade he wouldn't. Hence, the vicious JToma scolding.

Another trader, Mozart Light, was waiting to short CVX below 75c. Mozart Light hit the 59c bid to get short. Again, you must ask whether hitting 59c bid 1,000 times will be a profitable technique with his given setup. And watching the trade back 59c was not a good enough entry. 65c would have been fine in front of a huge 68c offer. But 59c was not good enough. And Mozart Light should have let the trade run without him if he could have gotten short at 65c.

Wharton Junior risked an extra 21c on his trade. Mozart Light risked an extra 6c on his trade. If you are going to write 2 million shares a month then 27c on two thousand shares is a huge deal. Even for a less active retail trader, this is an extra $540 on one trade. And for active intraday prop traders, you can't be in these trades at the prices above.

Learning to get stocks at the right price is a skill that good intraday prop traders learn. And it's a very important skill. Do the math. If you learn to save 1c on average for every trade, and you write two million shares in a month, how much extra will you make? That's an extra $20k in your pocket.

If you just watch your screens patiently all day, plays will emerge. Good risk/reward setups will appear. Consistently profitable traders do not force trades. They embrace the important part of their job—just waiting for a setup to develop.

As you gain experience, you will learn that success will require more than simply opening a position in a stock that you have watched. You must establish your position at a good price with the proper timing as well.

"Patience, young fella, patience."

A DETAILED PLAN BEFORE EVERY TRADE

"The best trader is a prepared trader."
                    —Evan Lazarus-Partner, T3 Capital

A prop firm leader identifies a new trader in a position. He has spotted his next potential victim. Slowly, this partner approaches unnoticed behind the new trader. And then, like a cobra, strikes with, "What is your trading plan?"

That is one of my favorite teaching techniques. If it takes a new trader more than two seconds to respond, then this is a bad sign. This is assuming, of course, the new trader was not just flustered by my sneak attack. A developing prop trader should in one sentence be able to explicate his detailed trading plan for every trade. Quiz yourself. The next time you are in a trade can you summarize your detailed trading plan in one sentence? Call it a trader's equivalent of corporate underlings' "Elevator Pitch" to the CEO of his firm. Let's discuss.

First, you need an exit strategy. One of our great advantages is flexibility. We can exit a position in a millisecond and even flip our position if advisable. We are not a behemoth Mutual Fund or Hedge Fund with millions of shares to unwind. It may take such a market powerhouse a month to unwind their position. We are light and nimble. You have to decide when to exit if a stock goes against you. As our good friend and author of the best-selling momentum technical analysis text in history, "Technical Analysis Using Multiple Time Frames," Brian Shannon from alphatrends.com preaches, "You must have a backup plan for every situation." And you must do this before you enter your every trade.

Likewise, and this outcome is more fun, your plan should also include an exit strategy for if the stock trades in your favor. What will make you cover your position favorably? Will you exit if it trades at a certain price? Will you exit after a substantial move or when a large order appears? The details of the plan are important, but actually having a plan is most significant.

Here is an example of a plan: I notice that NYSE is offering ADM at 30. If NYSE lifts, I will buy ADM and hold until either the offer is 29.90 or the stock trades at 30.50. I will also consider selling if a new large seller appears before 30.50.

But you may need a few more details than that. Let's try this again. I notice that NYSE is selling at 30. If NYSE lifts, I will buy ADM and hold until either the offer is 29.90 or ADM trades at 30.50. I will also consider selling if a new large seller appears before 30.50. If NYSE lifts 30 and the futures begin to rapidly decline, I will consider selling ADM.

And now even more detailed: If NYSE lifts 30 and the futures quickly worsen, I will consider selling ADM if I notice bids have disappeared from the NYSE Open Book.

Look, if you are a developing trader, and you do not develop a detailed trading plan before every trade, please do me a favor. Go find all of your trading records. Secure a fireplace and a match. Take these "trading records" and light them on fire. A paper shredder would be just as effective. Your "trading records" are meaningless. Your trading results are only significant if you have followed the fundamentals used by all consistently profitable traders (CPTs). And a detailed plan for every trade is one of them. Now go and extinguish that fire, please.

DISCIPLINE

"Some people say, "I can't sell that stock because I'd be taking a loss. If the stock is below the price you paid for it, selling doesn't give you a loss; you already have it."
         —William O'Neill, Founder, *Investor's Business Daily*

Trading is about skill development and discipline and not understanding dark matter. So it figures that this is going to be an important section. Simply put, you have no chance, trading any market, at any period, with any stock, in any country, making money as a trader without discipline. Let's discuss.

Discipline is executing your plan as you set out to do it, without altering it in the middle. Discipline is executing your detailed plan *every time*.

If your plan is to buy a stock at 30 and hit it if it fails to hold that level, and the stock fails to hold 30, *then hit it*. And hit it immediately. As James "RevShark" DePorre of thestreet.com and star trader counsels, "Sell is not a four-letter word." Hit the stock and reevaluate. Pay attention to how easy it is to get out. Then find the next trade.

There are going to be days when you follow your plan and the stock trades higher after you hit it. In fact, there will be times when your sale will be the low print of the day. But consider these two points: (1) Do not judge your trading system based upon one trade. Executing your plan, being disciplined, will lead to long-term success. (2) A good prop trader hits the stock and reevaluates. Not just hits the stock. Hit the stock and reevaluate. It is always your option to formulate a new plan. You can always buy the stock back. You might recognize that after hitting the stock below 30 that it didn't go down the way you thought. For example, you may exit easily at 29.98, when you anticipated you would at best clip 29.90. In this case, you may gather information that this stock may still be strong. So develop a new plan to get long and only exit after a significant move up or a move to a new low.

As we have discussed, new prop traders often make the mistake of overvaluing one trade. They develop a plan and hit the stock executing their plan, and then watch in frustration as the stock trades higher. They conclude that they were wrong to hit the stock. In effect, they conclude that being disciplined was wrong. Wrong. You are developing a system that will produce consistent results over a long period of time. One trade is not the measurement.

Execute your plan. *Hit your stock* if it reaches your exit point. You will never be a successful trader if you are not disciplined. I do not know one successful trader who is not disciplined. Heed the advice of Jesse Livermore, who said, "A loss never bothers me after I take it. I forget it overnight. But being wrong—not taking the loss—that is what does damage to the pocketbook and to the soul." Do not let the market teach you this lesson by taking your money.

Mad Max

Just a word about discipline and what I have learned as a mentor. You can't try to be a disciplined trader. You must be a disciplined person to be a disciplined trader. Let me explain.

One of the most talented traders we have worked with used to trade with us (let's call him Mad Max). And he had stretches when he was the best trader on our desk. This tended to be when the market was very volatile. Mad Max craved action. He loved fast-moving stocks that would trend for points on end. But when the markets were the way they are normally—selectively volatile, filled with fake breakdowns, and fake breakouts—Mad Max ripped up an awful lot of money. Almost more money than he made when the markets were volatile.

And I really liked this trader. Honestly, I miss Mad Max. He was original. But he got away with breaking more of our rules than anyone on the desk. We would overlook them sort of like Jerry Jones overlooked TO's behavior for a few years. This was a mistake.

When Mad Max started to struggle, I moved my schedule around to work with him personally. Not to be overly dramatic, but I did everything I could to help. I watched tape with him personally. I created rules for him to follow to help with his discipline. I made sure I pointed out good trades to improve his confidence and offer an idea of the best trades for that particular time period.

And this trader was super smart. Mad Max loved trading. He was very talented. We are talking top 1 percent talented. And again Mad Max had some monster trading days.

But this was just not enough. The market demands more. He just wasn't a disciplined person. For example, he liked to stay up late at night playing Madden Football instead of getting the rest necessary to be alert during the next trading day. I know this seems like a small matter, but stuff like this screams, "I am not disciplined." And the market will respond, "Not in my house, Mad Max. Next!"

He would show up late to our AM meetings, which again may not seem crucial, but it is. It's a testament to how disciplined you will be during the trading day. If Mad Max couldn't discipline himself to come in on time, then how the hell could he discipline himself not to jump into trades that did not offer him an excellent risk/reward? He couldn't.

I do not enjoy sharing this anecdote with you. Not any of it. When he left (He quit. I never would have fired him.) I was really upset. I thought it was my fault. Maybe partly it was. And he quit, in a huge whole. And I wasn't the least bit upset about the firm's losses. I was losing a friend. Mad Max was someone who had the confidence in me to help him become the trader that he wanted to be. And I couldn't do it.

This is the worst part of prop trading. Due to the difficulty of trading, and how many fail, one day you look up and your friends are now not sitting next to you. You spend 10 hours a day, for many years, and build relationships with traders who become your close friends. You stand in their wedding party, are present for the birth of their first child, perhaps you introduce them to their wife, or console them after the death of a parent. And then one day they move to the suburbs, start coaching or something like that, and the best you get is the occasional "how are things?" e-mail. Prop trading can steal your friends.

The deck was stacked against me, perhaps. One day Mad Max got into a serious traffic accident. He gets taken to the hospital. A girl he started seeing shows up to check on him. That's nice. But then like a bad afternoon soap, the story gets more complicated. An hour later, his longtime girlfriend shows up, unaware of this other girl. This trader just did what he wanted to do when he wanted to do it. It's the main reason why you loved the guy so much, and the exact reason why he struggled as a trader.

I have thought a lot about this trader leaving and what we could have done better. There were some things that we could have improved on our end. But after careful introspection and analysis, the truth is that this trader cannot become a great trader until he becomes a more disciplined person. In fairness, toward the end, he made significant strides toward improving in this area. Mad Max just started so far behind. He can certainly become a great trader. And that is just the way it is.

I will end with this simple suggestion. One way to keep a better sense of discipline is through vigorous exercise. A healthy body leads to a healthier, dare I say, more disciplined mind. Another firm with whom SMB is friendly and respects, T3 Capital, sponsors a triathlon team to get their traders in better physical shape, and they continue to perform well on the desk. This is well done by them.

At a good prop firm, the floor buzzes with trading ideas. How does this work? And which ideas should be shared?

COMMUNICATION

"No man's opinions are better than his information."
—J. Paul Getty, Founder, Getty Oil

A solid prop desk shares valuable trading information with each other. We consider sharing such information as a trading fundamental. Sixty pairs of eyes are better than one. As Roy Davis, director of SMB Training, explains, "We teach our desk how to work as a team so they make more money individually." As I've said already, just before starting SMB, it was all very "every man for himself" with no culture of intellectual collectivism.

The purpose of speaking on a trading desk is to share *relevant, factual* information (I will skip the specifics of how we define relevant and factual information). I have found that such sharing increases the profitability of all the traders on our desk. Case in point, one Friday afternoon, one trader, SPA, called out AIG dropping below an important support level, and consequently the desk made chops. That communication carried our desk on this trading day.

Not only must a prop trader communicate their best trading ideas but they must review their trades.

REPLAYING IMPORTANT TRADES

"Find the trading plays that make sense to you and make more of them with more size."

—Mike Bellafiore, SMB Blog

Good prop traders constantly strive to improve their performance. Let me remind you of the JToma Review, an old school self-improvement technique: Replay important trades in your head.

When the market slows, this is the time to think through your important trades. Do this multiple times during the trading day. Ask yourself these questions:

- Was there a spot where you could have added more size?
- Did you sell too early?
- What made the stock go up?
- Was there a catalyst for the move?
- Did you assume too much or too little risk?

Replay the trade and construct improvements for the next similar trade. We watch a lot of video of our trading. Professional coaches review hours of game tape. They review their team's performance so that they can improve their strengths and eliminate their errors. Professional athletes, on teams and competing individually, do this as well. They concentrate on improving their technique. A pitcher might view tape to see if he is tipping his pitches, or if his arm angle is consistent. If he spots a mistake, he works to correct it.

Traders who watch video can find setups where they can add more size, plays that are not working for them, patterns that they did not discern initially, gain screen time that improves their skills, and imprint their best setups in their mind.

Also, talk to other traders on your desk who are trading your stocks. Ask for their thoughts. You will get better as you gain experience, but you will get much better if you improve your technique while you are gaining experience.

Print out your trades. Were you disciplined? Did you execute on your stops? Did you do worse in a stock than you thought? Are you trading some stocks better than others? Are there some stocks that you just don't trade well?

Get into the habit of evaluating your more important trades during the day.

MONEYMAKER'S ONE GOOD TRADE

"Rome was not made in one day."

—French Proverb

Learn to judge your trades based on how closely you followed your trading fundamentals. The following is a trade that MoneyMaker made in August 2009 in AIG and judged by the seven fundamental principles. (See figure 2.1). Your goal every day should be to make One Good Trade, and then One Good Trade, and then One Good Trade.

Proper preparation: AIG had a strong move from 34 to 37 on heavy volume in the last 30 minutes of the Close the prior day. The next day, AIG gapped up above the high from the prior day on news that AIG's founder would work with the current CEO to help rescue the company.
Levels: Res: 41.50, 42.25. Sup: 40
Average Volume: 38m
Short % of float: 20%
52-week range: 6.60–99.20

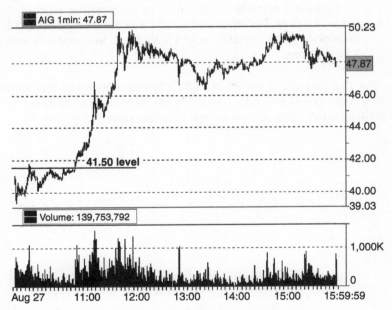

FIGURE 2.1 MoneyMaker—(AIG)—One Good Trade—8-27-09

Hard work: On the Open, the stock consolidated in a range between 40 and 41.50. AIG began to consolidate around 10:45 AM in a tighter range close to 41.50. I noticed, however, that the stock could not hold above 41.50. When 41.50 finally started to hold, and buyers stepped up, I bought 3,000 shares.

Patience: Got long at 41.58 as soon as I saw buyers step up and hold above 41.50.

Have a detailed plan before every trade: The plan was to get long as soon as buyers stepped up and held above 41.50. I would scalp part of my position initially but if I saw significant buying above 41.50, I would buy back the shares I sold and hold a core until there was a reason to sell. Conversely, if the stock traded below 41.45, I would exit my long position and re-evaluate.

Discipline: Sold half of my position between 41.70 and 42.00. Held a core and bought back the shares I sold when the stock got above 42.00. Held a core to 50, when I sold.

Communication: I shared this level with the desk.

Replay Important Trades: When the stock held above 41.50 and then 42.00, I could have held more size for a bigger move. I knew that there was a high short interest in the stock and the shorts would be squeezed if the stock continued its upward momentum. The stock also gave a clue the prior day into the Close that it had the potential to explode. I actively traded most of my position catching 20–50 cents at a time, but after seeing offers being paid aggressively and buyers stepping up, that should have given me confidence to hold a larger core.

Now that you are an expert in trading fundamentals and the characteristics of some excellent traders, let's discuss the concept of a good fit. Who lands these dream jobs at a proprietary trading desk?

CHAPTER 3

A Good Fit

Angel is the most persistent prop firm candidate in the nation. He's probably been rejected for positions at every single firm in the New York area, but has yet to stop banging on doors.

First, he persuaded a friend of mine, a well-known financial reporter, to forward his resume my way. Angel did not receive an interview. Next, Angel followed up monthly for six months with e-mails and his resume. Still, no interview. Apparently none of this deterred the ever-vigilant Angel. No meant maybe. No response meant possibly at a later date. I could only imagine what yes would mean!

A well-regarded prop firm head with whom we used to share office space (call him Strategic) stopped me in the hallway one trading session. Strategic inquired how trading was going for us, and then lobbied me to take a look at "an excellent candidate." Strategic runs one of the most successful prop firms in NYC, and with limited personal time, pleaded for me to read this candidate's resume. Seeming personally upset for this recruit, he explained that his firm had to retract this candidate's invitation due to current trading conditions, but thought he might be a good fit for us. A few minutes later Strategic e-mailed me a resume. The name at the top was Angel Cuevas. The third time was not a charm, though. Angel again did not receive an interview.

A few more months pass until one day I received an instant message. Actually, four of them:

Angel: Hi Mike! It's Angel Cuevas. Wanted to follow up on possibly meeting for an informational interview on prop trading.

Angel: Hey Mike, tried contacting you earlier today, figured you might have been busy. I wanted to follow up on my e-mail. Do you think it might be possible to meet up for a few questions on prop trading?

Angel: Mike, got to run. Please let me know at some point if the informational interview will be possible. I would appreciate the pointers on breaking into the business. Plus I'd like to hear your stories on when you got started.

Angel: got to run. Bye!

And then, a few hours later, now apparently back from wherever he went:

Angel: Hi Mike! Any chance that we can meet for the informational interview?

Unlike a lot of folks who break into prop trading and Wall Street in general, Angel did not come from a family of great means. He was scraping by just to fund his own personal trading account by working the night shift at a New Jersey factory. (Frankly, it's a touching story, and not all that uncommon. Bruce Kovner, founder of multi-billion dollar hedge fund Caxton Associates and considered one of the best traders in the modern era, funded his first trading account with a loan from a credit card while driving a taxi in New York City. As I write this book, Kovner is 164th on the World's Billionaires List published annually by *Forbes* magazine.)

Angel worked at a factory by night, slept for a few hours, and then took his cuts trading the S&P mini futures by day. Since he could not fully devote his time to develop the right skills, he was not consistently profitable. Though I was able to share some words of encouragement with Angel, he still remains without a spot on a prop desk. Why? Well that is a lot of what this chapter is about.

Great Wall Street firms often mention the concept of "fit" when doing recruiting pitches. So how does this whole recruiting process work? Who is a good fit for these plum jobs? What things will harm a candidate's chances? What about the recruiting of experienced traders? And what about after the dream job is landed—how does a person know he will remain a good fit?

Each prop firm has its unique recruiting process. Some place an emphasis on elaborate math tests and some heavily weight your performance interacting with their traders. Each prop firm has a set of characteristics most important to their trading style. Some prefer Ivy League graduates with excellent grades. Others seek former college athletes, with a history of competitiveness. All prop firms are really just looking for people who will be a good fit for their firm.

At many prop firms the recruiting goes something like this:

- Resume Screening
- Testing
- The Interview
- Second Round Interview
- Meeting with Firm Traders
- Comparison to Other Candidates
- Background Check
- The Offer

Each firm is simply looking for the best candidates who fit their trading system. Who presents the best risk/reward to trade their money in their trading style? Is it likely that the firm will see dividends from the time teaching and capital allocated for your development as a trader? It is that simple.

WHO GETS HIRED?

For Angel and others like him, it's important to ask the question, "So who gets hired?" Examining the differences between the trader who lands the job and the one who keeps looking is a valuable step toward breaking into the industry.

Not Necessarily Persuasive

There are many traders walking around the streets of New York City and Main Streets convinced that they can be the next Steve Cohen or Paul Tudor Jones or Bruce Kovner, just to name a few industry legends. All they need is a chance. One such would-be superstar recently sent this e-mail to a prop firm:

I've been bothering you for months now for a job because I know I can be successful and you won't meet anyone who wants to work harder or be more successful more than I do. I am confident in saying that there is no one who wants this more than I do. NO ONE! All I need is a chance and you guys will never regret it and that's because you will see that I am working my tail off and that I love this job. THIS IS MY DREAM JOB! I don't want to do anything else but trade. I'll trade any style you guys want. I'm a fast learner and can adapt to any style or technique. If my style of trading isn't accepted with you guys then that's ok because I can trade whatever style you want.... The fact of the matter is, most successful people do well because they work hard and they love what they do. If you think about it, most people who do well at any job work hard and love what they do and that's how I feel about this career. If hired, I WILL MAKE AT LEAST $7K A DAY! I understand I am inexperienced but you guys look for smart, driven, hard-working people who are educated, THAT'S ME! I can't see how you could find someone to hire over me due to the fact that I have unmatched drive and ambition. In all seriousness, what do you guys want from a trader that I don't have?

Some cite paper trading results as proof that they are our next top producer. Another recent e-mail ended with:

I have been paper trading for the last couple of months with remarkable results.

For example, during these volatile months, from 08/07/08 to 10/10/08, total net profit was $13,417.00 with 100 trades using 5 ES contracts. Seventy-one were winning trades and 29 were losing trades.

One self-proclaimed experienced trader badgered me every day for two months requesting an interview, e-mailing me his trading results. One day he made $30,000, the next $15,000, the next $18,000. We invited him in for an interview, but quickly learned his results were all based on paper trading. Ripper.

Some share that they have read every trading book and, naturally, they must be good. Most interviewees claim to watch CNBC religiously, assuming that this fact is dispositive of success. Some say that they just have a feel for the markets because they frequently predict intraday which way the market will close. One interviewee originally insisted that since his father was a good trader, trading was in his blood. Unfortunately, none of the above is determinative of success.

Many hopeful future traders plead with their body language "just give me a chance bro, I won't let you down." They dream of earning a nickname reflecting their superior trading skills, perhaps Iceman, MoneyMaker, or Franchise. They dream of becoming mega-rich and living the life of the trader rich and famous. Their toughest decisions would be how to show off their newfound wealth: Lamborghini or Ferrari? Blonde or brunette model?

Vacation in St. John or Cap Ferret? Sushi at Nobu or steak at Peter Luger? But really, all this is exactly that . . . day-dreaming.

And few of those dreamers would be a good fit for us and many other prop trading firms.

Becoming One of the Chosen Few

Contrary to popular belief, trading is a craft. Like an artisan who develops a craft over a lifetime, it requires a discipline to be exercised daily. Just to get started, it takes 10 hours of work every day for months and maybe years to become a consistently profitable trader (CPT). Becoming a CPT is like joining an exclusive country club: they do not let everyone in and you must follow all of the rules or else your membership will be terminated.

Few are willing to pay the price required to join our club of successful proprietary traders. There are many people who presently do not have the personal skills, which help develop the trading skills, to become a CPT. Or more accurately, many do not offer a good risk/reward to a prop firm that they can develop into a CPT. Possessing certain characteristics shortens your learning curve and improves your chances of success. Simply put, there is often a disconnect between those who *believe* they can trade and those who actually can.

Personally, I agree with Charles Kirk of the Kirk Report who said, "It is my view that everyone has the capacity to become a successful trader provided that they put in the time, effort, and dedication over a lengthy period of time." At SMB, we could motivate many of these would-be traders to change, but this would be a bad use of our time and energy. Why take the chance that those who needed to change would ultimately resist change? We use the same risk/reward concepts in making human resources decisions as we do with our trades.

Conversely, many institutional trading firms hire mostly those from top-ranked colleges and universities, with a heavy emphasis on the Ivy League. Kevin Hassett at Bloomberg.com highlighted the tremendous increase in Harvard graduates hired by Wall Street firms since the 1970s in "Harvard Narcissists With MBAs Killed Wall Street." Many are former Division 1 athletes, with certain desks making a concerted effort to keep the pipeline flowing from the sideline to the trading floor. But in the end, despite the hiring practices of the big boys, or what remains of them, trading is about skill development and discipline, not understanding the theory of relativity or throwing a football. So contrary to popular belief, you don't have to go to an Ivy League school, run fast, or live in NYC to become the next great trader.

Ok, so where does that leave us? As I said earlier, there are many who *mistakenly* believe that they can become a CPT without serious personal skill development. These people could change but the risk/reward for a prop firm is not in our favor. And there are also many not getting hired by the big banks who absolutely fit our profile. So whom exactly do you hire, Mike?

Most smaller trading firms know their place in the trading hierarchy. Prop firms do not carry the recognition of Goldman Sachs. They are not SAC Capital. Prop firms may not get many candidates with math SAT scores of 800 or cum laude GPAs. But they do offer something unique.

At more prestigious firms, you will most likely have to sit on the bench for a few years. You may be in charge of filling orders for the Asian markets at 2 AM. You may fetch more than your fair share of venti lattes for your boss. With us and other prop firms, you start developing a trading track record almost immediately. At SMB you start trading live on Day 26.

Let me be clear. There is nothing wrong with being a gofer to start your career. For two years after graduating from college, I worked for the legendary chairman of the Judiciary Committee at the Connecticut General Assembly, Richard Tulisano. My job was to do whatever he asked, whenever he asked. Some days, my biggest contribution was to sneak cognac in a paper cup to the chairman during sessions that ran into the early mornings. And I loved every minute of that job.

Some recent graduates only want to trade. They simply love trading, and do not want to sit on the bench, so to speak. They want to start developing their skills now. Some may not buy into the byzantine cultures of Corporate America. Our head trader, GMan, lasted at a big bank for two days. He quit because he couldn't stand their culture. Some want to keep a larger percentage of what they produce. The payout at a proprietary trading firm often allows the trader to keep a larger split of her profits than a big bank would, and the payments are much more frequent than an annual bonus. Some were passed over by the big banks, but only want to trade. And these are the people whom we recruit.

Smaller firms also often offer their new traders more in the way of education. In my obviously biased opinion, SMB offers the very best short-term equity training program on the Street. We and other reputable prop firms will teach you to trade well. Now a prop firm offers a lot more but that comes later.

Excellent prop firms have developed a unique culture. We have a distinct culture at SMB. We grind it out. We judge our trading performance not by our P&L, but by our trading progress. We work on our game every day. We work as a team. We respect the market and our competitors. We communicate our best trading ideas with our desk and in our own language. We prepare with a sense of urgency that we must find the best stocks For Us on that day. We make One Good Trade, and then One Good Trade, and then yes, another One Good Trade, with no celebrations after a profitable trade, or "chop." We work very hard, but we enjoy our time away from trading, and often together.

As I write, one of our traders, Franchise, is gunning to be an elite trader, and he is driving up to the University of Connecticut to interview some candidates. He asked me before he left: (1) What should I look for from a candidate? and (2) Can I borrow the corporate credit card? I told him: I want those who are "one of us." I want to train only those who are passionate about the markets, bright, competitive, conscientious, mentally tough, hard working, willing to work with the team, and able to demonstrate a history of success. And most importantly, that he should go see Steve about the credit card.

We have developed a series of questions and processes to find such candidates. But simply, we are looking for those who are a good fit for us, a candidate who offers an excellent risk/reward for our trading style, those who are one of us. And this is what is done at all good prop firms.

A RECRUITMENT PROCESS

Since I couldn't get on the phone and compile a summary of every prop firm's recruiting process (and if I did, this would be exceedingly uninteresting), I developed a Plan B. I am going to share some about how our firm recruits and sprinkle in some anecdotes to highlight what is most important. But I offer you this thought to consider during every step in the recruiting process. The head trainers at a prop firm spend all of their free time working with their students, they sacrifice trading opportunities to teach, and their salary depends largely on the success of their students. They better get this part right. A few great traders can carry a firm on their backs for months. Imagine if GMan landed at another desk.

Just to use SMB Capital as an example, we trade a unique style—stocks "In Play" on a short-term basis. While there are many different ways to make money in the stock market, we do it in a way that has worked well for us over the years. There are certain characteristics that best suit our style. Plus, it's my desk! You are trading my money! And I spend a great deal of time teaching you. I am a former competitive athlete and law school graduate who enjoys the company of the intellectually curious. Naturally, we hire people we like. What is the point of running a desk if you cannot hire the people with whom you would enjoy working?

But for those who are not invited to trade with us, I tell them very clearly, that we are just one desk. If you are truly passionate about trading, then please keep searching. If you do not receive an invitation, this should not be viewed as a huge rejection. It certainly does not mean that you cannot become a great trader. The fact that Angel was not offered an invitation to interview does not mean he cannot become a CPT.

SMB holds three classes for new trainees every year, beginning in January, June, and September. We receive thousands of resumes for each class. Only about 10 percent of those who send us their resume do we wish to learn more about. We send them questions, an essay test, to this "Talented Tenth." Our HR staff reads all the answers sent back to us and then decides whether a candidate will receive an invitation to interview at our office. Most who interview with us are not a good fit or do not value what we offer, but some do, and those candidates are asked to return for a second interview. The surviving few are then asked to return for a third interview where we offer access to an SMB Tradecast. Here, the candidates watch us teach and trade, meet with traders from our desk, and interview with a partner.

During the process, we evaluate each candidate based on the characteristics that are most important to us. We have developed a recruiting matrix and each candidate receives a numerical score, kind of like the Wonderlic test for the NFL draft. After meeting dozens of candidates, we offer invitations to those who receive the highest scores.

Submit a Resume

Like just about any company, when you send us a resume, we either send you a follow-up questionnaire to answer or a generic thank-you letter for expressing your interest. A young person came up to me after I spoke at the 2009 International Traders Expo in New York City. He was one of those people whom you like instantly, with an easy smile and excellent listening skills. He had played college football and graduated from a top university. This young man explained that he had applied to SMB and received the generic thank-you response. He mentioned that he had not heard anything after that. That is not a good sign. I explained that that means he did not get in the front door. Our HR had rejected him. Bastards!

Not one to turn down a polite go-getter, I asked him to reapply and copy me on his resume, and instructed HR to set up an interview. Unfortunately, I cannot possibly give each resume that we receive the attention that it deserves. And during these turbulent economic times, we receive thousands every quarter. But every once in a while I will read a resume and check to see if HR is missing a good candidate. I mean, look how they screwed that nice young man above! As a partner, I do have the pull to get you an interview. It turns out that HR had been correct after all about the former college football player. We were not a good fit for him.

I often receive e-mails from candidates expressing their surprise that they were not offered an invitation for an interview. On paper, they admittedly were more than qualified. But let me make a few things clear. I am not the ultimate decider of who will become the next great trader. We can, and do, make mistakes about a candidate's chance of success. We are merely looking for those who would fit in with our desk, personally and philosophically. And this is the same at most prop firms.

We either send you a generic thank you (remember, you don't want this reply) or a document titled "Questions for New Intraday Traders," our version of an application essay.

The Essay Exam

Here are thirteen questions that are important to us initially. And if answered correctly as defined by us, will get you in the front door.

1. Is your first interest trading?
2. What is your favorite trading blog?
3. Do you own a personal trading account? If so, what were the last three trades that you made and why?
4. Is there something about yourself that you have wanted to change and have in fact changed recently? If so, what?
5. What is your greatest accomplishment?
6. Share with us the last thing that you failed at. What was your response to this failure?
7. What in your past demonstrates your competitiveness?
8. Are you willing to spend a year focusing on learning our trading system and everything that we teach? Your reward will be trading skills that can make you $1–4k a day.
9. There is a learning curve of 6–8 months when you begin. Can you psychologically survive this learning curve?
10. Please share a life experience that demonstrates your ability to be patient.
11. Many traders fail. On a scale of 1–10, how confident are you that you would succeed?
12. Please name a public figure that you admire and why.
13. How did you learn about us?

The First Interview

If HR likes your answers, you will get an interview. Again, we are searching for that reciprocal good fit. We start with questions that are important to us, and explain what we offer. Some questions that we typically ask are:

- Have you ever traded before? Do you own a personal account?
- What do you do daily that demonstrates your interest in the markets?
- Is there a favorite trading blog that you read? (Hint: SMB Blog is a really good answer here)
- What is the best trading book you have read? (Hint for the future: the book you are presently reading.)
- Where do you see yourself in five years? (Hint: On a trading desk.)
- Describe the last incident that caused you stress? What was your response?
- Describe the last time you were angry or frustrated? What caused your reaction? (My last question is not a good answer.)
- Who is your favorite professional athlete and why? (Hint: Michael Vick, Pacman Jones, Plaxico Burress, Stephan Marbury, or another me-first athlete is not a good answer.)
- If you were to fail as a trader, what would be the reason?
- What was the cause of the recent housing crisis that required a bailout from our federal government? (Barney Frank is incorrect.)
- We interview hundreds of candidates for a few spots; why should we give you an opportunity?
- Please describe something that took a long time for you to be good at.
- Dr. Steenbarger describes a Trader A and a Trader B in his article that we asked you to read. Would you be Trader A or Trader B?
- Would you describe yourself as conservative, moderate, or entrepreneurial as it relates to your job career? (Hint: the last choice.)
- Why did you decide to go to (insert their college)?

I have a distinct interviewing style. I like to call it "Unrecruiting." And this is an interview strategy used by many prop desks. I start the interview trying to convince people that trading is too hard for them or that there are better jobs for them to take. I will spend the next eight months of my life working with these trainees every day. I do not want anyone who does not have two feet in the door, has a doubt they would rather work another job, or trade at another firm. But if near the end of the interview, the interviewee is still fighting for a chance on our desk, then I shift gears. I start to share what we offer and why trading is the best job in the world. We make sure that the candidates learn the advantages of training with us. We answer their questions, and thank them for visiting.

If you survive the first interview, then you are off to a very good start when interviewing at a prop firm. Most prop firms can tell very early if you are a good fit. As I said earlier, survivors of a second round interview are then invited to an SMB Tradecast. Two Saturdays a month our desk meets to review tape of our trading. During these sessions, we combine recruiting. Candidates are invited to attend a Tradecast and get a feel for how we trade and teach. We assign them hosts with whom they grab some thin-crust pizza and ask questions. They can ask how our traders are doing, their thoughts on our training, what they most enjoy about trading, and so on. But many just sit there, listen, and enjoy the pizza, which is totally fine as well.

Then we watch some more film. Candidates are pulled out one by one to meet with a partner as we restart the Tradecast. At the end, we meet with all of our candidates in a conference room. The partners, head trader, and senior traders share why they love trading. We thank the candidates for visiting, and they wait for our invitation. Dum-duh-dum-dum. Who do we choose? Obviously, the best mutual fit. No shocker there.

My Favorite Interview: Penny

Sometimes the quest to find the right fit for us is a painful one. I started SMB with my best friend, I train everyone who comes through the door, and I am determined to hire the best people. Even if it means taking the recruiting trip from hell to get what we need.

I don't get sick very often. But one week in 2008, I was under the weather with an utterly unbearable cold. After the Close, I was scheduled to travel to the University of Virginia for on-campus recruitment (OCR). To get there, I hopped aboard Amtrak to DC, and then drove close to three hours to my hotel near campus. We're a newer firm and haven't quite gotten to the point of being able to afford a NetJets account (unlike my good friend Jim Gobetz, @aiki14, a great fundamental trader and managing partner at Wallinford Trust), but hopefully some day.

On my trip down, I could not stop coughing. At our first stop, my fellow riders were praying that I would get off the train in Jersey/Philly. I didn't. They were stuck with Mike the Walking Petri Dish for another two hours. I took another swig of NyQuil to help remove some of the stares being sent in my direction. I could hear their internal monologue: "What are you doing on this train if you're so sick? And if I get sick because I am trapped on this train with you. . . ." When we arrived in DC, the doors were held for a few minutes. Those poor souls who spent the last few hours catching my cold were antsy to get out as much as I was. Why couldn't we exit? Why were there Bomb Dogs being led down the aisle? Was Senator Joe Biden on the train or something? And then out the window I saw a recognizable, distinguished, white-haired gentleman striding quickly, with an entourage of a dozen. It *was* Joe Biden. Apparently, he really does take Amtrak.

After humming down I-95 in my rental car, I checked into a hotel which shall remain nameless because of what I am about to write. This was one of those hotels that looks very different online from in person. Perhaps the owners took pictures of a hotel they wished to own. This two-star posing as a four-star was not what I had booked.

I had not eaten. The NyQuil shots had lost their effectiveness hours ago. Six hours on a Biden-delayed train and crappy and cramped rental car had drained my sense of well-being. I needed a snack and some new sheets. I picked up the phone to call room service. The phone was dead.

Perfect. I am the furthest thing from a demanding traveler, but I normally stay at the Westin (@aiki14 probably stays at the Four Seasons) and have become accustomed to the Heavenly Bed and their ultra soft, cotton sheets. In fact, I bought all of the above for my apartment in Manhattan. Let's just say the Heavenly Bed wasn't an option at this place. OK, fine, let's just watch some TV and go to bed, I decided. There was no cable. Just a few local stations on their circa 1985 Sony. OK, I figured, I will just log in and get some work done. There was no Internet hook-up.

As John McEnroe would say clamoring at some poor official, "You have got to be kidding me!" I just gave up and slept fully clothed on the comforter.

The next morning I awoke and headed to campus. I felt worse. I was starving. I was late. I was about to be pleasantly surprised. My trip was about to become more than worth it. For those of you who have never been to an OCR, most are held in a nondescript 10x12 room, usually painted a dull prison color, with one window if you are lucky. UVA was different. UVA instantly became my favorite campus for an OCR. Interviews are not held in a glorified prison cell. They are held in the box suites at UVA's Scott Stadium.

I got a whole luxury box! I could walk around! I had my own bathroom. I had couches. I had a view of the football field. I could open the windows and let some fresh air in. It was awesome.

So I started the first interview. A nice young man entered, but he was not a good fit. The next interviewee entered. Again, very bright, but not a good fit. The next showed up late, next.

And then a candidate we will call Penny walked in.

For those unaware, Penny Hardaway was one of the best high school basketball recruits ever. But make no mistake; he was not a six-foot-eight athletic stud. Far from it. Penny's tie is too thin. The collar on his shirt was sticking up. He was in need of new shoes. His suit was two sizes too big. English was not his first language (he is Vietnamese). When he speaks, he looks down too easily. My mind wandered, thinking about breezing through the interview quickly, and then spending some time banging out a few e-mails before my next interview. But I had made the grueling effort to get down there, so I decided to give him a chance.

I asked, "What do you do daily that demonstrates your passion in the markets?"

Penny responds with a vengeance, better than I had ever heard. "I trade frequently. For example, last week I bought GS because at $60 it is showing support. I find it hard to believe that GS will not trade up near $100 since $115 was such an important level just recently after Buffett struck a deal with GS. At the very worst it should trade back toward $98, another support level, before it cracked. Also, I really enjoy your blog, and Trader Mike's. Yesterday, you talked about stock selection. I have never considered trading In Play stocks. I always just traded the same stocks. But I can see now how In Play stocks are best to trade. Further, on campus I am the Long Position Manager for the McIntire Institute of Investment."

Every ounce of whatever energy and attention I had left, due to my sick-induced stupor, was now owned by Penny.

Penny went on to explain other recent trades, a recent article he had read in the *Wall Street Journal*, and closed with the effectiveness of Mariano Rivera as he asked a thoughtful question about a line from a recent blog I had written. If you're interested in getting the attention of a partner, this is how you do it. He was one of us.

I was not impressed with Penny because he had read our blog. I was impressed because he was sincerely interested in our blog. He grabbed my attention because at such a young age, and obviously someone of modest means, he was actively trading. He found a way to trade. Penny was hungry. He talked about specific trades he had made. He scored very well with the other attributes that we seek. We identify with candidates who are aware of what they really want to do. And Penny really wanted to trade. We made him an offer and he accepted. Despite the odyssey to Charlottesville, this trip was more than worth it.

The Worst Question   The worst question you can ask during an interview is also the most commonly asked question: "What does the average trader make when they begin?" If you ask this question, you ought to be thrown out of the interview immediately. But I'm too nice to do that.

First, there isn't an easy answer to this question. There are those who make it and those who don't. Of those who make it, everyone is different. Trading is an individual sport, like tennis. There is a high failure rate with this job. Some say the failure rate is 95 percent, others 90 percent. Second, what elite performers do you think aspire to be average?

We met a college student who flew across the country from California about three years ago to visit us and wrote a dissertation on this singular topic. This student concluded that the failure rate was a slightly more generous 80 percent. Maybe that is true if you include everyone who has ever attempted to intraday trade. But as the tech bubble showed, many were not qualified at all. So are they relevant in calculating the failure rate?

I have also heard that the failure at a big bank is 50 percent. Our failure rate is simple. In an ideal world, my partners and I have done our homework in the recruiting process and won't have one. Mind you, I understand that's unrealistic. If trainees listen to what we teach, work hard, work every day on developing the skills to be a CPT, then they have an excellent chance to determine just how good they can be. This is all we can offer. Any other answer is incomplete at best and dishonest at worst.

The results of others have no effect on your trading. Trading is about personal skill development, discipline, and controlling your emotions. If the person to your left has developed his trading skills and your skills are not as developed, then naturally your results will be worse. If the person to your right is disciplined and you are not, then your results will be worse. If the trader behind you remains calm during most of the trading day, yet you are easily frustrated, then your trading results will be worse. As much as a prop firm may emphasize teamwork, at the end of the day, trading is an individual sport. Let's look at an example. To illustrate this point, Table 3.1 shows results from a random trading day for those in our firm who traded FAZ.

Not every trader's results were equal. Most interesting, let's examine the results of two traders who started at the same time, JPA and EKA. (They're all SBC, so for reading ease make it just the last three letters. Or use code names so as to not confuse with stock symbols) EKA made more than $1,300 more in FAZ than JPA. From our viewpoint, he did so because his trading skills are more developed at this stage of his career. And if COH never develops his trading skills, then the results of those on our desk who made over $1,500 in this one ETF will not be relevant to him. But COH happens to work very hard, so he just might.

Frankly, this idea that you can figure out how much you will make based upon someone else's numbers is silly. It reminds me of a hysterical "Seinfeld" episode.

George and Jerry are waiting to hear from NBC about how much the network will offer for their pilot for a show called "Jerry." When NBC

TABLE 3.1 FAZ Traders' P&L

Trader ID	Open Shares	Open P&L	Closed P&L	Marked P&L	Max MoneyInv	MoneyInv	Intraday	Max Intraday	Ticket Ave	Volume
SBCIEL	0	0	2500.21	2500.21	0	41070.75	0	41070.75	13.98	178800
SBCYIP	0	0	2079.04	2079.04	0	39460	0	39460	9.48	219388
SBCGME	0	0	1613.97	1613.97	0	29988	0	29988	8.48	190414
SBCEKA	0	0	1538.71	1538.71	0	18722	0	18722	10.94	140600
SBCDOV	0	0	1487.73	1487.73	0	22440	0	22440	9.59	155200
SBCZGA	0	0	1200.64	1200.64	0	19510	0	19510	11.68	102800
SBCSTE	0	0	647.91	647.91	0	39500	0	39500	9.21	70380
SBCGDI	0	0	303.21	303.21	0	22850.63	0	22850.63	3.15	96400
SBCCMU	0	0	276	276	0	32000	0	32000	7.23	38200
SBCJPA	0	0	227.88	227.88	0	5905	0	5905	7.12	32000
SBCHCH	0	0	176.9	176.9	0	4002	0	4002	8.27	21400
SBCMCL	0	0	−51	−51	0	7782	0	7782	−12.14	4200
SBCCOH	0	0	−117	−117	0	7564	0	7564	−8.73	13400

eventually offers Jerry and George $13,000 for both of them, George yells, "That's insulting! Ted Danson makes $800,000 an episode."

Jerry: "Oh, would you stop with the Ted Danson."

George: "Well, he does...I can't live knowing that Ted Danson makes that much more than me. Who's he?"

Jerry: "He's somebody."

George: "What about me?"

Jerry: "You're nobody."

George: "Why him and not me?"

Jerry: "He's good. You're not."

George: "I'm better than him."

Jerry: "You're worse. Much, much worse."

Long story short, you will make what *your* skills allow.

CAN A FIRM ALWAYS SPOT THE NEXT GREAT TRADER?

No. But a prop firm can tell who has a poor chance to become a CPT. Keep in mind that there are two very important pieces of information that a company does not likely have during the recruiting process. They can't know how hard a candidate will work during training, nor do they know if that person has any trading talent in his style to speak of. Let's discuss.

Everyone claims in her prop firm interview that she will work hard during the training process. One frequent statement I hear from an interviewee is, "I will outwork everyone on the desk." Actually one interviewee took it a step forward, much to my amusement. The interview was over. Ten minutes had passed and I had shifted gears to writing my blog. He knocked on my door, flung it open, and pronounced, "Mr. Bellafiore (he butchered my name), if I am honored to receive an invitation from SMB, I will work harder than anyone." I did interview one less-than-modest person who told me that recently he had to learn how to work hard. He relayed that things had come very easy to him during his first two decades.

Don't ever share this during an interview, please.

To be good at anything will take everything you have. Not having developed the skills to work hard is a turn-off. We did not invite this young gentleman to train with us. I make it abundantly clear that if you do not work hard during our initial training, then you will be asked to leave. And I don't do this with a smile on my face. Once we start our real training, then I learn who is really going to work hard.

With one of our most recent training classes, two trainees had barely left before I went home. Often, I leave the office after 7 PM. They worked so hard that on multiple occasions I actually had to order them like a boot camp drill sergeant to head home. One of these traders was living in Connecticut, with a two-hour train ride ahead of him. That kind of commitment always reminds me that despite the alleged grandeur of trading, this is a grind-it-out sport with lots of sacrifices to make.

One notch below those two who were seemingly chained to their desk were those new trainees who left right on the nose at six. Some had the audacity to leave before six, indicating it was unlikely they were completing all of the scheduled tasks built into our training program. However, during our painstakingly thorough interview process, they all told me they would work really hard. In fact, all of them told me, "I will be the hardest worker on the desk." Yet only *two* turned out to actually be hard workers. Not surprisingly, when this class started trading live, the two hardest workers were the best traders.

In order to mitigate this problem of hiring "alleged" hard workers, many prop firms have an internship program. We do. It was only a natural next step as so many of our Wall Street peers use this method to attract and retain talent. Young people now compete for internships as if they are reapplying to selective colleges and universities, and once they get them, most realize that the experience is a ten-week interview. We watch them closely, and see it as an opportunity to evaluate their work ethic and trading talent. If they pass muster, like most peer programs, they have a high chance of being invited back for a full-time position later on.

We started the internship program because I cannot determine a candidate's trading talent from an interview alone. Trading is a skill learned by doing, not just by reading a lot, theorizing, or the faux art of "paper trading." But there are some who are better suited to developing this skill. And I cannot verify this by asking you questions in an interview.

As an example, MoneyMaker is one of the hardest workers we have trained. He has made money from Day One. But in addition to his top-notch effort, he also just has a feel for trading, able to read the order flow better than his training class peers. But when I interviewed MoneyMaker, my impression was that he was a marginal candidate. I saw no evidence of a passion for the markets. He did not even own a retail trading account. He struggled relaying his favorite trading book. His grades were average.

Steve loved him. But Steve loves everyone. Sometimes I think that Steve is so tired by the time we interview that mentally he cannot withstand being disappointed. For Steve, any second wasted is annoying. Thirty minutes spent while hungry and exhausted with no reward to his business would just be too much for Steve. So he convinces himself that he loves everyone. I take his recommendations in this context. GMan liked him but wasn't blown away. Steve had it right, if you do not discount the fact that he loves everyone. If I had known MoneyMaker would work so hard, and that he had exceptional trading talent, I would have graded him differently. Today, I pray for candidates like MoneyMaker.

One of Steve's roles in the interview process is to ask candidates questions that test their mental acuity. In our business, five seconds can be eternity, so the ability to process information quickly and react appropriately is crucial. In his book *Liar's Poker*, Michael Lewis writes of a big bank's recruiting technique where a candidate is instructed to crack a window that cannot be opened. This is a test of how a candidate will react under pressure. We do not go to these extremes but we do search for evidence. My favorite of Steve's questions is (try to answer in five seconds):

You have 16 socks in a bag. 8 are white and 8 are black. How many socks must you remove from the bag to be statistically certain that you will be holding a pair in your hand?

Not every candidate can do this well, even those who look good on paper. Some stumble. They're so nervous for the interview that they either outthink themselves or answer so quickly and cockily to mask their nervousness. For those who can handle tough questions in tough spots, they show an implicit passion for the markets in doing so.

By the way, the answer is two.

Not to draw on another extended sports metaphor, but *Moneyball* is one of my favorite books. It shares how the Oakland A's, or more accurately Billy Beane, Oakland's general manager, discovered inefficiencies in Major League Baseball. For example, Beane recognized that batting average was not as important as on-base percentage.

Similarly, Tom Verducci in *The Yankee Years* shares how the Cleveland Indians have developed a proprietary database to find new inefficiencies. What is important is that some baseball teams were not using new statistical data to find players who would fit their system.

I think about *MoneyBall* a lot as a partner at SMB. We need to find those who are best for our specific style of trading. At our company's inception, we were awful at finding these people. So one day GMan, Steve, and I started working on improving our methods for identifying good candidates. Like Beane in *Moneyball*, who developed algorithms to find players who fit Oakland's criteria and much-less-than-the-Yankees budget, we created a recruiting matrix of our own. We identified specific characteristics of candidates that are most important for how we trade, and assigned them numerical values. Once the interview process has ended, we gather all the data from our matrix and use it to compile more objective criteria with which to make hiring decisions.

We used to recruit like old school scouts. We would evaluate based upon what candidates said and their body language. One of my favorite lines from *Moneyball* is when Billy Beane dismisses comments from an old school scout who advised to pass on future Boston Red Sox slugger Kevin Youkilis because he does not have a good body for the game. Beane retorted that the team was not selling designer jeans. Similarly, we are not trying to find people who look and sound like they will be good traders.

There are some firms who believe you really just cannot tell who will be great until the training begins. So they bring in a class of trainees, and in Darwinian fashion, the strong survive. If you do not show promise early, then you will be cut. As long as firms are up front about this process, this is certainly fair.

Outlier #1: Psycho

As important as it is for a prop firm to develop an effective recruiting matrix, and as advanced as our methods have become, we will still miss some traders. Some will be outliers, lacking the most important of personal characteristics like the ability to control your emotions, process information quickly, or fit into a firm's culture.

Not every good trader I have met or developed meets the general characteristics of a CPT. For example, one of the best traders I know is probably certifiably insane.

One of the criteria used in most prop firms' recruiting matrix is a calm disposition. For the first two years of SMB, I slept about four hours a night. Some days, I would just rise and head to the office in pre-dawn hours. There were videos to produce and lectures to write, and it was calming to me to just be getting work done instead of lying in bed fretting.

So one day I headed into work around 6 AM. As soon as I got off the elevator and tagged my security badge to enter the trading floor, I stopped quickly like a driver who just spotted a deer. Someone was screaming at the top of his lungs. I couldn't hear what he was saying, so I just stood there frozen, unsure what to do. I did not want to walk in on someone who was arguing with a girlfriend. But I also didn't want to walk in on someone who might shoot me.

So I stood there for a few more minutes. The trader screamed at the top of his lungs, "You are the reason I am in this situation. I cannot believe you did this to me." I recognized his voice. Not only was he a trader on our floor, but he was the best trader on our floor. He wasn't mad, he was emotionally unstable. Think Christian Bale's character in *American Pyscho* or Christian Bale as himself on the set of *Terminator Salvation*. I have never heard someone that distraught in my life.

I took the elevator back down to the street, e-mailed someone to check out the disturbance, headed over to Starbucks, ordered a green tea, read the *NY Post*, and waited. I wrote a new lecture, packed up, and headed upstairs. Psycho was staring at his screens and grinding out profits. He was up over $10k before 8:15 AM. And that was just chump change, hardly a huge day for him. So much for needing to be calm and emotionally stable to be a good trader.

Psycho is an outlier.

Outlier #2: Tebow

One of my favorite people of all time had to beg his way into the prop firm where I started. Tebow (Tim Tebow, the Heisman Trophy–winning All-American quarterback for the University of Florida reminds me of this former trader) had gone to a mediocre state college, played on their football team, and could not get an interview there through the conventional channels. In fact, he probably couldn't have gotten an interview anywhere. I think it is fair to say that Tebow would not impress an interviewer with his ability to process information quickly. Some hedge funds and other prop firms administer mental math tests as part of their weed-out criteria. Should he have had to take one of these tests, he would probably have been asked to leave the interview within a minute or two.

You know what, let's let Tebow tell his story:

Finding a job was a bit of a struggle for me. I had a good GPA 3.4 overall (3.6 in my major, Finance, and 3.8 in my minor, Economics) from TCNJ/Trenton State. . . . I had put in for a few jobs, but didn't get a call from Goldman or Merrill and was a bit discouraged. I knew that I wanted to work . . . with stocks. I did receive interviews from Thomson Financial and some financial planning place, both of whom seemed very interested. However, that was not what I wanted to do.

An upstart trading firm granted me an interview in the fall of 1997. They sent this well-dressed Italian guy named Dominic with a last name that started with a D (I will remember it later). We sat in a room on my campus and he began to tell me about my dream job. He liked that I was a college football player and that I had good grades. He said that a good trader could make at least $100,000 their first year. That was all that I needed to hear.

Weeks and then months went by and I heard nothing. . . . Maybe this company wasn't really interested?

Over two months later, I received a phone call setting up my long-awaited meeting with the firm's managing partner in NYC. I got all dressed up in my one and only suit. I even bought a pair of Rockports that set me back 150 beans, threw on my red power tie and was ready to meet Wall Street's elite. What I got was not what I expected. The traders weren't dressed like me, they were in jeans and t-shirts. This couldn't really be Wall Street, could it? Then I met the managing partner, he was dressed in jeans and a collared shirt. He took me into his office and we started to chat.

The one thing that I can remember vividly about the interview was that he asked me what else I would want to do if I couldn't be a trader. I answered that I would want to be a proathlete (football player, specifically). The interview was short (15 minutes or so, but enjoyable). I knew that I would enjoy working for this firm if I was offered the job.

The good news is that I didn't have to wait two months this time. They offered me the job within a week and told me that it was contingent upon passing a Series 7 exam. I graduated in May, would take the test July 6, 1998, and start July 20 IF I passed the test.

I did pass, but barely. I celebrated like any New Yorker would by buying a 22-ounce Heineken and drinking it in the street with the bag still on while walking down the sidewalk. Beer never tasted so good. I was going to be rich!

When Tebow first started, he was moved to sit next to one of the firm's great traders to try to improve by osmosis. But he was struggling hard. You didn't get fired "back in the day" but if you struggled enough, you would get your draw cut. Often a draw cut would prompt a resignation, and a draw cut was imminent. He had one foot out the door.

Despite the dire circumstances, he would not let anyone outwork him. He kept at it. Slowly, he got a little better, and a little better, and a little better. Then the market improved and offered more opportunities. Today, this trader is retired, paid for his house in full, and teaches and coaches in one of the nicest areas in New Jersey. Tebow was an outlier. But he did it!

Outlier #3: Tickster

For a training class, we hired a trader who demonstrated a passion for the markets and exceptional intelligence, with an SAT math score of 800 to boot. Tickster (named for his superior ability to read the ticks in a stock) had traded somewhere else, but was not happy with the training offered.

He was a little quirky. Later I would learn he subsisted on Burger King and candy. He had trouble keeping still during his interview. Tickster would answer my question before I finished it. He did not exhibit the calm demeanor essential to be a CPT. But we gave him a chance.

During the first week of his training class, two separate traders from our firm asked to talk with Steve in private. They relayed that this new trader had been complaining about his payout structure. It was the first week!

Apparently he was bad-mouthing his deal to the others in his class. His strong show of nerve continued on his third day when he plopped himself at the table of our more experienced traders while eating lunch, and cut them off repeatedly. Most newbies are like freshmen on a college team. They do not sit with the seniors until asked, and that is certainly not on the third day. These two traders made it clear in no uncertain terms that they did not want someone in the firm like this.

Steve asked to speak to this new trader privately. He shared what he had learned. Now let me explain the dynamic at SMB. I do most of the teaching and coaching. I am really hard on our guys early so they learn the standard that I expect from them, or more accurately, the standard that the market will expect of them. And also behind closed doors, I am the one between Steve and me to react viscerally. And Steve knew that when I learned of this, my response would be something like, "Get him the hell off our trading floor."

This new trader apologized and apologized and as Steve explained, was sincerely sorry. But Steve ended the discussion with, "I sincerely doubt that Bella will have any interest in training you going forward." And then Steve called me. He instructed me to sit down and told me the story. What was my response?

"Get him the hell off our trading floor!"

At our firm, we give you every resource to succeed. We will eat six figure losses if necessary to help a trader become a CPT. But we only work with those who highly value what we offer. And this new trader did not value what we were offering, and was infecting his new class with negativity, hence my reaction.

Over the weekend, Tickster sent us a long, contrite e-mail. After reading it, it occurred to me that he was young, perhaps socially undeveloped, and may just have been running his mouth without malice. I told him to show up on Monday, work hard, and we would forget the whole thing. It is possible that I had a bottle of Pinot Noir in me when I wrote this e-mail, heightening my compassion. But that is off the record. Anyway, that was my decision. It is not fair to cut a new trader based upon one transgression, and when you give them another shot, it breeds loyalty in some traders.

Fortunately, I gave Tickster another chance. What was the result? This individual has been nothing but hard working, helpful, and positive. He has worked on his game every day. Tickster picks up others when they are down. And he has come into his own as a solid trader. Recently, he was recognized as our most improved trader. You could not ask for anything more from a trainee than what he has given. He was an outlier. And we were lucky.

THE PROS AND CONS OF RECRUITING EXPERIENCED TRADERS

Landing an experienced trader at your prop firm can be a huge win. But too often prop firms undermine their culture for increased profits. We have learned from this mistake. Often those who claim to be experienced professional traders are failed traders grasping for another chance. It is all about finding an experienced trader who values what a firm offers and who is a good fit for the prop firm.

We receive inquiries from experienced traders regularly. We will not recruit a profitable experienced trader unless they have already left their firm. We do not poach. Wall Street is saturated with legendary stories of poaching. Headhunters make a living on this very practice. Conventional wisdom says, "Get a new job while you still have your old one." But our line of work is hardly conventional. We believe it is not fair to the firm that developed this trader, took the risk on him or her, and has spent so much time and energy working with him or her. That firm deserves the rewards of their work. The reality is, though, that sometimes traders need a new place. They just do. Before I started SMB I had to leave a firm, and I landed in a better place because I did.

Many years ago, I traded at a firm that had recently relocated. At this new location, our trading platform went down almost daily at 9:35 AM, for extended periods of time, and into the Close. The platform failed whenever the volume spiked. So I voiced my concerns to the firm. They assured me these technical problems would be fixed, and I know they tried very hard. However, the new building handicapped their ability to make infrastructural changes, and they just couldn't get the problems fixed expeditiously.

Like any rational trader, I had to leave. I hadn't been able to do my job for months, and the problems were not going to be fixed soon. I couldn't afford to sacrifice more months of lost profits because of the supposed simplicity of back-end infrastructure. In all honestly, I felt awful about leaving. This is where I got started, and they deserved my loyalty. Loyalty is a good thing to a point, but it cannot trump logistics and reality.

So while every now and then traders need a new home, and I know this all too well, we at SMB have found it difficult to integrate some experienced traders into our firm. Our style is a specific one whose philosophy may not be shared by others. But we have done it.

When we first started, we found a trader who needed a new home. The first day he sat down he made more than anyone on our desk. But he fought off a lot of what we did and taught. He made money and at the time it was still worth it for us to look the other way when he refused to act in his self-interest. He was uncoachable. And there came a time when he needed guidance. Today he sells insurance in Central New Jersey.

The House: A Different Definition of Consistently Profitable

While new experienced trading blood can be welcome, it can also come with headaches and nuisances we wish to keep off our desk. We once hired an experienced trader named The House. But his nickname had nothing to do with his looking for a new home. He was The House because he could have very well been the world's largest trader. (Famous hedge fund manager Larry Robbins has earned the nickname "L-Train" for his size, but even he isn't as big as The House.) The House was more likely to play in the NFL at his prodigious 6′ 3″, 350 pounds. The House had had a disagreement with his last firm (often the party line in trading when leaving somewhere, whether justified or not), but he was willing to buy into our system, and we liked that. While some firms welcome varying styles, we mostly prefer everyone to be on the same page.

However, once The House started trading, he redefined "consistently profitable." He lost money for thirty days in a row! I suppose I can give him credit for being consistent.

Just to offer some point of reference, on average, I lose money on 10 percent of my trading days. Sometimes I go 30 days without having a negative day. But losing money 30 consecutive trading days is not a slump, it's an infectious disease. Along the way, I asked him if anything had been bothering him. He said no. What made it worse was that he was not particularly bothered by this losing streak. The legendary trader Paul Tudor Jones said it best: losing money should really bother you. If I am negative three days in a row, I spend a long evening on my couch with a bottle of red wine and comfort food. This guy was weighing down his ship in more ways than one, sinking further into the abyss.

As traders, we can all recite the memorable line from *Wall Street:* "A man looks in the abyss, there is nothing staring back at him. At that moment he discovers his character. That keeps the man out of the abyss." I appreciate that trading can be tough at times. However, our new traders were all making money during this period, and it was clear what the real disagreement had been at his old firm. We let him go.

Billy Bucks: Good Trader, Bad Fit

While a consistent money loser like The House is unwelcome on any desk, some firms are willing to sacrifice professional culture for the bottom line. We are not one of them.

Take Billy Bucks, for example. When he walked in to start with us, we read him the riot act about fitting into our culture. He said that he understood, and would buy in to our way of doing things. Unlike The House, Billy Bucks could trade. He made money pretty much every day, demonstrating the skills of a seasoned pro.

But Billy Bucks would show up in game jerseys, as if every trading day were game day at Giants Stadium. T-shirts are one thing, but game jerseys are unprofessional in the intraday trading community. They are to be reserved for weekend warrior activities followed by drinking games. Billy Bucks did not get this memo. But what compounded his unprofessional dress were his late arrivals. He was part of the nonprofessional day trading culture from the 1990s when you came and left as you pleased. One time he arrived at 9:35 AM, sat down, and asked GMan what he was trading. GMan responded, "(STFU!) I am trading. Why don't you try showing up on time!"

We are a professional desk that works hard, shows up early, prepares with a sense of urgency, and relies on each other. And Billy Bucks was just not one of us.

Refusing to Join the League of Lesser Firms

We ended up hiring a semi-experienced trader who was very talented but lacked discipline. We will call him "Ungrateful," or UG. To remedy the problem, Steve took UG under his wing for three months. For two of those months, he talked UG through every one of his trades.

"Be careful, the stock may reverse," cautioned Steve. "Do not be so aggressive here, the stock could go either direction," Steve would bark. UG ended up making $15k one month and over $20k the next. Previously, he had been nothing but negative.

Now to talk through every trade with another trader means sacrificing a great deal of your own P&L. During the Open and Close of every day I talk through my trades with our new traders via our audio feed. I explain why I am buying, why I am selling, and what I am thinking. I talk with more detail when a new class begins. As such, my P&L suffers with the start of every new class, sometimes up to 50 percent. When the class is over, my results immediately improve. But still every morning I try to trade easier stocks so that my commentary over our training call is most useful for teaching. And this is what Steve did for UG.

So now here is Steve, who has sacrificed the last three months of a great portion of his trading for UG. Another firm had learned of UG's recent success, and started poaching him. They eventually persuaded him to switch, promising a better deal structure.

Look, I do not want to hold anyone back. But switching to this other firm was not in UG's best interests. Steve had carried him. UG was not ready to trade without attentive mentorship. And since Steve is one of the better traders I know, and certainly one of the best teachers in our space, it was doubtful this trader would be better in a new home.

I had a choice. I could have wished UG the best of luck. Or I could have told him the truth. I opted for the latter. I told UG that Steve carried his P/L for months. I told UG that he was very talented. I told UG that switching was not in his best interest. I told UG there was no chance he would succeed at this other firm. In fact, I said, "If you go to another firm without the direction from Steve, you will with a hundred-percent certainty blow up your account within a month."

Even after all that, I failed to persuade UG to stay. Next, I called up the partner at the poaching firm and explained the situation; call him Harpoon, the weapon of whale poachers. Harpoon replied that he was sorry, that some of those under him approached UG without his consent, and had just found out about the situation. I was waiting for the moment for Harpoon to tell me that he was so disgusted with the practices of his rank and file and that he would revoke the offer to UG. He just said he was sorry how this all came down and that there was nothing he could do about it.

I was embarrassed for that other firm. Nothing you could do? You're the managing partner of the firm! How about after you found out your guys were poaching a trader, you tell them to stop? How about you refuse to join the league of lesser firms?

One of my favorite TV shows of all time is the *West Wing*, written by Aaron Sorkin. One of my favorite episodes finds President Bartlett making a life-or-death decision over how to deal with an international terrorist. President Bartlett has been advised to assassinate this terrorist before he endangers the U.S. But there are international rules on how we can assassinate a terrorist. And a plan is devised that technically does not breach international law. President Bartlett is debating with his Chief of Staff about a go ahead and offers this objection: "Doesn't this mean we join the league of lesser nations?" To me, poaching, while it can be financially rewarding, is joining the league of lesser firms. Harpoon could learn from the classy Andy Kershner, CEO of Kershner Trading Group—a firm 3xs the size of Harpoon's, who personally called me to ask my permission to talk to a former SMB trader, who had already left our firm and the east coast.

There is an unwritten rule amongst friendly prop firms to advise every experienced trader to first talk to their firm and work things out. It takes a great deal of hard work to develop or find an experienced and consistently profitable trader. Most prop firms will only talk to traders who have already left their firm. Once we take this shortcut to success, we will rationalize others. I am not joining the league of lesser firms.

Anyway, UG left for this other firm. The result? Unfortunately, I heard that two weeks later UG blew up his trading account.

Z$: The Gold Standard

While The House and Billy Bucks are extreme examples of transplants gone away, I love stories like Z$. At his last desk, he was sitting around a bunch of traders who could not adjust to the new hybrid system for NYSE stocks, a mix of traditional market making by specialists and human-free machine trading. Being in the wrong environment without strong support around him, Z$ was not making money. We talked about our culture and he claimed he could fit in.

So Z$ went through our training program. We showed him how to Read the Tape with the hybrid system, find Stocks In Play, and compete in this different market. Z$ started slowly, but eventually he started making money. Steve pushed him harder, to be more aggressive, as Z$ had a tendency only to wait for certain setups. The pushing apparently worked, as Z$'s trading profits increased 300 percent.

This new home, with us, was a great fit for him. This is another one of the guys that we work with that just brings an immediate smile to my face. You can't hope to work with a nicer person. There are low-maintenance traders and then there is Z$, who is non-maintenance. Z$ speaks so softly, that like megafund manager John Paulson in front of Congress, we often have to ask him to speak up. He has become one of our core guys even if we can't understand him half the time.

If you are an experienced trader looking to switch firms, it is important that you consider the culture of the new firm first. And as a firm, you must consider whether a new trader would fit in. It is not enough that a trader is consistently profitable; he must also be a good fit. If not, he will tear away the culture of your firm. And this is a loss. And that loss is often more than the income this trader is producing.

A GOOD FIT FOR THE TRADER

Hopefully, so far we have offered an inside view of what a proprietary firm seeks, at least one example, anyway. Not everyone has a choice between firms, but for those who do, take the following into account when making a decision.

Training is most important. The two types of training available for new traders are what I call, quite plainly, old school and new school.

Old school training consists of a new trader sitting next to a mentor for a few weeks. There are no classroom training sessions or daily take-home assignments. Just watching and learning while trading a demo alongside your mentor. This is how I started, and at the time, the late 1990s, it worked just fine. My mentor, after all, was considered one of the greatest day traders of all time. In our world, he was a superstar, as if I was getting personal lessons from Tiger Woods on hitting a Stinger (his famous low-flying tee shot), or Michael Jordan on how to take it strong to the hole.

The problem was he was too good. He would have five different open positions with 10k plus shares on each. Meanwhile, I didn't know a bid from an offer! How was I supposed to follow five different positions? But things were different back then. First, the market was not as complicated, as programmed algorithmic trading had not become a common practice just yet. Plus, the market was more directional. Second, this was the best training that could be offered, considering technological limitations. Third, there was no competition back in the day. We were one of only a handful of firms day trading. Today, some firms have carved out a competitive edge through their training. So for that time period, I was fortunate to receive the best training available.

But today, we can train new traders better because of enhanced technology, online interactive platforms, more reams of data available, and better access to psychological support. Proper training now includes mentorship, classroom instruction, access to a trading simulator, videos that explain trading setups, hundreds of written lectures, an audio call where in real time you can hear what senior traders are trading and why. Without giving away the recipe for the secret sauce, that's essentially what we do.

Oh No: Why Talking Yourself Into a Firm Is Not In Your Self-Interest

Take the example of a gentleman we recently had to fire. We'll call him Oh No. This ambitious, bright young man was a broker who wanted to trade. (I don't blame him. Cold calling 400 strangers a day to sell some dog s&%tt stock is no fun.) Oh No initially sent us his resume and HR rejected him. He mailed in his resume, I passed the resume to HR, who again rejected him. Not to be deterred, Oh No showed up at our office one day, charmed HR, and gave them his resume. HR asked me if I would speak to him. I replied, "What is this, Denny's? There are no interviews without an appointment."

But Oh No was relentless. He even befriended one of our traders and when that trader came to speak to me about letting him at least interview, I reluctantly agreed.

After five minutes, it was clear that he just was not cut out to be a trader. At one point, I actually told him this. But again, he kept pushing forward, not taking no for an answer. He talked about how hard he works as a broker and how hard he will work for us, all in a very likable way. His slick-talking broker skills were coming in handy. He fooled a few others on the desk before the interview as well. I, too, wanted to believe in this young man, and I convinced myself that we could make him into a good trader. Perhaps he was an outlier I spoke about earlier. At the time, I had been reading Nassim Taleb's book *The Black Swan*. Maybe I did not have enough information to conclude he was not really cut out to be a trader? I decided to give him a shot.

But when Oh No showed up for training, my initial reservations were vindicated. One morning, he showed up late. A week later, I asked him to answer a simple question during a classroom lecture and he was lost. Once we started trading, his results were consistently poor. At one point, I caught him playing Internet games at 10:15 AM, our peak trading time. But Oh No was staying late every night. Unfortunately, the staying late was all for show. He wasn't doing any work, just flipping back and forth between screens making it appear as if he was working hard. One of our senior traders also told me Oh No would be off the desk for long periods during the day.

This was my fault. I over-believed in my outlier theory. Oh No's past history told me all what I needed to know about him, and it just continued during his training and subsequent live trading. He lost the firm a lot of money, hurt the morale of his classmates, and senior traders resented having to mentor him. We had to let him go.

In the end, it was not in this young man's self-interest to talk himself into our firm. He made no money, and could have been learning a skill that was better suited for his talents. He is obviously very talented, likable, and bright, and he will be successful one day. But he wasted six months of his life on my time. What good did that do him?

Funny postscript—Oh No recently reached out to HR to ask if he could have another shot.

A GOOD HOME

Alexander Elder, in his book *Trading for a Living*, writes about the danger of the cost of trading to the developing trader. Dr. Elder theorizes that trading is not a zero-sum game, but rather a minus-sum game. Your parent firm housing you as a trader may make money on commissions, yet you may not make a dime. You want to avoid a situation where your payout scenario makes it impossible for you to make money. Most prop firms charge you for your trades and then split a percentage of your profits. At SMB, new traders trade at close to our cost, which is very low, and we split their profits. If you are going to be charged more than $8 per thousand shares and then split your profits, it will be difficult for you to make money if your firm advocates a high volume trading style.

It is important to find a firm that is ethical and patient with its new traders. New traders don't often take this into account, searching mostly for the highest payout. It is likely that at one point in your career you will need a negative balance erased or that you need some help financially, perhaps an advance or draw. Recently, a veteran SMB trader needed an advance and started to explain why. I cut him off: "The check will be on your desk by the end of the day." It is probable that you will need a firm that believes in you though you are not yet a CPT. A good prop firm will help you, if not take care of you before you become profitable. They will treat you fairly and not just look at what you are presently producing. They will reward your hard work and contribution to the firm.

And if you are curious about what you can do, or what you can say, or what you should wear, or place on your resume to land a spot on a prop desk, then I have this advice: Be yourself. Prop firms know who they are looking for and where to find you. Let them do their job.

But if trading is your passion, then open up a trading account as soon as possible, start trading small, and put that on your resume. Scour the Internet for trading blogs of most interest to you, and plaster that on your resume. Read books about trading and smack them on your resume. When you interview, highlight specific trades that you have made recently. In short, demonstrate your passion for the markets. Traders don't talk about how they want to trade, what they want to read about trading, or how they wish they could talk about trading. Traders trade, read about trading, and talk about trading.

Visit a bunch of firms before you decide who may be the best fit for you. Meet their traders. Question them about their experience at the firm. Ask if you can sit in on their teaching, as this is of utmost importance. Talk to the partners or whoever runs the firm. And make your own decision on who offers the most value to you.

Ok, so after you land your dream job at a prop firm, what things are truly important to focus on to become consistently profitable? Let's go build a pyramid of success together.

PART II

Tools of Success

CHAPTER 4

Pyramid of Success

I t is Day One at 11:30 AM for a new training class at a prop firm in lower Manhattan. A team captain leads his fellow trainees into a training room lined with seats stacked closely together to maximize space, plastered with neutral beige paint colors, a plant in the back of the room that can never die, and a $4k supercomputer which is linked to a gorgeous 65-inch flat-screen TV, hanging from the wall at the head of the room. On the screen is an empty pyramid.

A prop firm leader enters the room, dressed in jeans, Dallas Maverick Adidas sneakers, and a striped Paul Stuart dress shirt with its sleeves rolled up like a politician on the campaign trail. All conversations end, these new traders affix their eyes on a tall, knocking-on-the-door of 40, experienced market veteran some have traveled from as far as India to learn from. This is their first lecture.

In a comforting and compelling voice, this prop trainer pauses at certain moments, lets the silence linger, and then accentuates a point not to be forgotten. He starts, "What is important for you (pause here. . . . and now the accentuation) to *succeed* as a prop trader? Work together in a group to fill in this blank pyramid. And then come find me so we can discuss what really is important. This is the best job in the world but only for those who do all the things necessary to succeed. Ok. Good luck!"

So you start trading at a prop desk. This is your dream job. Failing is not an option. There are literally thousands of trading books you could purchase with helpful hints. The Internet is flooded with educational trading blogs. Bloomberg, CNBC, and Fox offer endless hours of pros pontificating their opinions. And there is the *Wall Street Journal* and IBD and the

Financial Times. And then there is *Business Week, Fortune, The Economist,* and *SFO,* and on and on. What is important? With all this information, what do I watch? What should I focus on to reach my trading potential?

I know of many new and developing traders overwhelmed with information and empty with ideas to improve. Certainly, I have witnessed too many prop traders start their careers focusing on all the things that have nothing to do with making money.

One common question that I am asked during an interview is: Who is the worst trainee? My answer? "Anyone who thinks they really know what they are doing."

I do not mean to be condescending with this remark, but as a developing trader, it is imperative that you work on the right things. You must focus on the process and learn how to trade from those who have done this a lot longer than you have.

Preconceived notions about what is important before you trade professionally can be harmful. So this Pyramid of Success exercise is offered to make sure that everyone is focused on what is truly important. If these traders indeed do focus on what is important, in time they will find out how good they can be. If they take another path, the market will eliminate them with no exceptions.

But first take a stab at filling in the Pyramid of Success. If you were in that room, with all those ambitious, passionate, new traders attempting frantically to fill out that blank pyramid, what would you offer as answers to what is truly important to succeed as an intraday trader? Once you've done that, read through this chapter for a discussion of what is really important to the intraday trader. Good luck.

FIRST, BE UNORIGINAL

Often, new traders mistakenly believe that trading is about developing some brilliant new strategy or making bold predictions. At some point, I have to remind them that at 22 years old they are not yet a market guru. They are not Jim Rogers, or Warren Buffett, or John Paulson. Perhaps one day they will be stars like these guys, in which case, I might demand a cut of their billions. But for now they should come in with an open mind.

My sense is that this falsehood is propagated by the new trader's misinterpretation of what they learn to be important from the media. If we are not sure, blame the media, right? Every day, "experts" go on CNBC or Bloomberg News and propagate grand theories, more often than not "talking their book." Some are legitimate; some got placed there by good publicists. Please do not mistake what they do with what most meat and potatoes intraday traders do. We do not make grandiose predictions on the direction of the US economy. We do not have billions we must invest like hedge fund and mutual fund managers. We are not long-term investors.

Successful prop firms first and foremost emphasize trading skill development. Simply put, you do not have to develop a brilliant new trading strategy, as we teach you proven ones. So before you start calling yourself a market wizard, learn how to trade. When you gain experience, after you have developed good habits and skills, you will be able to create new plays that work for you. But not at the beginning.

My advice to any new traders is to seek a mentor who will offer you trading skills that will allow you to adapt to any market. (See more in Chapter 12.) What works one month may not work the next. But with fully developed trading skills, you can make the necessary adjustments. Let me offer an example.

No Longer Hitting the New Low

In the Fall of 2008, hitting the new intraday low in a stock would work in the financials (see Figures 4.1 and 4.2), which were bleeding daily. By hitting the new intraday low I mean getting short a stock in an intraday downtrend when it makes a fresh intraday low for the day. There was a

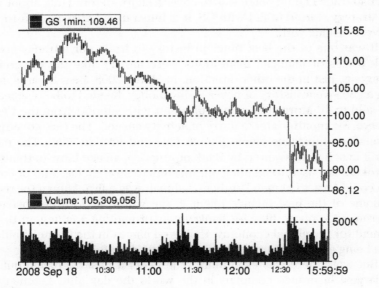

FIGURE 4.1 Goldman Sachs 9/18/08

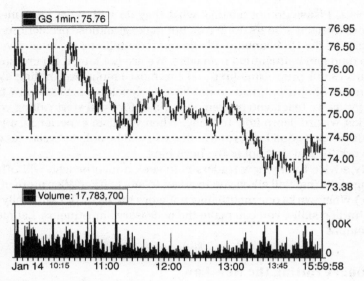

FIGURE 4.2   Goldman Sachs 1/14/09

run on some, if not all of the banks. Of the big banks left, the market kept asking who would be next. During the Fall of 2008, sometimes I felt the only bad trade I could make was to cover a short. Before I talk about when this strategy started to fail with GS, it is imperative I give context to what we were dealing with.

It was one of the best times in history to trade our intraday style as stock prices of financial institutions were moving like the dot-coms of yesteryear, just in the other direction. In March 2008, Bear Stearns, a firm with an 80+ year history of never losing money, needed to be rescued and was sold to JP Morgan at a deep discount with support from the Federal Reserve. Six months later, a flurry of activity ensued. The U.S. government nationalized mortgage giants Fannie Mae and Freddie Mac. The mighty Merrill Lynch was acquired by Bank of America, an ego blow to thousands of brokers not used to handing out toasters to new clients. And of course, who could forget Lehman Brothers. Lehman was a firm known for recruiting some of the best finance talent in the world, and in the absence of government support, filed for bankruptcy, prompting a falling-off-the-cliff moment for the global economy. Hallowed names in the financial industry were being eliminated one by one, seemingly day after day.

But wait, there was even more. The Federal Reserve bailed out AIG, the largest insurance company in the world the day after Lehman went under. Morgan Stanley and Goldman Sachs, the two whitest shoe names in the investment banking world, would soon join their Merrill peers in handing out toasters, as they reincorporated to bank holding companies. These Wall Street icons would now be subject to more intense regulation as depository institutions. Washington Mutual, a thrift that had grown by leaps and bounds in recent years was seized by the FDIC, creating the largest bank failure ever. PNC Bank soon bought Ohio-based stalwart National City, and California megabank Wells Fargo bought fast-sinking Wachovia.

With Wall Street and Main Street simultaneously collapsing, SMB must have gone out of business, right? No. Mike, you blew up your trading account? Nope. This was the best intraday trading time period since 1999. And let me say that I hated every day during this crisis, even with the outsized trading profits.

Your job as a trader is to exploit excellent risk/reward opportunities, but this not how I want to make money. Good people lost jobs that will never return. Historic firms were just destroyed in a blink of an eye. On my desk, I wondered if it was possible for our entire banking system to go down. Was the money in my bank account safe? Did I need to withdraw it all and put it in a safe in my apartment? Would all of these trades I was making eventually clear? I didn't really think any of this was what might happen, but I did have these thoughts. The whole thing made me sick.

It is a very strange feeling to sit on the trading floor of a firm you built from nothing, see your traders flourish, and wish it would all just stop.

And there was still more to come. The financial crisis spread to Europe, which was apparently more overleveraged than America. The Fed cut rates to 1 percent, and eventually to practically nothing, a "target rate" in between 0 and 0.25 percent. The Central Banks coordinated cut rates. China ordered a stimulus package. And the US government passed a $700 billion bailout of the nation's banks. Yes, this all really happened in less than a year, actually, more like a few months. Talk about a trading opportunity.

Anyway, enough of the painful history lesson and back to trading. At the start of 2009, shorting the new intraday low, particularly in GS, would manifest a 50c rip (see chart on the right below of GS). With just this trading play of hitting the new low, you would frequently lose money. But with fully developed trading skills, you would adjust, and we did. We waited for GS to spike after the new intraday low and shorted into an upmove. When a new intraday low was created, then we covered.

As you progress, you will get better at the plays that you are taught or learn. You will learn to trade with more size incrementally. You may stumble across a new play here and there. But almost all of the money that you make as a new trader should be from statistically measured, basic trading plays. Think of it as the first few pages of a high school football playbook, basics up front, advanced stuff later on. On our desk, these are the plays that our partners and senior traders use every day to make money, and have been using for over a decade: Support Plays, Breakout Trades, Consolidation Trades, Range Plays, Momentum Trades, Trades2Hold, etc. . . . Master the basic trades first.

When traders overlook the basics when confronted with low-hanging fruit, I can't help but get angry. One time, Steve and I met with our core traders about missing a trade in MON. MON offered three easy trades, and the partners and our Head Trader were in all of them. The core was not. Unacceptable.

It was not so much that our core traders missed the trade. Hey, that happens. Trading is not easy. Rather, it was their poor listening skills. Steve, GMan, and myself called out these trades on our internal intercom. Our desk ignored the guys who have made millions over their careers. They were yapping with the other guys on our desk who have, well, not made millions in their career. This concerned me, so we had a talk. Let's just say it was a one-way conversation.

Our desk is saturated with talent. But talent absent hard work and good listening skills is not rewarded by the market. Our desk was not listening to a suggestion from their bosses on MON. They were in some dopey BAC support play and some mediocre MGM trade. They were doing "their own thing," all against their self-interest.

TBone: The Ticking Time Bomb

Let me offer another example. When SMB first started, we ran our desk more loosely, and our barrier to entry was not what it is now. You cannot build a trading desk without traders, after all. So we invited some folks to join who claimed to be experienced traders and gave them the benefit of the doubt.

Along those lines, an experienced options trader joined our desk. Let's just call him TBone for the Seinfeld fans and the sake of this story. TBone made $1,500 the first day he traded with us. Great, profits! Before the Close, I checked TBone's work to see how he did it. His work was horrendous. He shorted a strong stock and happened to make money and got long a weak stock and by chance profited. He doubled down with positions. He sold the top and bottom a few times in thinly traded stocks. He was a ticking time bomb. An intervention was necessary.

Steve and I took TBone into our conference room and gingerly offered our analysis. His response? "Guys, I made $1,500 on my first day. Obviously, I know what I'm doing. Thanks for your thoughts, though."

Those were not exactly the words that I was hoping to hear. And what was worse was TBone's body language, which said, "What the hell are you morons talking about? Why are you bothering me?" This from a guy with one day of professional short-term equity trading experience. Not good.

Now to put it in context, TBone was arrogant. He was surly in this meeting, but he had been arrogant in his interviews as well. We took him on because we were looking for an experienced trader, and we didn't know any better. It would be hard for me to think of someone I found more unlikable than TBone. Very, very hard.

Sensing potential disaster, Steve and I set an amount that we would allow TBone to lose. We then estimated just how quickly he would blow up his account. Steve set an over/under on how long he would last. I was forced to take the over as Steve beat me to the under, and Steve won the bet.

TBone just ripped it up from that intervention on. We let him go.

If you pretend to know what you are doing when you start, you will quickly just prove that you don't. You need reps. Experience will be the cure. There is only one outcome for those who pretend they know what they are doing. And that result is not a long-term future on a trading desk, or even as an individual trader.

Spend your first three years just mastering basic trading plays and pushing yourself every day to get better. Save the new strategies for after you have learned how to trade.

Be unoriginal.

SURVIVE THE LEARNING CURVE

Most traders struggle when they first begin. The great news is the worst you will ever be as a trader will be when you first start, just like anything else. You have to hang in there and focus on improving. Remember GMan, one of the better intraday traders to hit the Street in a long time, once walked into my office to quit. He soon went from "I quit" to Head Trader to Partner. I was negative $36k eight months into my career and am writing this book. Steve did not make money for his first six months. One of the best intraday traders on the Street was absolutely one of the worst at my original firm. This trader was in the bottom 10 percent of our firm and today he is in the top 1 percent of all intraday traders. Our most improved trader in 2009 floundered for his first seven months and now is headed to becoming a star. It takes time to get good.

I see this time and time again. Those who can give trading more time when they start have a better chance to succeed. Eight months is better than 6, and 12 is better than both. You need reps. Like Hall of Fame basketball player Michael Jordan, who did not make his varsity basketball team when he was a sophomore in high school, you must be patient. But your time will come.

At the start of your trading, you should trade with small size and with one stock. You should not increase your tier size until you are positive 7/10 trading days. You should set a small max loss when you begin. You should be limited in your buying power. For example, when a new trader begins, he should not write more than 10k shares in a day, total.

Let's visit a column, "Genius: The Modern View," written by David Brooks of the *New York Times* to offer clarity for a trader's need to be patient when they begin. Mr. Brooks once wrote insightfully about the modern genius model. Basically, we are not born great at anything. It takes concerted practice to become great at something. He wrote, "The key factor separating geniuses from the merely accomplished is not a divine spark. It's not I.Q., a generally bad predictor of success, even in realms like chess. Instead, it's deliberate practice. Top performers spend more hours (many more hours) rigorously practicing their craft," wrote Brooks. We are not born great at anything. You were not born a great trader (sorry to that interviewee who claimed trading was in his blood.)

Tiger Woods was not born great. Tiger had a father intent on improving his physical and mental skills. And today, after numerous Majors, fame, generational wealth, this is his daily practice routine:

6 AM:	lift weights for 90 minutes
7:30 AM:	breakfast
9–11 AM:	hit balls on practice range
11–11:30 AM:	putting
11:30 AM–12:30 PM:	play 9 holes
12:30-1 PM:	lunch
1–3 PM:	hit balls on practice range
3–4 PM:	work on short game
4–5 PM:	play 9 holes
5–5:30 PM:	hit balls on practice range
5:30–6 PM:	putting

Not convinced yet that you are not going to be a great trader on Day One? Let's check out Malcolm Gladwell's page turner *Outliers*. Mr. Gladwell explores the commonalities amongst the uber-successful. Those that Mr. Gladwell studied all worked at their craft for at least 10,000 hours before they were great. Microsoft founder Bill Gates, Tiger Woods, musical sensation The Beatles, and Intel founder Bill Joy all had extraordinary opportunities to practice their craft, which was responsible for their greatness. Gladwell explains, "Working hard is what really successful people do."

And in yet another example of analysis, Geoff Colvin in *Talent is Overrated: What Really Separates World-Class Performers from Everybody*

Else, wrote that deep practice, often with continuous feedback, is necessary to become great. Concentrated practice is key.

Not to digress too much, but let's explore the world of tennis with my friend Daniel Coyle in *The Talent Code: Greatness Isn't Born. It's Grown. Here's How* for further evidence that you must remain patient to become a solid trader. Russian women accounted for half of the top 10 ranked players in the world in 2007. Wow! Three of those players were produced by Spartak, a dumpy club where they felt lucky if the heat worked. Their secret? Deliberate practice on technique, constant critical feedback, and improving weaknesses. At Spartak, passionate instructors focus on the brickwork of developing the skills of their students. Players start at five years old, so they have practiced for at least 10 years before we ever meet them at Wimbledon or better yet, the U.S. Open out in Flushing Meadows. If you want to be good at something, practice. Practice deliberately, and do so for many years.

Ok, so you don't like sports; let's use an example from trading. After all, this is a trading book. In Edwin Lefevre's classic *Reminiscences of a Stock Operator*, we read, "Years of practice at the game, of constant study, of always remembering, enable the trader to act on the instant when the unexpected happens as well as when the expected comes to pass." So I guess you got to practice as a trader also. Sorry.

FOCUS ON IMPROVING EVERY DAY

"I know of no more encouraging fact than the unquestioned ability
of man to elevate his life by conscious endeavor."
—Henry David Thoreau

As a new trader, it is tempting to focus solely on your P/L to judge your progress. There is a big scoreboard on your trading platform that is hard to ignore. Plus $300. Negative $700. Plus $1,500. This scoreboard never stops offering feedback.

Do yourself a favor, and cover up your P/L. It is not significant when you first begin trading. On most advanced trading platforms, there is an option offered to etch out your P/L. If yours doesn't, then go old school and use some masking tape. Seriously, go find some masking tape and slap in on your trading platform. Your goal is to develop skills first, make money second. You have to focus on getting better *every day, day after day*.

Let's bring in a former trading colleague of mine.

Back in the day (I love saying that, by the way, but it reminds me too that I'm older than most of those I work with), the trader who ended up best was at first considered a wuss. He was hesitant to enter the high-flying Internet stocks. He was timid to size up with certain plays. But you could always find him talking to the better traders. He was always working on strange things that others weren't. I remember small things, like getting a glare guard for his computer, so he could concentrate better. He started making the spreads in his own stocks with size, like a market maker. He would write down reams of notes in his journal. He started dipping his toes into the big boy stocks. He started adding size that others could not handle. And soon he was the top dog.

Your goal every day is to improve. Each day is a gift from the market to improve. Work hard. Each day is an opportunity to get better. Focus on the process.

ASK THOUGHTFUL QUESTIONS

I understand that there are many retail and individual traders who work from home. Not everyone has or wants the opportunity to start at a prop desk with experienced mentors. But for the individual and retail trader, let me share some advice from an expert. Dr. Brett Steenbarger at TraderFeed once wrote, "There is no question in my mind that, if I were to start trading full-time—knowing what I know now—I would either join a proprietary trading firm or would form my own "virtual trading group" by connecting online (and in real time) with a handful of like-minded traders." Borrowing an idea from Secretary of State Hillary Rodham Clinton, it takes a village to raise a trader. You need a network that can add value. To whom can you turn to ask trading questions?

Your mentor or trading community does not know what you do not know. They cannot read your mind. If you do not understand something, then ask. You must understand one concept to understand another. It is like building a house brick by brick. One well-formed brick helps support the next brick. If one is weak, then the others are in jeopardy.

Traders cannot skip steps in the process. It is one foot forward and then the next. Master one topic, and then and only then move on to the next.

When I lecture our new traders, I instruct this is not an exercise for me to practice my presentation skills (and if you have ever watched me on StockTwits TV, they are obviously superb—kidding). This is an interactive learning experience for my mentees. Questions are encouraged so that we teach better. Also, thoughtful questions improve the learning experience of others in your class. It helps others on our desk learn.

In this day of thousands of trading blogs, StockTwits, Twitter, Facebook, IMs, e-mail, Blackberries (and by the time this book is published, whatever new social networking application is hot—the iPad?), you can reach an expert in any field. Bloggers will respond to your questions. I developed a relationship with Dr. Steenbarger by e-mailing him questions, which lead to a phone call, and then a personal introduction. Without embracing this new technology, we may have never met. Jack Welch, the legendary former CEO of GE, once informed me on Twitter that his wife, Suzy Welch, and he were to speak at the 92nd Street Y. I instantly bought tickets. Mr. Welch didn't actually inform me personally, but what's the difference? I had an evening with Mr. and Mrs. Welch. I would never have known they were speaking at the Y if I did not embrace Twitter. I gained an opportunity to ask them questions about running a business.

We have access to people whom we didn't in the past. You must take advantage of this wonderful technology to interact with experts. I had a question about a trend day, so I reached out to Corey Rosenbloom of AfraidtoTrade. Steve had a question on psychology and reached out to Dr. Steenbarger. He received a quick response. I am asked questions by new traders every day and I answer every one. (Boy, am I going to regret that last sentence.)

Your learning experience is as good as you make it. There will be things that you do not understand. This is common. What is not ok is to ever leave a lecture, or move on from a topic, without mastering it. And if this means questions asked to your mentor, then this is your responsibility. Please ask.

TALK SHOP

Outside the office at social functions, there are inevitably those who only want to talk about what they do for a living. When traders gather, since they tend to be passionate about what they do, there is little discussion but trading, other than the game on the TV in the bar. When these moments happen, whether informally or formally at some industry function, you ought to discuss trading setups. What did the others in your community see? When you talk to other traders, concentrate on exchanging important levels in stocks, how your orders were treated by the Specialist or market maker, your best play in a stock, what they noticed that you might have missed. Especially share the patterns that you notice. By offering your advice, you get great advice back to you tenfold. It's a karmic exercise like anything else.

How Do You Spend Your Time?

GMan, Joe P, and I traded QCOM After Hours (chop!) and then I hopped on the subway much earlier than usual to head uptown. It was a road trip for SMB to experience Avatar on the IMax with 3D glasses. On my ride uptown,

I overheard some new day traders from another firm talking. I found their conversation unproductive.

Three 20-something new traders stood bantering away. Did they discuss QCOM after the Close and the repeating ARCA and then NASD sellers who would not lift? After chopping up this play, GMan exclaimed, "That was a 3k play." And then he sat and started to replay how he will make that happen next chance he sees this pattern. Joe P joined in GMan's quest to better trade this Afterhours trading pattern.

Did these new traders discuss the downmove of CAT below 53.50 and the double bottom at 51.25 that fueled an impressive upmove into the Close? Did they discuss crazy AAPL today? At one point, I thought we might see 225. At another point, I thought we might find 195. At other times, a few thousand shares moved AAPL 50c. I tweeted:

> if you want to know how the mkts would trade if we passed transaction tax watch $AAPL no liquidity $$

How about the bounce into the Close? How about the failure to close below SPY 109? How about the amazing new iPad to be offered by AAPL? How about Congress grilling Geithner? The President's State of the Union? The Toyota recall? The Bullwhip effect on the front page of the Journal and that Steve highlighted during our AM meeting? The Fed decision to leave rates unchanged? What to trade tomorrow?

After this day, these new traders with an audience of other well-educated traders, and a 30-minute subway ride ahead of them decided to talk about what?

You learn so much from talking trading with other traders. Right after the Close is the best time to talk trading, as your mind is fresh with specific details about trading patterns. By listening to others discuss their trading, you can learn a trading pattern that perhaps you can use. You can gain information about important levels in stocks you may not have traded. You can learn how some stocks may trade. You can get a different perspective on perhaps the same stocks you were trading by swapping war stories. And on and on and on and on. . . .

And look these guys were very polite, bright, ambitious traders. They work at a very good firm and I wish them nothing but the best. But they had a choice how to spend their time during that subway ride. And they chose to talk about? It wasn't anything to do about making them better traders. They talked about how much others at their firm were making. It was impressive how much knew about how much others were making.

Your life is what you do and not how much you make, where you sit on an airplane, who your parents are, or where you live (it is also partly how hot your girlfriend is). If your goal is to become an elite trader, then your time is a very valuable commodity. It is the most important commodity that you have. Use it wisely. Act in your self interest. Be focused on all things becoming a better trader. Talking trading with other traders in your firm is a great way to get better.

BTW, SMB loved Avatar. Amazing visuals. An incredible movie experience. I would tell you what disappointed Dr. Momentum about the movie but I am not sure if that is even appropriate for a blog let alone a book.

A great gift of the Internet is the many excellent trading blogs out there. See the box for a list of blogs I recommend.

Trading Blogs

Traderfeed	http://traderfeed.blogspot.com
Alphatrends	www.alphatrends.blogspot.com/
Afraid to Trade	http://blog.afraidtotrade.com/
Trader Mike	http://tradermike.net
Kirk Report	www.thekirkreport.com
Seeking Alpha	http://seekingalpha.com/
ChrisPerruna	www.chrisperruna.com/
Quantifiable Edges	www.quantifiableedges.blogspot.com/
Blog for Trading Success	http://tradingsuccess.com/blog/
Wall Street Cheat Sheet	http://wallstcheatsheet.com/

Post comments on these blogs. Start a conversation. Go to Twitter. Follow traders whom you respect. Read the articles that they suggest. Comment on their tweets. Barry Riholtz in an interview with Damien Hoffman from Wall Street Cheat Sheet shared, "...One of the things I've loved about Wall Street is people are incredibly generous with their time and expertise.... There is a mentoring relationship you can develop with people, and they're top notch." You don't have to work at Goldman these days to have access to quality traders. Talk trading.

DEVELOP A DAILY WORK PLAN

Trading is not a 100-hour a week job. At least, it isn't for me. It certainly shouldn't be. Trading is as close to being a professional athlete as I can think of. You must be well rested. Your performance changes from day to day. Trading—like sports—is performance based. Traders who trade well, just like athletes who play well, are paid more than they deserve. A trader must recharge after the trading day. You must be fresh and alert for the next session. Save the 100-hour work weeks for the investment bankers, lawyers, and analysts (and partners of trading firms like me).

Turning One Trading Day of Experience Into 10

Improving as a trader requires skill development. As traders, we may arrive at our trading desk, sit down, and trade. That is one day of trading experience. But what if you could take that same trading day and turn it into 10 days of trading experience. Interested?

Well, developing a daily training schedule does just that. We have learned from prominent authors Gladwell, Colvin, and Coyle that to become great at anything requires deliberate practice working at your craft. As traders we can develop such a learning schedule to improve our results. We can find ways to simulate trading to get better.

Traders can do the following to simulate trading:

- Keep a detailed Trading Journal.
- Replay trades in your head like old school traders.
- Talk trading with other traders.
- Use video review individually, and as a group,
- Practice on a trading simulator—Secret Project X.

This simulation can turn one day of trading into 10-plus days. Shaun White, the Olympic snowboarder, used simulation before the Vancouver games and exclaimed after a day of optimal practice that he experienced "a couple years of riding in one day." Let's use a trading example to demonstrate how we as traders can turn one day into 10 plus.

Example Toyota-TM   One trading session, Toyota had a full-blown crisis on its hands. As had been widely reported, sticking gas pedals and potentially dangerous floor mats caused Toyota to recall 5.3 million vehicles since the fall of 2009, including some of its most popular models. TM was gapping down.

During this intraday while I was babysitting LXK, Carlton, one of our hard-working new traders called out TM, Toyota.

Quietly, he asserted, "Watch Toyota, it is below 75."

I punched up TM. Below 75 was broken on the long term and intraday charts. We had fresh news with their recent large-scale recall. Spencer chirped 70 was a downside possibility. TM would not trade below 74.75 on the tape. A significant buyer was supporting TM, though broken and fighting awful breaking news. Finally, the buyer left and I started a Trades2Hold short. Three points of trending downside opportunity followed. I made a chop on this trade.

This may appear like a layup trade at first glance. The best trade was below 74.75 after the buying stopped. Skills to Read the Tape and enter with the best risk/reward were required. There are subsets and nuances to learn for this one trading setup. It takes practice to develop the skill to handle the subsets to all of these trades. Simulation is how we can practice as a trader.

Once in the trade, a developing trader needed to ask: when do I exit?

A trader needed to decide when to cover. Perhaps when the intraday downtrend was broken? Perhaps after the first significant downmove just below 74? Perhaps when any strength was spotted on the tape? A trader needed to read his charts to confirm the downtrend using multiple time frames (1 minute, 5 minute charts). A trader needed to be glued to a newsfeed in case of an announcement of an unexpected upgrade or defense of the stock by a Tier 1 bank, which would have caused a reversal. Some traders may have been poised to cover if they spotted significant buying on the tape so they did not lose an excellent risk/reward setup. What was the overall market doing? TM is an ADR, so how does this matter? What was the automotive sector doing as a whole? Was the overall market strong, making it less likely for TM to trade lower?

This was a short below important technical support play.

If you hopped on the subway, came to work, found this setup, and made this trade, then that was ONE experience, One Rep trading this play. It would take an awful long time to master this trade at this rate. You might only see this trade once a week. But with simulation, a daily learning schedule, you can turn that one experience into 10 plus. As a trader, you can transform one day of trading experience into 10.

What if you did the following before you left work on this trading session?

- Made detailed notes in your trading journal—that's two experiences.
- Discussed this setup with others on the desk in the play—now three experiences.
- Replayed the trade in your head—and four.
- Watched your video recording of this trade—now five.
- Met in a training room and watched video of this trade with a group—and six.
- Visualized making this trade after the Close—and seven.
- Practiced this trade on a dedicated simulator such as our Secret Project X—and 8 and 9 and 10.

With just this one trade, you can turn one trading experience into 10 plus. Developing a daily learning schedule can transform one trading day of experience into 10. In six months you can gain three years of trading experience following a daily practice routine. Or you can head home after the market closes, flip on ESPN, play video games, grab drinks with friends at a local pub, and let one trading day of experience linger as one day of trading experience.

BOUNCE BACK FROM DEFEAT

All traders have bad days. There are still days when I feel abused. There were days where I would just go home, sit on my couch listless, and watch the Yankees. A sense of failure and guilt would consume me. I was a prisoner in my own guilt house.

CPTs will be profitable 80 to 90 percent of their trading days. But that still leaves 10 to 20 percent of trading days when they will lose money. Some days you will get stopped out. They are inevitable. There is a very fine line between a good trade and missing a trade, especially when your trading time frame is as short as mine. A second can be an eternity in intraday trading. We are talking many fractions of a second, which may be all we have to enter at an excellent risk/reward opportunity with some trades. And some days you are just off.

In the past, I have sulked after a poor trading day. I can remember sitting on my couch, sick to my stomach, mentally abusing myself with, "How can you be so stupid? You call yourself a trader? You ought to stop that. It is not possible that anyone could be worse at their job than you." Traders are great at really beating themselves up.

After one of my favorite athletes, Phil Mickelson, blew a chance to win at Winged Foot by overcooking his driver on 18, he said in the press room afterward, "I'm such an idiot. I can't believe I did that." I knew exactly how he felt. This is the raw emotion right after combat.

But then you have to move on. You must take some time, let go of these feelings, and start to work on getting better. And when you gain maturity as a trader, you will learn the importance of seeing your failure as an opportunity to learn. What can you do starting right now to get better? How do you eliminate your mistakes from today?

Every rip can make you a better trader. Embrace these tough days as a learning experience. Thank the market for offering this opportunity.

One of my favorite traders we will call Playmaker. He is 300 pounds plus. He was a starting defensive lineman on his college's football team. Playmaker bounces at a bar on the weekends. I doubt there are many scuffles where he works in Hoboken. And he knows I love it when our guys fight till the end of the day.

Often I challenge, "The day doesn't end until 4." If you are down on the Open, you make One Good Trade and then One Good Trade, until the bell rings. You don't pick up your stuff and head home for the day. You don't complain, or pout, or feel sorry for yourself. The market doesn't care.

Let me offer a few "back in the day" trading anecdotes to give you some inspiration to sit in your seat the next time you start being negative. I have seen Steve down on multiple occasions more than $100k. Once he finished positive. One of the best day traders from back in the day, let's call him Happy Prints (he was known for getting ridiculously good prints), was down close to $100k one trading day and approached his manager. Happy Prints announced, "I think I am going to head home." This manager recommended that he stick around and chip away at his losses. Talk about a great recommendation. Happy Prints down near $100k finished up $65k.

So one day Playmaker starts down $1,200. And he stays with it. By the Close he finishes flat. We talk after the Close and he says, "The market doesn't close till 4:00, right, Bella?" That is some good stuff. That is what I like to hear. That is showing some heart, hanging in there and showing the toughness, the resilience to be a good trader.

One trading session, a new trader started down $100 and then finished up $200. He had just started. I made a loud huge deal about the skill he was now developing. His P/L swing was not important; it was that this talented new trader had now learned how to fight back trade after trade to prevent a stop out. He showed resilience.

Resilience is a skill developed. And it reminds me of my favorite Thomas Paine quote, ". . . the harder the conflict, the more glorious the triumph. What we obtain too cheap, we esteem too lightly: it is dearness only that gives every thing its value. . . ." The day doesn't end until 4 PM.

Adam Guren, one of the best young prop traders in the business who once made *Trader Monthly*'s Top 30 Under 30 list said in an interview with the popular trading blog, Wall Street Cheat Sheet, "As a novice trader, it is important to be resilient. You are never going to be right all the time. That's hard to swallow for a lot of novice traders." Mr. Guren, a former professional soccer player, who trades international equities around the clock at First NY Securities, counseled that you must learn to accept you are going to be wrong often and bounce back.

Dr. Ari Kiev, a leading trading psychiatrist best known for his work with Olympic athletes and top equities trader Steve Cohen of SAC Capital in his book *Trade to Win*, wrote, "The trading arena has produced its share of select 'super-traders,' market practitioners who set themselves apart from the rest of the field with one distinct advantage: mental and emotional toughness. Like outstanding athletes who stay focused, remain calm, and stick to their game plan, these master traders in this highly risky, highly competitive arena possess an edge that keeps them from being distracted by fear, self-doubt, greed, and other emotional components that can cause major losses and prevent gains from soaring to new highs."

Resilience is key.

A trader must be like Mariano Rivera after a tough day. They must have the mentality of a closer. After blowing a save for the Yankees, Mo, unlike fanatical Yankees fans, forgets it. The next day he does not remember his last blown save. He goes back to what he does well. Hard cutter in, hard cutter in. Just like you ought to as a trader. One Good Trade. One Good Trade.

Yesterday's past rips have nothing to do with today. If we make One Good Trade and then One Good Trade, then the rips yesterday will have no impact on our trades today. Go back to work the next day with the attitude that today will be a great day. Because this is what a consistently profitable trader does. And this is your goal.

ELIMINATE YOUR MISTAKES

"The definition of insanity is doing the same thing over and over again and expecting different results."

—Albert Einstein

As a developing trader, you must note what works for you and continue to do more of this. But you also must eliminate your mistakes. At the end of every day in your trading journal you must make a list of things that do not work for you. And then eliminate them.

I learned the importance of this exercise from a former trader at SMB who we brought on in the beginning. We were lucky to have him as long as we did. He was a former market maker, trying to transition to electronic trading. Often, former NYSE Floor traders, sales traders, or hedge fund traders struggle transitioning to electronic trading because of their weak bidding and offering skills, or getting executions at the best prices. But PK learned quickly.

PK was one of those guys who seemed to have it all. He was handsome, with sandy blond hair and boyish looks. He was a great tennis player, who had played in college. He was very bright, a graduate of RIT. And he picked up electronic trading faster than anyone we have trained who made the transition.

PK's work got better every week. One day, I went up to him and asked him how he improved so quickly and he said, "I just eliminate my mistakes every day." Oh. Here I was waiting for a complex response and PK offered something so brilliantly simple. PK left to help his wife with her business and we fell out of touch.

Let me offer a quick exercise to help with your trading. No matter what your skill level, go get your trading journal and place it next to your trading station. Draw a line down the middle of your trading journal. On the left, keep a list of the things that do not work for you. Trading setups that do not work. Premarket routines that are not effective. Trading rules that are not helpful. On the right, keep track of what works for you. Do more of what is on the right-hand side and don't do any of what is on the left-hand side.

For example, some developing traders start a position with their biggest size, instead of scaling into this position after confirmation to load up. This you must eliminate.

One of our best developing traders was trading WFC. He saw a pattern change by reading the tape. The stock was in a downtrend. He started a long position at 20c. But he just started with 2k shares. GMan, our head trader, called him out for this.

GMan instructed that when you see the pattern change, buy just 600 shares, or one lot, for this trader. When 30c holds the bid, then you add another 600 shares. When the SPY spiked, then you add another lot. When the 33c seller lifted, then you add another lot. Hold your biggest position only when more indicators are in your favor. But you don't just start with 2k shares.

Most people go to work and do an excellent job. At some point, they have an annual review. Their boss will come into their review and compliment them on their performance. They will laud the employee on how hard he or she works and the value that he or she adds to the company. And then the boss will say something like, "It would be nice if you took more initiative." But if that's the only thing to nit-pick over, the boss will conclude with, "You are doing a great job. I do not know what we would do without you."

After the review, that employee will go home. He or she will have dinner with his/her significant other. And a conversation will begin about the review. The employee will say, "Do I have something to tell you! Can you believe that my SOB boss complained about me taking more initiative? Tomorrow, I am going to take more initiative to point out what a moronic boss he is!"

And if you are any successful significant other, your job now is to look flabbergasted. And try adding, "What a jackass, honey!"

That employee will then go back to work, do nothing about taking more initiative, and feel contempt for the boss. The company will not care that much since overall this employee is doing a great job.

Well, the market is different. Let me introduce you to our boss, the Market. The market has a much more cut-and-dry performance review. First of all, performance is not reviewed annually. It is reviewed after every trade. If you do something wrong, the market does not wait till the end of the year to let you know. She tells you right away with a rip. Thank you market. Also, if you choose not to change your behavior, then the market will just reach into your bank account and take your money. Simple. Honest. Unwavering.

Barring a broker's execution error, there really is no appeals process. You cannot go to the market and say, "Oh, now I know you were serious. Can I have my money back, please?" The market will take your money, care less about doing so, and be on the alert to take more.

The great gift of trading is that you must learn to change. You must eliminate your mistakes. And you must do so immediately.

A CPT sees a loss as a learning opportunity. After the 2001 PGA Championship in which Phil Mickelson three-putted on 16 to cost him the tournament, he worked on his lag putting. Phil hired Dave Pelz, who offered him a series of drills to improve this skill. Soon after, Phil won three majors.

It is a gift to learn what we need to work on. And there is always something to improve. You will never get it. You will just get better and earn more chances to get even better.

RESPECT THE MARKETS

Again, you have one boss—the Market. The market will disrespect those who disrespect her. If you are unprepared, you will be punished. If you lack discipline, you will be reprimanded. The market eliminates those unworthy of participation.

Some examples of being disrespectful as an intraday trader? If you are doubling down, then you are being disrespectful. To double down means to start a position, for it to trade against your stop-loss, and then double your position. If you fail to hit stocks that hit your predetermined exit price, then you are being disrespectful. If you are unprepared to trade, then you are being disrespectful. If you ignore the price action of a stock or the market because they are disharmonious with your predictions, then this is disrespectful. The result of such actions are heavy fines from Mother Market.

When you actively trade like we do, you compete against the most sophisticated people in the world. Many are former DI athletes. Most are Ivy League—educated. They may have more money and experience than you. They probably are armed with more information than you, supported by analysts and hungry trader-in-waiting clerks. They sit around their mahogany conference room tables, nibbling lunch catered by the firm, and group-think about ways to take your money. This is a full contact sport. Anything less than your complete focus is disrespectful.

Who the hell are you to think you can roll in at 9:20 AM, sit down at your trading station, check out a few websites, glance at your filters, and think that you can compete against them?

"The market can remain irrational longer than you can remain solvent," wrote John Maynard Keynes at the beginning of the 20th century. This is still true today. I cannot think of a quote that has been more helpful to me during my trading career. So now you know this. There are going to be trades where you watch the price action and think, "What the (expletive deleted) is happening here? This move is ridiculous." You will watch stocks sold at prices that you are convinced are crazy. And it probably is.

But you have to survive these irrational moves in a stock. You can wipe out your trading account on ONE crazy move. Over the course of your trading career, you will develop thousands of excellent risk/reward opportunities. Why jeopardize your career, your passion, on one trading idea? Thinking you know best, or you are bigger than the market is disrespectful.

A Raid on Amaranth

Let me share a famous trading anecdote. Brian Hunter was a star trader at Amaranth Advisors, a massive multi-strategy hedge fund at the peak of the hedge fund heyday in the mid-2000s. This 32-year-old Canadian cowboy was up $2 billion trading natural gas for 2006. There was not a bigger natural gas player than Mr. Hunter. But when all was said and done, there would be a new biggest player, Houston-based trader John Arnold of Centaurus Energy.

Did I mention that Mr. Hunter was a star? A trading superstar with an impressive track record. For years, he took home more than eight figures, and even got into a lawsuit with his old employer, Deutsche Bank, over how many more millions they supposedly still owed him. (He left for Amaranth soon after.) He was so good at what he did that Amaranth let him trade from his hometown of Calgary, Alberta, Canada, over 2,000 miles from the firm's Connecticut headquarters.

Mr. Hunter's fortune quickly unraveled (see Figure 4.3). From up $2 billion, he quickly lost $6.6 billion in a matter of weeks in August of 2006. How? Mr. Hunter repeatedly double-downed on a risky, volatile bullish position called in energy trading circles "The Widowmaker." On the other side of this trade? John Arnold. Natural gas plummeted from $15 to below $4 in a terrible, unusually steep downmove, on a weak hurricane season. Amaranth went from $10 billion in assets under management to near $4.5 billion. The Feds were raiding Amaranth's headquarters shortly after. Arnold ended up taking home over $1.5 billion for himself that year.

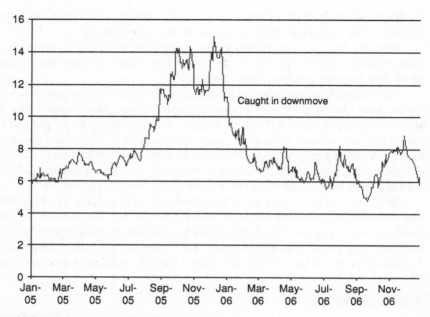

FIGURE 4.3   Natural Gas Prices 2005–2006

And remember that Mr. Hunter had billions to allocate to protect his position. And even with these unusually deep pockets, he was forced to liquidate his positions. (JP Morgan, Hunter's prime broker, only exacerbated the process. The bank kept calling for more collateral to support his humungous positions, and once the collateral didn't arrive, his credit was pulled, the JP Morgan prop energy desk crossed the Chinese wall, and took the trade off Hunter's hands for pennies on the dollar, only to make an absolute killing in the next few weeks once natural gas prices rebounded.) For the trader at home, or at a prop desk, with many dollars less than billions, you cannot withstand such draw downs.

SNDK Ripper

I have to share a personal trading story involving Steve, me, and a stock the very mention of which causes my mood to turn dour. GMan is afraid to mention this stock to me whenever it is In Play for fear of upsetting me. I had to research the specific facts of this day because I think my brain has protectively blocked this day from my memory. This was one of the worst trading days for Steve and me personally. We got hammered. The whole thing makes me upset just rereading what happened.

One day there was an announcement that INTC and MU were going to enter SNDK's space. SNDK was killing it at the time and Steve and I did not see the real threat. SNDK gapped down. For us, this was a classic bounce candidate. The premarket had just gotten this story wrong and we would get long and ride SNDK up so it would fill the gap. SNDK was down big.

SNDK opened near 54, there was some buying, so we got long. SNDK traded lower, we hit the bids and took a loss. There was some more buying, we bought, SNDK traded lower, and we hit the bids. We repeated this process more times than I care to share. We should have just followed the downward trend of the stock after the fifth time buying, and hitting SNDK lower. It opened up down big and just went lower. It never bounced intraday. Steve lost so much money he received a call from higher-ups concerning his account balance. I will leave out how much I lost, but it was considerably less.

I had numerous opportunities to double down and I passed. As much as this day was a rip, I did live to play another day. I would have blown up my trading account if I had doubled down. SNDK never bounced (see Figures 4.4 and 4.5). It closed near the low of day near 46.50ish (Steve hit the very bottom).

The story gets much more painful. Less than two months later, SNDK was 30 points higher (see chart below) than where we were hitting it. We are intraday traders, so we would not have held it overnight and captured

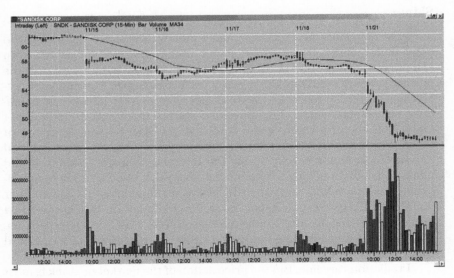

FIGURE 4.4 SNDK 11/15/2005–11/21/2005

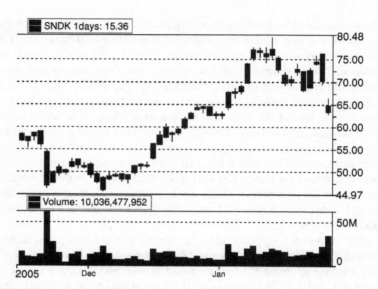

FIGURE 4.5 SNDK Nov 2005–Jan 2006

this move. See, we were right after all. But this is not relevant. SNDK was going to trade lower on this day.

Skippy

Some would rather be right than make money. These are the types who conveniently forget that the market can remain irrational longer than you can remain solvent. One of the smarter guys we have traded with over the past decade, let's call him Skippy, is a perfect example. The guy knew everything about the markets. He was a hopeless market intellectual enamored with fundamentals, PE ratios, and market theory. And if you didn't know this, then he would make sure that you did. He was from one of those European countries where the stereotype is that everyone is blond and of old Teutonic stock. During the Internet explosion, Skippy would chirp about YHOO being overvalued at $50, yet it went to $500 (split adjusted). Skippy would warn that BRCM was overbought and it had another tenfold to go. He instructed that AMZN would be out of business in a few years. I am loving my new Kindle purchased from AMZN not a month ago. Skippy focused on shorting during the entire Internet Bubble. Ooops. And for those interested, Skippy doesn't trade anymore.

Predictions are fine. But the price action of the market or stock is most important for intraday traders like us. If you have what you believe is an irrefutable trading opinion and the price action does not confirm your bias, then do not make the trade. Predictions absent validation from the price action are not advisable if you wish to enjoy a long intraday trading career.

We were watching tape on a Saturday one day. A hardworking new trader asked, "Bella, would that have been a place to double down?" I had the tape stopped.

I responded like a Judge while pounding his gavel, "Please never ask me that question again. Doubling down does not work for the intraday trader. I have tried it. Eighty-five percent of the time you will profit when you double down. But the 15 percent of the time you are wrong, you will get smoked. The losses during these trades will far outweigh the gains from the 85 percent. The math does not work. And I even tried to master this technique during a range-bound market where this should work best. Just forget about it. It is a waste of your mental energy to master doubling down." And then we restarted the tape.

So, for every trade, you must be prepared for anything. Remember my SNDK disaster. Play defense if a stock trades against your exit price. The unexpected will occur. Live to play another day. Respect the markets.

MASTER BASIC TRADING PLAYS

When you begin you must master basic trading plays. You cannot trade 70k SKF until you first learn how to trade a support play in a MCD or BAC with 100 shares. To learn this play, you must develop if-then statements for this trade. There are subsets of a support play, not just one. Trading is not learning to buy at a specified level and then just holding. Sorry, it is not that simple. If it were that easy, there would be no need for trading mentors, this book, and me.

Let's talk about a day I traded STI. It held the bid at 16 and never dropped (see Figure 4.6). This is an easy trade. Sixteen was a level. We got long and we held until the uptrend was broken.

On the same day, MCD hit support at 60. JToma had offered this support level the day before on CNBC's "Fast Money Half-Time Report." In true JToma form, he came back from his appearance reporting how "stunning" Michelle Caruso-Cabrera was in person. We bought MCD at 60, the level dropped (see Figure 4.7). I hit the bids. The Specialist came right back to the bid at 60 and I reentered long 2k shares.

Again, on the very same day, V was In Play. Seventy was resistance. V met this level. V would hold the 70 level a bit and then drop (see Figure 4.8). I bought 70 and then hit the bids when the stock dropped the 70 bid. I recognized that the buyer(s) would drop out of the stock, and then come back

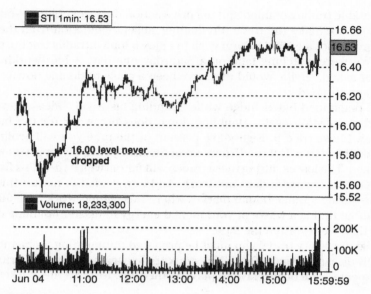

FIGURE 4.6 STI 6/4/2009

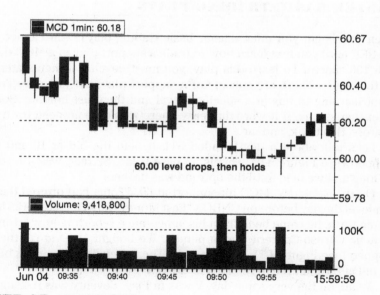

FIGURE 4.7 MCD 6/4/2009

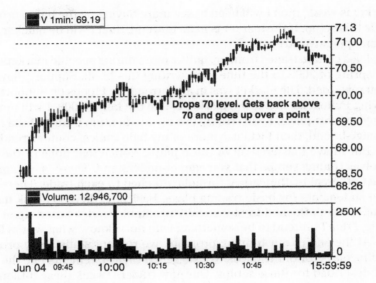

FIGURE 4.8 V 6/4/2009

to the 70 level. The buyer(s) would not immediately come back to the 70 bid, like MCD did. They would drop buy down to 69.85ish and then slowly buy V back toward 70. So I made an adjustment. I bought at 69.85 when the buyer(s) dropped it out. And I held till V showed weakness near 71. Chop.

This was the very same trading day. This was the same trading play, a support play. MCD, V, and STI each offered different subsets for this play. Any trader can make the STI trade. Some can make the MCD trade. Few can make the V trade. As Alexander, who sits to my right on our desk would kid, "Who is better than you, Bella?" And I have different if-then statements for each subset of this support play.

For STI, my if-then statement was: If the 16 bid holds with significant volume, then get long and hold. If 16 drops, then exit.

For MCD, my if-then statement was: If 60 drops, then exit. If the buyer reappears automatically, then this is just a shakeout and rebuy.

For V, my if-then statement was: If the buyer(s) is dropping out the bid, then buy into the dropout and then hold until the uptrend is broken.

And this is just for this market, with one play. I have a thick playbook of trading plays. I am always looking to add plays. In fact, I think my next book is going to be called *The Intraday Trader's Playbook*. Watch your back, Dan Brown.

But the market will change. And with just these three simple subsets of a support play, the market will demand that I make adjustments. If the market is weak, then I will need to see more buying on the bid to profitably trade this setup. If the market is in an uptrend, then I will be quicker to buy when I perceive strength.

I use certain trades from my quiver more during specific markets. Since the spring of 2009 to the time I am writing this book, Support Plays have been rewarded. The market was in an uptrend. So I focus on Support Plays, Buying Pullbacks, etc. If the market is like the fall of 2008, I will not make many support plays. I will strictly use my momentum trades. If the market is range-bound, then I will use more of my fade trades, countertrend plays.

But I have mastered all of these plays. Notice that none of the above involves trading setups that you cannot understand. There is not some abstract ethereal mathematical formula attached to each trade. There are if-then statements for basic trading plays. Basically, there is a risk management system attached to statistically profitable trades based upon how I trade. I don't pretend to be something I am not. I know what works for me.

At the end of our training program, we roll out statistically profitable trading plays for our trainees. We suggest if-then statements like the ones I just described for these setups. Our new traders tweak these if-then statements so they are best for them. As the market changes, our traders must again tweak these plays. Consistently profitable traders adapt. But when you start, you must master basics.

Becoming a CPT will not depend upon you mastering complicated new trading plays. These are plays that traders have used for over a decade. They have always worked, will always work, and need to be mastered. Work on them.

LEARN TO EXECUTE ORDERS QUICKLY

Most prop players trade electronically. We are not on the NYSE trading floor or in a live futures pit. We do not call our broker to execute our trades. Everything is done on a keyboard, and we must train ourselves to have fast fingers. The single most important reason why former NYSE floor traders, hedge fund traders, and institutional traders fail to successfully transition to electronic trading is their lack of speed entering orders. You can't be that guy in our game waiting for a stock to trade below an important level, and then it does, and not be quick enough to get short at a good price.

Practice your execution skills daily. Create speed drills for yourself. Our traders practice 15 minutes every day during their initial training to get faster on the keyboard. Being fast and light is an advantage that the intraday trader must learn to exploit. We can go from long to short very quickly and easily. That is, unless we are not fast. As a way of incentive, the world markets will only continue to become increasingly electronically based.

As such, learning to be fast with your orders is a skill that you will have to master.

For Vanguard to unwind a few million share position may take weeks. But you are not Vanguard. You can exit your positions with the tap of a keyboard. You can flip your position in less than a second. Understand that this is a huge advantage. The good intraday trader maximizes this advantage over other larger market players.

Point-And-Click

Let me offer an example. Steve and I used to sit next to a trader who entered his orders by pointing and clicking with a mouse. I had heard some talking head on CNBC bragging about how he was talking with his hand on his mouse to enter a position while he was being interviewed. To the active intraday trader, this is suicide. This would be like taking a 50-pound weight jacket, attaching it to Kobe's back, then seeing how well he plays. This is a huge disadvantage.

This very solid trader would sometimes trade the same stocks as us. One time, we were all trading MON. It was In Play, and near an important intraday level: one where we are short as long as MON is below this level and long if MON is above the level. MON was in an intraday uptrend but this level was offering significant resistance such that we were temporarily short. This recent resistance with significant volume trumped the intraday uptrend indicated by our charts. And we were all short. I was short, Steve was short, and Point-and-Click was short.

The level lifted. Steve got flat, then long 3k. I got flat and long 2k. Point-and-Click was still short and cursing that he could not get filled. In fact, after he covered he smashed his keyboard into pieces (impressive keyboard smashing, by the way). There were only a few letters left. Old School traders will tell you that if you are going to smash your keyboard, then do it well. Smash the living crap out of the keyboard. It should be rendered useless. If not, then take your sissy keyboard smashing elsewhere, because now you are just making noise and distracting the rest of us.

Now this was not a case of us, Steve and me, taking Point-And-Click's prints. Steve and I could have bought 5k each if we wanted. There was that much available. He was just much slower than the rest of the marketplace. MON traded up another 50c where we sold. Steve made $1,500, I made $1k (why does he always have to make more than me?), and Point-And-Click lost $1k.

We all were using the same technique of short below and flip above the level. But the fast traders made money and the slow lost.

I presently sit around 20-somethings right out of college, former athletes. Not a week goes by where we are trading the same stock, I get stock that they cannot because I am fast on the keyboard. This is usually followed with my shaking my head at these slowpokes with this line, "Guys, I am thirty-nine years old. How is it possible that I can get stock and you cannot?"

There is no substitute for speed.

FINE-TUNE YOUR FOCUS

Steve is one tough SOB. If you met him for the first time, you would walk away concluding he was a Wharton intellectual. He is so damn smart. But Steve will grind it out like Tiger. He will take a loss and fight back. The day for him doesn't end until the bell rings. A bad start is just an opportunity to make a comeback. You would have to literally drag him away from his trading station to end his fight. Steve's trading mentor, a market veteran, said about Steve, "I have never seen anyone so comfortable on a trading floor." And he fights with every tick, every day, sick or not, tired or alert, hungry or well fed. Do you know how many times he has picked himself up after the Close and announced he was heading to get some lunch?

And he doesn't miss one tick in the 10 different stocks he is watching on a given day. He can tell you important prices from two weeks ago. Like Derek Jeter, you cannot tell from watching him if he is having a bad day or a career trading day. This is what I mean by focus.

During the fall of 2008, we traded every tick during the day. Dr. Momentum was not six months into his trading career. At the end of the day, he looked like he had been through a war. He had to leave at 4:30 every night because he had nothing left. Twenty-three and less than six months into his career, he had focused so intently during the trading day that by the Close, he was wiped. This is the focus required by the market.

CONTROL YOUR EMOTIONS

Me: I have noticed that you have trouble controlling your emotions.

Notorious Underperformer: I do, but I am getting better.

Me: Ok, let's work on this. For the next three days, keep a list in your trading journal of all the things that set you off. Send me that list and then we will discuss it.

Notorious
Underperformer: Today, I told myself not to get upset about things and I traded better.

Me: This is not something you can will away. You have to work on developing the skill of controlling your emotions. This is not a big deal. Most intraday traders at one point must work on this.

I can't tell you how many times I have had a conversation similar to the one above. Active intraday traders deal with rejection more than longer time frame traders. We trade more, so we are wrong more. If a losing trade sets you off, then this can affect your trades going forward. And this is dangerous.

We call this trading on "tilt." You are in an temporary emotional state where you are not thinking as clearly as you can. You are angry, or frustrated, or disappointed. And then you make decisions that you normally would not. And rips result. In short, you manifest trading data that does not reflect your ability.

A few days later Notorious Underperformer, a bright Ivy League graduate capable of much better trading results, sent me his list of things that set him off. They were a typical list. One of them was getting upset when he exited for a loss greater than he expected. I suggested the following visualization exercise (shortened considerably below):

Find a quiet area. Breathe deeply in and out for a few minutes until you are calm. Then visualize not getting out of a stock where you expected. In as much detail as possible, remember the last trade like this that set you off. Then expose the logic of getting upset. Something like if I let this upset me, then I will miss easy trades in this stock about to come. Then breathe in and out deeply again until you are calm. Repeat this process a few times.

I recommend you read Dr. Steenbarger for more about trading psychology and this topic. My sentiment about learning trading psychology can be summed up with this past tweet:

after readin @steenbab often I consider whether I should end my future blogs w/ thxs 4 reading but 4 a really awesome blog visit TraderFeed

Controlling your emotions is necessary to recognize your trading potential. Most on our desk spend 15 minutes every day working on their mental weaknesses utilizing visualization exercises. You will not rid these issues in one session. It takes weeks of repeated practice. But you can get better. And remember, this issue is so important that GMan went from "I quit!" to Head Trader to Partner by improving controlling his emotions.

THE GOOD NEWS

Mike, that all seemed very difficult. As Teddy Roosevelt inspired, "Nothing in the world is worth having or worth doing unless it means effort." The good news is that you can learn it all. This is your opportunity to do something great!

Many intraday traders have successfully navigated very different markets. Whether it was 1999 or 2002, the intraday trader has been able to profit. Most got killed during the 2008 market collapse, but for the intraday trader, this was our best year since 2000. I share the reticence of Andy Kershner of the Kershner Trading Group to talk about doing well that year, "You have to be careful of how much you talk about it. Everybody else is having tough times. You feel a little bit guilty about it when everybody else is losing money." But the reward of fully developed trading skills is that we can profit in any market.

And we get to do so doing the very best job in the world!

Now, let's examine past traders who have failed and why. They make for some entertaining stories and trading lessons.

CHAPTER 5

Why Traders Fail

Y ou are at a local bar drinking with your buddies and cannot take your eyes off its prettiest patron. You approach confidently and start working this lovely young woman. After leading with some of your best material she asks, "So what do you do?"

You smile, pause and answer coolly, with a George Clooneyesqe twinkle in your eye, "I am a trader."

The young woman flips her hair, unconscientiously wets her lips, and now focuses her eyes squarely on you, "Really?"

The evening ends at worst with this young woman's phone number in your iPhone, all in full view of your drinking pals.

The failure rate is too high in this industry, with too many traders failing for the wrong reasons. There I said it! And this is all unnecessary. In this chapter, I will share my experiences working with traders who failed or simply should have never started in order to help future and present traders avoid these obvious but common mistakes.

Reasons for failure include: not listening to the market, failing to hit stocks that trade against you, a need to be right, the unrealistic learning curve, thinking as an investor instead of a trader, and simply not loving trading.

The last reason seems obvious, but there are pikers who grab a seat in our industry without a passion behind what they are doing. They become traders for the perceived social prestige of being a trader (see the opening pickup scene above, which, by the way, I have personally observed on numerous occasions). Trading is only for those with an ability to sustain their energy of working day in and day out at their craft—the discipline of trading. Trading is only for elite performers committed to a long journey of ups and downs, where you learn just how good you can be as a trader. The others, well, they are in this chapter.

THEY DON'T LISTEN TO THE MARKET

Too many new traders think they know how to start. If Jim Cramer can throw tantrums on TV and be right half the time, why can't I? Let me give you a sports analogy.

I love golf. And despite its snooze-inducing pace to some, I love watching it on TV. But just because I watch it on TV, like I might catch Cramer in the evenings, does not mean I have the slightest idea about how to become a professional golfer.

One of the more common statements from those trained on our desk is: "I wish I would have just listened earlier." I do not offer this quote for any other reason than to save you some aggravation.

You have a choice. You can spend the first six months of your trading career not learning anything because you don't listen, or you can start the right way. After six months, you can possess the skills that you need to trade profitably in any market, from anywhere, and for the rest of your trading career. Or you can be frustrated, unskilled, with a decidedly negative trading account. Do not be one of the thousands who needlessly loses excessive amounts of money when he begins and worse still, never develops career-making trading skills.

We will share in the following pages some stories of mainly former traders who already made the most common mistakes so you don't have to. As a result, you will vault ahead of 95 percent of those who seek to trade.

One of the written lectures most important for the new traders who I train is: "Be the Best Listener." If you are fortunate enough to join a solid trading firm, first things first: listen. And here's another reminder: when you begin your trading career, despite all the books you've read, charts you've examined, balance sheets you've picked apart, or profits you've experienced in your PA, you do not know what you are doing. Listen and learn. Evan Lazarus, chief information officer at T3 Capital, teaches that this first stage is "unconscious incompetence." You do not know what you are supposed to know and you do not know this. The market is our boss and punishes those who disobey. Let consistently profitable, experienced traders share the rules communicated to them from our boss, the Market.

There is a direct correlation at prop firms between those who listen best and those who perform best. Our top five new traders presently were the best listeners during their training class. At the firm that taught me, the best traders were those who hung around the best traders hungry to listen. One of our best listeners, Dr. Momentum, parrots lines that I have spoken months ago. I walk away astounded after a chat with Dr. Momentum thinking to myself, "How the hell did he pick that up?" Dr. Momentum had understood an incredibly complex idea taught to me by the market that I conveyed in passing weeks ago. With such superior listening skills, it is no surprise that he has grown into a solid trader.

How to Be the Best Listener

Lesson number one: be the best listener on your desk.

My favorite political show is *HardBall*, hosted by Chris Matthews. Mr. Matthews recently offered some great advice for new traders (and those who are single) unbeknownst to him in his new book *Life's a Campaign*:

"When he was a Yank at Oxford, Bill Clinton had a reputation as someone who knew how to get the girls. A fellow Rhodes Scholar who was waging a losing battle for the woman of his dreams asked Clinton for advice. "Have you ever thought about listening?" the expert from Hope, Arkansas, told him authoritatively.

Later in the book: "Clinton used the same tactic to score good grades. As a college student at Georgetown, Bill was famous for being able to read the professors. He would wow his classmates by predicting just what questions would be on the exams. That's because he listened in class, really heard what the professor most cared about. This is something I've been telling my kids: Pay attention to what the teacher personally is trying to teach."

To use Clinton's prowess with academics and females as an analogy, the market is our professor. A prop firm mentor in turn shares what our professor has taught us in the last decade or so. It's not that we are egomaniacs and demand to be the center of attention on our respective desk (though it is our money they're trading). Personally, I couldn't care less if a new trader listens to me. But I am just sharing what the market has taught me over the past 12 years. We ask that they listen because if they don't, their chance of failure dramatically increases.

I don't mean to be cavalier about this. Let me be clear for those who may have missed my point. The Market has rules. Experienced prop traders have spent many hours, days, months, and years learning these rules, at times very painfully. I've spoken endlessly to new traders about what happens when one disobeys these rules, i.e., Mother Market reaches into your pocket and takes what is hers. And she doesn't give it back.

Trent: Great Guy, Poor Listener, Former Trader

If you are still a non-believer, let me share an anecdote with you. One of my favorite traders was, and I emphasize *was*, a guy we will call Trent (think "Swingers"). I really did like Trent. Everyone liked Trent. I was so fond of him that I still remember the sleepless nights following his departure. He was the first trader to ever fail with SMB.

As an aside, my favorite Trent story also involves GMan. We all went out for St. Patrick's Day on the Upper East Side. My alma mater, UConn, was playing Albany in the first round of the NCAA tournament. The atmosphere could not have been any finer for a bunch of alpha male traders: college hoops, beers, wings, and a barroom full of women. Trent invited his girlfriend and her sister, who just happened to be an ex-Miss Florida. (Who doesn't enjoy the company of an ex Miss Fill-in-the-Southern-state?).

Miss Florida apparently fell for GMan immediately. Sensing that there was chemistry, Trent arranged for all four of them to go to dinner. But the dozen or so beers GMan had imbibed did him no favors. Over dinner, GMan blurted to Miss Florida that he had a girlfriend. When these words came out of GMan's mouth, Trent apparently looked at him like he had committed a felony. "I just laid you up with Miss Florida and this is the thanks you give me," read the expression on Trent's face. I don't care if you are the Head Trader. This is one awesome risk/reward opportunity you just sabatoged. Sadly (tragically?), GMan never did get together with Miss Florida, since we severed ties with Trent not too long afterward.

But why did Trent fail? As much as we enjoyed his company and his access to former beauty queens, he didn't listen to us. Or more accurately, he didn't listen to the Market. During one of our Midday meetings on risk management, we discussed a subtopic on the danger of trading heavily shorted stocks. In particular we mentioned Travelzoo, symbol TZOO.

I strongly recommended staying away from TZOO because its short interest was too high, a ridiculous 62 percent! When stocks are under heavy short pressure, anxious market makers and opportunistic buyers like to engage in short squeezes that start and end without warning. The stock often spikes and drops, then spikes and spikes and spikes . . . and then plummets. Under these conditions, the stock is unreadable, unpredictable, and too dangerous for a new trader. Almost like trapeze artists and fire eaters at the circus telling kids "Do not try this at home."

Not three minutes after the end of our meeting did I sit down at my trading station and take notice of how our desk was doing. Trent had red all over my risk monitor. I clicked to see his positions. This Miss Florida-toting favorite of his trading peers was long 800 shares of TZOO! Did I not just say to stay away? It would have been one thing if he was up on the trade, but it was two points against him, and the stock never rebounded.

Well, that was certainly a rip. And that was the last trade that Trent ever made (though he does have a good job now).

If you want to recognize your potential, then be the best listener on your desk or in your trading community; listen to experienced traders. Listen to what the market has taught us.

Boy Genius

Let me offer another anecdote that any trainer at every prop firm has experienced. The names, dates, and locations may vary, but the ending and reason for termination is always the same. Some extraordinarily bright new prop traders possess poor listening skills.

One of the brightest traders I trained had poor listening skills. Come to think of it, it wasn't that they were poor, they were non-existent. Let's call this new trainee Boy Genius. More accurately, he did not listen to the senior traders, the head trader, or the partners, including me. And not listening to me incurs a hefty penalty.

If I sense a new trader is not listening, well, I initiate a discussion behind closed doors that is rather unpleasant. In this meeting, I am brutally honest, like all good coaches must be. And despite all the love I have shown in the recruiting process, I am not shy about telling you that if you do not pick up the pace, we will move forward without you. It is my job to tell the truth.

Boy Genius was academically bright. His math SAT score was 800, and had graduated from a top-ranked liberal arts school in the Northeast. As a former college athlete, he had a history of competitiveness. Interestingly, he had paid the bills as a professional blackjack gambler for close to a year (yeah, I am not sure how this is possible, either).

Before I can continue offering you the perfect example of how not to start as a trader, I must give some background about how new traders often get started at a prop firm. When a new trader begins trading live, they are usually assigned a mentor. This mentor reviews the trainee's trades after every close. The mentor will check whether you are in the right stocks, overtrading, following the trend, keeping losses small, and answer specific questions. There is a mentoring document that you must fill out after every Close on these points.

The new trader must focus on skill development and forming good habits when he first begins. Losing money is not a big deal when you start. However, it is not acceptable to make certain fundamental mistakes. You hit the cutoff man in baseball. You box out the player you are defending in hoops. You keep your head still in golf. And in our sport, fundamentals must be honored by the new trader.

For example, letting stocks trade against your exit price or trading too many shares from the start are not acceptable mistakes. If a mentor spots this, reprimands are likely. And with this newbie, he was letting stocks trade against him. Boy Genius's punishment? The DEMO! There is no greater insult on a prop desk than being banished to the demo for a day. It's probably worse than getting demoted from the majors to the minors. Cowboys have to learn to ride a horse before a bull, so to speak.

As intraday traders, we have a distinct advantage over institutional traders in that we can exit our losing positions instantly. Before every trade, we must determine our exit plan for if a stock trades against us. A new trader might start out trading 1 standard lot, 100 shares. One hundred shares is low risk for the firm, and although it's low reward for the trader, he needs to start somewhere. Many great traders started out on "one lot." If that loss barrier hits, they really have no excuse about why they couldn't get out. Even for an illiquid stock, 100 shares is nothing.

Institutional traders, on the other hand, may have a 1,000,000 share position with which to work. It takes some time to unravel such a large position, not one click of a mouse (or in the case of most active intraday traders, a tap of a hot key, exceedingly faster than clicking a mouse), and losses can be significant. Intraday traders trade with much smaller size and can hit the bids for a very small loss. In fact, a good intraday trader can take numerous losses of as little as one penny. So we must learn to exploit one of our huge advantages. And this means hitting a stock when it trades against our exit price.

Boy Genius's mentor instructed him to stop letting his losses run past 20 cents. His book was littered with these. When the problem continued, I had to call a private meeting with him. We discussed some of his trades from the day before. I explained the importance of hitting stocks that trade against him, even though Steve and I had covered this in his training. (When we teach this principle to new traders, I always ask with my voice raised, "What do you do when a stock hits your exit price?" And our new traders respond quickly and in unison, "Hit the stock!" And I animatedly growl, "That is right. You HIT the stock!")

After our talk, Boy Genius still was not convinced. I asked him, "Do you understand why this is important?"

Boy Genius replied, "I am not sure that that is the most efficient way to trade."

Did I just hear that? This genius has been trading for a few days and all of a sudden he is an expert on trading efficiency? I bit my lip, restrained what I really wanted to say, and patiently discussed the following trade.

Boy Genius had bought a stock in front of a support level. This was excellent! Just as we teach it in our training program! However, the support level broke and the stock traded lower. I re-taught that when the support level broke that he must sell. And he said, "But how do you know that the stock is really going to go down?" Right then, I knew we had a problem. He had not been listening. We had covered this probably 50 times already.

I patiently explained again, "You bought the stock because it was holding a support level. This is the reason why you entered the trade. When the support level drops, your reason for being in the trade no longer exists and you must exit. You cannot be sure that the stock will go down, but that is irrelevant. We play the percentages. We make trades where our win rate is 60–70 percent with a downside of one and an upside of five. When the stock does not act like we expect, then we exit and start over. And we are not in the business of losing money to prove that we were right. So when the stock drops below the support level, you have no other choice but to hit out of the stock. Holding a stock below support is now gambling. And that is not what we do here."

Before he left, I really laid into him. He was the most talented trader in his class yet his results were the worst. Didn't it occur to him that this didn't make any sense? I let him know that questioning the validity of such a fundamental trading concept concerned me. It was a sign that he was not listening. There's always time to experiment later, but at the start, it's most important to just learn how to trade. He agreed and commented that he would get better.

A few weeks later, Steve called Boy Genius into his office to discuss a trading mistake. I had something to discuss with Steve and walked into his office not knowing he was talking with Boy Genius. I stuck around and listened to their discussion. I quickly noticed Boy Genius would cut off Steve whenever he made a point, and didn't stop. Finally, I cut Boy Genius off from cutting Steve off and angrily interjected, "Why do you keep cutting Steve off? When I was in law school we learned to immediately stop talking when an Appellate Judge spoke. When Steve talks, do not interrupt him! Just listen."

Clearly, I was furious at Boy Genius. A lack of disrespect shows up in your trading. If you disrespect a partner and your financial backer, then you will do the same to the market. And not to sound street-ish in a gangster sense, but if you disrespect the market, it will not respect you back. Consider these memorable lines from Jules Winnfield in the movie *Pulp Fiction:*

> *The path of the righteous man is beset on all sides by the iniquities of the selfish and the tyranny of evil men. Blessed is he, who in the name of charity and good will, shepherds the weak through the valley of darkness, for he is truly his brother's keeper and the finder of lost children. And I will strike down upon thee with great vengeance and furious anger those who would attempt to poison and destroy my brothers. And you will know my name is the Lord when I lay my vengeance upon thee.*

A month later, Boy Genius's mentor asked to talk with me again because Boy Genius was still making the same mistakes. His trading losses compiled. Compounding his trading losses was Boy Genius's nerve to write his mentor and Steve an e-mail explaining his disagreement with some of the fundamental trading concepts we preached. Excuse me? Two months into trading, no profits, and he's questioning the lessons the market has taught us? Now this will certainly test one's patience. I would have liked to see Gandhi work with this know-it-all.

Steve was thinking along the same lines. He sent me an e-mail commenting on Boy Genius's theories with simply, "If all of those things make sense, then why is he the least profitable trader in his class?" I suggested we have another meeting with Boy Genius, this time with his mentor at his side.

I was not prepared to be as surprised during this meeting as I was. His mentor started with a review of Boy Genius's work and his weaknesses. Now not only was Boy Genius refusing to hit stocks that traded against him, but he was doubling down. He was making progress. At getting worse! His mentor reemphasized the importance of cutting his losses, but Boy Genius still wouldn't do so. And then it was time for Boy Genius to respond.

He replied with what he had said a few months ago, "I just don't see how it is efficient to hit stocks that trade against me. The stock may come back. So why hit the stock?" His mentor rolled his eyes. I was experiencing deja vu. Was there a window we could throw him out of? Would we get caught? What the hell do you say to someone like this?

For about the one hundredth time, I explained why he needed to hit stocks that traded against him. His mentor supplemented my points. Our logic was irrefutable. I said, "Look, you can try to figure things out by yourself. And since you are exceptionally bright, you just might. But it will take you years. I am teaching you the fundamentals that I was taught by the market. I am not making this stuff up. Steve and I did not sit around our office and say, 'Wouldn't it be hysterical if we made up a bunch of arbitrary fundamentals, made a bunch of people follow these rules, and let them trade our money?' You can fight what we teach. But in time you are just going to learn that what we teach is correct. These are just things the market has taught us. I do not ask you to follow our instruction because I am some egomaniac. I could honestly care less whether you listened to me or not. But if you don't, then you are going to struggle, and struggle needlessly."

I ended our meeting with "You are exceptionally bright. You have a background that normally excels on our desk. I am looking forward to seeing your progress."

A few days later, this new trader sent me an e-mail resigning. Thoughtfully, he remarked that he did not want to lose the firm any more money. I was surprised and disappointed. We were prepared to keep working with him, perhaps foolishly. Boy Genius had too much talent to fail. And I actually liked him personally.

It's hard for some new traders to understand that trading may not be something their skill set will allow them to just figure out. And my sense is that this was the issue with this new trader. The fact remained that he should have never failed. It bothers me to this day that we could not persuade Boy Genius to just listen. What a needless waste for us and more importantly for him.

THEY DON'T LOVE TRADING

I sit in my office interviewing an ambitious trading prospect. He looks me squarely in the eyes and declares, "I will outwork everyone on your desk." At this point I rub my eyes, experience a nasty case of deju vu and try not to show skepticism. You see, no one has ever left an interview without uttering the phrase above. Never.

"I will outwork everyone on your desk" is a statement most frequently uttered during any interview at a prop firm. There is no greater line an employer can hear other than "I'll work for free in perpetuity." (Mind you, that would probably violate some kind of labor law, but as you know, I'm not a practicing lawyer.) What boss doesn't want a hardworking rank and file? But then they start their training class. By the simple laws of physics, not everyone can work the hardest, but those who do earn a firm leader's respect immediately.

Based on the routine I'm about to describe, you would think traders are professional athletes who train six to eight hours a day in the off-season preparing for a lucrative season both statistically and financially. Well, they kind of are. For example, at one prop firm, they watch film of their trading daily. They keep a detailed trading journal. They prepare with urgency for every Open. They review their work in their heads religiously. They spend 15 minutes every day performing visualization exercises. They watch tape of their trading on the weekends. On the weekends! When most are playing touch football and getting drunk, these guys are watching film! We often hear stories of how a zealous work ethic pays off in spades in school, sports, and life. It's the same in trading. Prop traders have learned that their performance when the bell rings is determined by the work that they do before the market opens.

Some teachers become frustrated by those who do not work hard. While most encourage a mentoring culture, at the end of the day, the teachers want to see an effort. But I have a different theory. Those new traders who do not work hard do not do so because they do not love trading.

Few know what it is really like to be a trader until they trade. A prop firm can share a typical day in an interview. One of its traders can explain his day during a phone conversation. But there is no way of simulating what it is really like to trade professionally until you do it. And one thing that some interviewees gloss over is an explanation of the work that is required. Some just do not understand how hard their firm will work them. New traders train from 8 AM to 6 PM every day at firms that offer rigorous training. And they cover a lot. At the end of the day, most trainees have given it everything they have.

As we introduced at the inception of this chapter, some like the idea of simply *being* a trader. It seems cool to them. They've read back issues of now defunct *Trader Monthly* and see themselves on the cover with a model in their arms and a private jet in the background. It's as if it brings ultimate respectability in the eyes of their peers. And let's be honest. On more than one occasion, women who have just met me got a lot more interested when I told them I'm a trader. Some would-be trainees envision the rich trader lifestyle that they will lead. And this dream can become a reality. But none of this will happen unless you are willing to pay the price.

And some just are not willing to work hard. There is grunt work that needs to be done every day. At the end of the trading day, your eyes are tired. Sometimes my eyes start twitching over the weekend from a week of staring at my screens. My wrists constantly throb because of the excessive typing I do searching for the next great trade. I often have to stop trading and just rub my wrists to relieve the pain. By the end of the trading day on Friday, I feel like I have taken four consecutive Constitutional Law exams on. Some just do not want to watch some more tape of their trading after the Close. This requires a serious commitment. Some just do not want to go through all of their trades after the bell. There is so much to do before and after the Close. You will not do all of this work unless you love trading. You just won't.

The problem is that if you do not do all that the market requires, you will almost certainly fail.

The Butcher: A Hard Worker Who Never Worked Hard as a Trader

Let me introduce a new trainee to highlight the difficulty of succeeding if you do not love trading. He was a former college basketball player. Let's call him The Butcher, for reasons about to become apparent. The Butcher graduated from an excellent liberal arts school. He was unusually calm during his interview. Controlling his emotions would not be an issue. I liked him. He swore to a trading Partner he would work hard. As proof of his work ethic, he cited his improvement as a college basketball player. The Butcher progressed from a freshman his coach warned would be cut to a solid contributor by his senior year. I was convinced.

There were no red flags with The Butcher during his training. Word starts to spread from our core traders to the new traders that if they do not work hard they will be asked to leave. One of our traders, G, likes to guess which new trader is most likely to be fired first. (Even though we make market bets for a living, side bets on who will be fired are only a natural extension of what we do.) Sometimes he greases me for insider hints. I had nothing.

I did remember The Butcher stopping by my office and asking if I was happy with his work. I thought this was odd. We let them know if their work is subpar immediately. But new traders do not seek me out to ask if their work is satisfactory. And as Steve explains, our new traders are usually scared to death of me. Most keep their distance in the first few weeks. Like some coaches, we break our trainees down when they start training and then build them up before they start. Yet here, The Butcher was sticking his head in to talk with me.

Once his class started to trade live, his results after the first week were not as good as expected. Worse still, The Butcher was not positive a single day. After the end of the first month, The Butcher was negative every day save one. At the end of the month, The Butcher popped his head in again. After that kind of month, he needed to talk with me, and I was impressed how he offered himself up so easily. Following The Butcher's lead, we spent the next 30 minutes going over the process for being fired. Like some bizarre masochist, The Butcher was fascinated with exactly how this would work. He was searching for clues whether he was in jeopardy of being asked to leave.

Look, no one gets fired in the first four months unless they continually do stuff that is unacceptable. Doing poorly is not grounds for termination. But now we are 11 weeks into our relationship and the only conversations The Butcher initiated were related to my impression of his work. Perhaps it's a millennial generation thing where people The Butcher's age need constant feedback about whether or not they're doing well. Thankfully, his mom didn't call me. Yet there were no questions about what he could do better. There were no specific trading questions. The Butcher just fished for clues about whether he was on the hot seat.

But just by witnessing his behavior, I could tell he wasn't long SMB.

Our traders watch tape after the Close. The Butcher was out too early to be watching tape.

Our traders have a serious premarket routine, arriving to the office around 7:45 AM to prepare. The Butcher arrived at 8:30 AM. We do not consider this late. We allow for the possibility that some may prepare at home.

We hold a special training call for new traders before our AM meeting to ensure that they understand how to find Stocks In Play. Each new trader is asked for his best trading idea. The Butcher often offered the same idea as a new trader who went before him.

I asked a Senior Trader to check his trading journal. He did not keep one. During the trading day he led the desk in checking ESPN's NBA home page. During his second month, he was positive one day. We could train a hundred traders and The Butcher's results would still rank at the bottom. In fact, I propose that 80 percent of the general population could sit on our desk without any formal training and generate more positive trading days. Moreover, The Butcher was stopped out, trading parlance for reaching one's loss limit, close to 50 percent of his trading days.

We would send over traders to offer suggestions. He would listen, but The Butcher rarely asked follow-up questions. He was never spotted actually enacting the recommendations of other successful traders.

During our Tradecasts, I challenge our traders to expect more from themselves. For example, we suggest traders keep a detailed trading journal. I will remark, "If you are not keeping a detailed trading journal, then please do not pretend that you are competing." At other times, when I learn that some traders are slacking, then during a Tradecast I will remark, "If you do not love trading, then please go find something else to do. There are others begging to train with us. Give your spot to them."

We talk with our new traders at the end of each month. I was ready to tell The Butcher that his results were like nothing I had seen. Before we had a chance, I received an e-mail from him offering his resignation. He shared that trading was not his true passion. Amen.

Now The Butcher is a hard worker. He became an excellent college basketball player through hard work, and he is a very good person. I heard he landed a good job following his resignation from SMB. Of course he did. He will be successful when he finds his true passion. But trading was not it. He loved basketball. That is why he spent hours working on his game for no pay, and little recognition at a liberal arts college not known for its basketball program. But he never had a chance as a trader because he did not love trading. And there is nothing that a trading coach can do to overcome that.

THEY CAN'T HIT STOCKS THAT TRADE AGAINST THEM

If you examine the work of most successful intraday traders, they all take many small losses. Their results are littered with numerous small losses of 7c (cents), 5c, 3c, and even 1c. Most good intraday traders have few losses of more than 30c. Most trades work for you right away. One of the fundamentals taught by active trading prop firms is to hit stocks that trade against you. Those who never master this fundamental will fail.

Before every trade, you must develop a trading plan for where you will exit if your stock trades against you. For example, in the spring of 2009, I was trading WFC. WFC had just released positive earnings. WFC had gapped up on the Open and then started an intraday downtrend. At 18.25, WFC would not lift the offer, indicating a huge sell order was pending. So I shorted WFC. If it hit 18.30, I was exiting, gathering information, reevaluating, but moving on to my next trade. For those interested, it did not touch 18.30, and I covered WFC at 17.60 when the selling pattern dissipated. With this trade, my exit price didn't hit, but my plan was firmly in place if 18.30 was breached.

Smiley: Smiling Back to Hong Kong

One of our former traders, Smiley, brings a smile to my face as I remember him. He wore a perpetual smile, with positive energy that spread across our trading desk. Smiley loved trading and had an uncanny resemblance to Ichiro Suzuki of the Seattle Mariners. I can imagine him now, smiling, on the trading desk trading his GOOG. But he had one big issue. He could not hit stocks that traded against him.

Smiley loved his GOOG. What's not to like with the volume and volatility GOOG offers? We had just started as a firm and allowed our new traders more autonomy. This was our mistake. Certainly today, we would not permit a new trader to trade GOOG, as it moves too erratically for a new trader to handle. But we were young and learning. Smiley was not trading other stocks well so there was not much to lose for either party.

Smiley is perhaps one of my top 10 favorite people who have ever traded near me. I have never seen anyone so happy to be on a trading desk. Our upstart desk was grabbing drinks after the Close one day, and Smiley offered a long soliloquy on how he loved trading. English was not his first language. Think Eddie Murphy on *Saturday Night Live* saying, "Baseball has been very good to me!" in broken English, but Smiley would replace baseball with trading. At times, it was challenging for Smiley to communicate with us. Maybe that is why Smiley smiled so often, masking his inability to communicate.

So we are having drinks and this quiet guy just couldn't stop talking. Smiley explained that back in Hong Kong he was a video graphics expert. He had worked on numerous movies. In fact, Smiley had recently turned down a job to work on *Mission Impossible III*. Smiley mocked even the thought of accepting this job. Proudly, he exclaimed, "I want to do what I love. And I love trading."

We worked with Smiley on hitting stocks that traded against him. We first started with the simple instruction, "Smiley, if a stock trades against your exit price, then hit it please."

He nodded his headed energetically. Then when we noticed Smiley had opened up a position, I would ask, "Hey Smiley, what is your exit price for GOOG?"

He would yell back, "Three eighty-five, Mike."

Ten minutes later, I would notice GOOG at 383 and Smiley with an open position 4 points against him. "Hey Smiley, I thought your exit price was 385?" I directed at him.

"Yes. I should have hit it," he replied agreeably.

Generally, a head trader or partner should reluctantly order a trader to exit a position that they themselves are not watching. I had not watched GOOG's downmove to 383, so I was not in a position to offer advice as to whether here at 383 GOOG was a good sale. But as a partner, one must demand that his traders follow trading fundamentals. You must expect that they have an exit plan for their every trade. If they disregarded this plan, then you should start a dialog with your trader to exit this position. So I would ask, "Smiley, where are you going to hit GOOG if it does not go back up?"

"Bella, I am gonna hit it if it makes another downmove."

Ten minutes would pass. GOOG would trade up three points and then back down. I would look over at my risk monitor and Smiley had not sold GOOG into the upmove. And in fact, it was now lower than the original 383.

"Hey Smiley, isn't GOOG lower now?"

"Yeah, I should have hit it."

And so obviously talking with Smiley while he was trading did not work.

Steve offered visualization drills to help him solve this mental block. We tried technique after technique and we still could not get Smiley to hit out of the stocks that traded against him. Smiley wasn't really losing money. He would trade GOOG very well 80 percent of the time. But then when it traded against him he simply could not pull the trigger and exit the bad trades. In turn, he would wipe out all of his gains from his positive trading days.

GOOG would be four points against his exit price, and four hours after this exit price was violated, there would be Smiley still long. What is most memorable about all of this was that Smiley would be glued to his screen. Smiley never missed a tick in GOOG, his hands affixed to his keyboard in the ready position to smack the bids if GOOG moved lower. Then his exit price would arrive, but still Smiley would be locked into his screens, with his hands affixed to his keyboard, not hitting the stock. It was as if he was in his "ready position" as a middle linebacker fixated on the quarterback's signals, but never reacted to the snap. He would still be long.

In fact, the only thing that got Smiley to hit GOOG was if Steve ordered him to exit, or the bell was about to ring, as we did not allow Smiley to take out overnights. But even the bell did not get him out of GOOG. Now in the after-hours session, Smiley would sheepishly ask, "What should I do?" Of course, he was still smiling as if he had just seen supermodel Giselle Bundchen pass in front of him.

Steve and I would just shake our heads. Once Steve scoffed, "You should hit it when it trades against you. Or at least before the bell rang." Now GOOG had spread out. There were not fair prices to sell GOOG in the after-hours market. We would try to figure out the best price to exit, but since we were not trading GOOG ourselves, we were not in a position to know whether the price was a good sale or not.

I can still picture Smiley at his trading station, in his trader position, ready to smack the bids like he was in charge of setting off a nuclear device if we were attacked. But HE WOULD NEVER SELL. It was like he was the great Warren Buffett and just did not believe in selling.

This is a common problem amongst new traders. You must work at this. One prop firm runs their new traders through extensive drills during its training program to instill the habit of hitting stocks that trade against you. This firm reviews all trades of new traders, and if they see a trade with a loss of over 20c, their new traders must explain why. If they fail to hit a stock that hits their exit price, they are placed on the demo the next day. And we know how demeaning the demo can be. As such, we teach visualization exercises to ensure our traders do not have this issue when they start trading live.

If you struggle with this issue, start with this simple visualization exercise. Find a quiet place. Concentrate on your breath. Breathe in and out deeply. Concentrate on your breath flowing through your body. After a few minutes, start to visualize your trading station. In detail, recreate the sounds and visual stimuli you encounter while trading. Picture yourself long in a stock that you trade, with a predetermined exit plan. Imagine this stock trading against you, and see yourself hitting the bids. Pick another stock and repeat this process. Feed your mind with the ability to immediately hit stocks that trade against your price.

I still love Smiley. It was just that trading was not for him. But I hear he is back in Hong Kong making kick-ass action movies and still smiling.

THEY HAVE UNREALISTIC EXPECTATIONS

I have some great news for those who have just begun their trading careers. This is the worst you will ever be. (Actually, that's not true.

Unfortunately, a few traders are just bad all the time. Back when I started there was so much prop money floating around that traders who had blown up would simply convince whoever would listen that they just needed a new environment. Like degenerate gamblers, they just churned through more of other people's money. Those days are over for the most part. See Andrew Spanton.) It takes time to become a consistently profitable trader. There are many things that a prop firm does to speed up a new trader's learning curve. But they cannot make the learning curve disappear.

Often, HR at a prop firm is asked in an interview how long it takes to start making money as a trader. Many interviewees offer that they have heard it can take a year. Some state that it is not possible to make money for two years. We have found that most of our better traders consistently make money before the end of their third month. But it can take a year for some others. But on average at a prop firm, it takes about six to eight months.

Now there are outliers. Some take even longer than a year. And as long as these traders are working hard and improving every day, then most prop firms will stick with them. On the flip side, there are a few who just start making money in their first month.

Your reward after all this training time and underpaid apprenticeship is the trading skills to trade profitably in any market, from anywhere, and for the rest of your trading career. Essentially, this is a license to print money. But it takes time and experience to develop these skills. I compare this development to that of an All-American quarterback entering the NFL. How many make the Pro Bowl in their first year? How many for that matter have a successful season? Joe Flacco and Ben Roethlisberger are the only ones I can think of recently. Most take years to develop, including the Manning brothers, who have each won a Super Bowl.

New traders, like NFL quarterbacks, need reps. All the weightlifting and film work goes only so far. You need to play. You need experience deciphering market patterns and tweaking your if-then statements for your trading setups. You must start recognizing patterns and developing trading systems for each setup. And these patterns must be practiced trading live. A trading simulator can help, but there is no substitute for trading "when the lights are turned on," where your results count.

At most prop firms, developing and experienced traders often have succeeded in almost everything they have done. They are ambitious. They expect a lot from themselves and early. They expect to be the best. Success has been their history, so why should trading be any different? When you begin as a trader, you most likely will be horrible. Let me be clear if I haven't been already: Boy, will you suck.

This does not mean you should lose a lot of money when you trade live. A good training program will only place you in setups where you can succeed. You will trade the easiest setups when you start. For example, for the first week live, new traders might only trade support and resistance levels. The next week, new traders then shift to breakout trades exclusively. The next week, they focus on momentum trades. After that, they focus on consolidation plays. But they start with one trade at a time.

Some new traders expect to make money immediately, and when they don't, they let this affect their work. When they do not see the results that they expected, they start to focus on the wrong things. Some increase their tier size, hoping that this will help them make more money. Some do not prepare as hard because they are discouraged. "What is the point of preparing hard if I cannot make money?" they ask themselves. They start to take chances that an experienced trader would not take. This leads to big rips and only compounds the problem. Now they are in a bigger hole.

While there is no one right way to make money trading, there is a right way to begin your trading career. When you first begin, you must focus on the process. You must allow 8–12 months to become consistently profitable. If you are not willing or are unable to do this, then you should find another occupation. Some are not able to commit this much time either financially (at best, you will be on a small draw) or psychologically to this pursuit. If this is the case, then again, please find another profession, because the market couldn't care less about your finances or mindset.

I cannot express to you how unimportant the results are from your first six months of trading. Like spring training, they do not matter. For example, I lost $36,000 in my first eight months of trading. During these nascent months, you are building the foundation for a 20-plus year career. Do you think in year 10 that your results in your first six months will be significant? They weren't for me. When it is time for you to buy a house, do you think you are going to do that from the money you made in your first six months as a trader or Year Three? Bet the latter.

Becoming a consistently profitable trader just might be the hardest thing you will ever do in your life. Respect the process. You are not entitled to make it. You are entitled to work very hard for 8–12 months, be trained well, and find out how good you can be.

Hollywood

In 2008, we trained a young person transitioning from the corporate world. He was dubbed Hollywood by a Senior Trader on our desk and this nickname stuck. (I'll explain further on.) Hollywood had worked at an established financial institution and was looking to trade. In his eight months of trading with us he did very well, including two over-the-top months. And Hollywood had just begun. He was one of the top three young traders on our desk.

Like his early trading days, Hollywood had plenty of success with the ladies. He was one of those guys who you wonder ever ate a carb, since he was so fit. A female photographer came in to shoot our desk one day and before leaving asked, "So what is Hollywood's deal?" I responded that he had a girlfriend. The photographer seemed disappointed. She added, "He doesn't take a bad photo. Let me know if things don't work out with his girlfriend."

Hollywood was exceptionally talented and did well early. But he had unrealistic expectations about the start of his trading career. Mind you, he had come from the corporate world, so he was probably making over $100,000 a year before he started with us. But his take-home pay in his first eight months was excellent for a new trader. Most traders do not hit their stride until between their second and third year. So making this kind of money this early was excellent progress.

And remember while he was making this kind of money the world was changing. Investment banking was in a free fall. The big banks were obliterated. Even Goldman had to restructure its business model. Most were just trying to hang in there. Many rank-and-file Wall Street employees were fired or about to be axed. It was hard to imagine the big bonus jobs returning soon. So he was not only doing well at the start of his career, but comparatively he was doing better than most on the Street.

But he had met a girl. (I don't want to say that women with nesting instincts are the undoing of traders per se, but this one halted Hollywood's progress.) She lived closer to Philadelphia than NYC. Hollywood moved out of the city to be closer to her, and traded remotely. Remotely, his work was just not the same. He was still making money, but he was away from the action. He did not have the younger traders around him pushing him to improve, like MoneyMaker, Dr. Momentum, and Tickster. He could not see how they were making money. He was away from the environment that would force him to compete and get better.

One day out of the blue, Hollywood sent me an e-mail resigning. He was unhappy with his progress of late. He thought a different career would be better for him. Hollywood, do you think it might have had something to do with that move you made for the girl?

I sicced a senior trader on Hollywood to talk some sense into him. This was a task for his older equivalent and CNBC star JToma. JToma has an appreciation for women not found in a million other guys, and he couldn't understand why a young, talented, good-looking 20-something would move out of the city for a girl. There were scores of them in the city, JToma reasoned. It was as if JToma's rationale for getting him back on board had NOTHING to do with trading, but rather the opposite sex. JToma blasted Hollywood for giving up the chance to meet all of those other women. His exact words were, "Why would you give up a chance to meet all that a$$?"

JToma has made a lot of money trading and in other investments throughout his career, and he likes to go out with the young guys. The young guns particularly look up to JToma regarding all the stuff that you might imagine traders did when they first come into money "back in the day." At the bar, the guys gather a round him to hear all his stories like grandchildren on their grandfather's lap. Plus, he is still an excellent trader. And he gets on them about seizing this opportunity to make a great deal of money so young and doing something so interesting.

JToma reamed Hollywood out for giving up on this opportunity. He relayed that he had just begun and would only get so much better. Hollywood agreed to keep trading. Order had been restored in the world to JToma. But a short few weeks later, Hollywood quit again. There was nothing else we could do.

Steve and I talked about Hollywood during some slow periods. When our desk went on a good run I sometimes thought of Hollywood and guesstimated how much he would have made. Steve and I saw his talent. There was little doubt that he would have made a great deal of money trading with us. He was that good. We just could not convince Hollywood that it would take some more time. Hollywood had unrealistic expectations about how good he should be so early.

Not a trading day goes by that I do not think about Hollywood. He should have been a success story and had a whole subchapter about him with Dr. Momentum and MoneyMaker in the chapter These Guys are Good. He could have been the best trader on our desk. He already had the great trading nickname. Our desk, and apparently our photographer, misses him. He was a great guy and a ton of fun. But he possessed an unrealistic learning curve. I wish Steve, JToma, and I did not fail to convince him of this.

A quick note here is in order. Prior to publication I received a call from Hollywood. He wanted back in. I was getting a little worried about JToma there for a while.

THEY'D RATHER BE RIGHT THAN MAKE MONEY

There are some traders who just cannot admit that they are wrong. They develop a bias about a stock. When the stock does not trade as they expected, they are paralyzed. They insist that the stock will start acting as they expected, and refuse to exit their positions. As I've explained earlier, successful intraday traders exit losing positions quickly. They are not emotionally invested with the market, proving their thesis correct about a stock.

Consistently profitable traders are interested in making good trades. They accept that they cannot control the results. And holding a position that is trading against them because they are most interested in being proven correct is bad trading. Your job is not to be correct. Your job is not to make money. At the best prop firms, a new trader is taught to just focus on making good trades (see "One Good Trade").

The Mayor

When we first started, we worked with a colorful trader (HBO could develop a series after him) we will name The Mayor. Uniquely, he would either show up to the office in a sweat suit or a gorgeous Armani suit and tie. Maybe this should have been our first hint. The sweat suit was, I must say, really nice, something Michael Jordan might be seen wearing at the Atlantis. It was one of those fancy Puma, extra comfortable sweat suits. We were so young as a company that we had not created a dress code. Today, we don't allow sweat suits to work. More important, we also do not allow a suit and tie.

The Mayor was a successful options trader. Once he began with us, we saw he had a great feel for stocks as well. The Mayor held stocks for the entire move like a superstar trader. He had no fear.

One day when he first began, The Mayor made over $4k. He made sure that everyone on our desk knew. "Look, I made $4k!" exclaimed The Mayor to the most attractive woman on our desk. Then to Steve, "I made $4k!" Then to GMan, "I made $4k!" Then to me, "I made $4k!" You get the point by now. We were very happy for him. He had a child in Europe that he was supporting. And though boastful, his energy was contagious.

Not to digress too much, but The Mayor reminded me of my first boss when I worked in politics, the legendary and brilliant House chairmen of the Judiciary Committee in Connecticut, Richard D. Tulisano. Rep. Tulisano was dubbed "King Richard" because no substantive piece of legislation could pass in the State of Connecticut without his approval. Richard and I would walk down the streets of Hartford, often in an undesirable area as was his habit. No matter what street we walked down people would call out to my boss. "Hey Richard," locals would yell out from their apartment windows. Richard, also intellectually curious, would yell back and ask how so and so was, or one of their relatives. He knew everyone and everyone knew him. The Mayor was the type of guy who would have his name called out as he walked down a street. And he loved trading.

After The Mayor showed his promise, he asked to trade from home and that was fine with us. We were happy to add a successful trader to our young desk. But then one day trading PD, we noticed he was holding a position many points against him. Steve e-mailed The Mayor, cautioning him about his position. The Mayor explained that the stock would turn around and was still confident in the position. Steve asked for his exit price. The Mayor said another 50c. The stock did not rebound, the market closed, and The Mayor was still long.

Steve called The Mayor and asked him to close out his position. The Mayor predicted PD would open up tomorrow. Steve remarked to just close the position and start over the next AM. The Mayor did this, but was noticeably unhappy with us. PD opened up a little and The Mayor expressed his disappointment at being ordered to close out, with an unusually long e-mail explanation supporting his PD bias. Steve explained that he could have exited PD points before the Close and gotten a much better price than the opening price the next AM.

Despite this hiccup, The Mayor continued to trade and show promise. Then again we noticed he was holding PD well against him. He and Steve went through the same rigamarole, but this time Steve let him hold on.

The next AM PD opened up down. The Mayor was still long. Steve e-mailed to hit the stock. The Mayor pleaded to keep the position, explaining why he was correct. Steve asked for his exit price and The Mayor gave it. A few hours later, PD had not rebounded. Steve e-mailed The Mayor again, who explained that he was still correct with his position. We did not trade PD so we listened, but as a young firm we were still held hostage by his talent. Steve again asked for his exit price, and The Mayor again gave it.

PD did not rebound, the stock hit his exit price, but The Mayor had not exited. So Steve put him out of his misery and closed his position. Unsurprisingly, The Mayor sent us an angry e-mail. Steve offered his empathy about the loss but explained that the price action was most important. Despite all the theoretically valid reasons The Mayor gave for his thesis, it was not as important as the price action. The Mayor insisted that he was still correct and for us to watch PD trade the next few days. The Mayor was so upset that we hit out of his position that he never traded with us again. We were down some money on him, and we were no longer going to overvalue his talent.

Ultimately, The Mayor would have rather been right than make money on PD. Not as a personal vendetta against us, just for his own ego. He failed to let the price action be the ultimate arbitrator. Developing a bias can be helpful when trading a stock, but when the price action contradicts your theory, then you must exit.

Unfortunately, we never learned how good The Mayor could have been as a trader. For those interested, PD did not trade higher over the next few days. For those who are not interested, now you are thinking like a trader.

DON'T FORGET: YOU'RE A TRADER, NOT AN INVESTOR

Often, I remark playfully on our desk to new traders, "It's called trading, not investing." We do not care where RIMM or AAPL or GS trade in two years. We do wish personally that they are higher (perhaps for our PA) but as a trader, our personal wishes are irrelevant.

When I first started making money, I proudly bought a basket of the best technology stocks for my personal account. I bought AKAM, AMZN, INTC, MSFT, BRCM. I had all of the best. And I waited till these stocks pulled back considerably to important technical support levels. I remember buying BRCM at 85, and declaring that this was a steal. I was pumped. I was counting the cash in my head. But I couldn't have been any more wrong.

Even when the Internet Bubble burst and I lacked shorting skills, I have never suffered serious annual losses as an intraday trader. The largest losses I have ever suffered were in my personal account as an investor. Not a wimpy "down 10%" either. I'm talking substantial losses. I bought on margin. I did not create exit prices for my stocks that traded well against me. I lost 80–90 percent in some instances. I suppose I had a strategy. It was to buy, hold and pray. I was just long and very wrong.

Like many investors in 2000 and 2001 when the bubble had burst, I would just not look at the statements in my PA. During this period a common phrase heard at a cocktail party, your local diner, or gym was, "I don't open my statements anymore. It is too depressing." It was too painful.

I remember riding the subway with my dad talking to some stranger on the way back from a Yankees game.

(Side note about the Yankees, my favorite team: During the great Yankees run, my dad and I had season tickets. We were at Game 7 when Boone hit the series-ending homer against Wakefield. We were at both Arizona games when Tino, then Brosius, tied the game with two outs in the ninth. We were also there when the young Marlins pitchers of Beckett, Burnett, and Pavano stymied the thunderous Yankee bats. And I remember vividly talking to this gentleman whom we struck up a subway conversation with about stocks.)

During the Internet Bubble, it was common for people anywhere to talk about stocks. At cocktail parties. After attending mass. On the subway after work. Often, you barely knew these people. And when people found out that I was a trader they automatically assumed I was as knowledgeable as Jim Rogers.

Non-professional traders hunted for tips about the next hot stock. This Yankees subway stranger asked, "What should I be in?" And I told him what I had bought. I prefaced my advice with an explanation that I was not a financial adviser and that I was a short-term trader. Despite my efforts, this distinction was lost on this particular New Yorker. Then I remember saying the stupidest thing I can ever remember saying. Nonsensically, I uttered, "These are the stocks that I own. They are risky, but I am young (here it comes) and I can afford to withstand substantial losses."

Intellectually, I understand that a young person can withstand substantial losses in their PA more so than someone who is retired. But I just remember the way that I said it. I was not concerned that I would suffer these losses. It was like a throw-away line. Like those financial advertisements where at the end of the ad some guy verbally sprints through the mandatory risk disclosure.

Why I thought it was ok to withstand substantial losses I cannot answer. This is illogical. I was a dope, and a horrible investor. I was swept up in creating my American dream. People owned stock during this time period, so I owned too. There was little reflection on my true downside risk or the consequences if I actually lost a substantial amount of money. I probably lost more investing than my grandfather had made working his entire life. Why did I think this was acceptable?

So I remember this life lesson: I am a trader and not an investor. The risk of investing is much greater than my own trading, nor am I trained as an investor. I do not study long-term trends. I have never developed a long-term investing strategy. There are professionals whose advice you are better off relying on.

During this latest near-collapse of our banking systems, I received calls from average investors asking for my advice. Most of these calls transpired near DOW 6700. Soon after the DOW bounced to almost 9600. And I told each of these callers that I was not an expert in long-term investing.

Many were worried that their 401(k)s were being obliterated. What a terrible thing to fear. During 2008, many watched helplessly as much of their retirement evaporated. When I hung up from these calls, I know that on the other end some callers were confounded how I could not offer advice. How can he be a trader and not be able to offer investing advice?

This is not what I do. And I learned this lesson very clearly back in 2001. My investing thoughts are probably not much more advanced than the average investor. But sit me down on a trading floor, let me look at some charts, provide the news for some stocks, and I can make money 90 percent of any trading day. These are my skills. This is what I do.

In fact, sit me down on a trading desk, and give me access to the Level 2. Cut me off from the news. Turn off CNBC. Shut down my charts. Limit my access to capital. Seclude me in a room without any information from fellow traders. And I can still grind out a living. I am a trader.

There is a right way to start your trading career. And there are things you can do to ruin your dream. So much of your success depends on how you approach your learning curve. Prop firms are littered with so many who failed who never had to. I hope you have learned from the failings of some others that we have shared. There is a right way to start your trading career. And if you do then you will learn just how good you can be as a trader.

There are too many failed prop and individual traders walking around Main Street and the blocks of NYC who could have made it. If only they found a way to persevere.

CHAPTER 6

Live to Play Another Day

Y ou are in your mid-thirties, married, with three beautiful girls. You own a private equity fund which you financed from a small percentage of your trading profits. You own multiple apartments in NYC and commercial real estate throughout the country. You have walked every golf course you have ever longed to play. You took your wife to Fiji on your honeymoon for a month. Of course, you also own a Porsche. Your personal trading account is flush with working capital. You are paid to make frequent television appearances on the country's leading financial network, CNBC. New traders crowd your desk after every Close, hungry for tidbits of your market knowledge. Your prop firm entrusts you with as much buying power as you need. Every day you wake up and get to do exactly what you love to do: trade. Who are you?

You are JToma, Senior Trader at a prop firm. You are an experienced trader, who lived to play another day.

One of my favorite trading expressions is "Live to play another day." This simple saying says so much about the mindset of a market veteran. If you can just find a way to hang in there, then the good times will come. If you can find a way to stay in the game, then you can become an experienced trader. But you have to survive. And some just can't.

In this chapter we will discuss some typical landmines that the new trader must avoid such as not believing, making predictions, of course getting fired, and starting too quickly. You will meet some of the traders I have worked with at prop firms spanning my career, including JToma, to highlight some pitfalls to avoid. Perhaps one day you will earn the privilege of being a successful market veteran.

JTOMA: FROM THE ABYSS TO CNBC

A young trader, not yet 24, sits on the couch of a prominent psychologist and starts, "I am afraid to trade. I just lost 80 percent of my trading capital. I don't know what to do."

Sitting on the couch of a shrink? What is wrong with this guy? Suck it up, you wuss, and start making money. This is not talked about a lot by veteran traders but the scene above is not uncommon. But what is commonplace is for the market veteran—whether it is visiting a professional, taking up yoga, changing his diet, or breaking up with a distracting girlfriend—to find a way to survive.

When JToma first began as a prop trader, he made 10 to 30 percent of his P&L. His goal was to trade his own retail account where he could keep 100 percent of his trading profits. JToma needed to make about $250k his end to trade his own account. $250k was not even enough money so he had to borrow another $250k at 12 percent to sufficiently fund his trading account. So essentially he had to make millions before he ever had enough of his own personal money to trade his own retail account. And when he did, he got to keep 100 percent of his profits after paying commissions on his trades (which were as much as 600 percent higher than they are today... ouch!)

JToma made enough to trade his own account. What an accomplishment for a young man not yet 24! And then the merciless market entered the room. In JToma's first three months trading his own account, he lost almost all of his money, more than $200k. The market ripped into his trading account with the ferocity of a tsunami. He was down to his last $50k.

The average trader might have become depressed. Would you? But JToma remarkably just shrugged it off. He sought out a prominent performance psychologist and worked to improve some emotional issues which were hindering his trading. JToma had become afraid to trade. And these sessions, which many professional traders sit through yet never talk about, worked. More than a decade later, he is still doing what he loves: trading.

This well-known sports psychologist offered training techniques to improve JToma's trading performance, which he still utilizes today. A daily journal was suggested and implemented. A plan for every trade was discussed and now is followed. Ambitious goals were set and surpassed. Favorite setups were identified and exploited.

In our game, the market will demand that you change. In our ring, the market will, with thunderous blows, often unforeseeably, knock you to the floor, leaving you bloody and beaten. And it will look down at you mercilessly daring for you to get back on your feet for another beat-down. And you will have a choice. You can quit, like many of my former colleagues have done over the years. Or you can find a way to hang in there. And if you live to play another day, enormous trading opportunities will come.

Let me share an old school trading anecdote often shared to new traders by JToma. A Lafayette graduate in his trading class walked into the Managing Partner's office at our original prop firm to quit and proclaimed, "There is no more opportunity in this market. We cannot make money anymore how we trade." This was September of 1998. The Internet Boom was just about to begin and rain cash on its market players. JToma went on to make a million plus that year while his classmate left to work for his father's plastic (or something like that) business.

DON'T FOCUS ON MAKING PREDICTIONS

One of the more difficult trading scenarios for me is the presence of an overly aggressive seller or buyer. After trading for 12 years, I've watched enough tape to know where a stock should be trading intraday. I can sense by the PENNY where a stock should be trading 98 percent of the trading day. Now, stocks are often close enough to being properly priced so that I do not make a trade. But as an intraday trader, I exploit short-term inefficiencies. When I sense a stock is too low, then I either cover my short or get long. When I sense a stock is overbought, then I either sell or get short depending on the intraday trend of the stock. Sounds simple enough, right? Buy low, sell high. Isn't this what we first learned about the stock market during our 7th grade trading competition?

But sometimes institutions enter orders to the market in a state of pure panic. And the traders executing these orders are incompetent. These pikers will indiscriminately drive the price down, only exacerbating their mandate to "Sell, sell, sell." (Who could forget Randolph and Mortimer in the Frozen Concentrated Orange Juice pits in the 1980s classic movie *Trading Places*, propping up their fainted trader who got caught long to the tune of hundreds of millions?)

One of my trading plays is to start a position when I sense the wrong price and assume the stock will revert to its mean. This is called a Fade Trade. Remember, I spend $6^1/_2$ hours every day, and have for the past 12 years, watching stocks trade intraday. My expertise covers where stocks should be priced intraday. My training has left me as good at this as Tiger's ability to read the way a putt ought to break. And yet sometimes we are met with lesser traders who just cannot trade, traders who just cannot see the break like I can. And they pump or dump stock at the wrong price.

The problem occurs when these jokers have more capital at play than I do to move the market. I take a loss because I hit out of my stock as it hits my exit price. And then after the order is filled, after the panic subsides, the stock reverts to the proper price. But I am out of the position. And I have essentially lost money because someone is not good at his job. This is very frustrating. But this happens every day, every hour, in multiple stocks.

I do not make many predictions. I develop biases. But if my biases are not confirmed by the tape, then I don't bite. Mark Douglas in *The Disciplined Trader* wrote, "If you believe it likely to have a definite bullish or bearish effect marketwise, do not back your judgment until the action of the market itself confirms your opinion." If I get caught long, spot an overly aggressive seller, the stock hits my exit prices, then I sell. I do not hold because I think that this overly aggressive seller is a putz. If I did, I would have blown up my trading account on multiple occasions by now. Once a stock hits my exit price, then I exit. I live to play another day.

"The markets can remain irrational longer than you can remain solvent," said economist John Maynard Keynes. (While Keynes is long since dead, at least doom-and-gloom economist Gary Shilling and his protégé Dennis Gartman borrow the saying from time to time.) And I do not get to set the prices for stocks, the institutions do. The markets couldn't care less what I think about the proper price of a stock. New traders sometimes make the error of believing that trading is about making predictions and that they can move the market with their 1,000 shares, or worse yet, their young opinions.

Crabby: How Predictions Harm the New Trader

We had a really smart trader with us a while back. Crabby loved the markets. But he was obsessed with predicting the markets six months out. That is not his job, nor mine. For example, Crabby would ask me where the price of oil was going to be in six months. I would answer, "I have no idea." And Crabby would look back at me funny as if I ought to know that. I could sense him thinking, how can a partner at a proprietary trading firm not have an opinion on the price of oil in six months?

Then Crabby started asking me essentially the same question daily but phrased differently. For example, he would ask, "Do you think oil can top $60 by the end of the summer?" And I would answer, "I have no idea." And Crabby would look at me funny. After a while when Crabby asked me the same question, I would look at him funny. I wanted to beat him to looking at me funny. And he would respond by looking at me even funnier. I had no response to his funnier look. Dammit.

Crabby spent all his free time scouring reports predicting the future price of oil. Crabby spent none of his time after the markets closed working on his trading skills. As a short-term trader, even if you develop the correct bias about the direction of the market, stock, or sector, you still must possess the trading skills to capture these moves. Wasting your time on predictions is energy and time lost for what will truly make all the difference, skill development. Derek Jeter does not spend time working on his fastball (he is not a pitcher), and you should not sharpen your skills as an analyst (you are a trader!).

Also, as a prop trader, you must sit and process the data the market offers with an open mind. Too many traders color the data the market offers with their own biases. I saw this with too many traders in August of 2009. Traders developed a bias that AIG should trade lower since its future prospects were glum. Identifiable buyers and intraday uptrends were dismissed because these traders colored the data, only seeing that which supported their preconceived short biases. Thus, they missed the AIG move from 14 to 50. And they got caught in too many short squeezes.

Crabby eventually moved on, as he couldn't make money as a trader. Prop traders crushed the tremendous trading opportunities in oil in 2007 and 2008. We did so short and long. At no time, did any of us intraday prop traders ask where we thought the price of oil would be in the next six months. Frankly, we had no idea and didn't care. We were too busy making money. It's called trading, not predicting.

The Market Doesn't Care What You Think

Making predictions is just not what we do as intraday prop traders. We leave that to the hedge funds. A more cynical writer may have rewritten the previous sentence to something like: We leave that to the hedge funds who lost 40 percent in 2008. We are intraday traders interested in what stocks will move the most today. How we can make money today is our obsession and expertise.

With all humility, there is a great scene with this author from the TV documentary *Wall Street Warriors* that magnifies this point. With the cameras rolling, a new class that we were training gathered around my desk to discuss the importance of the prints. I made this fundamental trading point, "the institutions set the prices and not me. GS is not calling me up on the phone asking me where I think a stock is headed. No one cares what I think." And this is an important point to understand as a new trader. Dr. Steenbarger (the godfather of trading psychology, author of three trading books, including his latest, *The Daily Trading Coach*, leading blogger at TraderFeed, and the most giving trading coach who sets the bar for all of us) colorfully offered in a recent blog: "The market doesn't give a rat's posterior about your economic and political views. Trade what the market is doing, not what you'd like it to do in your nihilistic fantasies." No one cares where you think a stock is headed.

Macro-Strategist Barry Ritholtz in an interview with Wall Street Cheat Sheet offered these thoughts on positions not working your favor: "When it's apparent that something isn't working out, just move out. That means just sell it and redeploy capital elsewhere. Just don't marry a position. Bill Miller (star mutual fund manager) was a great trader for many years. But it seems that his model says if something isn't working and it's going lower, buy more. He did that with Freddie Mac and got killed."

So if no one cares what you think about a stock, then you shouldn't. Just trade. Watch the price action. If your stock confirms your bullish bias, then get long. If your stock confirms you were wrong, then trade your stock from the short side. Too many new prop traders never embrace this philosophy and as a result never experience the best markets.

I received an e-mail from a very accomplished young man recently with an obvious passion for trading. He had traded different products and still had not finished his studies. I was looking forward to meeting him. When we are interested in a candidate, we ask that they answer some questions. This young man answered one of our questions (below) which I would like to discuss. And it helps delineate one clear advantage of being an intraday trader. Intraday traders **can** make money whether our predictions are accurate or not.

> Please share a life experience that demonstrates your ability to be patient?
>
> I would like to take an example from my trading experience to demonstrate my ability to be patient. I had the feeling that the commodities prices were being driven up incessantly and part of it was speculation. When oil was at $136, I felt it was overpriced and thought that there will be a sharp drop in commodity prices. As lower oil would support the dollar, I took a long dollar position. Oil prices continued to rise and even touched $145. I still was convinced that there would be a fall in oil prices and did not close out my position. Soon after, oil prices dropped drastically, which led to a rise in the dollar strength. I booked profits when oil had dropped to $120. I think this example shows that I have the ability to be patient even when the chips are down.

As an intraday trader we are not beholden to the accuracy of our predictions. GMan blogged about the top in oil right before it turned. Pretty good call, GMan (I think he also called the bottom of the dollar, by the way). Steve is also scarily talented at calling tops and bottoms in stocks. But GMan pointed out that he would seek confirmation of his thesis from the inside market. This is the point. As intraday traders, we develop theories daily. And those are great. But our P&L is not dictated by our predictions but our trading skill. And when you develop trading skills, it does not matter whether you accurately predict the top in a sector. It just matters that that sector is active. As long as it moves.

If you were to take a look at GMan's trading records, you would see at a minimum 17/20 net positive days per month. It is almost like something really strange needs to happen for him to be negative. GMan recently ripped it up three days in a row, and he was banging and cursing. Steve sent him on vacation. He just needed a break. This was the something strange that was interfering with his trading results.

Our trading skills enable our consistency. Presently, CNBC is full of very bright people predicting that oil is going back to over $100 a barrel, even $200. I tend to think those who believe we are headed for $100 a barrel are more persuasive, but honestly, I really don't know, nor am I going to pretend that I do. I do know that if oil goes to $100, I am going to make money. And if oil goes to $200 a barrel, I am going to make even more money. I leave the predictions for others and just take advantage of the readable moves along the way toward those predictions. If you do not, then you will never be in the game to take advantage of the outsized trading opportunities.

YOU MUST BELIEVE

There is something that cannot be taught to new traders. Just like those pesky New York Mets fans (who, by the way, my father prefers would stop calling in to his favorite sports talk station, WFAN, and ripping his Yanks), you must believe. You must believe that you will become great. I am sensitive to discuss intangible things because trading is mostly about skill development and discipline. What does this mean that you must believe? What does this have to do with skill development? Actually, it has a lot to do with it. Let's discuss.

The market will carpet bomb trading data when you first begin proving that you cannot become a successful trader. At the start, you will most likely be net negative your first three months. You can look at this data and easily get discouraged. You can let this typical beginning data affect your fourth and fifth and sixth month, which will manifest more data that can convince you out of the market. If you do not believe, you will use this data as proof that you cannot become a successful trader.

You can be a consistently profitable trader using a system that starts not yielding profits. You will have to tweak this system just a little to make money once the market changes. If you do not believe instead of tweaking the system and then measuring your results, you become consumed with your bad results. You lose confidence. You start to question whether tweaking your system will work. And then this lack of confidence affects your every trade. Since you do not believe, now you have data to support your conclusion that you are destined to fail.

With any trading system, the market will offer you exits for your trades that are poor. If you are starting a position, the market may try to shake you out. If your confidence is low, you will most likely give in to the market's bullying and take your loss. This is what you have prepared your mind for since your confidence is low.

On the contrary, if your position starts to work for you, you are more likely to exit too early. Once you have a chance to lock in a profit, you do so sacrificing further significant profits. Or there is the chance you will hold a position too long, being offered the opportunity to exit like you had planned, but in the mindset of losing money. So you are more likely to let that stock reverse and wipe out your profits. The market demands that you believe.

You can train at the best prop firm in the country, but if you do not believe that you will succeed, then you will not. If you cannot visualize yourself as a successful trader, then you will never become one. If you never obtain the confidence that you will succeed, then you will not survive to enjoy the most opportunistic markets.

Credit Derivatives Trader (CDT): She Did Not Believe

I read the resume in front of me as I sat behind my office desk, beneath a framed picture of Derek Jeter barreling face first into box seats at the old Yankee Stadium. The candidate waiting nervously as I learned was an Ivy League graduate, held a master's degree, was a former credit derivatives trader (let's call her CDT) and oh, also sported a nose ring. After answering a few of my questions, I instantly placed her in the category of people much smarter and hipper than me.

As I remember this interview, I liked everything about her, save one thing. She was indeed brilliant, talented, and loved trading. But there was a hesitancy about her, about her and this job. The best traders at most prop firms would sign their contract a second after an invitation. I hoped perhaps she was just doing her due diligence, but I was left with a different impression. She was not sure she could succeed as a prop trader.

What was CDT doing in front of me? One day CDT walked into work and was down $14 million on a position she could not exit. (Note: We cut our traders off a lot earlier than $14 million!) There was no market for her positions. She could hold or hit the bids at effectively zero. They fired a bunch of people in her department at the big bank where she worked, so CDT was now in my office. Chop SMB!

On a side note regarding female traders, I was talking with a woman at the Traders Expo in New York who had visited some prop desks. She asked why prop firms don't have more women trading with them. As I write, less than 5 percent of prop traders are female. Not many women apply to prop firms, with fewer than 2 percent of our applications sent by women. I wish there were more. While trading has often been a man's domain, there are several success stories of female traders.

When I started my career, I sat next to an excellent one. In fact, she made so much money that she is now semi-retired. She bought a house in the suburbs, works on her gardening, and enjoys playing tennis.

I posed the question to the Twitter and StockTwits community as to why more women do not apply to prop firms. A respected trader of the StockTwits community, AnneMarie2006, a must-read blogger and friend of our firm (speaking about most, but not all, women) offered an explanation:

AnneMarie2006@smbcapital: Trading has gr8 uncertainty associated w/it. It's also a place that gives little to no security... key elements in female psyche

AnneMarie2006@smbcapital: Also, trading is confrontational ...u have to stare at ur mistakes...women hate that too...most women are avoiders

Sadly, at the same time, some male traders need to be educated at prop firms about how to behave. Firm leaders have to say things like "Take down that wallpaper on your screen," "put the strip club passes out of public view," or "watch your language." A prop firm is not a boiler room.

CDT was too talented to pass on because of one partner's hunch. At least, that is what my partner Steve scolded. CDT followed all of what we asked. She was the last person to leave the office during her training. When she started trading live she often remained the last person to leave. She was well prepared, and stayed focused during the day. CDT went out of her way to ask excellent trading questions to our Senior Traders and me. Her results, not surprisingly, were at the top of her class. But she had a weakness. She did not believe.

Before CDT was to trade live, she asked to speak with me before the Open. She started, "I am not ready to trade live. I need some more time." Let me be clear, she was trading firm capital. Whose money did she think she would lose if she indeed was trading a few days early? Also, she was ready. Her work was excellent, dare I say impeccable. This was my second major whiff of her uncertainty.

Now this may have been because of her recent past. CDT had an excellent job at a Tier 1 bank that blew up. CDT worked hard her whole life to secure such a job. She went to the right schools, received the right grades, and learned the right way to act in a corporate culture. Heck, she was allowed to trade products that produced a 14-million-dollar loss overnight. And then that world was destroyed.

Managing partners at prop firms see this quite often. Some people just have doubts, and it is our job to remove them before they impact their trading. So, during a subsequent sitdown with CDT, I said, "You have all the ability in the world to do this job. It is natural to doubt your exit strategy. I do of my own at times. What is most important is to be asking the right questions. What is most important is to be thinking about the right stuff. And you are. You need experience exiting stocks that trade in your favor. After months of practice, you will improve. Just keep thinking about your exit strategy. This is excellent work."

One of the things you had to love about CDT was that she enjoyed even the inappropriate banter on our desk. When one of our traders said something over the line, I would scold, "I don't know if you have to use language like that." And then CDT would retort, "Oh Bella, please. I have heard a lot worse." And then she would continue with a comment more inappropriate than one of the guys. And the traders on the desk loved that. Apparently, I cannot control the guys OR the women on our desk.

Prop firm partners have had many talks with new traders to boost their confidence. After all, many of us are trading coaches. One of our better traders I had to fire up every day for two straight months. "You are going to be the best trader on the desk," I encouraged. Once he got to where I thought he'd be, I stopped with the talks. And he slipped a notch. Another talented trader I repeatedly told, "You can become an excellent trader." This developing trader knew nothing but negative months. But I had to keep telling him that he could succeed. He finally became a solid trader. So these talks with CDT did not necessarily say anything about her. It was simply my job to get her to believe.

In her last month CDT traded with us, she was net positive. Her results that month were outstanding for such a young prop trader. Early one morning, she asked to speak with me. Traders often ask to talk to me about everything from their clearing account to the pizza we are providing on Fridays (seriously, I once had a 30-minute sitdown about brick oven with fresh mozzarella over "anytime-anywhere" NY style). This conversation could have been about anything. Anything save what it was actually about. I had no idea what was to come next.

Choking with emotion, CDT announced that she was leaving. A job too good to pass up had been offered and she felt uncomfortable turning down this opportunity. I didn't know what to say. She, without a doubt, would have become a consistently profitable prop trader. I told her that. She was very upset, like she was concerned that I would be disappointed with her for her decision. Personally, I just want what is best for everyone. I didn't want her feeling bad about her decision so I kept the discussion short.

Right after CDT left, our desk went on a tear. She would have killed this next opportunity the market gifted. But she did not believe and I had failed to convince her to believe. If you cannot stay in the game, then you cannot take advantage of the good runs.

STOPPING YOURSELF OUT (GETTING FIRED)

When a prop firm spots new traders not buying into their system, they talk with them. A good firm explains, for example, that they are not working hard enough or they must listen better. (At this point I feel like a broken record, "Work hard." "Listen.") The prop firm gives them an opportunity to correct their behavior, and explains exactly what we expect from them going forward. If they do not correct their behavior, then the firm will ask them to leave. Hey, we're not running the local Little League.

AI: No Practice, No Play

During a recent training class, two of our trainees were asked to leave before they started trading live. (Does one try to get fired within the first five weeks of a job thousands would kill for? Do they realize the opportunity they have?) One of these traders was asked to leave because he refused to do the work. First, he often showed up late. That's a big no-no in an environment as competitive as ours. He was a former mortgage broker, who was his firm's biggest producer over the past three years. He had scored an 800 on his math SAT and graduated from a local state college. On his resume he wrote: "Highly coachable, and looking for a collegial environment where ideas are shared in a team orientated hierarchy. Very confident in mathematical ability (assuming high level of Mathematics is relevant). My expectations are very realistic and I'm prepared to go 'all-in.'" Sounds good to me, on paper anyway.

He (I'll call him AI, short for NBA star Allen Iverson, who once made it clear to the media and the fans that practice was not a priority for him) asked very few questions to his Senior Trader or the partners. He would not pay attention during video reviews. (Before you trade live, we review your work. We can tell how well you have listened by doing this.) If your demo trading shows large losses, then this is a signal that you are not listening. If your work shows that you are doubling down, then you are not listening.

If you are trading too many stocks, then again, you are not listening. If you are trading the wrong stocks, then you are not preparing properly. Your work does not lie, and it best reflects your training effort.

Three separate traders offered their concerns without solicitation about AI's work. I asked someone whom I respect on our desk, Charlie, to watch over him. Charlie reported back to me that AI's work was "not good." I wish Charlie had been more descriptive, but it was forceful enough that I sat AI down and let him know what we had learned. I cautioned that the information I was given concerning his work product did not look promising. It was not the work of a successful trader. I offered AI an opportunity to improve his work over the next week. If his demo trading did not improve, then we would not let him trade live.

AI, in some convoluted, self-delusional logic, explained that he would do better if he were allowed to trade live. AI expounded that he would concentrate better trading live. He shared that he was never good in school, so he had trouble concentrating during lectures and our video review. (I should have let him go right then and there.) AI was offering these words hoping to persuade me to let him trade live. Did he really think by making the excuse that he was never good in school because he had trouble concentrating that I would magically turn over keys to our money? He couldn't pay attention during a lecture? Then how would AI pay attention when trading live with the firm's money? He would concentrate better while trading live? The first document you receive from us explains the importance of practice. That's right, AI. I'm talking about *practice*. We argue that how you train will determine your results. We teach that how hard you work during training will determine your results on Day 26, the first day you trade live. He apparently concluded this document was optional.

I am not a big fan of forecasting the success of a new trader. That's Steve's job. Those who work hard I know will work hard. Those who do not work hard, I have no interest in predicting whether they will start working hard. Apparently, this new trader believed that when we turned the lights on that he would just change. Why would a prop firm take this chance?

But what was even worse about our discussion was that AI communicated, "I feel you guys have had it in for me from the start." Had it in for him? It was his choice to show up late. It was his choice to be lazy. It was his choice to not read our training materials carefully and be embarrassed in front of his classmates when he didn't know something he should have. What in the world would make him think that I had it in for him? This was disconcerting.

AI was hired out of the many that we interviewed. As I've mentioned, it is very hard to get invited to train with a prop firm. If you receive an invitation, then you have jumped through many hoops and your firm really likes you. You have stood out amongst the thousands who have applied.

And a partner's time is valuable. They do not have enough of it, and cannot buy more, unfortunately. Why would I want to spend five weeks teaching a new trader if I did not hope to receive the financial benefit of his success? If AI was asked to leave, then I just wasted an awful lot of time working with him when I could have been working with someone else who wanted to do the work. Goodness knows I have more than enough resumes from which to choose. And we just keep getting more and more as more learn about our training. I have a huge incentive for our traders to succeed, and a huge disincentive to waste my time.

We let AI correct his work over the next week. Then came some unsolicited complaints from some core traders about his lack of seriousness on audio calls. At a prop firm, when your core traders have concerns about a new trader, then you, as a partner, listen. Something about singing and nonsense chatter. His work did not show improvement. Like a good reporter, I relied on multiple sources to verify his work. We had a chat. AI, of course, was expecting to hear that he would be trading live the next day. I let him know otherwise, repeating that his lack of work was not acceptable. AI pleaded for a chance to show us that he could do better if he traded live. I was having none of it.

I felt like I was talking to someone from a different planet. We do not believe that you just turn the switch on. Our culture is about hard work and skill development. We preach that your results are based upon the work you put in before every Open. And he wanted to just trade without any demonstration of the skills necessary. Not at our firm.

I suggested that the best thing for AI was to leave. He had been trained. AI could try to hook up with another firm. And with an 800 math SAT score, he probably did. But we were not going to let him trade with us. AI again started with the nonsense about us having it in for him. I told him I was sorry that he felt that way. He was given almost two months to demonstrate that he was one of us, and he failed to do so.

Know It ALL (KIA): How to Get Fired on Day One

On the first day, in the first two hours of a new training class, a new trader asked to speak with me. He had been trading on his own for the past several months. We had met him a year before and he was not ready to trade. He (KIA, for "know it all"; please do not confuse him with a cheaply made, highly efficient Korean car) was one of those interviewees whom you can tell is really interested in trading. The second time around, he seemed ready to work with us.

So we start with what amounts to Trading 101. On Day One, we talk about the Prints. It is a simple topic, yet important. The prints indicate where a stock is trading exactly and whether the stock was bought on the bid or the offer. This is the first indicator that we teach to our new traders to learn how to Read the Tape.

During the Open, new traders listen to me discuss the prints as I trade live. They are attached via a mumble audio feed, and access a trading simulator that they watch to see what I am talking about. When I see something significant, I mention it. I'm discussing the most basic concepts in active equity trading, the foundation for these new traders. For the first hour on Day One, noobs simply listen to my explanations and watch their simulator. I then have them read something for 30 minutes, followed by a group exercise. I know what you're thinking: Didn't I go through a similar routine in either first grade or for resident advisor training in college? Probably, but not to worry, it gets much more exciting. This is just Day One, and only a few hours in.

On to the group exercise. We don't do the cliché trust falls from middle school outdoor education trips or corporate America "off-sites." But we do bring our new traders into our smaller conference room and ask them to develop, as has been discussed, a pyramid of success. (I know, sounds lame, but there is a method to my madness.) I draw a blank pyramid on our white board and ask them as a group to determine what is most important for their success as a trader. I leave the room, ask them to appoint a group leader, fill in the blank pyramid of success, and instruct them to come find me when they are done. This is an excellent exercise. First, it allows the new traders to get to know each other and learn how to work together. Even though they are green in experience, they are trying their darndest to figure out what's significant. Finally, when we reveal what is important, they remember it better since they have tried to figure this out themselves. In the end, our new traders are glad they do this exercise.

About 10 minutes in, there is a knock on my closed office door. I open it. It is KIA. I say, "Done already? That was fast." KIA remarks that he wants to talk to me privately, and I ask back if it can wait until after the group exercise. KIA says no. Despite Steve's perceived aura of intimidation over the new traders, I guess it didn't make an impression with KIA.

KIA starts, "I am not interested in doing this group exercise with a bunch of young kids." It's not even lunch time and KIA is not happy about how I've designed my training program. (I wish I could tell him that it took Steve and me only two years to develop this, but I'm too amused by KIA being indignant.) He explains that he never focuses on the prints when he trades and feels this is a waste of his time. He abhors being involved in this group exercise with a "bunch of young kids." (Granted, he was older than the rest in the training class. Generally, we hire recent graduates, but occasionally we do hire transitioning professionals who show a passion for the markets.) KIA continued that it seemed like we were guessing too much while we were trading on the Open. KIA wants to make trades where he "knows he will be correct."

Now before I begin, let me be clear that I like KIA. Again, he stood out amongst the thousands that we chose from. And I respect that he had the guts to take the plunge into prop trading. But we cannot train traders who will not listen, or for God's sake, question the training regimen two hours in! Imagine joining the Marines and on the first day of boot camp telling your drill sergeant "You know, I really don't like tucking the sheets in this way on my bunk," or "I don't like the method you use to take apart the rifle and put it back together again," or, "I don't see why we need to shine our shoes." This is how I felt when KIA disrespected our processes.

We explain that it is the new trader's job to listen, and my job to teach. We don't have meetings about content on our first day. If after you have become a consistently profitable trader, with a few years of experience, and would then like to offer a critique of our training program, I will be grateful for your input. But dissenting about our content on Day One is a sign that you are just not going to listen. And I mean this nicely; a new trader has no idea what the hell they are talking about. Seriously, you have no clue at all about what you are talking about. And the quicker you learn this, the better for you. You just don't. I know I didn't in my first eight months. It is common for experienced traders to acknowledge that they did not know what they were doing until after three to five years.

Now I understand that some have trouble learning how to Read the Tape at the beginning. This can be frustrating. The Level 2 quotes move quickly. It is a lot on the eyes at first. You feel like when you were a kid, you closed your eyes, and your friends spun you around quickly. When you opened your eyes, you were dizzy. That is how a new trader ought to feel.

I am a very patient teacher. But there are some things that I just will not tolerate. The idea that a new trader thinks he knows best how to start a training program, or had enough knowledge to critique a training program within the first few hours, is ridiculous. In fact, it is so absurd that when I explained why we started with the prints, internally I was saying, "Why the hell are you engaging in this discussion? Get rid of the moron!" But I calmly and patiently explained that we can never be sure of a position. I remarked that trading is a game of probabilities and that sometimes reading the prints, for even an experienced trader, was not clear. All I am trying to do is spot trading setups that offer a good risk/reward opportunity, with a downside/upside ratio of 1:5, and a win rate of 60–70 percent. The results I cannot control. All I can do is enter trades with these criteria and see what happens.

Anyway, he kept with the questioning even as I explained what we were doing. I could sense that this guy had some emotional baggage that

I did not have time to solve. He lacked the self-confidence necessary to succeed as a trader. That was why there was all this questioning of our teaching.

I called Steve into the room. I told KIA that I would bet him anything that when I told Steve about his concerns that Steve would first laugh. I wasn't trying to be disrespectful to KIA, but rather I was hoping he would understand that his actions were absurd. I asked KIA to relay his concerns to Steve. Steve, of course, laughed, and then said bluntly, "How would you know what we should teach?" We both didn't mean to be rude, and I can see how it might come across that way to the reader. But it was just so inane for him to be questioning us at this point. Steve politely asked him to go take a walk and decide whether he wanted to continue. I told Steve to get rid of him. Continuing was a waste of our time. I had no interest in working with this know-it-all, know-nothing new trader.

Late Guy (LG): I Am Not Running a Cafeteria

We started training a pleasant NYU student for a class in January 2009. He (LG for late guy) begged his way into the firm. He was a marginal candidate at best. But he was persistent. His math background was impressive. We were doing very well as a firm, so there may have been a touch of *whatever this guy lacks I can fix* going on here. He had a calm demeanor and a passion for trading, so we decided to give him a chance.

On Day One of training LG showed up late. On Day Three of training LG showed up late again. Like with a handful of others, I told him this was unacceptable. Showing up late is disrespectful to the others in your training class. Here is what I said behind closed doors, with our floor manager, The Enforcer, present, to this new trader, "Your training peers rely on your participation to improve their learning experience. It is also disrespectful to the market. You must be prepared before every trading day, and showing up late leaves you unprepared. Being disrespectful to the market will cost you money. If I were a manager of a cafeteria I might expect an employee to show up late. But I do not run a cafeteria. I run a trading firm. We compete against some of the most competitive people in the world. This might as well be the NFL."

On Day Six, LG showed up late AGAIN. I asked GMan to stay behind after our AM meeting with me and LG. I include GMan in these discussions because I want him to learn how to handle these situations, as one day GMan will have to give these talks. I explained that if you cannot show up on time, then you will not enter positions on time. If you are not respectful to the markets, then you will experience huge rips. If you are not respectful to your classmates, then morale will suffer. We had given him a second chance already. But now LG was fired.

LG started to say what you would expect about it not happening again, but I cut him off. I told him there was nothing to talk about. We liked him very much. He was very talented but he had thrown away his chance to trade with us. I wished him the best of luck.

STARTING TOO QUICKLY

You get hired at a prop firm, your dream job out of college. You are eager to show the firm's partners your ability. You are not going to be some ordinary trader. You will be the firm's next star. From Day One, your talent will be so clear that a buzz will generate on the floor about you. Why was the managing partner making such a big deal about the steep learning curve? That obviously applies to lesser traders. I am going to crush this market. Let me at it.

Ok, well, confidence is good. Prop firms like that. But no offense, you almost certainly will struggle when you first begin. This is good because the best educators counsel that you learn through struggle. Your goal is to improve every day, and slowly. If you sprint out of the gate too quickly, you might not be around for the finish, the best markets. Let's discuss.

Bolt: A Sprint Out of the Game

One of the more talented traders I traded next to started too quickly. Bolt (named after the great sprinter Usian Bolt) was passionate about the markets. On his first day trading live, he was calling out levels in 10 different stocks. An experienced trader remarked, "Why is he calling out all those levels? He just started. Exactly why does he think he knows anything?" He was a Carnegie Mellon graduate, had worked at a Tier 1 bank, and just wanted to trade.

I know in this chapter I've sounded like ex-Georgetown coach John Thompson during the NBA draft (i.e., "I really like this kid."). At the same time, I could be accused of emulating the ageless NBA lifer Hubie Brown (i.e., "This kid has tremendous upside."). Well, I could say the same about Bolt. I liked him, and yes, he had tremendous upside. He exuded positive energy. We wore a bright smile, laughed easily, and was so into the markets.

The first day he traded live, Bolt wrote 50k shares, with a 100 share max position size. Do the math, and this means he made 250 round turn trades! And there are only 390 minutes in a trading day. I'm surprised his keyboard didn't catch fire with all that rapid-fire trading he did. Thankfully, we have a good clearing deal and he didn't kill the firm on commissions.

Under our rules, no trader is allowed to trade more than 10k shares a day when they begin, save under special circumstances. So Steve had a chat with Bolt and politely told him to trade less. Bolt gave the normal Ok and headed back to his seat. So what does Bolt go ahead and do the next day? Trade 60k shares! So much for that persuasive, Tony Robbinsesque talk that Steve had with him. I had a talk with him.

I promptly brought him into our conference room (we were still not a year old as a firm, so actually we talked in more of a storage room) and told him: "You know there is no reason for you to continue as a trader. You are going to fail."

You could see that he had no idea what I was talking about. Fail? He knew so much about the markets. He knew all the levels. He loved trading. He went to one of the best undergraduate schools in the nation. He was practically a genius. He knew and I knew that he was much smarter than me. I explained: "Look, I don't make the rules. The market does. And at the beginning, you must go slowly. You must concentrate on improving every day. If you don't, you will rip up so much money you will not last to find out how good you can be." He nodded and went back to his trading station to prepare for the next day.

Bolt clearly was not listening (see earlier part of this chapter), because on Day Three he upped the ante to 65,000 shares! Two days in a row we tell him to cut back, and not only does he trade more, but he rips it up. We had to talk with Bolt again. He was so anxious to trade. He had all these levels to trade off of, but he was not seeing the differences between a good trade and a mediocre trade. Plus, he was trying way too hard. Like many of our trainees, Bolt had never failed at anything important he had ever done, and he expected to be the best trader on the desk. Needless to say, we loved his ambition. But he was never going to find out how good he could be if he did not focus on the process.

Trading is just a game of math and probabilities. We make fewer trades during the middle of the trading day because statistically our win rate is lowest. We do not trade with size when we first begin because our win rate will be poor. We focus on the process when a new trader starts because they are developing their playbook. Each trader must learn which trades offer the best win rate FOR THEM in THEIR style.

As a trading coach, there are times when you just cannot rein in a trader. We put restrictions on Bolt's buying power, tier size, loss limits, and so on. We had numerous talks with him. Bolt just could not control his need to be a great trader immediately. Nothing really worked.

After a two-month review, I told Steve to let him go. There was no point for Bolt to continue. If he could not start slowly working on the things that were most important, he would never make it. Steve got rid of him. Bolt accepted our decision agreeably.

The sad thing is that Bolt is walking around the streets of NYC thinking that he failed as an intraday trader. His few months of trading provided him all this data to support this conclusion. However, that data is not relevant. He simply did not start properly. He pressed too much, too early. Bolt judged his trading based upon data that did not include developed trading skills. Bolt is a trader who should have never failed.

DJ: Go Big And Go Home

Fast starter Number Two was an experienced trader when we first began with our firm. We will call him DJ, for Delta Jackass. DJ was an experienced options trader (hence Delta) who was transitioning into equities, and demonstrated a good track record. We figured we could work with him.

The first day DJ traded live (he did not take our training class because he was an experienced trader) he made over $1,500. During the trading day, both Steve and I had checked his work. It was a mess. He doubled down and held positions against him that happened to rebound. He just so happened to sell a long position in a stock that was in a downtrend for a two point gain just before it plummeted five points. These results were nothing short of miraculous.

Steve and I called DJ into our conference room, or more accurately, our conference closet posing as a conference room. Steve started by pointing out his fundamental trading errors. DJ scoffed, "Guys, obviously I know what I am doing. I just made $1,500." Now let me add some color to this dialogue. DJ was the biggest jerk we have ever hired. He was the most unlikable person I have ever met as a trader. (I was the anti-John Thompson in this case.) Just thinking about him now upsets me. We made a mistake hiring him. He was just a miserable human being.

Steve replied that his mistakes would catch up with him. He laughed. DJ stated, "I have made money trading options. I am not sure why you guys are worried about my making money trading equities. But thanks for the advice." I got the feeling that DJ felt like we were keeping him from something. That we were a nuisance in his day from which he wished to be extricated.

The next day he came in and ripped it up. There was some flaw with our loss limits admin on this day, so his loss limits were not triggered. Steve and I were busy ourselves and missed how much he lost. Let's just say it was an awful lot of money.

I took DJ into the office and told him this would not work for us, and that our business relationship was over. I told him that I wished him well. But really, that was a lie. I really hope DJ is at some dead-end job at the DMV or something, taking people's photos or telling them which line to wait in. OK, I don't really hope this, but arrogant jackasses like him don't deserve to touch other people's money.

DJ was not qualified to trade equities so aggressively. Options are not equities. Switching products takes some time, and DJ did not respect the process.

Playmaker, a trader on our desk, likes to say, "Go big or go home." This is a great trading expression. But I know when to add size. And our guys know that what I mean is to load up when you see it. But we don't load up when we are not ready to do so. You must pay your dues first before you can "Go big or go home." And if you go big before you are ready, then I am going to tell you to "go home" and not come back.

NOT EVERYONE GETS INTO AUGUSTA

We have talked about all the things that traders do to their own detriment, but a discussion of prop traders failing is not complete without one last fact: You may not be good enough. There are some who no matter how hard they work and how well they listen cannot become successful prop traders. Over the years, I have traded next to, trained, and heard stories about traders like this. These new traders worked hard and did what they were asked yet were not successful. Becoming a successful prop trader is like joining an exclusive country club. You may not get in. Unlike the other reasons I outlined in this chapter, this is actually an acceptable reason to fail as a trader.

Most traders do not fail honorably, as I've outlined earlier. They do not work hard, start too quickly, or do not listen. And almost all who have underperformed can do better. Almost all who fail are not properly trained. Almost all with better guidance would dramatically improve their results. And most just need to improve a few skills to make the jump from merely good to great. There are too many who fail who never should have. There are too many not doing as well as they can. But having said all of that, some are just not talented enough to trade for a living.

Namath: Just Not Good Enough

We worked with one trader who possessed the confidence of Joe Namath, the cocky former Jets quarterback who predicted an improbable Super Bowl victory. We would talk with this developing trader every quarter to check his temperature and review his work. He (let's call him Namath) had been continually negative. I am not sure why we really kept him around. We hoped Namath would turn things around, but that's all it was ...

hope. We let him go six months too long. There was no evidence that he would succeed.

But Namath would show up every day. He would attend our video review sessions. We would reduce his tier size and buying power and he would still come to work. Namath would offer an e-mail here and there protesting, but he accepted our decisions.

What strikes me as most peculiar about Namath is that he never seemed stressed about his lack of success. He was cocky and not the most popular guy on our trading desk. Honestly, I personally didn't like him very much. I guess I am old school. Think Larry Bird. Act like you have made a shot before. Think Emmett Smith. Act like you have been in the end zone in the past. Cocky without merit is not a laudable attribute. He certainly was not the hardest worker on our desk, but Namath did his work. Working harder would have helped but I cannot suggest that he failed because of his work ethic.

We would hold our quarterly reviews with Namath, and would encourage him to pick it up. He would agree with what we said, but had a tendency to cut me off before we finished. He did this with everyone. For example, we would talk about picking better stocks. I explained that you are only as good as the stocks that you trade, and that his results were significantly better when he was in stocks that were moving intraday. Namath would sit there and then before I had finished my point, would authoritatively say, "Yeah I need to trade better stocks." He would state this as if this was his idea, as if he had diagnosed his weakness. As I stated before, he was difficult to like.

Namath showed some signs that he could make it. He would put up some good days. When the market was directional, he would post solid results. In fact, during the best trading days he was regularly at the top of our leaderboard. Most traders who are just not good enough never show signs that they can make money, but this was not the case with Namath.

Namath would end every review asserting, "I know I am going to become a good trader." He didn't seem concerned that he was continually negative. He was supremely confident that he would turn things around. In fact, he was more confident that he was going to make a lot of money soon than I was about my own trading. And I have been doing this really well for 12 years. Namath had never made a dime as a trader. It was a little odd.

We gave him a few more quarters to make money. He didn't. We had a particularly bad month in December of 2008 and had to make some cuts. Namath was at the top of the list. We couldn't carry him anymore, so we asked him to leave.

Namath traded for about 18 months with us. He never made money consistently. Overall, he lost us a significant amount of money. I cannot say that we were particularly upset by the losses, because he did what we asked. Namath just was not good enough. Joe Namath correctly predicted the Jets' Super Bowl win. But our Namath's prediction that he would become a good trader was wrong.

Before Namath, left I told him not to look at his time with us as a failure. It takes a lot of guts to trade professionally. It is one of the hardest things you can do. We trade a specific style with a short-term outlook. This is just one style in one time frame. Underperforming with our style in our time frame did not mean that he couldn't succeed in a different trading system or time frame. Trading teaches you a great deal about yourself. I was sure he learned a great deal about his mental weaknesses and strengths. This alone ensures that trading is a valuable life experience. And he had developed some skills that might be useful to him down the road, perhaps as an execution trader for a portfolio manager.

Namath agreed. He included in his warm thank you e-mail, "I know I can become a profitable trader." He still was not all that concerned about his results and apparently was not affected by being asked to leave. You know what, good for him. We are one firm that trades one style that he traded with for a short period. Good for him to think he can still succeed. But he wasn't going to with us. Maybe we were not a good fit for him.

There is no shame in failing as a trader. The real shame is never trying if trading is your passion. If you are passionate about trading and you never give it a run, then you will live your life wondering what could have been. Having the nerve to take a chance and trade will serve you well later in life. Perhaps the next chance you take will work out. What you will learn about yourself is invaluable. What you soak up about the markets lasts forever. To try and fail because you were not good enough is honorable. It would be refreshing if this was the reason why all new traders failed. Unfortunately, as we have learned, that is rarely the case.

For those who stay in the game, the reason is often superior fundamentals. Review the seven fundamentals of One Good Trade presented in Chapter 2 as a starting point.

PART III

Getting Technical

CHAPTER 7

Stocks In Play

Y ou are only as good as the stocks that you trade. There are too many developing prop traders who do not know what a good stock is, how to find one, and waste too many trading days mistaken that the markets are devoid of opportunity. In this chapter, I will define what it means when I say "Stocks In Play," explain why we trade them, share how we trade them, and replay some memorable anecdotes to support why we trade these stocks (thanks, Reader Chuck).

Let me say again: you are only as good as the stocks that you trade. You can be the best trader in the world, but if your stocks do not move, nor are liquid, then you cannot make money consistently. (As an example, one trader from my early days made $18 million one year, trading only stocks under $5. The next year, he lost $20 million.) Intraday traders must be efficient with their time and buying power. We are not blessed with $50m trading accounts like some at the big banks. (That is, of course, if these types of accounts still exist after the bloodbath in 2008 and 2009.) So we must find the stocks that are moving to perform well with our lesser buying power. And we do.

I get a ton of e-mails like this one from a trader named Chuck:

> Hi Mike,
>   First off, you continue to inspire me with your discussions on StockTwits TV. Thank you, good stuff!
>   My question: I am clueless when it comes to finding the right stocks to trade (despite reviewing charts at night). Any advice?
> Best,
> Chuck

First I am not sure about the inspirational stuff. I am not Lance Armstrong, but I appreciate the kind words. Second, I do get this question quite often via e-mail. There is more than one way to select stocks to trade, but in the end it's always best to choose Stocks In Play.
    You are in the wrong stocks!

WHAT IS A STOCK IN PLAY?

What is a Stock In Play? This could be, in no particular order:

- A stock with fresh news
- A stock that is up or down more than 3 percent before the Open
- A stock that does more than one million shares of volume
- A stock that will move more than 3 points intraday
- A stock that will have real order flow and develop important intraday levels, which we can trade off of

I received hundreds of e-mails in August 2009 from traders struggling. You are in the wrong stocks! I regularly receive e-mails from experienced traders who have been underperforming. You are in the wrong stocks! I am often approached by a frustrated prop trader carping about continually getting shaken out. My response? "You are in the wrong stock!" Developing traders frequently complain to me that they are not doing well. You are in the wrong stocks!
    There are many different ways to intraday prop trade. But all must be in the stocks that offer the most opportunity. We are graded on our production. And too much time spent without trading opportunity because you cannot find Stocks In Play is a flawed trading system.

We trade Stocks In Play because they:

- Allow us to be most efficient with our capital.
- Offer MORE excellent risk/reward opportunities intraday.
- Ensure additional opportunities to load up.
- Allow us to execute our ideas and trading rules with more consistency.
- Help us combat algorithmic programs.
- Allow us to utilize our superior trading skills.
- Help the developing trader develop faster.

I can count on one hand how many days in three years there has not been opportunity with such stocks.

Some prop desks trade baskets of stocks, but not us. Some trade ETFs exclusively. Many have developed proprietary filters to find stocks. Others concentrate on trading the markets as a whole with index futures. Still others, especially at the prop desks of the big banks, just trade a sector like Gold or Oil or Tech. There is more than one way to make money, and definitely more than one correct way. Many prop firms use their strategies successfully, but remember, we are intraday traders with limited amounts of capital. Further, I want to be where the action is. I crave for the ball to be in my hands. I live to hunt the largest game, that best test the trading skills I've developed over the course of my career. So we trade anything that is moving. (*Trader Monthly* titled a profile of Steve and me "Motion Detectors", after all.) After 12 years of trading, there are some mornings when I am trading a stock for the first time ever. But as long as it is In Play, I can make money with it.

Unfortunately, I still get far too many e-mails from people unwilling to move away from their normal basket of stocks. They struggle and complain that there is less opportunity than before. Again, I can count on one hand the days the markets did not offer opportunity on the past three years. You do not need the markets to be active, just as long as one stock is a Stock In Play.

WHAT IS A GOOD INTRADAY STOCK?

TRADERS ASK: "TELL ME MORE ABOUT INTRADAY STOCKS"

I received this quick, simple e-mail from Reader Sam:

Bella,
    What characteristics make a good intraday trading stock?
Sam

A good intraday trading stock offers you excellent risk/reward opportunities. It is a stock that you can regularly read is about to trade higher or lower from its present price, offers good prints, and moves. And these moves are predictable, frequent, and catchable.

A good intraday stock offers numerous excellent risk/reward (1×5) setups. Trading opportunities where your downside is 5c and your upside is 25c, or your downside is 20c and your upside is $1. With a good intraday stock, you surmise that your risk/reward is 1×5 and it actually is. As opposed to your risk/reward really is 1×1. Sometimes, stocks look like they offer an excellent risk/reward. But then the stock trades against you and you cannot get out ("What the hell. I can't get out of this piece of s&%t"). And this is not because you are slow to exit or stubborn. You quickly and painfully learn your risk is much larger than you had calculated. Succinctly, a good intraday stock is a Stock In Play.

A Stock In Play offers us many excellent risk/reward opportunities intraday. This is the whole game. These stocks gift numerous trading setups, where your downside/upside ratio is 1-to-5, and your win rate is at least 60 percent. And as I mentioned, a Stock In Play actually offers you opportunities where you conclude your downside is 1, and it is actually 1, as opposed to stocks where your slippage is underestimated or unknown.

For example, if you buy JPM at 30 and you set an exit price for 29.85, can you actually get out near 29.85? Or are you hitting the 29.50 bid to exit? If you are trading JPM and you conclude you can exit at 84c but really you cannot exit until 50c, then this is not a good trading stock intraday. Stocks In Play are liquid such that you can exit without unexpected slippage.

Again, you are only as good as the stocks you trade. If you are the best trader in the world but your stock does not move, then you cannot make money. Trading a stock that doesn't move is a trading day wasted. I look for a stock that will move intraday 3 to 5 points at a minimum. For example, at the start of 2009, I selected WYNN before a trading session. WYNN traded from 23 to 21, then 21 to 23, then 23 to 21, then 21 to 22.50 (see Figure 7.1). WYNN moved about $7^{1}/_{2}$ points intraday. This is the movement I need to make money. This is excellent intraday movement.

The next trading session I traded FLS on the Open. FLS moved from 50 to 53, then 53 to 51.50, then 51.5 to 53 before 11 AM (see Figure 7.2). FLS moved about 8 points intraday before lunch.

Now, I don't want stocks to just move. I seek stocks where I can identify that they are about to move in a certain direction. It is possible that a stock that moves 50 points intraday may never offer me excellent risk/reward opportunities. Some stocks move too much intraday without

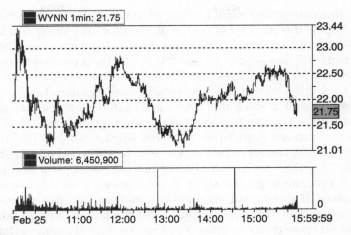

FIGURE 7.1 WYNN 2/25/09

foreshadowing their direction. BIDU and GOOG are two stocks that are difficult for the new trader to read the direction of its next move. I forbid new traders from trading either stock. POT and CME are also outlawed. When the new trader is wrong, the rip is such that it wipes out any gains. Thus these are stocks to avoid.

There are some stocks that are easy to read. WYNN and FLS were easy to read at the end of February 2009. I could identify the direction they would trade. And I like stocks like this. There were some stocks like GS

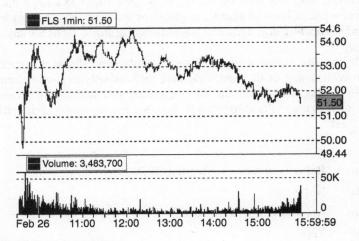

FIGURE 7.2 FLS 2/26/09

during this time period when I struggled to determine the direction of the stock. During this month, GS was so difficult for me I swear that if the GS Specialist jumped in a cab, came to my desk and told me where GS was going, I might still lose money. I guess this is why I was positive 90 percent of the trading days when I passed on GS. And why I was negative 100 percent of the trading days when in GS. Are you sensing a pattern here?

Lastly, I seek a stock that offers good prints. A stock that gives you prints near the bottom. A stock that gives you prints near the top. Some stocks move up and down in 50c clips. But when you bid for the stock near the bottom you cannot get hit on the bid. And when you offer the stock near the top, the Specialist and other market players will not take your offer. If you cannot get the stock at good prices, then this impacts your risk/reward. If you cannot get good entries then you may not be able to execute excellent risk/reward trades. The stock may move up and down without an opportunity to make good trades. And sometimes that is just the way it is.

A good intraday stock is a Stock In Play. During my trades, I feel like I am in control. If I focus and wait for my setups, I can find enough opportunities where my downside is 1, my upside is 5, and my win rate is 60 plus percent. I will have to do something horrid to finish negative. It will not be the stock. A Stock In Play will be flush with opportunity.

If you want another perspective, let's hear it from the guy who runs the SMB AM Meetings, Steve, where we identify the Stocks In Play before the Open. It is funny because on the way home from work in the spring of 2009 Steve was bragging about an idea he lifted from the SMB AM Meeting. He crushed MGM during an Open by listening to a new trader offer 10.80 as a level. MGM held this level on the Open; Steve bought 3k shares and held it for over a point. He was slightly negative at the time. But this trade turned around his trading day. This was a good trading stock, or as we say, a Stock In Play.

During the summer of 2007, as the subprime disaster struck, I had never even heard of Countrywide and its famously orange-skinned CEO Angelo Mozilo, who at the time of this writing still stands trial for securities fraud. Corporate malfeasance aside, here's a conversation I had with GMan back then.

GMan: Bella, have you ever traded CFC?

Bella: Nope.

GMan: Are you going to trade it?

Bella: Yep.

GMan: Spencer, have you ever traded it?

Spencer: No.

GMan: Anyone ever traded CFC?
Silence.

GMan: Should we trade it?

Bella: Yes. It is In Play. We will figure it out.

As long as the stock meets my criteria (as a rule, we do not trade stocks with an enormous short interest, nor with a daily volume likely to be less than 600k shares intraday), no matter if I know the way it moves well or not, I will trade it.

Stocks In Play are that ace for your favorite MLB team, that menacing defensive pass rusher that pressures a quarterback, and that NBA 4th quarter scorer who can put the ball in the hole when it most matters. You can talk all you want about trading strategies and setups. You can talk about moving averages, and MACD, and Fibonacci levels. A Stock In Play is easier to trade. Just how easy? With a Stock In Play you can wuss out of a good position, take a rip on the Open, miss 20 percent of the best intraday trades, and still be exceedingly profitable. All of this is because your margin of error is much higher, your upside is much greater, and your risk is lower. This is all possible because you are in a Stock In Play.

WHY TRADE STOCKS IN PLAY?

Steve and I did not always trade Stocks In Play. As I discuss in Chapter 12 we moved toward this strategy out of necessity. In 2003, we began trading Stocks In Play because previous methods of making money were no longer working. Back then, this was just Steve and me sitting next to each other trading at ETrade's prop shop (which was voluntarily eliminated—very long story, which if we ever meet in person you can ask me about). There was no SMB Capital. There was no thought of SMB Training, or SMB Capital Management (I think we are up to five separate entities that we own now, but I lose count). We were just trading unnoticed, leaving at 4:05 every night, not working on the weekends, and enjoying lots of free time (what the hell was I thinking, starting SMB?). We were, during this time period, two fledgling traders figuring out how to make money after the Internet Bubble had burst.

But we recognized we needed to be smarter than the go-go late 1990s. We noticed there was opportunity again in the markets if we chose the right stocks. So we started selecting our trading stocks more carefully each morning. Previously, we had just traded semiconductors, tech or Internet stocks, mainly because they had traditionally moved the most on an absolute basis. It didn't really matter which specific names they were. I could have thrown darts at a dartboard with "SEMIS" "TECH" "and "INTERNET" embedded in a pie chart. But now we started trading anything with unexpected fresh news, anything that moved. We were able to use our considerable trading skills to capture significant moves, moves that maybe some traders were too slow to catch, in stocks that perhaps some were not able to trade on both sides.

We forfeited familiarity for opportunity. We eschewed comfort for greater profits. We developed a trading strategy that propelled us to make money again in the markets. We originated a stock selecting system that we later used to build our firm and is what this chapter is all about.

Percentage Returns for Day Traders

I mentioned that at most prop firms we are not trading with $50 million accounts. And that is probably a good thing since that would add more stress than necessary to my days checking the inflated positions of our young guns. But we, like most other prop traders, must be efficient with our buying power. A typical new intraday prop trader starts with buying power of $100k. (Recall "buying power" consists of capital from prop firm partners plus leverage offered from our prime broker. While leverage enhances returns, it also enhances losses. But since we don't hold positions for very long, almost always intraday, we do our best to minimize those pesky annoyances called losses.) A good intraday trader has access to $800k in buying power. Only the superstar intraday prop traders use more than $1m.

Not many people understand how efficient the intraday trader is with his buying power. I actually stopped answering questions about our ROI (Return On Investment) because no one believed my answers. The last time I answered this question I was met with a quizzical stare and "How is that possible?" I certainly can understand how crazy it might sound to the outsider when we quantify our ROI. But remember we are not a private equity firm, buying whole companies and holding them for profit and eventual sales. PE firms even throw in another stat with an I and R, IRR (Internal Rate of Return). I don't know what it means, and I'll leave that to the Excel jockeys.

We are traders, and not investors. More specifically, we are intraday traders. And we are really good at it. A talented developing trader can make over $500k-plus a year after payouts with daily buying power of less than $250k. I warned you, the whole thing sounds absurd initially. I thought I would let our resident engineer, Head Trader, and original non-believer tackle this subject. If you ever wondered how much an intraday trader could earn, you will not use ROI as a metric. Asking an intraday trader what his ROI is will elicit a blank stare followed by a rant, like the one earlier, about how you just wouldn't understand.

Near the end of 2008, GMan received an e-mail from a blog reader inquiring about his performance for that year. And we are often asked during interviews what kind of returns we generate. Almost every day, GMan, on Facebook and some blogs, sees traders posting their percentage returns for a particular stock. Well, just as we are not a private equity firm, we are not a traditional hedge fund either, judged by short-term returns. It's better if I let GMan explain in his own words.

As active intraday traders, we place many, many trades. On a very volatile day, I can put on as many as 250–300 trades. For me to try to add up all the little percentage moves for the different stocks is inefficient. Similarly, for me to talk about the overall percentage return on my account on a daily basis is silly and almost misleading.

In the simplest terms, as a trader for a proprietary firm you ought to have a bankroll. At the end of each trading day, whatever net gains/losses you incur gets added/deducted to your bankroll. At the end of the month, any surplus to your original bankroll is essentially your paycheck. Any losses incurred in that month need to be recouped in the following month before getting paid again. (In this regard, we are like a traditional hedge fund, in which we cannot get paid our performance fee until losses are made back.) Every trading day, you start with the same amount of buying power determined by your level of experience, needs, and trading skill. This amount is independent of your performance from the previous day.

With that said, here is where the math gets silly, as I stated earlier. Say Trader A has a bankroll of $10k and has $100k of buying power. Now, say that Trader A has a very good day and nets $3k in one day—a very reasonable target. Essentially, Trader A makes a 30% return on his bank and 3% on his buying power that day. If Trader A continues to have a good month and he/she makes $50k, then essentially he/she has made 500% return on his bank and 50% on his buying power. At the end of the month, Trader A gets his/her check for $50k and his/her numbers get reset for the following month. Put together a few good months in a row and those numbers just look staggering but are they meaningful or relevant?

Thus, the most efficient metric to evaluate our performance monthly and yearly is by net P&L. However, one day/week/month performance should not determine your trading career. There are many other things that we use to judge our performance on a day-day, week-week, and month-month basis. We are interested in our growth as traders: learning to adapt to the changes in the market, learning to eliminate that which does not work, and further developing our trading skills. Placing too much emphasis on our results just causes unnecessary anxiety. The bottom line is that if we are trading well, working hard, and spending all of our mental energy to get better as traders, then the results will follow.

Percentage returns are not a relevant metric for us as intraday traders. I didn't have a clue this was the case when I first interviewed with SMB. I remember Bella just rolling his eyes at this question from me. I guess as an engineer and math geek I just wanted to know all the little details. . . .

The numbers that GMan uses here are possible only because we actively trade Stocks In Play. With very little buying power, we are able to book sizable profits. Stocks In Play offer us more opportunities, and trades that we have to hold for only short periods of time.

Opportunity All Day and All the Time

Dr. Steenbarger wrote a blog in August 2009 about the limited opportunities that he was seeing for day traders ("Why Daytrading Stocks in the U.S. is an Increasingly Limited Proposition"). Our desk reads Dr. Steenbarger so religiously that I received two e-mails before the Open from our guys nervous about our future opportunities because of his spot-on blog. I swear I thought these early AM e-mailers thought we were going to have to pack up and head to Hong Kong imminently. But this blog and the subsequent e-mails demonstrate the power of Stocks In Play.

No one on the Street who was intraday trading was making money, as Dr. Steenbarger astutely proffered. Large proprietary traders were not making money. Most hedge fund traders were not making money. But we were.

It was a tough month for those whose strategy relies on the market moving significantly. It was also tough for those who trade only certain sectors or baskets of stocks that lacked interest during this month. But it was not for me or those whom I had trained. Frankly, August 2009 was our best month of the year. And again, this is because we trade Stocks In Play.

A Last Week in August to Remember

August is historically uneventful. I went on StockTwits TV in August 2009 and said the same thing. I wrote in my blog "Vacation...Chop!" that you ought to take a break. I suggested that the last week in August or the first week in September are generally excellent weeks to vacation. I have some new information.

Steve has written many excellent blogs on Stocks In Play. Our trading philosophy as short-term intraday traders is to find the stocks that are moving and use the trading setups that work best with these stocks. The advantage of this strategy is that we can count on one hand the days that do not offer opportunity in a given year. To be more accurate, we can count on one hand in the past three years the trading days that have not offered opportunity. And a week in August 2009, a week that has been traditionally slow, was the best week we had all that year.

Huh? Bella, did you just say that you guys had a killer week the last week in August 2009? But the market did not move. It was the last week of the trading summer. Everyone was on vacation working on everything not related to trading. Young traders were in the Hamptons hitting on the models (oh, to be young again). Dads were catching up on important family time. People were having fun. Traders were not trading, Bella. What the hell is wrong with you?

The huge advantage of trading Stocks In Play is that you only need one stock to be In Play. Not only that, but you need only one stock to be In Play for a few days. And we saw that in the last week of August 2009. We saw this with AIG (see Figure 7.3). We saw this in the last

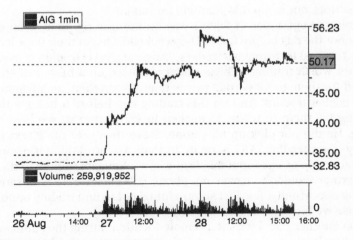

FIGURE 7.3   AIG 8/26/09–8/28/09

20 minutes into the Close on a Wednesday, all day on a Thursday and again all day on a Friday (and then the following week). Our desk made some serious chops!

A favorite baseball-ism heard on a baseball broadcast is: "You see something new every time you come to the ballpark." I went to the new Yankee Stadium during this same August 2009 and saw a grown man eat four sausage dogs in one sitting. Does that count? This last week in August 2009, we again saw something new in the markets. A last week in August that offered memorable opportunity.

I had planned to take Tuesday through Friday off from trading that week and focus on all things Partner. And then came AIG in the last 20 minutes on a Wednesday showing us the face of opportunity. I formulated a Plan B. Plan B was all day trading, all the time, in AIG. Good Plan B. GMan had planned a trip to Great Adventure for that Friday with a mess of the guys. Trip canceled. Profitable decision.

Like in professional basketball, there are runs in our sport. There are days that can make your week. There are weeks that can make your month. There are months that can make your year. This August 2009 was a month to make your year. If you missed it, you may have missed the best trading of the year. And this is part of the huge disadvantage of what we do. You have to be connected to the markets and ready to cancel plans when tremendous trading opportunities visit.

Trade with an open mind at all times. Expect the unexpected. Just because every August I have ever traded was slow does not mean there would not be opportunity in my twelfth August of summer trading. And this is straight out of the "Black Swan." We overvalue what we know and undervalue what we do not know. Eleven straight years of a quiet last week in August does not mean this year will be similar.

During September of 2009 I was on the trading floor of an excellent prop floor the day before Labor Day weekend. One of their floor leaders got up and started lecturing his traders, "Anyone who is trading is overtrading. It is not worth trading." These traders focused on a basket of stocks and waited for them to hit certain prices that offered them an advantage. They were basket traders. And on this trading day before a holiday there was nothing for them to trade. I checked in with Steve to see how we were doing. He did not pick up his phone. Steve then sent me a text message, "Sorry, I am trading. AIG is really In Play. We are killing it again!" While the leadership at one reputable firm was scolding its traders to do nothing, my partner wouldn't answer my phone call because he was saturated in trading opportunity. It is just so rare for us not to find trading opportunities because we focus on Stocks In Play.

On another day, I was at a remote location during the summer of 2009 doing firm business. I opened my risk monitor to check what our guys were trading. They had moved away from AIG and were trading FAS and FAZ. I shot GMan an e-mail: "Get our guys back in AIG! It is still In Play." Apparently on this same day, Steve was trading, remarking every five minutes, "Watch AIG." And "AIG is really good again." AIG had started slowly this morning, so most of our traders searched for new opportunities. But they just needed to be more patient. The action would return soon to AIG, like *Die Hard 2*. Our desk was making some money in FAS and FAZ but not anything like they had in AIG the past few weeks. GMan got them back into AIG. And our better traders crushed the Close in AIG again. This would not have been the case if they continued with FAS and FAZ.

Load the Boat

One of my favorite sayings from back in the day is "load the boat." During my first year of trading we would search for the strongest tech stocks into the Close and "load the boat." This means take a huge position. GMan likes to say, "If this stock holds above resistance I am going to buy unlimited." Unlimited . . . yeah, right. That scares me a little when he says that. This is not a video game here, GMan. But you get the point. There are times when we want to be uber- aggressive. And those times with Stocks In Play offers the highest win rate and risk/reward for the intraday trader.

After we find a Stock In Play, we then watch it trade. We watch the order flow. We search for points of inflection. We want to see the buyers and sellers come together and battle it out. We want an epic battle. The bigger the battle, the more we expect the stock to move after the buyer or seller has won. We had such a setup in AIG in August 2009.

AIG was trading in a range. AIG could not trade below 40.80 or above 41.50. AIG had traded strongly into the Close the day before. It rose 5-plus points in the last 20 minutes of trading. AIG gapped up on the Open. It pulled back slightly and found support at 40. AIG found more support at 40.80 and then resistance at 41.50 (see Figure 7.4).

Our intraday fundamentals told us AIG had room to run since it was again in the news, everyone had an opinion on its worth, its volume was tremendous, and its short interest was high. Heck, I even had an opinion and was quoted in TheStreet.com: "Investors hope that if the two are on good terms, it could mean Greenberg will be willing to help the new CEO, who has more than enough on his plate,' Mike Bellafiore, a trader and partner at SMB Capital said." Did I say that? What does that even mean? Anyway, AIG was In Play and had room to run.

And when AIG got above 41.50 and held above this intraday resistance level, I loaded the boat. And I held for multiple points. The buyers had won the battle. My risk/reward was tremendous. AIG was holding above 41.50. And let me say this, not quoted in TheStreet.com: What a chop!

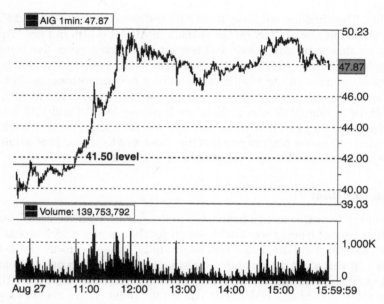

FIGURE 7.4   AIG 8/27/09

Consistency

Let's bring in my partner, Steve, and let him explain in his own words how trading Stocks In Play improve your consistency as an intraday trader.

SMB Capital trades Stocks In Play. Our traders are taught how to find such stocks. And during our SMB morning meeting we review the best Stocks In Play for a particular trading day. Over the past few years I have had quite a few conversations with interviewees, including "experienced traders," about this core trading philosophy. Some don't seem to grasp the importance of this principle. Let me explain.

Your ability to make money consistently as intraday traders relies on your high daily win rate. If you ask any professional trader how many days they are net positive each month, they can give you that figure. It is between 80–90% for almost all successful traders (a few on our desk are consistently above 95%—think GMan). How can professional traders have such a high win rate? There are three basic reasons for such a high level of success:

   1. They develop a skill set over time that allows them to get in and out of stocks efficiently

2. *They develop pattern recognition skills that enable them to accurately assess their risk versus reward*

3. *They are in the RIGHT stocks*

The RIGHT stocks are those that we have identified as Stocks In Play. These stocks will have greater order flow than normal. This does several things that gives you an advantage: (1) increased order flow increases liquidity, which allows you to risk less on each entry and exit from a position: (2) the greater order flow creates additional volatility, which leads to many favorable risk/reward scenarios during the day; and (3) the large number of orders will overwhelm the dopey algorithmic trading programs, which results in a stock moving more cleanly.

If a stock is In Play then there is a 95% chance that I will make money trading it. During our SMB AM Meeting on Friday in December 2008, we highlighted RIMM as a Stock In Play. 19/22 traders were net positive trading RIMM. I can even make three or four losing trades in a row. But by the end of the day, I will be presented with so many trading opportunities that I inevitably finish positive in the stock for that day.

Let me offer the example of another day in December 2008 when I traded MON and AAPL (see Figure 7.5). Both were In Play and I had no difficulty making money in them.

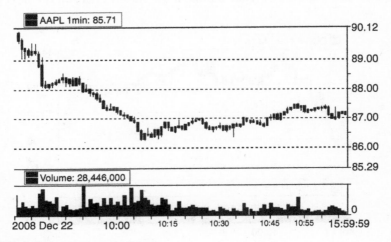

FIGURE 7.5 AAPL 12/22/2008

There is one other point I share about stock selection. I am sometimes unable to identify a stock that fits these criteria for being In Play and we will trade an ETF or a momentum stock because both have a tendency to make several good moves each day. But my first choice is always to be in a Stock In Play.

Earnings Stocks

As I mentioned, Steve has written extensively since our blog began regarding Stocks In Play. During earnings season, there are many In Play stocks to choose from each day. Traders should choose no more than two or three of these stocks each day to focus on. You can make a lot more money trading one or two stocks well than trading many stocks poorly.

Prior to the start of earnings season in April 2009, Steve was trading FAZ almost every day. But he made it clear to our desk that once earnings season began his focus would change to stocks with fresh news. This is where a skilled trader's edge exists. The increased order flow in stocks with fresh news creates greater liquidity, intraday volatility, and great risk/reward setups that are EASILY recognizable.

During seven trading days in April 2009 Steve was able to find a new In Play stock each day. His worst day during that period was finishing up over $3k. Certainly his trading skills played a large part in his success each day but a bigger contributor to his success was proper stock selection. Some of the stocks he traded during this time period included RIMM, AAPL, QCOM, AXP, GS, MS, and AMZN. Take a look at the chart of QCOM below from the day it released earnings. Even novice traders would probably have crushed QCOM if they were aware of the resistance levels at 42.60/43 (see Figure 7.6). Take a look at the AMZN chart on the next page

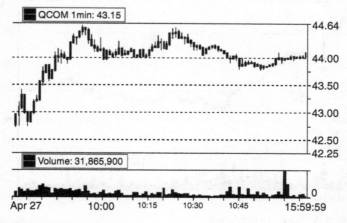

FIGURE 7.6 QCOM 4/27/2009

FIGURE 7.7 AMZN 4/24/2009

(see Figure 7.7). How difficult do you think it was to make money when it traded above prior resistance of 83? Not very.

THE IMPORTANCE OF PICKING THE RIGHT STOCKS

In this section, we'll look at two opposing case studies: Mr. Disciple and The Favorite. These are real-life examples of why picking the right stocks is paramount to your trading success.

Mr. Discipline: Stuck Picking the Wrong Stocks

One of the most disciplined traders I know was outstanding at playing up-trends. Aside from his market prowess, he didn't have an ounce of fat on his body. In two years, I never once saw him eat anything for lunch save a salad. Anyway, he would find stocks off of the filters that were trending up intraday and ride them patiently until they ran out of gas. This experienced trader—let's call him Mr. Discipline—was like a great jockey riding his stock for everything it would give him.

During some markets, Mr. Discipline outperformed the desk. But then the subprime mortgage mess hit. And most on our desk were trading CFC (Countrywide), MBI (MBIA), and ABK (Ambac Financial). CFC would move 8–10 points intraday. And this experienced trader was still glued to his filters looking for his uptrending stocks. We were short, long, short, long, then short, flipping our positions, just trading the crap out of these stocks.

By the end of the day I felt like I was suffering from vertigo. All the movement, and intense focus, just left me dizzy. On countless days, I would shake my head and blink to keep from losing my equilibrium. At the end of the trading day you had nothing left, sessions that left you so wiped, making it to your couch was a major physical accomplishment. Trading days where going to the bathroom would cost you thousands of bucks. Literally.

Mr. Discipline watched in disbelief as new and lesser traders skyrocketed past his results. Plus, he was starting to lose money. He had just gotten married, and I could sense that maybe the instability of intraday trading was not a good fit for his life presently. But he also was exceptionally stubborn. I had a talk with him about trading Stocks In Play. He was not interested. He did not like the way they moved. They were too erratic. I told Mr. Discipline that he was a solid trader, and if he tried, then he could make this adjustment. He was an excellent trader but not a good listener. Mr. Discipline was clearly more interested in proving his theories correct than making money. He merely tolerated people like me for offering alternative suggestions and ensured his access to the markets.

Mr. Discipline continued to struggle. I thought I would try again to talk with him. We were a young desk and we needed an older, experienced guy like him to succeed and become a leader. He was one of the better traders we had at the time. And really, this was so silly. All he needed to do was get in there and trade these stocks that were moving. They were hard, and fast, but there was so much opportunity. His mentality was like the basketball player insisting he can take the ball to the hole against a star shot blocker. Shot blocked. Shot blocked. Shot blocked. Greaaaat! I thought, if I were the star shot blocker. I always love playing with guys like this. But unfortunately, this guy was on my team.

Mr. Discipline thought these stocks were too erratic and fast? Too erratic and fast? Are you kidding me? Maybe it's just me, but I want the ball in my hands in crunch time. I want my trading skills tested. I love being challenged by the hardest stocks when they are littered with opportunity. These are the days that I live for as a trader. I pray to the trading gods for volatility like those subprime mortgage days.

Recall that I didn't know a thing about CFC and MBI before the mess. I had never traded them. I did not know how the Specialist treated the orders. Honestly, I had only a vague understanding of what a subprime mortgage was. I did not know the fundamentals of the companies. I had not reviewed their charts until the day I traded them. But I am a trader. I am not an analyst writing research reports for the public to read. And I trade stocks that are moving. Give me the information that I need as a trader (technical levels, news, average daily volume, short interest, average daily range), and I will go forth and trade. I learn very quickly. At the end of the day, I am going to figure out these stocks. As uncomfortable as they are initially to trade (think jumping out of an airplane with just the faith that your parachute will open), I take the plunge. And if they are moving, I am going to make an awful lot of money.

During our second talk I said much of the above, but Mr. Discipline wasn't really listening. I thought I gave a great speech. There was no "ask what you can do for your country" JFK moment, but still my points were persuasive. He was just not someone who learned from others. He was who he was. My words were as effective as taking my head and banging it against a wall. He thanked me for "the pep talk," and walked out.

The pep talk? He thought I was giving him a pep talk? I was giving him a way to save his career! I was offering him a way to avoid pushing a bunch of papers around a desk for the next 20 years. Or how to avoid getting on the phone every day and hawking some financial product that he knew was garbage to some strangers whom you would never want to talk to you. I was helping him stay in the arena. The trading arena where every day is new and your heart pounds with excitement with your biggest trades. I would color my hair gray if I thought this would keep me in the trading game. I would trade a toothpick company if you told me this is where the action was.

But I guess that is why I am still trading. It never really had to end for Mr. Discipline. He just decided his time was over and he would not make the adjustment. The market does not reward stubbornness. The market is not interested in how you wish stocks would trade. You adapt to the market. You do what the market demands. And that is the way it will always be.

Losing Mr. Discipline was a tough loss for SMB. I had a few too many vodkas with not enough tonic the night after he left. But an empty trading seat gets quickly filled. New traders filled in the void. Developing traders got better. Most importantly, SMB headed in a new direction. Younger, more agile, and hungry to crush these subprime lenders. Skilled and confident enough to crush the Stocks In Play.

The Favorite: The Importance of Being in the Right Stocks

For our next case study, The Favorite, Stocks In Play turned around his trading career. The Favorite joined our firm after being dismissed from a highly regarded prop firm known for its intraday momentum prowess. He was surrounded by some of the better prop traders on the Street at his last firm, so I knew he had some game. It was just a matter of putting him in the position so that his skills would be rewarded.

As way of background, The Favorite is one of the favorite traders amongst his peers (hence his given nickname here). The Favorite is also the only one who calls me "Michael" besides my mom these days. When he is in a Stock In Play and that stock moves suddenly, you can hear him smack his desk with both fists and exclaim, "Oh!". This "Oh!" just comes out of nowhere from a person whose English is not fully developed (which is also amusing since he has been in the States for years now, is extremely bright and likable, yet has not improved his English) and is generally quiet. Our desk erupts in laughter when silence is met with The Favorite's out-of-left-field "Oh!". More amusingly, when The Favorite makes a good trade, he moves his head forward and back like a clubbie bopping to the latest hip hop music.

The Favorite had a great run with us when he first started, trading the momentum in Gold while it was In Play. His results were in the top third of our firm. I wondered, what the hell his former firm was thinking, getting rid of this powerhouse? But then his trading reality appeared. The Favorite started to struggle for a few months, like an unwanted hurricane sweeping through your favorite beach destination. The Favorite went from one of the best to one of the worst traders on our desk. GMan and I checked his work. He was trading Gold every day and it was now not as In Play.

I sent The Favorite an e-mail instructing him not to fall in love with Gold stocks and to find better stocks, yet he kept trading Gold. The Favorite kept struggling, so I forged another intervention. I pulled him behind closed doors. I noted his superior momentum trading skills, and I explained that he was not taking advantage of these skills by trading Gold when it was not as In Play. The Favorite sat, listened, and ended the meeting with, "Thank you Michael." I thought I had gotten through to him.

No dice. The Favorite continued with this Gold bug like some end of the world conspiracy theorist, hoarding and converting his cash to hard assets. He continued to struggle. How was I going to get through to this young man?

I have to share this anecdote before we move forward. Back in the day I sat next to Gold prop traders who were the hard-core end of the U.S. theorists. Present-day parallels were openly discussed with the end of the Roman Empire. Their best example was the growth of porn with Roman excesses. One of these traders got on the phone to call his bank and asked, "If you go out of business will my gold plates be secure?" You see, the Armageddon scenario is for U.S. dollars to be worthless so you will want gold plates delivered to you. And since the banks then would be bankrupt, would his gold be safe? How did he know?

Ok, back to The Favorite. I had another idea. I moved his seat. I moved The Favorite to the back of our trading firm and surrounded him with our best momentum traders, who were crushing FAS at the time. This kind of worked as he stopped losing money. But he still was not trading as well as I thought he could. I talked with one of our better momentum traders and asked him to speak with The Favorite. And I sent another e-mail, making my best argument for The Favorite to get into the Stocks In Play and maximize his superior momentum trading skills.

FINALLY, one of his new deskmates got through to him; The Favorite started focusing on the AIGs (and in a former era CFCs) and most In Play stocks. He leapt to the top of our leader board, where he belonged. And he stayed there. It only took, what, five months to get him in the Stocks In Play? But I'm glad I did.

BLACK BOX ALGORITHMS ARE NOTHING TO FEAR

In July of 2008, I received a GChat message from a future trader, Reader Carter, who was interested in the impact of black boxes, or algorithms, on intraday trading. I had heard Carter's concerns from other future traders. Some believe that black boxes will rule trading and eliminate the intraday trader. I received this antisocial e-mail from Reader Gutless, who of course sent me this note from a fake e-mail account:

"Ah! I hate to ask a dumb question here, but how come you all are using people to trade instead of computers? Aren't you kind of stuck in the Stone Age here?"

There is all this talk about how black boxes are the end for intraday traders. To me, this is simply an excuse for not doing well. I heard the same thing when pricing went to decimalization in 2001. I heard the same when the market went hybrid in 2006. Anyway, here are my thoughts on black boxes and how to beat them. This is just another reason why you must be in the Stocks In Play.

A few thoughts:

- I have heard this argument for the past five years and I am still trading profitably. And our desk just had its best week ever in August 2009.
- Black boxes have made intraday trading more difficult.
- You must be more selective with your trading. But if you are, there are still many plays where you will have an edge. A momentum trade in a Stock In Play is a perfect example. If you are not selective, then the black boxes will certainly take your money.

- A higher percentage of black boxes fail than traders.
- Too many black boxes are written by programmers who have not learned how to actually trade and thus are destined to fail. Throw these nerdy quants in a futures pit and ask them to yell out bids and offers and they'd look like they were about to be run over by the 6'6'' ex-NFLer standing next to him. You can't just crunch numbers and expect to be a profitable trader. As mankind has proven time and time again, human emotion will trump even the best of automated intentions. And to understand that past data may not help you in a current market.
- You must be able to identify the different algorithmic programs so that you can trade against them. This takes some experience, good mentoring, and practice.
- I have seen many black boxes get destroyed and many that certainly will. The most disappointing black box program today is what we call the Buy the New Low Program. Actually, I have a fundamental problem with this black box as it disobeys fundamental trading principles (don't fade a weak stock!). A stock makes a new intraday low; so then many day traders get short and play the downside momentum. The program buys the shorts from the day traders, and then pushes the stock higher, causing all of the day traders to cover. The problem is that this program was turned on often in FNM and LEH and FRE during their freefall in the late summer of 2008. Ooops! The stocks were broken technically. And not only did intraday traders hit the new intraday low but so did huge institutional sellers. Thus these programs were obliterated. Programs should be respected but not feared.
- Anyone who has created a profitable black box is a genius. It is really that difficult to build one.
- Black boxes have to be turned on and off just like bids need to be placed and withdrawn. And what works today may not work tomorrow. And because of this, black boxes can never completely rule trading. There will always be the need for the discretionary trader who understands when he has an edge to buy or sell. And the market is always changing such that it is impossible to program all of the different variables that eliminate the need for trader discretion.

Black boxes will continue to become more prevalent. I have the utmost respect for those who have created successful ones. There is a fortune to be made in doing so. I know of one superior prop firm that started off the back of a few black boxes. But there isn't a program that can be developed to trade against the well-trained and disciplined trader. There are just too many variables in the markets. And I spend my day only making trades where I have an edge. If I recognize there are too many programs in a stock in order to gain an edge, then I move on.

But as some on my desk joke, I guess I am just a human black box.

Black boxes can be frustrating to trade against. Some algorithmic programs are designed specifically to take the money of the intraday trader. For example, as an intraday trader, we may get long AIG if we notice SPY explode. A program may get turned on to short the buying in AIG as it predicts these buyers are short-term traders. So suppose Trader A gets long AIG at 35.05, Trader B at 35.06, Trader C at 35.07, and Trader D at 35.08. An algorithmic program is shorting our buys. But then AIG does not trade higher because the only real buyers are short-term traders. There is no huge order from an institution. And then when AIG ticks down, Trader A hits the stock at 35, loss of 5c, Trader B at 34.95, another loss, Trader C at 34.90, a bigger loss, and Trader D at 34.85, ripper.

All that has happened is that the program took the money out of the pockets of these short-term traders (me and my peers). And there are dozens of setups where algorithms are set up to take the money of what I call the "weak hand short-term trader" (Traders only interested in holding if the stock ticks in their favor. Think of the Texas Hold 'Em player who plays only pocket aces or pocket kings). So intraday traders become frustrated, saying things like "That is BS. I can't beat these freaking programs." But is that true? Yes, you cannot beat most programs if there is no real order flow. But you can if there are real orders behind certain moves. And in Stocks In Play, there is often real order flow.

Let's take our example from above again. AIG is In Play. We get long AIG when we notice SPY explode. A program may get turned on to short the buying in AIG as it predicts these buyers are short-term traders. So again, let's use the same traders and price points. Trader A gets long AIG at 35.05, Trader B at 35.06, and Trader C at 35.07, and Trader D at 35.08. An algorithmic program(s) is shorting our buys. Ripper again, right? Not this time.

Remember with a Stock In Play, there is real order flow. Generally, when SPY explodes, a big order will flood the market and overpower the algorithm(s). So now assuming this is not a Trade to Hold, Trader A will sell at 85c, Trader B at 93c, Trader C at 94c, and Trader D at 97c. Chop, chop, chop, chop! And lifted straight from the cult classic movie *Swingers*, I ask: Who's the big winner now?

Now with a Stock In Play, when we identify strength, the stock tends to trade higher. The programs cannot shake us or get lifted off the box by real buyers. So this is one more reason why we stick with Stocks In Play.

And there is really a much larger lesson here. As an intraday trader, you can carp and complain about the annoying algorithmic programs developed to take your money. In their worst sense, they are predators and you are their game. If you allow them, they will take your money or for purposes of expanding this analogy, they will eat you.

But you have a choice. You can spend your energy complaining or you can compete. And to compete means figuring out how to use the programs to your advantage (example: riding a short squeeze of a program on the wrong side—delicious!). This means finding the spots where the algos cannot take your money, discovering stocks where you can beat the programs.

As traders, we can spend months making a list of all the inequities in the markets. We can find examples where we get screwed that we can discuss with our drinking buddies all the way into an early diner breakfast after closing down a bar. Heck, we could probably even write an entire book about all things unfair to the intraday trader (I will not be writing that book). Where will that get you? What will that accomplish? How will that help you make money?

As I said, you have a choice. The market is simply a pattern-solving exercise. The programs make it more difficult to decipher these patterns. But they do not make it impossible. Before programs, there might have been three subpatterns per trading setup and now there might be six. And no matter how hard they make the markets for the intraday trader, there is always an edge to be found.

When I first started, the markets were rigged by NASDAQ market makers. They paid billions in fines while they were lobbying the networks to put the word "day" in front of my job though we were doing the same thing they had been doing for decades (save the rigging the markets part). And we still made a small fortune, and that's with transaction costs that were $30 per thousand, a cut of our trading profits, and a platform that could go down for hours without an ability to close our positions.

There will always be obstacles. There will always be things unfair. And we ought to take steps to rid the markets of these scams. But what we cannot do, what a trader must never do, is make excuses. As long as I have access to the markets, then I can find the patterns where I will have an edge. If some firm's PhDs want to screw me out a few dollars here and there, that will not deter me. It is one thing for them to take my money outright; I cannot control every instance of that. But I can control how I react to these perceived unfairnesses. I can make sure I do not take myself out of the game for the trades where I have an edge. Because I can more than account for the screw jobs with the patterns where I have an edge. The little gnats who take my money here and there on certain trades do not determine my future.

And finally, as electronic traders, it is hypocritical to complain about algos. Algos are just an extension of technological advancement. We have access to the markets because of technological improvements. Our ability to trade actively, in and out of stocks, is the result of technology. In the future, I hope to gain access to more equity markets overseas. This too will only occur with technological breakthroughs. Also, there is nothing stopping my firm from creating black boxes, other than us.

SHORTENING THE LEARNING CURVE

Trading Stocks In Play benefits the new trader because it offers more trading reps. Just like any job, when you start out anew, you lack experience. The more market patterns you see, the better. One of the huge benefits to new traders in the fall of 2008 was all of the market patterns they saw in such a short time span as the VIX hit abnormally high levels. Dr. Momentum and MoneyMaker from Chapter 1 benefited at the start of their trading career from markets that offered so many market patterns. This made them better faster. The volatility of the markets transformed one trading day into the equivalent of five trading sessions of market patterns.

Well, this same principle applies with Stocks In Play for the new trader. Since you are trading a stock that is moving more intraday, you are seeing more market patterns. And as a result, you are gaining added experience over someone who might just be trading a basket of stocks. Using the "five trading days" equivalent from above, think of it as the difference between taking 250 free throws in your driveway before going in to dinner, instead of the normal 50, but in the same amount of time. Trading the Stocks In Play will speed up your learning curve.

Superior Trading Skills to the Rescue

When I am not out of the office doing partner-related things, you can hear me say on the desk from time to time, "This is not a good stock. It does not allow me to utilize my superior trading skills." I am half joking but entirely serious.

I have developed tremendous trading skills. I can short. I can get long. I can play both sides of a stock. (Remember in the late 1990s, they didn't teach us how to short. Well . . . we didn't really have to.) I have a trading playbook so thick with profitable trading setups that if I went through them here, all would undoubtedly find another author. It would take a painfully long period of time to sit through that explanation.

If a stock is going to move significantly intraday, then I am almost always going to carve it up like a succulent Thanksgiving Day turkey. I can Read the Tape and find enough intraday plays where I possess a significant edge. And these can be shorts or longs. They can be longer-term intraday trades or quick ones. If a stock is just sitting there waiting for an order or not doing much, then I am not able to utilize my superior trading skills. That is no fun. And as JToma might say, "That doesn't pay for my Porsche and house in the Hamptons."

FINDING STOCKS IN PLAY

Stocks In Play generally have unexpected fresh news, either positive or negative. News that most interests me is higher margins, better sales than expected, or increased market share. I check the news on all stocks up or down 3 plus percent premarket. Stocks In Play the day before often are still In Play. Stocks near important support and resistance levels are also considered. I ask this simple question: If I was a Hedge Fund and a sales trader called me to pitch a trade in this stock, would I be interested? If so, then this stock will be In Play.

If we choose properly before the Open, we often trade just one stock. If we choose very wisely, we often trade one stock for three days and squeeze every cent we can out of it. Short, long, light, loaded, millisecond-holding periods, positions held all day. It's called trading. ("It's called trading" is something Steve and I like to repeat on the desk over and over. Almost like Nike's "Just Do It.")

We choose our stocks before the Open so we can best prepare. We find the levels on our charts and from our trading notes that are most important and consider the different ways the stock may trade. Now often, we don't know the stocks we are trading very well so we must do research to ensure we are properly prepared. (Remember from Chapter 5: The Butcher, failing to prepare is preparing to fail.) We ferret out data about the stocks that is meaningful to us such as average daily volume, short interest, important technical support and resistance levels, average daily range, etc. After all of our morning preparation, we determine which stocks out of about a dozen with fresh news are best to trade.

We also use our filters selectively, most frequently when the market is very slow. In order to help, we use Trade Ideas. It is a very well-run company that has allowed SMB to do what we do. In fact, Trade Ideas is so on the ball that I once wrote a blog about trading V, right on the Open. I described the setup, and how to trade this scenario. Low and behold, David Afariet, who runs Trade Ideas, read the blog, created a new filter for these very setups, and posted a comment on my blog with a link to it. That is what I call adding value!

So how do we ensure we are in the Stocks In Play? Before every Open, every SMB trader submits his best trading idea to our AM Ideas Sheet. This is an internal document that all of our traders can access. Steve then reviews these ideas and chooses the best ideas from this batch. During our AM meeting, which begins at 8:30 AM, Steve highlights the stocks that are best to trade. Steve will offer his analysis of how these stocks may trade. The trader who offered this idea educates the desk on the daily volume, important levels, news, and premarket trading, etc. We also hold a Midday meeting at 12:30 PM to discuss the Stocks In Play into the Close. So after our SMB AM meeting and Midday meeting, our traders are armed with the tools they need. We are then prepared to compete.

If there is news in the middle of the day not covered in our AM meeting that will create a new Stocks In Play, we share this information immediately with each other. If an alert goes off on our trading platform indicating an important support or resistance level, then we yell this out as well. But almost always we chose one or two stocks to concentrate on for a trading day, and this stock(s) is the only thing we trade or need to trade. And then we just carve it up. Chop!

Experienced traders are hypersensitive about being in the right stocks, as we have learned we are all just as good as the stocks we trade.

A skill that too few developing traders have mastered is about to enter the room. Reading the Tape is the first skill that new traders should master, the very first skill! Let me explain in the following chapter.

CHAPTER 8

Reading
the Tape

I meet too many new and developing intraday traders who think trading is just about learning technical analysis, reading charts, and loading up. Here's what I've heard some of them say:

"I can see everything that I need to from the charts."

—An amateur trader

"I can't make much money reading the tape."

—A misinformed trader

"I can't Read the Tape."

—A new trader making excuses

"Reading the tape is extinct."

—An experienced trader who has given up,
believing the quants have won

"Reading the tape is for scalpers. It is for hyperactive, overly caffeinated, nicotine-addicted day traders exclusively."

—Someone who thinks my industry is a joke and probably works
for a shop that would rather be right than make money

"I need to find plays that I can hold to make real money."

—Another misinformed trader, perhaps not an intraday one

193

Little do these guys know that reading the tape can enhance their P&L by many multiples. Some cannot Read the Tape at all. Others, perhaps you, may not even know what reading the tape is. They are that guy you see at your local driving range who only hits Driver. There are a dozen other clubs in his bag, yet he falls in love with his Driver. My trader's playbook is like that bag full of clubs, but I use every one of them. As in trading, you have to develop beyond just one skill (say, technical analysis), and one of the most important is Reading the Tape. This skill will provide you with that elusive "edge" that traders always seek.

Reading the Tape is a skill that enables the intraday trader to predict more times than not whether a stock will trade higher or lower from a given price based on just examining the bids, offers, and prints. Some call it reading the Level 2. The prints tell us where a stock is trading at a given moment and whether this action is on the bid or the offer. You will not always be able to tell a stock's next direction, but you will identify patterns where you can more than 70 percent of the time.

Let me share a story with you. Back in the day, I went to our first firm party held to announce the big producers for the month and build comradeship amongst our traders. It might have been just an excuse for the firm to spend a small piece of the millions it was banking on us traders every month and for everyone to get drunk. Steve and I and the rest of our crew headed down to SPQR, a legendary Italian restaurant in Little Italy, where the firm provided everything on the menu plus an ocean of booze. I do not know what it is about traders, but give them something for free and you earn their everlasting loyalty, for a few months anyway. Ever seen a trader when the free pizza shows up to the conference room? It's as if they just won the lottery. As if these traders can't drop a few bucks on some slices and Coca-Cola? Anyway, after eating too much pasta, and talking to a bunch of rich 20-something traders (I myself was 20-something and not rich), I was ready to hear who were the top traders at the firm. I had some idea. But it is like American Idol. You think you know who is going to win but you still might be surprised (Taylor Hicks beat Chris Daughtry?). And it always fun to see people recognized and happy to earn the spotlight.

So with my gut busting, and anticipation mounting, the names and numbers started to be announced, starting at number 10:

> "At $212k for the month . . ." Some Russian dude whose name was unpronounceable even considering he was a top ten trader.
> "At $235k for the month . . ." I had never seen this guy. But man, was he tanked.
> "At number 8, Steve Spencer . . ."

Steve Spencer? Strange. That name sounds awfully familiar to my best friend from home. Did the firm have two Steve Spencers?

And then Steve, sitting next to me, rose from his seat and lined up with the other big producers. How much did he just make? Holy cow! My best friend, who taught me how to play tic-tac-toe at sleepaway camp when we were seven, had just made over $200k for the month. This was a very different world from our Merlin-the-Magician days. And this was before the Internet dot-com explosion.

During the Internet Boom, circa 1998–2000, to make the top 10 at our firm, you usually had to make over $500k. Our holiday parties were held in the Grand Ballroom of the Waldorf Astoria Hotel. Now, that is a palace. And it was hysterical seeing some of the short, unattractive, young kids walking around with tall, blond, Eastern European fashion models. I wonder how that happened. (I will let you figure that out.) For fun, Steve bought one of the first plasma TVs, 50″, for nearly $20k. Now, you can probably buy one at Walmart for $800. And that near $20k was on discount. JToma bought a Porsche, and a few apartments (very, very smart, given the real estate boom that would soon rise in place of the dot-com bust).

And we were all just reading the tape. There were no charts. CNBC was not broadcast on our trading floor. In fact, I am not sure if we even had TVs anywhere in our space. Interestingly, during a meeting with management, Steve asked for CNBC to be broadcast on the floor. At times, there were funny moves in stocks that came from out of nowhere. Only later would we learn the news on stocks causing these strange moves. Steve's suggestion was dismissed without much comment.

"Just play the momentum. We don't need to know the news."

And you know what? We really didn't need to know the news, because we could Read the Tape so well that news and charts were not really necessary. It was indeed a different era back then, but a skill learned that would not be lost.

JToma would eventually take a few years off from trading, start a private equity fund, and give bonds a shot to round out his trading. When he returned from the dark side, bond trading or anything other than equity trading for that matter, back to prop trading, in his first month, he made more than anyone on our desk. Why? He had never forgotten his tape reading skills.

In one of his blogs, Dr. Steenbarger talked about this skill. Dr. Steenbarger, aka the godfather of modern trading psychology, wrote: "My experience is that an understanding of (and ability to read) order flow is one important factor that separates the older, successful generation of day traders from the newbies who only know simple chart patterns and indicator readings." I am one from this older generation of intraday traders, but I'm not sure why Dr. Steenbarger had to remind me of my advanced age. And so I thought this "old-timer," me, could share his thoughts on reading the tape and how it impacts the developing intraday trader.

For years, I have disappointingly heard developing traders state, "I am just going to focus on the charts going forward. I can't Read the Tape." I have heard it too many times, and not one of these individuals, not one, became successful intraday traders.

The second part of our training program is called Trader Development, after five weeks of training and now trading live. After the Close during an initiation of new trainees, Steve and I answered their questions and discussed what was important on Day Six of their live trading career. (Oh, to be young again. I can't possibly recall what I was doing on Day Six of my trading career.) One of our promising trainees discussed a trailing stop for a trade in MS. "Trailing stop?" I thought. I didn't authorize any trailing stops. What kind of amateur trading books have you been reading, young Skywalker? This was a red flag. My impression was this talented new trader had trouble Reading the Tape, and was experimenting with these trailing stops to minimize this weakness. Experienced traders trading multiple positions can enter trailing stops, but I always advise new traders to trade with "both hands on the wheel" and enter limit orders. He was jumping the learning curve. I counseled this new trader to continue working on the skill of reading the tape and to sell the stock on the offer when the tape showed weakness. And I did so because this is what an older generation intraday trader, like myself, does.

In addition, I offered an analogy about not learning how to Read the Tape. To me, not learning this skill is like a basketball player not working on his free throws. This baller just decides to keep clanging his free throws and give up some easy points. This same new trader offered a better analogy. (Hey, we hire smart kids. Obviously, this analogy was much better than mine. In the future I will take creative license to just use his idea as my own. After all, what is the point of being a partner if you can't steal the analogies from your trainees?) His analogy: not developing this skill is like the amateur golfer hitting only irons during his round because he never learns to hit Driver.

I like that.

Still not convinced? Let's bring is some famous market players for further persuasion.

> Exhibit A: From Steve Cohen, one of the greatest traders ever, of SAC Capital in *Business Week*'s "The Most Powerful Trader on Wall Street You've Never Heard of": ". . . everything I do today has its roots in those early tape-reading experiences."
>
> Exhibit B: Jesse Livermore from *Reminiscences of a Stock Operator* (Lefevre 06): "A battle goes on in the stock market and the tape is your telescope. You can depend upon it seven out of ten cases."
>
> Exhibit C: Linda Rascheke from the essay "Tape Reading" on trader-slog.com: "If you can learn to follow the price action, you will be two steps ahead of the game. . . ."

Exhibit D: Paul Tudor Jones in an interview for *Institutional Investor* Magazine: "... at the end of the day, I am a slave to the tape and proud of it."

TRADERS ASK: "HOW DO I ·READ THE TAPE·?"

After my first blog on Reading the Tape I was left with a lot of questions from loyal readers.

From Chad:

Could you explain what you mean when you say "Read the Tape"? Watching price action? Could you give me an example of something you would watch for? I watch price action a lot and I've learned some things from watching but I'm not sure if that's what you mean (not familiar with the lingo). Thanks.

From John:

This is probably an amateur question, but what do you look at to watch the order flow? A Level 2 screen?
Thanks

From invNin:

Reading the tape is kind of tricky because of the lack of good material to study. Without knowing what to look for, we end up just looking for dancing number on the screen. Also, even in your blog, I sometimes get confused about what is reading the tape and what is watching the order flow...

From (another) John:

John—May I ask? What do you use to Read the Tape Is there a specific platform you use or is it the Level 2 screen?

And then I received this e-mail:

Hello Mike,
...My question has to do with tape reading skills, a question you obviously get a lot.
First, a little about my background. I have spent 16 years on Wall Street as an institutional salesperson (that's probably my problem) and have started, run, and sold my own research broker-dealers. I have

always let the prop traders and market makers do their thing, of which admittedly I knew little about but always tried to hire the best people I could find to manage it. That being said, I have recently (since last November) began to day trade. I have successfully been able to block out the fundamentals/perceptions and learned to read the charts but I am having difficulty reading the tape fast enough for it to make a difference in my trading. I can watch the Level 2 on the NASDAQ stocks and get a feel for demand but as a predictive value but. . . . Help! It's frustrating that such a skill eludes me since I know it's so helpful. What can I do to hone that particular skill?. . .

And so I sat down to answer the readers' questions. I wrote some stuff, wrote some more stuff, wrote some more stuff, and then stopped. Can I explain how to Read the Tape in a blog? No. Can I explain how to Read the Tape in a written chapter? Nope. Alan Farley of TheStreet.com wrote, "Reading the tape must be learned through personal experience and long observation." It is too difficult with just the written word, with too many variables, and too much to share to accurately teach how to Read the Tape. Start by reading this chapter, but keep in mind that nothing can top experience. Don't give up.

If I may use yet another analogous example from the sports world, learning to Read the Tape is like adding LeBron James to your favorite NBA team. It will improve your trading that much. Videos, written materials, individual questions, more videos, and practice are required to learn this important skill. I cannot emphasize it enough.

Just to give you an example of the complexity of this topic, we created a Reading the Tape training program for our commercial website. I was swamped with work, so I asked GMan to develop the curriculum. He sent me back a rough draft with 15-plus written lectures, and 30-plus videos. And after a brainstorming session, I sent him off with more videos to create and lectures to write to best teach this skill. Over many weekends, after he shook off the effects of a hard-drinking night on the town in NYC, he locked himself into our offices and cut tape after tape to partially develop this training program. But he did it. Here's a bit of what we came up with.

THE TAPE TALKS TO YOU

We were in a video review session with our June 2009 class (the best of breed whom we recruited for a year in 2008–2009). We were watching some nondescript play of a slow-moving stock (slow to me, that is). And I blurted, "Buy!" And then the following dialogue ensued.

Bella:	Why didn't you buy there?
Trainee:	I am not sure.
Classmate:	Bella, why is this stock a buy?
Bella:	You want to buy the stock. It is strong. It is in an uptrend. The stock has potential to trade much higher. The market is strong. You want to buy in to a pullback. Well, that was the buy signal.
Classmate:	What was?
Bella:	They stopped hitting the bids. They hit the bids at the whole, 95c, 90c, 85c, and then at 83c the bid did not drop right away. Buy!
	Roll back the tape, please.

And I showed them how the stock was different at 83c. We played the tape forward and the stock soared 50c in three minutes. It was almost like watching review of a football game with a quarterback and examining how to read a defense. With a quarterback though, I wouldn't say, "Buy at 83, the bids are not dropping," but rather something like "look to the post down the middle to split the safeties since they're in a Cover 2 zone."

I did not make up this buy. I did not know definitely where the stock was going. But I Read the Tape. And by doing so, I could see exactly where to start my position and I knew that this trade offered me an excellent risk/reward opportunity with a 60-plus percent win rate. And those are trades we make every time.

AAPL: Steve Jobs's Health

Let me share a pitch-perfect example of how reading the tape offers the best entry price for a position. At the end of 2008, there were rumors about Apple CEO Steve Jobs's health. Many had noticed during Jobs's 2008 WWDC keynote address that he was "thin, almost gaunt" and offered a list-less performance. Steve Jobs is one of the great CEOs of our time. If he were sick, what would this mean to AAPL? On a personal note, it is disconcerting and downright sick that some speculate on the health of an innovative executive for personal gain. And many of the comments about his health beforehand were cold and inhumane. But his health would move the stock and, though it is the worst part of my job, I am a trader.

AAPL had maintained that Mr. Jobs's health was a "private matter." On January 5, 2009, the company released a statement on Apple.com that

Mr. Jobs had been suffering from a "hormone imbalance" for a few months. Nine days later, after the Close, came this (news from Briefing.com):

> Apple CEO Jobs announces medical leave of absence until the end of June (85.33–2.38)—Update: Apple CEO Steve Jobs today sent the following e-mail to all Apple employees: "Team, I am sure all of you saw my letter last week sharing something very personal with the Apple community. Unfortunately, the curiosity over my personal health continues to be a distraction not only for me and my family, but everyone else at Apple as well. In addition, during the past week I have learned that my health-related issues are more complex than I originally thought. In order to take myself out of the limelight and focus on my health, and to allow everyone at Apple to focus on delivering extraordinary products, I have decided to take a medical leave of absence until the end of June. I have asked Tim Cook to be responsible for Apple's day-to-day operations, and I know he and the rest of the executive management team will do a great job. As CEO, I plan to remain involved in major strategic decisions while I am out. Our board of directors fully supports this plan." (Stock is halted.)

My first reaction was I hope he is OK. This was very sad news. I have to admit my mind wandered, concerned about this country's brightest CEO, running one our most innovative companies. But I had to focus. The stock was halted. During the halt, I considered strategies to trade AAPL. I considered all of the different ways that AAPL might trade. Were there support levels if AAPL gapped down? If it gapped down too much, would it bounce? When it re-opened, what would panic selling look like? And on and on I ran through the different possible ways that AAPL might trade. I made notes in my journal about AAPL's most important technical levels. And then AAPL re-opened. The price action was opportunistic. And by reading the tape chops short and chops long were available.

Let's use this example in AAPL as how reading the tape can lead the way for our determination of whether a stock is probably going up or down next. AAPL re-opened near 78, down over 7 points from its halt price of 85 and change. And the tape told us the story. It guided in its silent way, "Bella, I am going down now, short me, short me, short me now!" How? At 78, the offer was tested for size and would not lift. AAPL kept printing on the offer at 78. My prints showed repeating green at 78, which means that the offer will not lift at this price. On our desk, we call this a held offer. And this was after the 7-point plus gap down after the breaking news. The NASDAQ, the exchange where AAPL trades, would not lift the 78 offer. AAPL was a short.

At 77, the offer kept coming back to 77. A bid could not hold 77. "Bella, I am still going down, buddy. Why don't you short some more, Champ?" the tape announced. And AAPL traded lower indeed. At 76.50, NASDAQ would not lift the offer. This was another held offer. The same seller at 78, and the main seller at 77, was now selling at 76.50. "I am still selling, catch me if you can on the way down!" teased the tape at this 76.50 offer.

But then like John the Apostle spreading the word of God to his followers, the NASDAQ seller lifted. "Follow me no more, I'm out of here," communicated this 76.50 seller. The pattern had changed. This repeating seller had disappeared. He had done all the downward guiding he could. This repeating, not lifting, and stepping lower seller was no longer on our box. What did this mean? AAPL would most likely trade higher. So I got long.

At 80.25 AAPL met some new resistance. But this was some almost 4 points higher. When you learn how to Read the Tape, it is like the stock is talking to you. If you develop this skill and listen with an open mind, you will have an edge over your peers.

Reading the Tape offered an easy 1.5-point short and a simple almost 4-point rebound. There was a controlling seller. The tape indicated as much. And then he was no more, so AAPL climbed higher. And prop traders with tape reading skills were profiting all the way to the bank.

Brown Brad: Thinking Like a Trader

It is not always this easy to Read the Tape. But there are plays where it really is simple. And reading the tape will offer pattern recognition plays that you can exploit.

On his last day as an SMB intern, Brad, our rugby-playing, investment-obsessed, soon-to-be Brown senior sparked my interest in trading SYNA, which had gapped down one particular AM. SYNA, which had closed at 37ish, was gapping down 19 percent on bad earnings. And after a few months with us, Brad had learned to trade, so his thoughts were now actually relevant. Brown Brad liked 28.50 for a possible bounce. And I started to get him thinking. My job is not to mandate; it is to teach our traders to think properly. Personally, I was thinking long. What class did they teach you that trade in, you Ivy League pretty boy? Basketweaving? (I'm totally kidding here. Teasing is omnipresent on a prop trading desk.) The stock is gapping down and your dopey 28.50 is gonna get run over like roadkill.

So Brown Brad and I started a discussion. I liked him finding this 28.50 level. This was excellent detective work. This was a technical level to consider. But then I prodded him to consider other alternatives. What if the stock held a little above 28.50 and did not reach this support? Did he have a plan to trade this deviation? What if the stock traded below 28.50 and showed a seller? Would he short? And on and on I offered different variations of how SYNA might trade on this Open. I wanted Brown Brad to be ready for each of these possibilities, each if-then scenario (see "Maximizing Your Profits with Scoring"). I wanted him to be mentally agile. I wanted to make sure he would not suffer from confirmation bias.

But before I finish the story with Brad, it's important that we examine confirmation bias a little bit more. Reading the Tape can help us overcome this bias.

Overcoming a Confirmation Bias   On July 24, 2009, I remember battling confirmation bias while trading AMZN, the high-flying Internet retailer. I define confirmation bias as processing information in the market so that it fits your preconceived opinions. It's the deep down incorrect principle of being right rather than making money. When confirmation bias hits you head strong, you overvalue all the information that backs your preconceived thoughts. You ignore all the information that counters your belief. @steenbab(Twitter handle) and @thekirkreport have previously written about confirmation bias in their blogs. I want to share how I had to fight this mind-crippling disease for traders on AMZN. And what a fight it was.

Steve had written a killer blog the night before about how AMZN might trade on this day. Eighty-eight point eighty was the mother of all levels in the After Hours right after AMZN reported earnings. Those were some nice shorts for us. Chops for us intraday prop traders! With this in mind, 88.80 was a significant resistance level for on the Open (see Figure 8.1). And as per SMB protocol, Steve shared this important level with everyone.

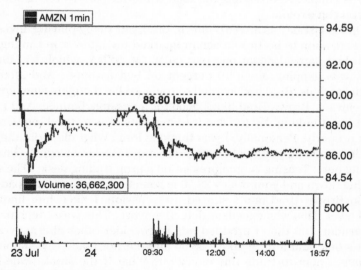

FIGURE 8.1   AMZN Aft-Mkt and 7/24/09

So what happened that day in AMZN? AMZN traded right to 88.80 and failed to push. How do you do it, Steve? We had been prepared with this significant resistance level. So I started a longer, term intraday short. I was not covering until there was a Reason to Cover.

In the after-hours session, AMZN held 88.80 and then traded down to 85.85 and held the bid after significant volume. So we had our levels in place. And now I am short AMZN after the fail of 88.80 on the Open and I am just convinced that 85 is AMZN's next stop. Every held bid HAD to get run over. My confirmation bias was in the house.

At 87.40, repeated buying offered support. And my confirmation bias strangled my thoughts: "These guys are idiots for buying here." But having struggled with confirmation bias in the past, I observed my behavior. I needed to see the screen objectively. So I acknowledged my confirmation bias, quieted my mind, and just read the order flow along with my charts. Seeing repeated buying, I covered some AMZN, booking a quick buck and change. Below 87.40 I would reshort some more. But right now, for my trading system, AMZN was a cover for 2/3 of my position. But only through observing my thoughts, with my tape-reading skills and recognizing that I can suffer from confirmation bias was I able to make a quality trading decision.

AMZN did trade below 87.40 and I reshorted the 2/3 that I had covered. But I was in complete control of my trade because I recognized my confirmation bias, let the tape talk to me, covered, then I reshorted when the reshort was proper. If AMZN had reversed at 87.40, I would have profited. When AMZN traded lower, I profited even more. Take that, confirmation bias.

And then came 86. Now remember my bias was for AMZN to trade down toward 85. What was this 86 buyer doing? Again I thought, "What an idiot." But AMZN would not trade below 86. And so I covered 2/3 of my position again. Another good decision.

In another example of kicking confirmation bias in the proverbial ass, I was perusing Twitter into the Close that day and noticed @downtowntrader chirp HGSI. My alerts were set for 15 in HGSI. I had concluded that it would not be ready for a new leg up until it held above 15. But then I started reading that @downtowntrader was long. And I typed up HGSI and gave it a look. At 14.70, I did not like how the offers were not being cleared. The tape was not bullish. So I did not buy. But this second opinion, my willingness to accept another's point of view, offered another buying opportunity into the Close. HGSI was back on my radar. And this is just another example of how I fought and conquered my confirmation bias during that trading session.

We all fight confirmation bias. But it will harm our performance if we do not overcome it. Let the tape talk to you. And use online vehicles like

StockTwits and your peers sitting next to you to gain second opinions. If you are fortunate like I am to be surrounded by talented traders, listen to their thoughts. This does not mean mimic other traders. Just consider another opinion. Do you know how many times I have heard Steve chirp a position that was the opposite of mine? That did not mean I automatically flipped my position. It just gave me some valuable color on what someone else was seeing with this stock. These other opinions will help you fight confirmation bias.

Back to Brown Brad. In the premarket, SYNA violated 28.50 support. Sellers held the offer below 28.50. The tape was talking to us. "Mike, I am weak. I am offering you an opportunity right here, buddy. GET SHORT!" SYNA spoke to me. I listened and got short. Brown Brad watched (I am not sure if we have clear rules on interns trading premarket, but if we did, they would forbid trading before the market opened, as this is only for experienced traders.). And when we opened, sellers held the offer, so I stayed short. This UConn Husky doesn't fight the tape. And the bids were hit hard, and offered little resistance straight down to 26. I made a chop on the short side. This is what happens when you listen to other smart people around you. Thanks, Brown Brad!

Brown Brad will make a great trader in the near future if he so chooses. And he did so many things well; he was prepared, he found a great stock, he had levels to exploit. All because he Read the Tape.

I HAVE A DREAM

I have a dream. Not a Martin Luther King dream. Not even a Bill Ackman at a Target shareholders meeting dream. I have a Bella dream. A tape-reading dream.

I have a dream that one day on my trading desk, one of our traders approaches me (heck, even an intern like Brown Brad) and declares, "Thank you for teaching me how to Read the Tape. I hit the bids in a weak stock and saved myself from a five-point rip." Perhaps by the time this book is published, my dream will be realized. But I doubt it.

I have heard of every trade where all of our traders have exited too early. It probably happens every day. Someone whines, "I got out too early." While no one ever goes broke taking profits, the angst for not holding for longer, the frustration about wussing out of a trade kills these guys. And yet, I have never been debriefed on a trade where one of our guys saved points for hitting the bids and getting one of the few prints before the stock plummeted. Never.

This all reminds me of the Orny Adams joke in "The Comedian," a documentary about stand-ups. I will paraphrase Orny's joke: 'Nine times out of ten when I see an attractive woman walking down the street, I turn and take another look. Ten times out of ten she does not turn around to check me out.'

Maybe one day a trader will approach. Oh, to dream.

A RIP SAVED

Here's an example of GMan saving himself from a 20-point rip. He still hasn't thanked me.

There was some great action in FSLR after reporting earnings in July 2009. The price immediately drove up from 175 to 187 (see Figure 8.2). There was a pullback to 180 where the bid momentarily held before dropping out to 179. Before you could blink, it drove up to 190. This powerful drive got us to start thinking about where to buy on a pullback. GMan was thinking 185. I, too, thought this would be his good spot to get long, and Steve agreed.

But then something changed. A seller appeared at 187 and actively held the offer. Steve thought to himself that this was still two points from the 185 area, so perhaps a long would still work at that price. FSLR started to

FIGURE 8.2   FSLR 7/30/09 After Market

trade down from 187 as sellers stepped down to lower prices. Then what appeared to be the same seller that Steve saw at 187 was at 185.25 holding the offer. Buying at 185 was no longer an option for Steve, so he passed, but GMan bought. Oh, to be young and bold.

When the 185 bid dropped, it traded down to 180 in about 60 seconds. GMan offered 184.75. Nothing. GMan came lower to 184.25. Nothing. The tape showed no buyers and screamed, "Sell, GMan, sell!" GMan smacked the 181 bid. Next stop? 166. Great bid hit, GMan. Great job of avoiding a disastrous rip! Did I mention he still hasn't thanked me?

The tape spoke to GMan. The 185.25 seller who stepped down from 187 told him that if 185 did not hold, then there was risk below. When this level dropped and his low offers were shunned by market plays at 184.75 and 184.25 he knew he was in trouble. The tape showed FSLR's weakness. And GMan's only option was to try to get out with as small a rip as possible. And he did (BTW, GMan re-entered FSLR and caught a five-point upmove from 166 to leave positive in FSLR and hit the gym. Now, *that's* mental agility!).

COMBAT HIGH FREQUENCY TRADING

In the summer of 2009 there was a huge controversy in the media and Congress over High Frequency Trading (HFT). HFT consists of computer programs automatically buying and selling shares faster than you can enter orders manually. Zero Hedge, a popular industry blog (www.zerohedge .com), six months young, exposed unfair advantages gained by firms using supercomputers to game the system. So successful was Zero Hedge that the 800-pound gorilla in any room deciding SEC policy, Sen. Charles Schumer, from the great state of New York, moved to ban flash orders, which are part of HFT strategy. And thus they were so removed. Score one for the bloggers!

Programs have been the nemesis of the intraday trader for many years. And many of those who claim you cannot Read the Tape anymore suffer from an inability to compete against these new algos. In all honesty, HFT does make it more difficult to Read the Tape. That's right, *more difficult.* Not impossible. At least not to me.

As soon as I dropped off this manuscript to Wiley, I started writing an article for *SFO* magazine on this very topic. Talk about topical.

Computer programs have been created by program traders to take the other side of trades made by active traders like me and force losses. I wrote about this in a blog (rant?) concerning a program I delightfully labeled the

Buy the New Low Program. GMan calls it the "Moron Piker Dopey Ph.D Has No Idea How to Trade Program." Both titles are accurate, and the strategy is defeatable if you know what to do.

Algorithmic Programs That Will Be Eliminated

Recently, I wrote about secondary plays, and a program we call Buying the New Low.* When a stock makes a new intraday low, algorithmic programs buy this new low because they predict that short-term traders will get short. These programs are betting that only light volume will enter the market when a stock makes a new low. They buy the new low, tick higher, and force the weaker short-term shorts to cover. Basically, they make pennies on many who are hitting the new lows in stocks. Let's discuss why this program, particularly below significant technical levels has not worked, will never work, and will be eliminated by the market.

I just want to say one thing about the dopey quants who employ this specific program: you are going to harm your firm. This program has not, cannot, and will not work. You need to take this program and toss it out with your left-over pizza boxes from Friday (for the retail traders, trading firms bring in pizza for traders on Fridays). And let me be clear, I am only writing about this one program, when stocks have broken very significant support levels. And obviously, we have a great deal of respect for the brilliant quant traders who run profitable ingenious algorithms.

One, it took us about a second to decode. Two, you can't play games like this below important levels. What are you going to do if a huge institutional order for millions of shares enters the market and you are caught long two hundred thousand shares as SAC Capital or T. Rowe Price hits the crap out of the stock for five points? Because a stock below a secondary price can cause panic selling.

What exactly is going through those brilliant mathematical minds of yours? Did they teach you this at algorithmic trading camp? Do you have so little regard for the market that you will disobey fundamental trading rules to make a few pennies?

Didn't firms like yours lose enough money when you tried these tricks when the subprime mortgage mess first hit? Your firms or firms like yours were decimated because you tried to get long very weak stocks when they made new intraday lows and force short-term traders to cover (think CFC . . . oops). For those at home, the programs bought the new intraday

---

* This section was adapted from a June 14, 2009, posting on Bella's Blogs (www.smbtraining.com/blog).

lows in the CFCs because they knew short-term traders would get short. The programs would buy and then quickly tick higher, trying to force the short-term day trader to cover. This did not work. Large institutional orders flooded the market. When the programs tried to uptick, the large institutional orders whacked some more of their bids and went low offer. The programs were forced to scramble and get out of their short-term positions. These programs recognized tremendous losses. These programs were eventually shut off by their firms.

Didn't you, your friends, or quants like you lose enough money when you tried this nonsense next with the financials? The financials made new intraday lows and you turned on the same dopey program. That didn't exactly work in GS, MER, LEH, BAC, and AIG. Again, oops.

I know a lot of traders who cannot trade against algorithmic programs and have been forced out of short-term trading. All it takes is some effort and thought to learn how to trade against them. There are things we teach to combat the programs. And I personally don't have a problem with programs trying to make spreads and quick money. I do have a problem with quants who have such a fundamental disregard for the risk of buying stocks that are technically broken. I do have a lack of respect for strategies that disobey very basic fundamental trading principles such as buying stocks below significant support levels. I do take issue with quants who keep trying failed techniques.

To the quants above, I understand that your math skills are genius. But superior math skills absent trading skills will not be rewarded by the marketplace. You are like an annoying gnat that requires nothing more than some bug spray. You are like that guy everyone can't stand on their pickup basketball team. You shoot every time down the court. You score a ton of points and your team with more talent loses. And then you think you have had a good game. Develop a new program or the market will eliminate you.

As I mentioned, this was just a rant. I was purposely rantish. Steve called me in a huff worrying about my incendiary tone after publishing these thoughts. I told him to go back to eating his oatmeal with walnuts and reading the Sunday *Times*. I wanted to start a discussion in the trading community (by the way our blog traffic climbed 2,000 percent on that day). And I sure did as this blog was linked and passed along to influential trading bloggers.

Since the inception of programs it has become harder to Read the Tape and thus trade because of HFTs. This is just something as traders we must learn to adapt to. The Buy the New Low Program discussed above is annoying but easily dealt with. But admittedly, there were more difficult programs which we compete against. Let's examine another day where adjustments needed to be made to trade against the algos.

High Frequency Trading and AMZN

On July 24, 2009, we had such an example of HFT that I have learned to avoid.* At 86.60, @smbcapital tweeted: "if you want a good example of HFT manipulation watch $AMZN around 86.60."

HFT was dominating trading around this level. I could not read whether AMZN would trade higher or lower. And my charts were not definitive.

A few times I thought I could Read the Tape and made plays around 86.60. The results? A short-term short in front of 86.60 ended in a loss of 25c (and my entry and exit prices were much worse b/c I couldn't get this seemingly liquid stock at the price I preferred). A long above 86.60 ended in a small loss. Ok, so now I see a pattern. The short-term longs are losing and the short-term shorts are losing. And our losses are greater than normal.

Now I had a choice. I could continue to pretend that I could compete against these difficult programs at this price. This undoubtedly would have concluded with me giving back all of my gains. Or I could choose a different path. And so I tweeted: "a great example also of when we shouldn't play in AMZN around 86.60 bc of HFT manipulation. Wait 4 it to trend then play, but not now."

I waited for AMZN to pick a direction. Around 86.40, I could Read the Tape again. AMZN was most likely headed lower. I reshorted. And I caught a nice move down to 85.90.

HFTs makes our trading more challenging. There are setups and time periods we need to avoid, such as AMZN 86.60. But trading is trading. We look for strong stocks and get long. We search for weak stocks and get short. Yes, HFTs shakes us out of more positions. Yes, it is harder to get stock. And yes, it would be nice if HFTs were not as prevalent. But guess what? HFT is here. And it will only grow. So as a trader I must adapt.

But we as traders can limit their impact through our own trading. We can choose not to play when HFTs eliminate our edge. If you go to a local restaurant and they charge too much for what they offer, then most of us choose not to revisit. And we can do the same when we spot HFT. If you do not play, then they cannot take your money.

Now that does not mean that adjustments should not be made to HFT. There are solid arguments being proffered that changes must occur. Manipulation has no place in the markets. And we should all have access to the same order flow. The market should reward the best traders and not those with an unfair advantage, such as access to exchanges some of us cannot reach. But we can all still compete, even with all this HFT.

---

*This section was adapted from a July 25, 2009, posting at Bella's Blogs (www.smbtraining.com/blog).

When we went to 1/16ths back in the day, I heard this was the end of intraday trading. When we transitioned to pennies, I heard that it was all over for the intraday trader. When Hybrid was introduced, this was supposed to be the final nail for us. When programs entered our markets, this was supposed to manifest our dissolution. Some traders were forced out during each of these changes. But good traders adapt. They find new patterns to exploit. HFT will not be our ruination. It is just another market challenge that we must learn to overcome.

I would like to see some changes made to HFT. But you know what? If things remain the same, then I will adapt. Today I am at the office (on Saturday), ripping through some charts for excellent setups on Monday. And now that SPY closed above 96.10 on heavy volume, I like the way the market is set up. This is a market overflowing with opportunity. I will figure out how to make money even with the HFT. I am a trader (see Figure 8.3).

Look, algorithms and HFT are here to stay. As traders, it is our job to exploit patterns and profit. We don't complain. We don't enumerate all things unfair in the trading universe. First, it would take us too long to complete this list. Second, that does not make us money. We take money from the markets by finding patterns, improving our skills (such as our tape reading skills), and adapting. Trading is a tough job. Algorithms and HFT make our job tougher. But we have learned to manage them. And so can you.

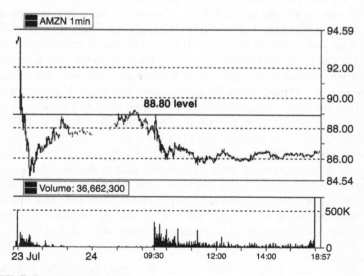

FIGURE 8.3 AMZN 7/24/09

READING THE TAPE 101

"There is only one side to the stock market; and it is not the bull side or the bear side, but the right side."

—Jesse Livermore

When we Read the Tape, we determine whether there are more buyers or sellers at a given price. We carefully watch order flow. We search for what we call held bids and offers, and unusual volume done at the same price that creates a key intraday level. Let's get to some definitions.

A Held Bid

A held bid is when a buyer buys 5–10 times more shares than we had expected on the bid. For example, if a stock creates a pattern where it does 5k shares on the bid before dropping and then 50k shares print at the same price on the bid and the bid does not drop, then this is a held bid. This is information that a huge order may be present. Why is this guy buying so much at the same price on the bid? Probably because he has a lot to buy. It is not 100 percent determinative that he has a huge order, but it is important information that he probably does. And if we spot a held bid often, we get long.

An Important Intraday Level

I make my best trades after I spot unusual volume at a particular price. We watch a stock trade and every 5k shares causes the stock to move up more than normal. And then say a quarter million shares are done at the same price (or around this price) and not in one singular print, for a Stock In Play. I am now interested. This is called an important intraday level.

The trading play after spotting an important intraday level? If the stock ticks above this level and bids hold, then I am long. If the stock ticks below this level, and the offer holds, then I am short. I am holding this trade for a longer-term intraday trade, say a few hours, instead of a few minutes. I expect the stock to move significantly away from this level. There was a huge battle. Now the fight is over. And now the stock needs to go find a new price. That might not be for a few points. So I hold.

The key to being a tape reader is locating where most of the volume is being done intraday. This volume may not show up on your charts until after a significant move. Remember, charts are at their core lagging indicators. Reading the Tape is a leading indicator. Use an unbiased principle to play both sides and be mentally agile.

So I am long when bids hold and our stock is in an intraday uptrend (unless the stock is near significant technical resistance), and short when offers hold and our stock is in an intraday downtrend (unless the stock is near significant technical support). To be most accurate, there are a few exceptions to the above but this then would move beyond Reading the Tape 101.

So often in the business of equities trading, there is a long bias, mostly perpetrated by the mutual fund and 401k industrial complex, and sales-focused commercials for T. Rowe Price of people running on the beach and the sounds of a baseball bat hitting singles. Do not let the popular financial media and fee-hungry asset managers influence you. That's not what we do as traders. A long hold for me is five hours, not five years. Make sure this is in your head when reading the tape.

PUTTING MORE TRADING PLAYS IN YOUR QUIVER

Intraday Prop Traders caught a nice trade in RIMM on the Open in the spring of 2009. We used an intraday support level from the previous trading session to start a core long in RIMM the next day. Again, we based this long thesis in tape reading. Let's discuss.

RIMM had finished up over 20 percent on a Friday afternoon. RIMM had trouble trading above 60 into the Close but still finished impressively. During the Midday, 58.50 was a huge level. This level was violated only temporarily when the market was weak on this day. The moves through 58.50 looked more like a shakeout. Yet RIMM did not trade below 58.31 on this Friday during this temporary move below 58.50. Then RIMM reheld the 58.50 level and traded toward 60, where its momentum ran out of juice.

After a long look at the prints on this Friday, we came up with some important levels. Sixty was resistance. Fifty-eight point fifty and 58.31 were support. On the following Monday, the market opened negatively and RIMM followed lower. RIMM opened below the 58.50 level, traded below the next support at 58.31, so I got short. I noticed too much buying at 58.25 and 58.20. If RIMM was weak, it would have traded down quickly below the 58.31 level. It did not. There was buying at 25c and 20c. There especially was some buying at 58.20. There was significant volume at 58.20. The 58.20 level held (see Figure 8.4 and 8.5).

For new traders, this can be a tricky trade. RIMM is below 58.31, the support level. Almost always we do not get long below support levels. But there was significant buying just below it. The tape communicated that RIMM was strong. I flipped my position and started a core long position. RIMM opened lower mostly because of the market. But significant volume

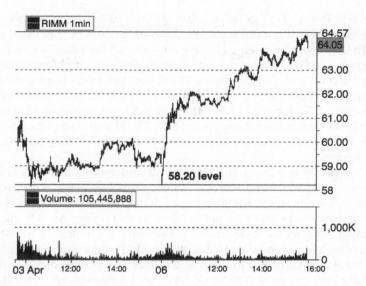

FIGURE 8.4   RIMM 4/3/2009 and 4/6/2009

was done at 58.20 and that level held. This is what an intraday bottom can look like.

This is a great example of why learning how to read order flow is most important when you begin. Learning this teaches us that the move below the support level, 58.31, did not signal a true breakdown. I did not just blindly short below the technical support level and expect that RIMM could

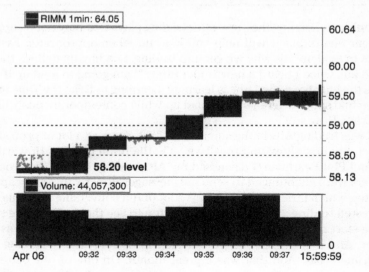

FIGURE 8.5   RIMM Open 4/6/2009

only trade lower. That is not trading. That is called being stubborn and overly simplistic, if not arrogant. If only trading could be that easy.

We trade with an open mind. We consider all the possibilities for how a stock may trade, during our every trade. We constantly evaluate if we are just wrong with our positions. There was too much buying below the support level. There was a held bid just below the support level. The short time period RIMM traded below the support level gave us pause to trust a break. So we got long. Now remember, RIMM was exceptionally strong on the prior Friday. Stocks after days like that one Friday tend to trade much higher.

Also, RIMM is a stock that we can all understand. The Blackberry is an awesome product that many of us use. This is an easy story to get as traders trading its stock. RIMM is one of the top five technology companies (though this could change by publication, as technology quickly changes). Top companies, with easy stories to understand, get bought en masse. With good news, hedge funds, mutual funds, the big banks, and retail investors want to own this stock. And I did. And others on our desk did as well.

Sixty was our next resistance level, so I lightened up in front of 60. Sixty did not offer much resistance that day so I reestablished a core long position. I lightened up near 62.75 into the Close as this offered resistance. I reestablished above 62.75. I held my core into the Close where I exited at 64. After all, RIMM had shown us no evidence that the top was near.

WHEN AND WHERE TO "LOAD UP" AND STILL LIMIT YOUR RISK

Not only can Reading the Tape offer trading plays that may not be apparent on your charts but it will help you load up when appropriate. Everyone wants to load up. It's why we get into trading. Loading up defines the thrill of the kill. Once I heard a new trader utter, "I am going to load up if ARCA holds the bid above 75c." She is learning. Learning to Read the Tape enables you to find spots where you can load up while contemporaneously limiting your risk. How so?

I was trading AIG in the summer of 2009. So were a lot of prop slayers. In fact, my first show on StockTwits TV, the brain child of Howard Lindzon and Phil Pearlman, I discussed my AIG trading. During the broadcast, viewers were encouraged to send me messages directly to @smbcapital on Twitter, which I tried to answer. It is a lot of fun conversing with this highly interested trading audience. And it was fun to see the desk trading so well at the start of August 2009. June had been a tough month. July was much better. And this August started like August of 2007, the beginning of the subprime crisis. And that was a great month. On one of our better days in August 2009 we traded AIG, the home builders, and ETFs. And AIG offered an excellent Trades2Hold that we should discuss. We spotted this by Reading the Tape around a key inflection point.

AIG opened and quickly traded down a few points to 25. It started a range between 24.90 and 25.10. AIG seemed to break out above, but it was a fake breakout. And then AIG appeared to break down below 24.90. But that was a fake breakdown. Greeeeat! Those damn quants are trying to steal our money again!

I started the day getting caught in a fake breakout and then a fake breakdown. Those PhD programming punks (geniuses?) were at it again. But the trading day doesn't end until 4 PM, so there was time to make it back. The nonsense of really just above 25 and below 25 continued some more.

But I hung in there. I kept my losses at a minimum. And then it came. The bullish flag was created. A gift from the trading gods had been delivered. I had a setup to crush.

AIG finally made an explosive move above 25.30, the intraday resistance, traded strongly on high volume to 25.75, and consolidated. As GMan would say, "It's party time."

AIG met some resistance at 25.75 but really, it was accumulating stock for its next upmove. By Reading the Tape I could see its strength. The pullbacks were nominal after an explosive upmove. When I bid for stock, I was immediately cut in front of by anxious buyers. It was impossible to get hit on the bid, a bullish signal from the tape that AIG was soon to trade higher. Would it?

AIG held above 25.75 finally (see Figure 8.6). By watching the bids, I saw that the buyers were now in control above 25.75. The bids were hit but holding and stepping higher. Again a bullish signal that buy orders were overwhelming the sellers and we were soon to be headed higher. If the bids had been quickly hit and they dropped below 25.75, then I would have had a signal that AIG was not ready, and GMan's party had not yet arrived. But the opposite occurred. The bids held, and they were stepping higher. Now was it Party Time?

Fortunately for GMan and the rest of us, it was. AIG started an uptrend to 29. This was a trade you must be in. Not only did Reading the Tape offer an opportunity to add more size but my risk was limited as my stop was just below the 75c inflection point. Furthermore, the held bid above 75c was my catalyst to pounce. So I knew to load up, had minimal downside, saw where and knew exactly when to load up because of my tape-reading skills. This is a powerful trifecta for the intraday trader. Long above 25.75 as a Trades2Hold was the play. And I loaded up because the tape confirmed what my charts were indicating. But still, to be safe, I needed to see the bids hold above 25.75. I was able to buy three lots when the tape signaled that

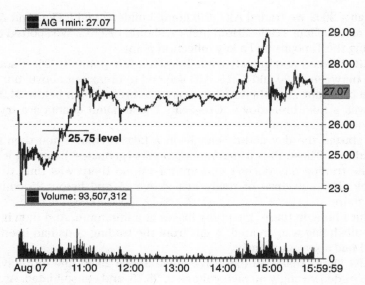

FIGURE 8.6   AIG 8/7/2009

AIG would trade higher. And I limited my risk. If the bids dropped the 75c then I would have hit out of two lots and started over. So now I had a large position, I had protection and a very tight stop that would have indicated my trade was not yet ready to work, and I never had to sweat.

AIG quickly traded higher. I was in the money every second of my trade. All because of reading the tape. (Have I not said that enough in this chapter? I'll say it again, all because of reading the tape.)

If I had just followed the charts I may have bought 75c and got shaken out below 50c, as occurred. But since I waited for the bids to hold above this key inflection point, I did not get shaken out, I had a nice position, and I was never out of the money. That is being in a position of strength as a trader. And I made a chop!

A LOVE AFFAIR WITH CHARTS

One of my favorite prop trainees at a nearby firm never bothered to learn how to Read the Tape. He loved his charts too much. All those deep reds and glorious greens were breathtaking to this young trader. To him, they never lied. But he was not trading. Trading is making plays where you have a statistical advantage of profiting. He was rolling the dice, effectively gambling. But it gets better. He did not even know how to read the charts! Like many developing traders, he thought he did. So he failed.

I received an e-mail one night during an epic Cavs/Celtics playoff game. I have to admit I was more interested in the game than responding to this e-mail. But I took a swing at it the next morning.

> Hey Bella,
>   This morning when you were trading USO on the Open and buying at the 32 level, initially 32 had dropped but you mentioned to someone else who was also trading USO that you did not hit out because you wanted to see the offer hold below 32. What was the reason for giving USO that little bit of time to see if it would hold an offer below 32 as opposed to just automatically hitting the bid once 32 dropped the way you normally would? Was it something you saw on the tape or was it just because 32 was a really important level and wanted more confirmation than just a bid dropping for the first time?

> My Response:

> I bought USO just in front of 32 yesterday a few times. Thirty-two has been a significant support level in USO recently. The first time USO traded up toward 30c, it slowed and I sold half. I bought some back when USO traded near 32 again. The bid dropped 32 and USO showed me the 98c bid. I did not hit it. Thus the question above.
>   I keep tight stops. I was long USO because 32 was the support level. So why didn't I hit USO when the bid dropped 32? Good question. My exit plan was not to hit USO until the offer held below 32 or the 31.95 bid dropped. Stocks often pretend to break levels and then trade much higher. I did not want to get shaken out in a fake breakdown. Further, I was holding USO for a large move. USO had bounced off of 32 the day before and hit 80c and even the whole a few times. This intraday there was some resistance near 32.50. So my upside at a minimum was 50c, perhaps 80c to $1. My risk/reward was still more than 5×1 if I gave USO to 94cish.
>   But there is a much bigger issue here. And it is something that we preach on our desk daily. Do not fall in love with charts. The order flow is more important than any chart. Use your trading skills to supplement your chart reading. Since I did not see an aggressive seller before that first time USO dropped the 32 bid, I did not hit out. If I had seen the seller, I would have been quicker to hit out.

It is easier to learn how to Read the Tape, or at least learn how to Read the Tape for signals to buy or sell than to learn how to trade with just charts. The traders I know who mainly trade off of the charts these days all learned first how to Read the Tape. And while they claim that they do not look at the Level 2 much these days, many are just mistaken. They have so mastered reading the tape that they do not even understand that they are using it to lighten up or where to enter with their trades.

GMan was offering his thoughts on a particular trading day on his Friday spot on StockTwits TV. After his appearance, I heard through back channels that young ladies from the StockTwits community started asking, "Who is that GMan guy?" Oh, to be young and single.

GMan discussed BBT. He highlighted a bullish chart pattern. BBT offered the opportunity to exit anywhere from 26.50 to 27 (see Figure 8.7). GMan started his position at 26.50 because he spotted the bid buying and holding at this price. He saw the bullish chart pattern and then found the best price with his tape-reading skills. If he had started his position at 27, this would have completely changed the risk/reward for this trade. If he entered at 26.80, he may have been shaken out of his position. But after he saw the buying at 26.50, he loaded up and was able to catch a significant upmove with size. Who is better than you, GMan?

Using charts is an art, not a science. It takes years to become a great chartist. As an example, I knew one prop trader at it for a while. He never

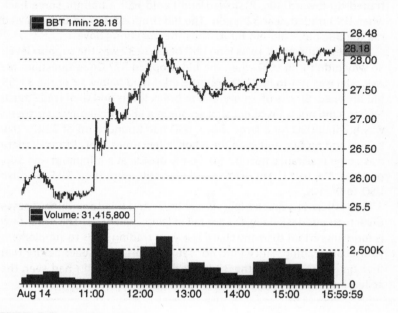

FIGURE 8.7 BBT 8/14/2009

made money! We would periodically IM about trading and I could tell he had no idea how to Read the Tape. He was absolutely mesmerized with his charts. He couldn't decipher a held bid from an orange. He failed.

Another trader I knew after a year proclaimed, "I have trouble reading the tape. It just is too fast for me to pick up." He didn't make it either.

I just don't get why people fall in love with their charts. There is so much more information from the prints, inside market, than the charts for short-term traders. And for long-term traders, reading the tape could dramatically improve their entry prices. How much more money would long-term traders make if they improved their entry prices making more per trade? And how much more would they take home if they improved their win rate by starting their positions at better prices, decreasing the trades in which they were stopped out? Much, much more! Again, it is like people are more interested in staring at their pretty charts than in making money.

If I told you I could offer information that would help you increase your win rate for trades, wouldn't that interest you?

Gary B. Smith in *How I Trade for a Living* offered some very interesting thoughts on charts:

> *Charts just weren't getting it done for me. They were great at telling me about the past, but were of little use in foretelling the future. Some who worship at the altar of charts may counter that the purpose of charts is not to predict, but to provide hints or clues to the future. Regardless of the semantics, I would have been much better off never looking at a chart. So it wasn't a tough decision in the spring of 1985 to throw out the charts and never consult them again.*

William Eckhardt, from *The New Market Wizards*, written by Jack Schwager, commented, "Most things that look good on a chart—say, 90 percent—don't work."

But with Reading the Tape, you can profit from Day One. In fact it's very simple. When we find a stock in an uptrend and then spot a held bid, this is a long. Easy, no? It will work more times than not. When you spot an important intraday resistance level cleared, you get long. Again, not difficult. And on the first day you trade live you can crush this simple pattern.

Mind you, do not discount the use of charts. We use them all the time. But it is hardest to start your career by relying solely on the charts. And the guys who do are great chartists. But remember, they have deeper pockets, so they can withstand a drawdown that you might not be able to. Please understand just how good they are at reading charts, and the years of experience it took staring at hundreds of thousands of charts to achieve this expertise.

When I catch some guys falling in love with their charts, I simply state, "All the best traders on our desk have learned how to Read the Tape. GMan, MoneyMaker, Dr. Momentum, JToma, The Yipster, Z$, Mr. Spencer, Franchise, G, Tickster, Roy. You will not become a good intraday trader if you do not develop this skill. It is up to you."

HOW DO I READ THE TAPE?

There are old school traders who have now transitioned to charts exclusively. Or so they think. They started reading the tape and then gravitated toward charts. But they still use their reading-the-tape skills. They undervalue these skills because they are so focused on their chart patterns. But they exit positions that are not working for them right away because of the tape. They choose entry points superior to lesser traders because of, yes, their ability to Read the Tape.

I know when I am making technical plays that I exit trades when I do not like the price action. I can just tell by the way a stock prints, or how the offers step down, if a stock may not hold an important technical support level. And so I exit. Sometimes my decisions are so fragile that if you pressed me, I could not verbalize exactly what I saw from the tape that made me exit. I kinda know it when I see it, based upon years of just watching the damn tape.

Every so often we invite potential candidates to visit our desk and sit in on a video review session. We were considering a middle-aged gentleman who had worked his whole life in IT at Goldman. On this Saturday, he sat watching film with our desk. As we watch, I will call out where a stock is a buy or sale so our guys learn where to buy and sell. After the class, this gentleman approached me.

IT Guy: "Mike, had you traded BBT on that day?"

Bella: "No."

IT Guy: "How did you know when it would go up and down? You kept predicting where it would trade."

Bella: "I was reading the tape."

He looked at me incredulously.

IT Guy: "But you were never wrong."

Bella: "I did have a good feel for that stock."

IT Guy: "That was incredible, how you did that."

(Did you really think I would leave this anecdote out of my book?)

If you are a trader who has started your career underperforming and have not developed the skill of reading the tape, then please do not get discouraged. And do me a favor, please. Go find your trading results, put them in the shredder, and move on with your trading career. It is too hard to start your career exclusively by reading the charts. If you do so, you are trading with the equivalent of one hand tied behind your back. You are missing an immensely important skill. Learn how to Read the Tape!

Remember that the best part of trading is that tomorrow you can start getting better. Well-rounded traders know how to Read the Tape. They also know all the little trading tricks to improve their P&L. A little something I like to call "Scoring," which will be discussed in Chapter 9.

Maximizing Your Profits with Scoring

S ome prop traders, as long as they take home a decent-sized check every month, are content. Not me. And certainly not any of the traders I employ. There are always ways to squeeze more profits out of each trade, just by some basic tweaking. I call it "scoring."

Scoring, simply put, is the skill of maximizing your P&L. Professional golfers often comment, "I struck the ball solidly but I didn't score well." Fortunately for me, I don't have this problem. Generally, I don't hit the ball well, thus I don't have the opportunity to not "score" well. Similarly, a basketball commentator often differentiates a "shooter" from a "scorer." As a professional trader, you can make good trades during the month yet not maximize your P&L.

Do you score well?

There are steps that you can take to ensure that you are scoring well. You can sit at your trading station all month, with the same skills as those around you, equal preparation, the same market opportunities, but end up with a P&L far worse than the guy sitting next to you, despite all things being equal. Economists call this "ceteris paribus" for any Latin geeks reading this book. So let's discuss a few things that will help you maximize your trading paycheck at the end of the month. Let's discuss how to "score" as a trader.

SETTING YOUR MAXIMUM INTRADAY TRADING LOSS

First things first: set a max intraday trading loss. There will be days when you just do not have it. Most traders trade 48–50 weeks a year, five days a week. Is it likely that you will be on every single one of those days? As someone who's been doing this for over a decade, I can tell you outright, no.

Traders are on par with professional athletes, as our job is entirely performance based. Win or go home, so to speak. Remember that great Michael Jordan commercial when he talked about how many times he failed in his career?

"I've missed more than nine thousand shots in my career. I've lost almost three hundred games. Twenty-six times I've been trusted to take the winning shot and missed. I've failed over and over and over again in my life, and that is why I succeed."

Just like Michael Jordan was off on certain nights on the court, so will you be on certain days in the market. Why do you think coaches pull their players when they are not playing well? They are more harmful on the field than off. When you are underperforming, you are hurting your team and your trading business. You need a system to yank yourself over to the bench. A stop loss is your answer.

When you first begin, set your max intraday loss for half of your median gross P&L. So if you make $1,000 gross on a median positive day, then set your maximum loss limit at $500. As you become more experienced, you can adjust this max loss limit to half of your last best trading day. But even the most experienced trader must set a limit.

Over the years, I have learned to become a very consistent trader. But in the Fall of 2008 I was having a horrid day. I got caught in multiple reversals—my kryptonite—and was down a lot for me. Make sure whatever trading platform you use has a loss limit feature. SMB uses LightSpeed, the best intraday equities platform available as I write. We had switched from another platform to LightSpeed about 12 months before this ripper of a day. And on this day, I went to enter some new orders. They were not going in. Then the following transpired:

Bella: Anyone having trouble entering orders?

Steve: Not me.

GMan: No problems, Bella.

Bella: What the (expletive deleted)! I still can't enter my orders.

The Enforcer: Did you hit your loss limit?

Bella: I don't even know what my loss limit is.

So I called up the LightSpeed help desk. Sure enough, I had hit my loss limit, but didn't know it. It took me a year on LightSpeed to have a day where I was marked down enough to even learn that I had a loss limit. Hey, I told you I am a consistent trader.

Bella: Can you raise my loss limit, please?

**LightSpeed
Help Desk:** Ok, have your manager call in the request.

Have my manager send in the request? This is one of those moments where you quickly calculate three responses. Two are not appropriate (One might be, "I am too rich and famous to deal with this nonsense, son. So get me some more buying power, pronto.") And then there is a third, which I chose.

Bella: Aren't I the manager?

**LightSpeed
Help Desk:** I don't know, are you a manager?

Bella: You know, I would hope so at this point, but on some days based on how my desk ignores me, sometimes I wonder.

The nice young man at the Help Desk raised my loss limit (apparently, I do have manager status). It had been much lower than half of my last best trading day. And thanks to my Lightspeed interlude, I actually saved thousands since my dopey orders, if executed, would have manifested larger losses.

Steve has a tendency to exceed his max intraday loss. We have code words—just like when we were playing high school basketball—which if spoken by me informs Steve that he is done for the day. Since we are SO creative my code word to him is "Mr. Spencer." When Steve hears "Mr. Spencer" from me he knows to trade out of his positions and then shut it down for the day. This saves him thousands every month. Even the best of traders like "Mr. Spencer" have set loss limits. So should you.

TRADING BASED UPON THE TIME OF DAY

I tailor my trading based upon the time of day, the Open, Midday, or Close. Dr. Steenbarger coached Dr. Momentum that each time period should be treated like a different business. I trade with the most size, most frequently during historically my most profitable time period. Makes sense, no?

I trade best on the Open, meaning I make the most money on the Open. My trading statistics confirm this. As such, I increase my size during this time and make more trades. The Open tends to last about an hour. My stats also show that during the Midday, I do the worst. So I lower my tier size and keep my stops tight. I only make trades that offer the best risk/reward during this period, and make fewer trades. Into the Close, stocks are more directional, so I stick with those that are trending up or down in the last hour of the trading day. I raise my tier size from the Midday, but not as high as on the Open.

The Danger of Midday Trading

As I said above, the Midday period (11:00 AM–3:00 PM) is the most difficult and least profitable time of day for me. I am not alone. Why? The market is slower. There is less volume and liquidity. A small order can cause a stock to move much more than you would anticipate. More strange moves in which you are not able to quantify, such as a surprise news announcement, do not allow you to calculate risk/reward as you would normally. A good trader makes note of what time of day it is, when he trades most profitably, and adjusts his trading to fit such times.

There will be favorable risk versus reward opportunities Midday, but much of this time for me will be spent finding stocks to trade into the Close when the volume picks up. Below is a list of adjustments you should consider for Midday trading if this is your worst time period:

- Increase your intensity and focus.
- Lower your tier size to the lowest size of the day.
- Wait for great entry points.
- Take your profits quickly.
- Don't double down.
- Lower your loss limits to the tightest of the day.
- This is the most dangerous time of the day. A small order can move most stocks significantly.
- Be disciplined.
- Sometimes good trading is not trading at all.
- Stocks purposely appear tempting, yet are in fact not favorable risk/reward scenarios.
- Most importantly, gather information for the Close. Watch the stocks trade.

Search for trading ideas. Check www.briefing.com for economic news releases coming out. Gather some ideas from the traders around you. Find support and resistance levels, and set your alerts for these levels.

New and developing traders tend to overtrade Midday, and we see this on our desk. As such, we have implemented rules to regulate this. Basically, Midday is just for exploiting our best setups and gathering valuable trading information for the Close.

If you are overtrading during the Midday, you are not maximizing your P&L. In fact, it's a great time to give back a lot of the gains you might have made on the Open. Your numbers at the end of the month will not reflect your true trading potential. Make the most trades with the most size during the trading periods that statistically are most profitable for you. Money saved during your weaker trading periods is money earned.

CONSISTENCY

Everyone knows someone at some firm making a killing. Everyone. Even the new traders. And new and developing traders tend to overvalue this information. *I want to be like so and so* (Big Man on the Desk) *at XYZ firm* (Chops, Bank, and More Chops Trading, LLC) *who makes mid-seven figures*. These newbies then develop theories about how to become that trader and bank that "mid-seven figures." Oh, do they develop theories.

"I need to learn how to take pain" is one thought entering their minds. One of our guys, Playmaker, believes this. This drives JToma and the rest of the senior staff nuts. The fact is that most trades you make will start working for you right away. But the new traders also hold stocks that are trading against them longer because they mistakenly believe this is how you improve. But common sense tells us that when a stock trades against your predetermined exit price, holding it only increases the chances that you will lose even more money.

Baby Steps

Marc Sperling of T3 Capital, considered one of the great day traders on the Street, came to speak to our firm in the summer of 2009. Marc is one of those traders who everyone wants to be, probably because his annual P&L is among the highest of those in our tight-knit community. Marc counseled that becoming great takes time. There is a process that every trader must go through. You cannot skip steps. When he first traded, he was positive every single day. He made sure that each day he stepped outside his comfort zone to get a little better. He got better slowly, incrementally, while remaining consistently profitable. (Stepping outside one's comfort zone, while initially painful, pays great dividends down the road.)

New traders mistakenly think that losing $5k is how they will learn how to make $5k. This is not true. To make $5k, you must first learn to make $500 consistently. Then you can gun for $800. Losing $5k in a day when you begin only teaches you how to lose $5k and how to trade irresponsibly. As Bill Murray said in the film *What About Bob?*, "Baby steps, baby steps, baby steps."

I am amazed at the new traders who have never made over $10k in a month who do not recognize that 17/20 days at $700 a day is a pretty good month. (Do the math here: 17 days at $700 a day is $11,900. Assuming the loss limit is $500 a day, typical for a new trader, the three negative days take the total down to $10,400. Still not a bad month while just beginning). There are so many traders capable of doing this. Yet they do not achieve this goal because they are focused on making the elusive $10k in a day, an opportunity that is seldom available, given their undeveloped skills. This five-figure-a-day goal is counterproductive. Your goal is to make as much as you can as you are developing and improving, not to show how much you can lose by trying to be a trader you are not ready to be.

Here is what I see too often from my seat. I spot a new trader with the ability to make money. He has two solid days a week. So I know he can do it. But then there are two other days when he starts negative, gets more negative, and then finishes much more negative. If you can learn to eliminate one day a week from too negative to flat you can substantially increase your take-home.

If you look at GMan's numbers at the end of the month, he is generally gross positive 17/20 days a month. (Same with me for that matter.) This should be your goal while building your trading account. Ask yourself how much can you make at this point in your career so that you are gross positive 17/20 days in the month? Achieve this goal. And then next month start working on an incrementally better P&L. Remember, baby steps.

PROPER SIZING

There exists a myth that you need to trade with huge size to make significant profits. Loading up on size is called for at times when the risk/reward is in your favor, but you need to be able to handle the size. There is plenty of money to be made trading with modest size, especially in active stocks.

You can make a lot of money trading in and out of an active stock with small size. Likewise, you can lose a great deal of money trading in and out of an active stock with too much size. Develop your trading skills, build your trading account, and slowly increase your size.

TRADERS ASK: "DO HIGH RISK
PARAMETERS AFFECT YOUR
TRADING APPROACH?"

Let's take a look at this e-mail I received from a developing trader:

> Mike,
>   Since you are a consistent profitable trader, what would happen if you increased your positions in AAPL, for example, from 2,000 shares to 7,500 at a time? Can you follow your set of rules with 3.5 times the additional risk with the same comfort? . . . . At what point does your consistent trading have to change because of the unusual high risk parameters?
> Neal

When determining my trading size I calculate first where I can exit if I am wrong. Remember, traders first have to ask themselves before entering a trade, "What's my downside?" I can often get out of 1,000 shares for a small loss. Rarely can I exit that same trade with 5,000 shares in an AAPL at the same price. And if this is the case, then my trade is completely different. I repeat, when making a trade our downside should be a ratio of 1 with an upside of 5. If with my extra size I now cannot exit with the same risk/reward ratio, I almost always cannot add this extra size. Also, it is a lot easier to exit if a stock trades in my favor for 1,000 shares than 5,000 shares. If it will be harder for me to exit if my position works for me with 5k shares, then I must factor this in as well.

Franchise: Finding Your Right Size

Listen in on this conversation between Franchise and me in the Fall of 2009:

Bella: What happened today?

Franchise: I am working on increasing my position size (by 100 percent). I can't figure out how to do this in some plays.

Bella: I like that. You will not be able to do this in all of your trading plays. To increase your size by that (100 percent) you will have to be more selective. You will not be able to exit that extra size while maintaining the same risk/reward with all of your trading plays. Some of them but not all of them.

We had an intern in 2008 who asked one of our traders why we just didn't Open all of our trades with 100k shares. Alan Farley said it well, "Experienced traders control risk, inexperienced traders chase gains." The intern did not last long.

When you trade with too much size, you do not prove that you can handle more size. All you do is prove you are not ready to handle this extra size. You should, as a trader, work on increasing your size with select trades. But again, this should be done incrementally. You cannot jump from 1k share positions to 5k without many steps in between. Again, do not pretend to be a trader you are not. The Steve Cohens of the world weren't moving markets on Day One with their volume.

And I know for certain that many readers trade with too much size on the wrong trades. My e-mail box is saturated with anecdotes of these mistakes. And you sit there discouraged because your results are being infected by these unwise trades. Sizing is a skill that must be learned, one that will impact your monthly results.

As you increase your size, your biggest obstacle will be psychological. Jonell Strough at West Virginia University in the *Journal of Psychological Science* highlighted the sunk-cost fallacy, a mental state in which you are more likely to make a poor decision the more you invest. You may see your position working in your favor and be tempted to take some off the table prematurely. Franchise has remarked to me that this is something he is still working on as a trader. This is a very common hurdle to clear when you first start sizing up. This will just require some visualization exercises. Simply spend five minutes every day visualizing these setups, manufacture the urge to lighten up (in as much detail as possible), expose the poor logic of so doing, and breathe through your fear. In a few months, you will rid your trading of these issues. Ari Kiev described this as skiing downhill and losing a little control of yourself, while maintaining overall control throughout.

WHY COMPARISONS CAN BE HARMFUL

Comparing yourself to another trader is not in your self-interest. Most successful traders are ultra-competitive, and it is human nature to want to be the best trader on the desk. But I just don't get it. Traders do not focus on how well they are doing, but rather compare themselves to other traders. This can be very harmful, and here's why.

If you read any history of business or Wall Street in particular, success tends to be measured relative to competition. But when businesses (and people) try to be something they are not, the results can be disastrous.

Just look at Lehman Brothers and Merrill Lynch, who tried to transform their businesses to be more like Goldman Sachs. How did that work out for them, again?

First, what makes you think that the trader you are comparing yourself to is in the same hemisphere as your trading talent? Just because someone sits next to you on a trading desk does not mean that his production has anything to do with your ability. Traders assume that since they are trained in a similar style and trade at the same firm, that they should do as well or better than the next guy. Let me be clear, the person sitting next to you, behind you, in front of you, a few rows from you is NOT you. They may miss trades that you don't. They may wuss out of trades that you don't. They may not see the screen as clearly as you. You are your own small business. How well you do depends on you, not comparing yourself to them.

This should be your attitude:

Steve: You are becoming the best trader on the desk.

The Yipster: I am?

Steve: You haven't noticed?

The Yipster: Honestly, and I don't mean to sound selfish, but I don't pay attention to what others are doing.

Steve once told me, "Before we started SMB, I never had any idea how others were doing. Cared how they were doing. Wanted to know how they were doing. What did that have to do with me?"

If you make $2k one day and you top the leaderboard for your experience level at your firm, this does not mean that you had a good day. You had a good day if you traded well. You had a good day if you took advantage of what the market offered you on this day. Who the hell cares what someone else on your desk did? What does that have to do with you? (You only care that one guy doesn't blow up all the firm's capital so that you can't trade any firm capital anymore. Otherwise, just focus on you.)

With all this said, there's a reason great traders have few peers. It's lonely at the top.

BE MENTALLY AGILE

If you develop a bias for a stock, and it trades the opposite of your bias, can you still make money? Of course you can. You just need to be mentally agile. This happens to Steve and me a minimum of once a week. We gather all the premarket information necessary. We have traded for over a decade. We are acutely attuned with the present market. Let's say we develop a short bias for FDX, yet it trades higher all day. We will still crush the stock. That's why we call it trading and not investing. I call this being mentally agile. Others might call it preferring to make money than be right. Once you get over this mental roadblock, becoming consistently profitable is within reach.

Traders are smart, strong-willed people. It is hard for them to admit when they are wrong. It is difficult to quickly take the opposite side of a trade. I am reminded of the applicable quote from legendary short-seller Jesse Livermore quite often, "There is only one side to the stock market; and it is not the bull side or the bear side, but the right side." While it's easier said than done, make sure you're on the right side.

Trading Both Sides

RMBS was In Play on a Friday in June of 2009 and we made some chops long on a slow summer day to its resistance, 17.80. Seventeen point eighty was an important technical level. RMBS collapsed from this level previously (see Figure 9.1). Seventeen point eighty was an inflection point for us on this Friday and on Monday. And we made money on both sides using our trading skills. Let's discuss.

Trading is not just about finding levels and then taking positions for most intraday traders. If it were that easy, you would not be reading this book. Trading skills enable the intraday trader to determine when some

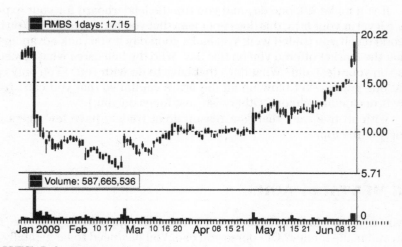

FIGURE 9.1   RMBS Jan 09–Jun 09

levels will be violated and when some levels will hold. We combine our tape-reading skills, with our charting skills and our short-term intraday fundamental analysis to determine which resistance levels will hold. For example, on this Friday we determined that the 17.80 RMBS level would hold because:

- There was more selling on the offer as RMBS neared 17.80
- There was a double intraday top at this level
- The longer-term chart showed significant resistance
- The buyers were hesitant to pay as aggressively above 17.75
- The news was not so important as to cause a violation of this significant resistance level on a first test

I lightened up with my intraday long position. Steve got short and caught a 50c downmove.

On Monday, we saw the strength from the tape in RMBS. The pull-back was shallow on Friday from the important resistance level. RMBS was heading toward the 17.80 resistance level again. The buying near this level Monday was aggressive. After 17.80 held the bid, we got long (see Figure 9.2). When the bid held 85c, we got longer. When the bid held above 90c, we got even longer. RMBS traded up another point. Chop!

We did not just rely on the charts to make decisions. We watched the order flow, used some fundamental analysis to weigh the new news in RMBS from Friday, and read our charts. Doing so allowed us to make chops on the short and long side trading RMBS on two separate days.

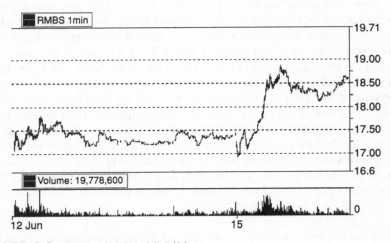

FIGURE 9.2   RMBS 6/12/09–6/15/09

When I write about reading the tape and learning how to trade, this is exactly what I mean. When I discuss developing trading skills to profit in any market, these are the skills that are necessary. Trading is not about making calls. Trading is not just about reading charts. Trading is about skill development such that you can trade a Stock In Play on either side. Just check out the trading in RMBS during these two trading days.

How Do I Make Money Today?

So, during our AM meeting October 13, 2008, Steve highlighted MS as his stock of the day.* Steve said, "I am going to look for a pullback right on the Open and then look for MS to trade in an uptrend for the day." Now that is what I call a great call. On the previous Friday, Steve mentioned MS as a stock to watch. He remarked that MS might see 18 during the trading day. Yet another great call. Steve played MS on the short side on Friday and MS on the long side today. He made money shorting MS on Friday and long MS today. So did our Head Trader, GMan, taught by us.

I preach for our traders to be mentally agile. We preach for our traders to follow the intraday trend on almost all occasions. SMB teaches its new traders trading plays that allow them to make money short and long. When I was taught how to trade, we did not watch CNBC during the day. We did not trade with charts. We had no breaking news feed. We were taught to watch the stock and determine its direction. Some of the most profitable traders on our desk could tell you Derek Jeter's road-batting average against right-handed pitchers on AstroTurf during the day. If you asked them the P/E of eBay, they probably would return a blank stare.

Now, obviously, times have changed. Charts, breaking news, and the backup vocals of CNBC is standard at most firms. But honestly, if you shut down my charts, turned off CNBC, and closed our breaking news feed I could still make plenty of money trading. I am a trader. If the stock were strong for the day, I would chop it up. If the stock were weak, my results would be similar. I don't care where a stock is going for the day. A short on a Friday of MS from 18 to 17.50 is the same as my long from 18.71 to 19.21 today. The first thing new traders can do to improve their results is stop pretending they have a feel for where a stock may go. It will take at least three years before you will be able to develop a feel just based on the news for where a stock may trade. Watch the stock and trade it. When it's strong, get long. When it's weak, get short. Your job is to make One Good Trade. Your job is not to make predictions. CNBC is not calling you up to make

---

*This section was adapted from an October 13, 2008, posting on Bella's Blogs (www.smbtraining.com/blog).

calls on the market or stocks. Leave your unbending biases and opinions at the door when you step on to the trading floor. Our trading floor is for traders. It's for those who can make money on either side. It's for traders who ask: How do I make money today?

It's Called Trading

Each day into the Close during the summer of 2009, our intern Krysten asked Steve to share a trading idea for our Twitter feed, which was shared with the StockTwits community of most interested traders.* On June 19, Steve told her that he would short AAPL below 138 but would cover above 138.15. AAPL had failed at the 138 level earlier in the day and had a significant downmove. Steve was risking 15c to make potentially $1.

About 15 minutes after he put on the short position AAPL began to hold the bid above 138.10. Steve covered his short and got long. Steve is somewhat reluctant to give our interns a trading idea each afternoon for Twitter because he recognizes that not everyone who follows our tweets is a professional trader who can capitalize on the important inflection points we identify. Brian Shannon, the leading momentum technical analysis expert in the trading blogosphere, shares these same concerns with his followers. The job of professional traders like Brian and Steve is to be mentally agile so that they can make money regardless of the direction of the market or the stock that they are trading. So when AAPL traded above his stop price of 138.10 and the price action indicated it was probably going to trade higher, then Steve got long. Other factors Steve considered were that AAPL had broken its intraday downtrend and it was trading above its afternoon high.

Within a few minutes of getting long at 138.16, AAPL traded up to 138.50, which had been a huge inflection point during the previous two weeks. Steve sold his long and in fact got short. Once he saw that an offer couldn't hold below 138.50, Steve covered his short. He got long again when the next upleg began. The next upleg was so powerful and on such heavy volume that I decided to hold 2,000 shares until the market closed. All of the evidence on his screen was indicating that there was a huge buyer that would not be satisfied until AAPL traded through its morning high of 139.13. AAPL traded up in the after-hours at 139.75 and Steve was still long 1,000 shares. Chop!

Another interesting point about the money Steve made long with AAPL is that he probably would have missed the entire move if he hadn't been

---

*This section was adapted from a June 19, 2009, posting on Steve's Blogs (www.smbtraining.com/blog).

willing to take the short position at 138. Observing the price action in AAPL while Steve was short gave him confidence to get long when it traded through his stop price. So the 15c loss he took on 1,600 shares allowed him to make about $1.50 on 2,000. I'll take that trade-off any day.

Trading is not about making market calls and being reliant solely on the accuracy of your biases. Trading is also remaining mentally agile and quickly absorbing that the market is sending a clear signal for the next move in your stock. Like today in AAPL above 138.10.

Amen Corner

Amen Corner often offers the most exciting holes of golf at the Masters.*
On April 9, 2009, 18.25 in WFC was our Amen Corner for WFC. There was an easy short below this level when WFC was in an intraday downtrend. There was an easy long when WFC held above this level when WFC was in an intraday uptrend. Let's discuss.

As intraday traders, we must be mentally agile. I couldn't care less where WFC finishes. When WFC is in a downtrend, then I look for opportunities to short. I shorted some WFC at 19 when it was clearly in a downtrend. I shorted some more when WFC broke to downside after consolidation at 18.50. I shorted some more when 18.25 sold a massive amount of stock. But then WFC's pattern changed near 17.50. The offers lifted quickly above 17.50. I had not seen offers lift quickly the entire downmove. Also, WFC stuck near the 17.60 level and did not make a new low. I had not seen this during the entire downmove. So I covered.

When WFC traded to 18, I shorted again. But when WFC showed me its strength holding above 18, I flipped my position. I started a long position. When WFC traded easily through the huge 18.25 resistance level, I added to my position. For the rest of the trading day, I bought into pullbacks, made the spread, and held my core long position.

I was mentally agile. When WFC was weak, I was short. When WFC was strong, I was long. For those interested in an excellent book on technical analysis that teaches the new trader the importance of following the trend, read Brian Shannon's book. I utilized the principles that Brian teaches to trade WFC profitably on this trading day. Though I can also not overlook the invaluable contribution that wearing my Masters Polo shirt, while trading that day, must have had on my results.

So the developing trader must learn to be mentally agile. Let's move on to another skill you won't learn anywhere but on a prop trading desk.

---

*This section was adapted from an April 9, 2009, posting on Bella's Blogs (www.smbtraining.com/blog).

STAY WITH IT

Consistently profitable traders get shaken out and then find a way to get back in to a good stock. Poor traders complain about getting shaken out. These lesser traders recall in detail how they were screwed. For example, I once had a conversation with a developing trader on our desk who got shaken out in OSK (chart below).

Developing Trader: Look what happened in OSK, Bella. I got long above the 18.80 level, OSK went to 19, and then had a sharp down-move to 18.67 where I hit the bottom (see Figure 9.3). What a screw job!

Bella: Did you get back in when it pulled backed to 19?

Developing Trader: No, I was done with it after that.

Well, ok. He got screwed. So? So does everyone else. Are you special because you got screwed? Do you think I, or the market, has any sympathy? That is not the approach you should take. A good trader hits the bid during the shakeout and takes his loss. But then the solid trader buys OSK when

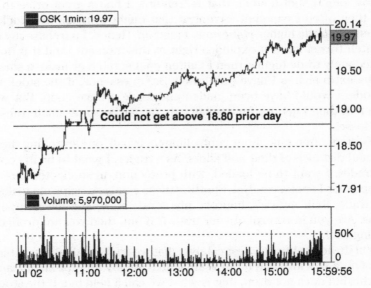

FIGURE 9.3   OSK 7/2/09

it trades above 19 again. And then a winning trader buys more when OSK pulls back to 19. The consistently profitable trader takes a loss during the shakeout but then catches OSK for a point upmove with two lots. And for those keeping score at home, that is a $2k gain minus a $250 loss. You can't ask for much better from a stock than that. A lesser trader's "screw job" is a consistently profitable trader's opportunity.

Some traders will require a few failed trades before they catch the move. This is the game we have all chosen to play.

IT MAY TAKE TIME TO GET ON THE RIGHT SIDE OF A TRADE

For the intraday trader, it is important to be on the right side of the stock *and* catch the move right before it happens. While easier said than done, there are reasons why this is true.

Understanding exactly what should make your stock move will enable you to load up at a given moment, and then if your stock does not start acting as you expect, you can lighten up immediately. Jesse Livermore counseled, "It isn't as important to buy as cheap as possible as it is to buy at the right time."

Essentially, as an intraday prop trader, I am buying very cheap options all day long. I spot a stock that is trending. I find a great price to enter. And then often I can spot a catalyst that ought to make my stock trade higher *and* trade higher *right now*. I load up. Hence, I purchase my option to catch this stock if it explodes right at this moment. And if it does not immediately trade higher, then I lighten up. I scratch or make a small gain on the extra shares I have purchased. So, in essence, if the stock was to explode, I would have been loaded and made a huge chop. But when it does not, then I get out for a small gain or maybe some small transaction cost losses.

Golfers often talk about controlling their ball, or controlling the direction and distance of their golf shots. As a trader, I want to be in control of my trades. I want to be loaded, with protection, in stocks that are trending up, after I spot a catalyst. Spotting these catalysts helps me make more in a trade, limit my risk, improve my consistency, and lower my mental stress. Are you in control of your trades? If not, then you are probably not scoring well.

On the long side, the best catalyst that we spot is called a held bid in an uptrending stock. When a bid is smacked quickly and for significant size, and this bid does not drop, that is what we call a held bid. If the stock was not strong, the bid would have dropped and the buyer would have bought cheaper. When we spot a held bid for a stock in an uptrend, we then add

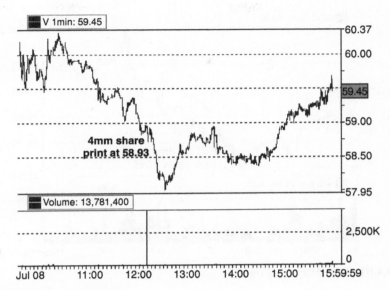

FIGURE 9.4 V 7/8/2009

size to our position and now expect an immediate upmove. This held bid foreshadows a large market order more times than not. And there are short-term shorts who are now caught on the wrong side who need to cover. We expect sellers to cover and the buyers to step up next.

But there are a series of catalysts, not just the bread and butter held bid in an uptrending stock. And these are different for the time period we are trading. But we must understand what makes our stocks go up and down so we can add size at the appropriate moment while minimizing our risk. Spotting catalysts helps us control our risk.

Another terrific example of a catalyst that I use is a huge print. The following is a chart of V where a 4 million share print went across at 58.93 (see Figure 9.4). Immediately after this print, V ticked down. I follow the direction of the ticks directly after such a huge print. I added to my short in V instantly after V ticked down, and held V to near its next support at 58. This was a chop. This catalyst helped me add to a position that was already working for me.

DEVELOPING IF-THEN STATEMENTS

For each of the trades that I make I develop if-then statements. For a Support and Resistance Trade, I have created if-then statements. Same

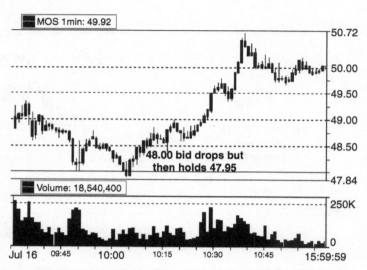

FIGURE 9.5   MOS 7/16/09

with a Momentum Trade. And that is not all. For the many subsets of each trade, I have also created if-then statements. There is just not one type of Support and Resistance Trade. There are at least 10 variations. For a momentum trade, there are a series of probable possible ways that a stock may trade. I have predetermined how I will trade this setup and in each possible way. And then after I spot the momentum trade, I have a framework for execution.

Let me give an example of when I was trading MOS. Forty-eight was support. I got long. If 48 dropped the bid, then I would exit. It did, so I exited. If there were a held bid just below 48, then I would get long again. At 47.95, there was a held bid, so I re-entered (see Figure 9.5). And I made a chop on this trade as MOS exploded higher. But what is most important is that I had predetermined plans of action with a handful of if-then statements. And I then I just did what I told myself to do. Simple enough, no?

Too many developing traders try to determine how to trade a setup in the middle of a trade. For the active intraday trader, In Play stocks move too fast for this. We do not have time to think about the best course of action intratrade. We have to determine our framework for options beforehand.

If-then statements should be different for each individual trader. We all process information differently. Some are faster. Some have a greater tolerance for risk. Some are more experienced. Some trade a different time frame. But I have considered all the different ways my stock may trade before I enter. So if my stock acts a certain way, I am not surprised. I have considered everything the stock may do. I may find a move to be unusual. But again, I have considered this. And now I just react to the trade I am ready for.

With well-developed if-then statements your results will be more consistent. I received a very disappointing e-mail from a college student who asked his professor about HFT and received "a half-hour rant on how intraday trading equities is reckless gambling." It can be if you do not develop thorough if-then statements. I will add a Warren Buffett quote here as well, "Risk comes from not knowing what you are doing." If-then statements help to make your trading more uniform on a monthly basis. Your results will be less based upon being right on a few big plays. With if-then statements and active trading, you, in effect, are running your own profitable gray box or black box in the marketplace.

Roy Davis: Director of SMB Remote Training

If-then statements are so important to the new trader that I was scolded by Roy Davis, SMB's Director of Remote Training, about their place in our training program. Roy felt that they were not being properly emphasized. And Roy started a heated debate internally about their best placement and insistence on trader compliance. Thankfully, Roy was right. We made improvements to our if-then statements analysis and location within our training program. We saw an immediate improvement in the results of our new traders.

Roy started this debate by proclaiming that the single most important task by the new trader during the first part of our training program is completing their if-then statements. In fact, he insisted our traders cannot go live unless they submit to their mentor their if-then statements for each trading setup. Not only do they have to submit their statements to their mentor, but their mentor must approve them, and communicate that to our Floor Manager. Now, no one trades a play live until their if-then statements have been submitted and approved by a mentor and our Floor Manager. And then after each week, our new traders adjust their if-then statements for the market they are presently trading, which is again reviewed by their mentor. It sounds pretty tedious, but this is the work required to compete.

We are always tweaking, adjusting, and rethinking our if-then statements for each of our trading setups. And no one enters a setup without understanding specifically, comprehensively, and automatically how he will trade each different setup. As Roy preached, this can make all the difference.

If-then Statements

Traders develop their own statements for Support and Resistance trades, but here are some good examples for new traders. Just to add some trader authenticity, they are not neatly written complete sentences that you would hand in to an English teacher. But they are all if-then suggestions for the intraday trader.

- If the 30 bid is tested, with significant volume on the bid, and holds, then... Get Long
- If the 30 bid holds with significant volume, then Trade2Hold
- If the 30 Holds, then ask who is the buyer?
- If the 30 holds and slows, then sell if the buyer is not near or thick offer near
- If 30 holds and slows and the buyer is near the offer, then hold
- If 30 holds and the bids step up, then consider another lot
- If 30 holds and the bids step up and hold higher, then add another lot
- If 30 holds and a ton of volume is done on the bid, then do not sell until a REASON TO SELL
- If 30 holds and a moderate or light amount of volume is done on the bid, then sell when slows, or significant upmove
- If 30 holds and then drops, then sell
- If 30 holds with a ton of volume and then drops, then sell and consider flipping
- Above 30 then long and below 30 then short
- If 30 holds and then drops, then the stock should trade lower and lower quickly
- If 30 holds, drops, and offers do not step lower to 30 or below and a significant bid is present at 29.99 or 29.98 or 29.97, then wait for the bid to decrement or disappear
- If 30 holds, drops, but significant bid within .03 and confident that you can hit that bid, then ok to wait for the bid to decrement or disappear if another bid right beneath at 29.96 or above
- If 30 holds, then drops, and there are some bids at 29.97 or 29.98 or 29.99 and the 30 offer is tested and holds, then get short
- If 30 holds and then drops quickly to 29.90 with a significant bid at 29.90 and you couldn't get out, then place order at 29.97 or lower, based upon your judgment to sell.

  a) Start at 29.97 and come lower quickly if not taken to 29.95

  b) Hit the 29.90 bid if can't get taken on the offer and bid decrements or little protection beneath the bid

- 30 holds and then drops and 29.90 is tested and holds the bid, then buy back and use 29.90 as support
- If 30 holds and then drops and 29.93 then holds on the bid after being tested, then buy back, and if 30 rebids and is tested and holds, then add another lot
- If you add a second lot, then trade the second lot as a momentum play and the first lot as a support play
- If 30 holds the bid and 30.03 holds the offer and 30 drops and you hit the stock and then the bid holds a little lower than 30 and then 30.03 lifts, then get long again
- If 30 holds and then drops and then rebids and is tested on the bid and holds, then get long again
- If 30 holds, then drops and rebids and the offer is not until 30.07 or better, then bid if underlying bid at 29.98 or better
- If 30 holds and you bid 30.01 and you can't get hit, then bid 30.02 and if you can't get hit, then consider taking 30.03
- If 30 holds and you bid 30.01 and 30.02 and 30.03 and you can't get hit and the offer is 30.10, then bid based upon the volume at 30

  a) The more volume the higher you can bid

  b) Risk versus reward should be 5 x 1

  c) If the volume at 30 indicates that the stock should trade to 30.50, then you can buy as high as 30.10

- If the 30 holds and the offer is 30.05 and you bid 30.01 and you are immediately joined, then this is a sign of strength
- If 30 holds and the offer is 30.05 and you bid 30.01 and are immediately cut at 30.02, then this is a sign of strength
- Best trades when you notice a ton of volume at 30 and the stock holds and then you step in front of the bid, get hit and hold until a REASON TO SELL

KNOWING YOUR BEST TRADING PLAYS

On a recent StockTwits TV SMB Unversity broadcast, I pounded the podium pleading, "To improve as a trader, you must determine which setups make the most sense to you! And then you must make more of them and with more size." Well, I know this is going to sound simple, but not enough traders make more of their absolute best trades. But how many traders truly understand their best trading plays and maximize the opportunities in these plays. Let me add some personal color to this section.

I do not make any trades with size, at any time, under any circumstances, in any market, (OK I am starting to pull a Michael Scott here from the TV show "The Office") no matter what is going through my mind, unless they are my best trades. I just don't. I know what my best plays are. I know exactly what I am looking for from the market. And I don't color the tape and my charts so that I falsely create a play that is not really one of my best trading plays. Call me a "Double Aces Only" player in Texas Hold 'Em, but unlike poker, I don't have to place a regular ante into the market. I can choose not to do anything and pay only for my infrastructure.

At the end of the month, I look at my trading results and I know that I did the best that I could. My month was spent in the trades that work best FOR ME. Knowing what my best is comes with experience. Now, not every month is outstanding, but what more can I do? I stick with my strengths. I risk my money on the plays that, statistically and historically, are most profitable for me. And this is how I score.

Here is one of my favorite plays. AMGN gapped up in the AM. It did not pull back much. Fifty cents as drawn on the chart below was a huge intraday resistance level (see Figure 9.6). And finally AMGN got above this level. I got long and loaded up with three lots. I sold one early because AMGN had not held above the level. I sold the other when it had trouble

FIGURE 9.6 AMGN 7/8/09

clearing the 80c level. But I held my last lot. And I was not going to sell this lot until there was a Reason to Sell (a predefined system for exiting our Trades2Hold).

I made a little on the first two lots but lost on the third. I cannot control the results. All I can do is make One Good Trade. And this was one of them. I was in complete control of this trade. I was loaded with one of my favorite setups. AMGN did not react as I had anticipated. But I can live with this trade. My job is to find these statistically profitable setups and execute. If I spend the month making thousands of trades like this, it will be an awesome month.

HOW TO END A TRADING SLUMP

We all slump. The problem is not slumping, but rather letting the slump last for an extended period of time. You must learn how to get out of the slump. Let's discuss.

One of our most competitive traders once initiated a meeting with me, apologetic about his recent slide. I laugh thinking about how many slumps I have been through in my trading career. How many times I have wondered if this was the end for me. Sometimes, I actually go home, sit on my couch, and wonder if I am capable of continuing as a trader. And I would say I have done this at least twice a year for the past 12 years. This is a healthy process, as long as these thoughts are then replaced by solutions. This is healthy because I do not want to feel this way. My personal disgust with my trading and inability to accept failure fuels an internal need to improve immediately. It forces you to focus on what you do best as a trader and then execute. You either get better or go home. Just like a pro athlete.

So, for this most competitive trader, I suggested that he make only his best trades for the next week, set a goal to just be positive, and lower his tier size. I wanted him to make things easier. He went right back to making money. This did not surprise me in the slightest. After all, I have 12 years of trading perspective.

One of our brightest traders was in a slump. We discussed solutions about lowering his tier size, sticking with his best setups, and visualizing a positive day. On the Open, I caught him with a large position in JPM the day after earnings on my risk monitor. I stormed over to his desk and ordered him, like a college basketball coach would to move the ball, to cut his position size in half. I reminded him that to get back on track he should cut his size, stick with his best setups, and just focus on being positive for the day. There are tricks to getting back on track. Letting a slump linger needlessly for an extended period can ruin a good quarter or in some cases, a good year.

Apparently, the prop trading public did not do as well in June 2009 as the spring of 2009 given the e-mails sent to me, phone calls I received, and anecdotes shared by other firms. Sometimes a trading year only offers 3–4 excellent trading months. The other months you grind it out and pay the bills. It is often in these other months that traders slump and dig big trading holes. Generally, this is because traders fail to adjust. They are trading with too much size for a slower market. They are assuming that setups that worked last month must work this month. They have unrealistic expectations for the present month. They are not making the best trades for them, and as a result they dig a hole for themselves.

June 2009 was a month that offered opportunity. Steve and I discussed why traders were struggling. A respected well-known trader friend of ours offered a hypothesis that traders had been too beaten down mentally from the fall of 2008 and the struggles at the beginning of 2009 to properly trade June. Interesting. But I have found that people have trouble shifting from struggling to making what they should because they undervalue the importance of confidence. You often just need to remind yourself that, yes, you can do it. You need to remind yourself of why you are a good trader. You must return to making only the trades that work best for you. Sure, the size of your winning trades may not be as big as they were in previous, better months. But you're winning again. Back to the sum of your best trades, the best of your trading.

If you have made money trading in the past, you will going forward with just a few adjustments. If you are a new trader and you do the things required, you will be fine. And the market is almost always ripe with opportunity. Anyway, I thought I would just offer my perspective.

THE CHEETAH AND THE TRADER

I had an interesting conversation with a young trader from another firm on January 15, 2009. This young trader pops into my office from time to time and talks trading. He is a very bright and competitive young man from the Midwest. And he was struggling. He killed it in October. But over the past two months, he has dug himself a huge P&L hole. I had been hearing a lot of stories like this at this time.

A trading friend of SMB told us that one of the best 10 traders we know gave back his whole year during this past month. While I was getting breakfast on this trading day, a few nervous young traders stopped me to ask how our guys were doing lately. They relayed that many in their firm were quite negative. I heard that a few Tier 1 day trading firms in January 2009 restricted trader losses going forward. I was at a holiday party the previous month and one of the best traders on the Street was practically crying to me about how badly he had been trading. I spoke with two energy traders during this exact time period at the Reebok Club in Manhattan who offered that they were probably going to be fired by their firms because of their losses. I know that for SMB, that month presented a challenge to some of our traders.

Personally, I don't have a bad month. I have traded through enough markets that I have created a trading system for myself that allows me to profit no matter what the market. That last month I was positive. And I will share what I shared with that young trader who was worried: You need more experience. You need to see some more markets. You need to make some adjustments. You need to go back to the basics.

One of our bright new traders, Joe P, who had been struggling, made a list of plays that he would focus on that month. Great work there. But there were a few plays on his list that I didn't even understand. They were technical plays that I did not use. And I will share what I told him. Trading is about finding weak stocks and getting short at levels that offer an excellent risk/reward. Trading is about finding strong stocks and getting long at levels that offer an excellent risk/reward. Do not make things so complicated.

We produced a video called "A Day on the Street," which tracks a trader for one day and was produced by Maureen Holohan from "$Game." On this video, you can hear me share, "The market offers you so much data to doubt yourself. And you must believe in yourself." And that is so true. The market provides you so much data that can convince you that you do not belong. But you must find a way.

There will be good runs and bad. Many traders had a nice run in October and November 2008. And from what I heard, December was an awful month on the Street for almost every trader. The good traders make the adjustments necessary and enjoy a long and prosperous career. And these adjustments are often minor. And those who don't find work elsewhere. That is the game.

It always amazes me how difficult new traders make trading. And during times like the above, the answers are simple. Go back to the basics. What trades work best for you? Make a list. Just make those trades for the next week. Make these trades with small size. What stocks are best for you? For SMB traders, it is the Stocks In Play. So make sure you are in these stocks.

JToma sent me a great quote on this subject: "The cheetah, while the fastest animal on the African plain and can outrun any of the prey it feasts upon, always chooses to go for the young, weak, or sick. Once identified, he/she attacks with laser-guided focus and effectiveness. It is only then that the kill is most likely. That is the epitome of a professional trader." Be the cheetah.

Having a slump is all part of the learning process. It is not supposed to be easy. Did you ever wonder why so few get to trade for a living? It is like joining this fancy golf club. They don't let everyone in. And to stay in, you must follow all the rules. Well, during this stretch those who were underperforming were not following all the rules. And the club doesn't like that. So they imposed a substantial fine on your membership. And now you need to pay it. Follow the rules and you will be back in good standing. Don't follow the rules and they will terminate your membership.

So, if you are underperforming, do not panic. The best part about this job is that the past is the past. And starting tomorrow, you can be positive every single day for the rest of the month. And have a great month. And then you can parlay that positive energy into an excellent quarter. And you are off to a great year. Along the way figure out the skills you need to better develop. Work on them every day. And the next time you underperform and need to go back to the basics, your list of trading plays will be longer.

When I first started, my account was negative $36k after six months. Eleven years later, I am still trading. How? I am a cheetah.

So this is how we score as intraday traders. Now if I could just get my jump shot to start falling again.

Let's take a peak inside a proprietary trading firm next and see what tools they use to improve their trading results.

PART IV

The Trader's Brain

CHAPTER 10

Trader Education

After I spoke at the 2008 International Traders Expo in New York, a well-dressed, older gentleman approached me and asked, "What is the advantage of joining a proprietary firm like yours? Is it the buying power you can offer?"

This Dapper Don explained that he had been trading for himself, and without hesitation proudly mentioned that he had been doing quite well. There was a hint of "What do I need someone like you for?" in Dapper Don's question. I liked his attitude.

I could only answer briefly, so I replied, "We do offer deeper pockets, which can help. But the main reasons are the ideas shared by our desk and the mentorship from experienced traders who have traded successfully for over a decade." I have been thinking about this conversation for some time now. I wish I knew this gentleman's name and could reach out to him. But my sense was that this developing trader was not sold on my response. So, to this impeccably dressed developing trader, I offer this chapter (and thank you, Dapper Don).

This chapter covers the main topics that make up our trader education program. We'll cover the reasons why it's beneficial for new traders to review their work, understand the emotions behind trading, and perhaps most importantly, find a mentor for much-needed guidance and support. These are just a few; read on for more.

USING VIDEO TO REVIEW TRADES

Traders, like athletes, should watch lots of trading tape. The best athletes and teams watch film of themselves to see what they're doing right and wrong, and how to improve. Word has it that New England Patriots head coach Bill Belichick, who has lead his team to three Super Bowl championships in the last decade, spends 12 hours at a time reviewing game film, all while scarfing down a whole pizza pie and a 2-liter bottle of soda. When asked what the first thing he would buy with his outsized signing bonus from the New York Giants, Eli Manning (now Super Bowl Champion quarterback Eli Manning), responded he would purchase a high-end video system to better watch film. By virtue of Belichick's meticulous analysis, his teams are often considered the most disciplined and best prepared.

I know of no other prop firm that does what we do, recording our screens as we trade and reviewing them later on like a football team. I'd like to think we are setting a trend, but it's up to our peers themselves as to how they wish to evaluate their traders' work. We hold three different Tradecasts: one on fundamentals, one for our experienced traders, and one for those not brand new but not yet experienced.

First, as the tape is rolling, I comment on what I see that is important on the trading tape (not to be confused with the video itself!). If I notice a big buyer from the tape (no longer literal ticker tape, it's all virtual at this point in time), I will point this out so our newer traders can learn. I watch to make sure our traders are trading with the trend. I make sure to point out spots where our traders are too aggressive. I mention trades that did not offer a good risk/reward and why. But like Belichick, what I most learn is what the trader most needs to improve. From watching a trader's tape I can see what errors he is making. Also, our traders get to watch how his/her peers are trading the same setups.

But my first goal for our Tradecasts is to teach our traders how to think. I challenge their trades. I ask them why they are long or short. I question their tier size. I ask them where they would add more. All that Socratic training in law school obviously paid off for something! Tickster describes this as "basically a trader getting mauled." They must understand the standard of thinking required to be a consistently profitable trader. And if that means these reviews are viewed as "mauling" their trade executions and egos, so be it. Remember, I am a trading coach. My job is to teach. Critical feedback is essential for trader growth. This is part of that process.

Trading setups change. Trades that worked one year ago, one month ago, or one day ago may not work ever again. On the flip side, trades that work the next day may be only slightly different from the day before. But if you learn *how to think*, and this is no easy task, then you can make these slight adjustments.

At SMB, as with most prop firms like us, we have a risk monitor. I can see the open positions of all of our traders at any given time. It's mine and Steve's money, as well as the careers of our rank and file, at stake here. We better have a risk monitor!

As I play Supreme Allied Commander with my all-powerful toy known as the risk monitor, I watch what stocks our traders are trading, while I am trading myself, and make sure they are not making fundamental errors. If a trader is shorting a strong market, I will call that trader out for fighting the trend. If a trader is in a stock that he cannot handle, I will order him to move on. If I miss something during the day, after the Close mentors review the work of new traders, who then brief me on the mistakes of these new traders. But I learn the most from watching the trading tape during the Tradecasts. Sometimes our guys are making mistakes that are not just putting their results into a recession, but rather into a full-blown depression. Let's meet G and Franchise to illustrate this point.

G: Improving Order Execution

G is one of the most likable guys on our desk. G never has a bad day in his life. Now he might lose money trading, but again, G never has a bad day. For G, every day the sun is shining. He also leads our desk in most vacation days taken.

G missed a trading day because he went to watch the Giants play Monday Night Football in Dallas. He missed one of the best trading weeks in 2008 because he found a great vacation deal in the Bahamas. He is one of the better-dressed guys on our desk in no small part from his two-week long visit to China, where he bought custom-made shirts. He also missed eight days of trading because he had to attend the Auto Show in NYC. I'm not sure, but does the Auto Show even last for eight days?

And, of course, who could forget this next anecdote? Steve and I got invited to attend a holiday party for another prop firm with whom SMB shares a close relationship. This firm asked us if we wanted to also invite some of our traders. We invited G. This might have been a mistake. G apparently hit on the wife of a partner of the firm that had invited us (he claimed ignorance).

Now that I am done teasing G, G is someone with whom I really enjoy working. He is, save Steve, the trader on our desk most interested in the markets. And when he isn't in the Far East, the Bahamas, Texas, or the Auto Show, he is one of the hardest workers on our desk.

G sits right next to Steve, who, if I haven't said so already, is an excellent teacher. A seat next to him is like a seat right behind home plate at Yankee Stadium, assuming you are not offended by the $2,500 price tag per seat. Steve provides a play-by-play of his every trade. And he trades all day long. Steve constantly attempts to get those around him into stocks that are moving.

In December of 2008, G was struggling with his trades, so we watched some of his tape. He had traded well that autumn, so his recent struggles were an enigma. After watching the tape of his trading, it became so clear why he was struggling: he was sweeping too much and not bidding and offering enough.

To sweep means to pay the offer plus a little extra, with that "extra" determined by you. So if the offer is at 30, then your sweep key will take the first trade it can at 30 and to as high as your sweep key is set. So, for example, if your sweep key is .04, or 4 cents, then your sweep key will attempt to buy at 30. If you do not get filled exactly at 30, then it automatically tries to take the offer at 30.01. If it cannot get that price, then it automatically sweeps at 30.02, then 30.03 if it could not get 30.02, then 30.04 if it cannot get 30.03. You also have a sweep key to sell. So if the bid is 29.90 then your sweep key will try to exit at 29.90, then 29.89, then 29.88, then 29.87, then 29.86. If you get the 29.90 print, then you are done. The key allows orders to be sent into the marketplace to get you the best price possible up to 4 cents. With a fast moving market, this is essential.

We watched some tape of G trading AAPL. He had found an important support level. And AAPL was trading a little above and a little below this support level. G was trading it on both sides. Below the support level, he was short, and above the support level, he was long. But we noticed in three quick trades that he had cost himself an extra $170 by sweeping when he should have been bidding or offering. To bid for a stock means you place a limit order at a specific price. For example, you place an order to buy AAPL at 75. You will only get AAPL if some market player hits your bid in AAPL. You can also offer AAPL for a specific price to sell. If you offer AAPL at 75.50, then you will not get this sale unless some market player takes your offer at this price.

Instead of buying AAPL at 75, G was sweeping and starting his position at 75.07. Instead of selling out of AAPL at 75.05 he was sweeping out at 74.93. And he kept doing this around this support level. Mind you, $170 is not a lot of money to lose for a trader of G's skill. But what was significant was that for the same trades, he could have saved $170. And this was three trades. Now, as active traders, we may write 2 million plus shares per month. Just to do some simple math, if you save just 1c every trade and write 2 million shares, that is an extra $20k a month.

So we pointed this issue out to G and he immediately started working on bidding and offering more. First, G eliminated his sweep key entirely. He just decided he would only bid and offer for the next few weeks. Doing this is like jumping out of an airplane without a backup parachute. You want to work on bidding and offering while also having your safety exit, your sweep key, but G chose a more extreme form of improvement. And improve he did.

Another trader who improved by watching the tape is G's good friend Franchise. G and Franchise are a modern-day version of the odd couple. G is short, stocky, olive-skinned, and new-age stylish. Franchise is tall, athletic, white, and preppy. The two are roommates, man-friends as we kid on the desk, in a swank Lower East Side bachelor pad. But enough about their out-in-the-open bromance . . . let's discuss how Tradecasts improved Franchise's game.

Franchise: Poor Position Sizing

Franchise struggled with position sizing which we could not pick up until we all sat down to watch his tape. Remember, Franchise is the former college swimmer who tried out for the Olympics in the 50-meter freestyle. That yearning to be the best has made him a driven, relentless trader.

We watched his tape and learned that his position sizing was poor. Actually it wasn't poor, it was nonsensical. Position sizing refers to how large a position that you take per trade. Some trades call for a huge position ("loading the boat"), some for a "large" position, some for your standard tier size ("one lot"), and some for much less ("just a taste"). Some trades for a developing trader can be as high as 3,000 shares, all the way down to the pedestrian retail of 100 shares. And learning when to have the most size is a skill that developing traders must acquire. Poor position sizing can lead to inconsistent results.

Trading is just a game of math. If you are long 3,000 shares of a stock and your win rate is 30 percent, yet you are long 700 shares when your win rate is 70 percent, then this will skew your trading results. It is not that your trading is poor, it is just that you need to get better at this one skill, position sizing. And this was Franchise's issue (other than living with G).

So we watched his tape, and he made a beautiful trade with 800 shares where his win rate was 70 percent, his downside was 1, and his upside was 5. (Just as we teach it in the training class! Somebody must have been listening!) And then about 10 minutes later, we saw another trader. BAM! He placed a trade with 2,400 shares where his win rate was 50 percent, his downside was 1, and his upside was 1. (This was Franchise slowly drifting into Chapter 5, *Why Traders Fail*.) We now had the answer to why his results had been inconsistent. He would have days when he was at the top of the leaderboard with superstardom possible. And yet there were too many days when he was stopped out before 10:15 AM. When you are on the top of the leaderboard as much as Franchise, you can trade for a living, and have tremendous trading talent. When you are stopped out so often, then generally you are disobeying a market fundamental.

Net-net, such add-ons will infect your trading results and reduce your P&L. You want results where you traded with the most size with your best setups. You do not want results where your good trades are mixed with other trades that did not offer you the best risk/reward. This is an example of reduced potential.

So we put Franchise to work on improving his position sizing. I am not sure you put a guy like Franchise to work per se. You suggest an adjustment and then wait, because with certainty you know he is working on it. Over the next few months he was our most improved trader. I was not surprised.

As I mentioned, we watch tape of our traders daily on our desk. Also, during two weekends a month, our desk comes in for a video review. The markets are closed, and there are few distractions, other than those beautiful sunny days when all your friends are at Central Park scouting the female talent or on the beach in East Hampton. Meanwhile, we are at the office working like all those snooty investment bankers we so desperately avoid trying to become. There is no other way to get better. There are no excuses in trading. To get better you have to work. And that is what our guys are doing.

And They're Not the Only Ones

To improve my own trading, I record my screens during the Open and the Close. Personally I look for new algorithmic programs that I must conquer. I search for spots where I could have added more size. This is one of my trading weaknesses. I do a poor job of holding stocks that ought to be held. So I consider trades that I could have held longer. I am not going to get better at this unless I do the work required.

Watching trading tape also shows me how easy trading is when I remove my emotions from a trade. When I review my work, I am not invested in a trade in real time. I, nor anyone else, can lose money watching tapes of my trading.

Trading live, the market seems fast. When you watch back your trading tape, you see that the market is actually very slow. There are so many times when I think I am trading a lightning fast stock, then watch my tape and learn the truth.

There are times when I see the pattern in a stock by watching my tape and recognize how I traded the stock backward. My pattern recognition was poor if not embarrassing, for someone of my experience. It was not that the stock was difficult to trade, but rather that while I was trading it I did not recognize its pattern.

Also, when I watch the tape I can see how clean some of the moves are in stocks. While in the trade. I overvalue the possibility that the pattern might change or the stock will reverse. But there are so many moves that are just clean. The stock is strong, it goes up, it never ticks down. These are the moves I must add size to, trades for which I must "man up" as GMan instructs to our developing traders. Watching the tape gives me the confidence to really size up with certain setups.

For me, I must identify the plays where I can load up, and hold for longer periods. I must prepare to accept these gains (gladly, I might add!). So when I spot a great setup live, then I remember my tape sessions, I remember to really load up with this trade and hold, and now and only now does it work.

Watching the tape is an exercise that can benefit all traders. In professional basketball, players have a shoot-around before each game. They arrive early to the arena and practice their shooting so that they perform better during the game. How well they shoot in the game is dependent on the skills that they develop during their drills. For a developing trader, watching tape is one way that he or she can practice and develop skills after the market closes.

Also, developing traders need experience watching the markets trade. Watching their tape multiplies their trading experience and shortens their learning curve. Easy enough, no? All it takes is a little time.

PRACTICING TECHNIQUES FROM TOP TRADING PSYCHOLOGISTS

I have read the works of all the top trading psychologists, including Ari Kiev, Dr. Brett Steenbarger, Doug Hirschorn (aka Dr. Doug), and Mark Douglas. What I learn from these authors is the importance of preparing your mind. Specifically, you must believe that you are worthy of making chops before you can. (Note: Kiev was the in-house psychologist for SAC Capital, a hedge fund firm that will go down in history as one of the best ever.)

I once heard Kiev say that traders should seek to "be in control while simultaneously being out of control a bit" and push one's comfort zone to find greater success. As if they are a downhill skier picking up top speed yet, having all the confidence they will complete the run without crashing and breaking both collarbones.

At SMB Capital, we dedicate a large part of our trader education program to practicing what today's top trading psychologists are preaching. We teach new traders the techniques we've found helpful for remaining calm and focused, whether it's taking a walk around the block or using visualization techniques.

As I mentioned, GMan, our Head Trader, walked into our conference room one day and announced, "I quit." Needless to say, Steve and I were shocked. Steve knew GMan better than I at the time and replied simply, "GMan, I think you're making a big mistake." Steve continued that GMan needed to learn how to control his emotions. GMan was prone to emotional outbursts and would bang the desk and curse when frustrated. He occasionally would break a keyboard.

(For historical context, when I started trading, it was commonplace for traders to break their keyboards and curse out loud. In fact, keyboards were broken so frequently that our tech support was trained to replace a broken keyboard in a few minutes. Traders were automatically charged for the new keyboard. There was little thought that maybe this was inappropriate behavior. Guys were making serious money, so boorish behavior was tolerated.)

Make no mistake, trading is stressful. Active intraday trading is the most stressful of all trading periods. One mistake can ruin your month. One missed print for 5k shares can ruin your week. As I've mentioned already, there is a fine line between being a good trader and a losing trader. And we do this day in and day out. We trade 48 weeks a year, five days a week, save the occasional holiday. This is not an easy job.

Unless you're Gandhi or the Dalai Lama, it's difficult to will yourself to remain calm. Unfortunately, verbalizing frustration does not improve one's trading. In fact, it usually compounds losses that are already being realized. When you are frustrated, your brain is chemically altered, and the only way to exit this state of anger is to, well, make an effort to calm down. I, along with many of my peers who run prop desks, instruct traders to take a walk to de-stress and not to restart their trading until they are focused and calm.

We also teach our traders visualization exercises so that they do not become frustrated as easily. For example, one of our traders gets frustrated when he gets long, has a short bias, and then takes a rip. Then he trades on tilt. This trader turns one small loss into getting stopped out. So we taught him how to use visualization techniques to control his emotions. The goal is to program his mind such that he does not get frustrated when he does the above. Again, you cannot just tell yourself not to get upset. This is not about self-control. This is about how your brain is wired.

In our training, we emphasize to new traders to perform visualization exercises to better control these emotions. (Women tend to be better at this than men, hence my desire to hire more women if they'd only send in more resumes!) I would urge those most interested to visit Dr. Steenbarger's blog TraderFeed to learn in depth the best visualization techniques. In short, and please don't think I'm some new-age yoga instructor by the following sentences, but all of this is important to our success as a firm.

We all have mental weaknesses that we must conquer. Some of us insist in showing the market that we are correct (remember about rather being right than making money?). Some cannot hit stocks that trade against them. Some anxiously take profits when there is no reason to do so. Some are afraid to pull the trigger with an excellent risk/reward setup. The only way to get better is to work on your visualization exercises as they relate to these weaknesses.

MENTORING

A good mentor can make your trading career. This was not always true. When I first started, the market was much easier to trade, as the markets were more directional. Some would say it was harder to *lose* money than make money. A simple "buy" of a tech stock on any given day would do the trick. The NASDAQ was in a steady uptrend to heights we have not even come close to since its peak in March 2000. But today, because of algorithmic programs and market volatility, it's much harder to navigate the market as a novice trader. Hence, a good mentor can make a huge difference.

Good mentoring is omnipresent on an excellent prop desk. At the beginning of 2009, I spoke with our desk as they slogged through a market where the volatility we had thrived on in 2008 was gone. They were struggling. I tried to explain calmly that this was an excellent trading market, and not as difficult as the previous month. I was that coach at halftime who was trying to communicate that we can do better, but without the chair throwing and fire-and-brimstone-win-one-for-the-Gipper speech. When they heard me explain that they could indeed make money, then they knew they could. Their doubts dissipated. It was like I needed to greenlight they could make money again and start running their trading offense, so to speak. And then a few weeks later, I heatedly challenged our traders to make more. I told them not to be satisfied; that they were capable of even more. And you know what? Then they magically made more.

GMan

After nearly quitting, GMan has stepped into the role as leader and mentor to our young traders. (After all, Steve and I can't do all the work.) Here are some examples:

Sometimes our traders try to get cute with a fading market. When GMan spotted this behavior one weak trading day, he yelled, "The market is not a long!" A new trader responded, "GMan, the market is not going down anymore." GMan replied harshly, "Stop getting long!" (Remember what I wrote about listening? There was a patented, vicious closed-door meeting for that rookie mistake.) Subsequently, the market tanked further. Traders on our desk hear this dialogue, and it helps them not do anything stupid like fading a weak market.

In another example of his mentorship, GMan was trading MS, which was in a downtrend. Again, the market was weak, and late in the trading day, 45 minutes until the Close. A few traders were fading MS and GMan caught this on our risk monitor. Again, he yelled, "Stop fading MS. The stock is not a long. It is probably going through 23. You should be focusing on a short below 23." Sure enough after a few fake breakdowns, MS traded below 23 and held. GMan was very short and very profitable. Those traders who listened rode MS down to near 22 and GMan had averted some rips for those new traders in MS. And even better, he had them and some others on the right side of MS into the Close. This is what a good mentor can offer.

And then, of course, there was the day when GMan was short LVS that was broken intraday. One of our traders, Z$, got short but covered too quickly. GMan caught this: "Mush, stop being such a wuss. Learn to take some pain. The stock is not a cover." Now you can't ever really hear what ZMush says because he speaks so quietly but word is he replied, "Shut up, GMan, and let me trade." ZMush has been positive every day for the past year, but it is still GMan's job to challenge him. One day, when he learns to hold and his results double, he will understand that GMan is making him a better trader.

Mentors will shout out important technical levels in the market, and will share when the market may turn. We often pull traders into our office and just tell them that they can make it. We build their confidence. A mentor demonstrates the professionalism required to be successful. We are in early and have scoured the news feeds for the Stocks In Play. Steve prepares for two hours every night before he starts his preparation for our AM meeting. We are at our trading stations with complete focus. There are no phone calls, e-mails, IMs, text messages, twittering, or any other new technology on the Open and the Close. We just trade. The preparation, focus, and discipline required to compete at this level is transferred to the young guns.

We watch their positions so they do not take unnecessary rips. We make sure they focus on the process. You can hear me implore daily, "Make One Good Trade, and then One Good Trade, and then One Good Trade."

Dr. Momentum

Experienced traders who know how to make adjustments on the fly mentoring the developing trader is vital. Let's take one of my favorite traders, Dr. Momentum. He killed it during the fall of 2008, but struggled at the end of that year and start of 2009. He had made so much money that financially he didn't need to make money for a long time. But he was starting to rip up his well-deserved cushion and most importantly, he was underperforming.

Dr. Momentum was so successful in the fall of 2008 because of his superior momentum trading skills. He was unafraid to smack GS, down 10 points, and ride it lower. When the banks were falling (and failing), he crushed them. When the banks were trading down, he was short. When the banks had a one or two day rally, he was long. In his first year, he showed superstar ability showing the mental dexterity to trade these fast moving bank stocks on either side. He had the nerve and gumption to ride the "crazy train" of GS, MS, MER, LEH.

But when the market stabilized, he started to underperform. So Steve and I offered him guidance. I offered, "Dr. Momentum, I have traded many different styles over the years. I have had to make many adjustments. This period does not indicate that you cannot make money as a trader. This is a learning experience for you. The market is testing whether you can adapt. You have the skills. Now we just have to work on when to be aggressive and when to be careful. And work on that."

And Dr. Momentum started thinking about the adjustments he needed to make. We pointed out some trades where he was being overly aggressive and how that would not work in this changing market at the start of 2009. He found FAZ (the 3x-levered ETF that tracks the financials inversely), which rewarded his aggressiveness again. He was selectively aggressive with the bank stocks. And he went right back to making money.

None of our mentorship works unless our traders like Dr. Momentum listen and then put in the work necessary to adapt successfully. He was receptive. Our experience and past success validates our instruction. And so instead of Dr. Momentum continuing to struggle, he turned it around. Instead of Dr. Momentum wondering why what worked in the Fall of 2008 now was not without a solution, our mentorship guided him through his next step and he found his stride again.

A Talk with the Newbies

One of my favorite discussions is with new traders who just go live. At the start, I gather our newest traders in our conference room and ask them how they are doing. At the initial sit-down with a recent training class, I was very impressed. Not one of these new traders judged their start based upon their P&L. They have been listening and learning. The first newbie, commenting on their progress, said, "I have to work on my if-then statements for support and resistance plays. I was not exiting some positions for small gains. Instead, I took small losses. I need to find ways to take small gains, be in the plays for the big gains, and not just so many small losses and only big gains." This was excellent analysis for a trader on Day Two of his trading career. Another former college football player and newbie commented, "I have to get faster pulling the trigger when I see a good setup. I was too hesitant on a few trades." Again, music to my ears.

In the past, I have led these meetings and some poor new trader makes the mistake of saying, "I got stopped out. I had a terrible day." At SMB this is like saying that you don't have a drinking problem at an AA meeting. Generally, someone says this in every class on the first few days of trading live. For effect, I pause a little while after this unacceptable analysis is communicated and then firmly say, "That is not how we judge our trading. Never judge your trading based upon your results. If money is all you care about, go join the league of lesser firms." And then I explain that their goal is to learn, to develop their trading skills, to gain experience trading live, and to get better every day. They get the point.

After about six months of trading live, there is a trader in each class I spot who can really take it to the next level. And these traders have no idea. Their numbers are OK, but compared to the rest of the desk, this trader does not think of himself as ready to become excellent...yet. I noticed this at the start of 2009 with EKA from our June 2008 class. This trader was absurdly bright but his numbers were very average. He was not making much more than $700 in a day. Every once in a while he would put up $1k. Again, please remember that he was about five to six months into his trading career.

But I could see how interested in the markets he was. When I gave a lecture to our desk, EKA looked right into my eyes. When I passed his desk after the Close he was watching tape of his trading. He was never late. Unlike G, he hardly ever took days off. (Though, like G, he has the funniest of trading quirks. In mid-trade he jumps from his seat, pokes his head above his trading screens like a chicken, looks around at the row in front of him, and then plops back down in his seat again. The other day EKA sprang from his chair, started bolting from his trading station, forgot his head-set was still attached, and choked himself.) EKA constantly struck up a trading conversation with our other traders. I just knew he was going to be good. He had laid the foundation.

But he didn't know. And so I started to work on him. I took him into our office. I said, "I don't want you comparing yourself to the others around you. I am not sure that they are the right comparison for you. They do not possess your talent. I want you to start visualizing days of $1,500 going forward. This is what you are capable of." And as he always does, he looked right into my eyes. He couldn't hide his smile.

The next few days, the encouragement was working. I noticed him put up $1k, then $1,200, then $1,400, then $1,600, and then $1,900. And this is a trader still only nine months into his trading career. And you know what, I had to go back and speak with him again about putting up more. I called him into my office, sat him down, and praised him on an excellent trading day. And then I planted an idea in his head. I left him with, "You know one day $5k will be a good day for you."

During his next good run, his better days went from $1,500 to $4k. It is all a matter of getting traders to understand their ability. Because EKA was capable of being one of the best traders on our desk. A mentor can lead you to discover the talent inside of you. Sometimes you just need to be told that you can do it.

My partner, Steve, is one tough trader. As I have said if you met him for the first time you would walk away concluding he was a Wharton intellectual. But Steve will grind it out like Tiger. He will take a loss and fight back. The day for him doesn't end until the bell rings. A bad start is just an opportunity to make a comeback. You would have to literally drag him away from his trading station to end his fight. And he fights with every tick, every day, sick or not, tired or alert, hungry or well fed. This is mentorship. There is not anything that Steve can say that is more effective than his actions.

I asked a former trader who writes exceptionally well, BLY, to add his thoughts about the value of mentorship. He shared his thoughts below:

As for talking with other traders, well, we all know it's extremely valuable to do so. Sure, one can certainly trade at home with filters and news feeds and the like, but generally speaking, a trader, especially a new(ish) trader, should trade with a group. Here's why.

First, there is always going to be someone else who has more experience than you. This is true of life in general and in trading in particular, and so you want to avail yourself of that person's knowledge, talent, and, yes, trading wisdom. People need other people, but traders especially need other traders because knowledge and experience don't exist in a vacuum. When a seasoned trader such as JToma or GMan (or you) says that a certain stock is approaching a key support or resistance level, it's probably a good idea to heed that information. Sure, jumping "blindly" into a new situation is generally not recommended, but because trading is a fast-moving, fluid

*enterprise, there's a strong likelihood that when a veteran trader says
he sees something significant happening, it's probably the case that
what he sees is for real and that what he thinks is about to happen
is likely to happen. Sure, predicting the future is a difficult skill but
it can be done. You want evidence? I give you evidence: if, for example, a monstrously large held offer, one that held for several previous tests, is finally decrementing—and decrementing fast—and it's
a seasoned and experienced trader who has called this out, it's probably a good idea to get in there.*

Not only can you learn from mentors on an outstanding prop desk but
you can learn from its traders as well.

LEARNING FROM TRADERS ON THE DESK

Let's turn to our rank and file for their take on why it's valuable to learn
from your fellow traders.

One of our most improved new traders is the best at engaging traders
in a discussion about stocks. I'll call him KW, for Kurt Warner, whose willingness to improve as a quarterback, especially when his college days were
over, when he stocked shelves at a grocery store, led to one of the most improbable rises to fame in sports history. Warner has played in three Super
Bowls, won one, and been robbed in the last minute in two others. KW
talks about FAZ with MoneyMaker, Dr. Momentum, and others above the
food chain than he. These conversations make them all better. But it's because KW initiates and then *leads* the discussion that they are benefiting.
KW recently doubled his trading output and has gone from simply good
to excellent. It is not so much his improved results that I notice. It is this
habit he has formed of seeking more information and learning from better
traders. Will he become the best trader on our desk?

KW (After Kurt Warner)

KW sent me his thoughts on how other traders on our desk help him:

*I try to seek out every trader I believe I can learn something from. If I
worked on a very poor desk, I would probably spend all day figuring
out what not to do.*

*At first, I asked every question I had to Steve, Mike, and GMan be-
cause it was early in my trading career and I wanted my basic*

questions answered right. As I grew as a trader, I moved on to a new phase in my development where talking with others in my training class helped me progress. The senior trainers cannot spend all day pounding the fundamentals into a new trader's head, but trainees can help each other stay sharp and focused.

I ask different questions to people from classes before me. I would ask YIP and DOV how they overcame problems associated with trading more than 100 shares. I would ask Franchise and G what they read on the weekends to prepare for Monday. I would ask JToma how he got out of a trading slump. On a successful prop desk, micro and macro trading issues are easily addressed because everyone plays a role and no one is embarrassed about asking a question.

Another benefit of talking with other traders is I can harass DOV and MoneyMaker every day on how they make so much money. If a trader on our desk is doing very well or has gotten very hot, you better believe that after the Close when that trader has a moment to spare I am going to be in his face asking every question I have thought of. That is because not only do I want to do what he is doing, I want to do it better, a lot better. In trading, the focus should be about being better than you. However, there is a lot of value in having a tangible comparison. I would not call it competition, but taking turns pushing each other, which could be the greatest quality a desk can have.

TBW (T. Boone Wannabe)

I also posed this question to our most talented new trader on our desk, TBW, for T. Boone Wannabe. He responded:

When I saw other traders last summer making money in those energy stocks, I started asking questions. Why and how are these stocks moving? What are the best ones to trade? What specific plays are you looking for? These are questions specific to that moment in the market, and you can only learn that from asking other traders the right questions and then putting in the time yourself.

So I think that being able to adjust to the market, and apply specific strategies at certain points in the market, is something I learned from other traders on the desk. The market is always changing. The market will always be a different one from the one you first learned how to trade in. Having mentors and other traders to work with is the best way to move through that process.

One of our disciplined young traders offered an example of how talking with others helped.

For example: February 13th, the 30 level in FCX was a big level. It failed there once before on the yearly chart, and that day, it gapped up hard in the premarket. I did my homework the day before knowing of this 30 level, and coming in premarket, 29.50 was support. I formulated my plan, telling myself that I wanted to be long FCX before it reaches 30, so I would look for any buying around the 29.50 level. The market opens and FCX has a very wide spread with few prints in between 60c and 80c. To make it short, I never got long near .50 and once it was at the 30 level, I did not feel comfortable getting long my max position size after the stock made a 50c move. Also, while the stock was making its moves above 30, I kept selling into the move. So when its stock finally made its move to 30.70, I had only 100 shares when I had 400 from 30. After the day, I went to talk with JToma about the trade, which he was in from 30 as well. I told him of my plan and what I saw in the morning. He told me that if I wanted to get long in front of 29.50, just risk it with 100 shares despite the lack of volume just so I can be in it. He told me that that 10c of risk was worth it since the real money is the stock above 30 and being in the stock before 30 allows you to be more aggressive. Also, he told me that if I had a strong long bias in the stock above 30, I should have kept a larger size as my core instead of lightening up as it moves up and buying the stock higher and higher. I remembered those concepts and both those ideas translated well into my trading of QCOM today.

GMan

GMan, our Head Trader, recently offered an example of how talking with other traders helped him and the developing traders:

Some of us went to Metro Hotel's rooftop for a couple of beers. The discussion quickly turned into how we all trade FAZ. The three of us have very different styles with our own strengths and weaknesses. There were plenty of arguments as to when to trade it with size on momentum and when to trade it as a trade to hold. After listening to them, I realized that I could be much more aggressive on certain momentum plays. They also realized that in some plays it is okay to take some pain buying into a pullback or shorting into strength to play the direction of the market, rather than trying to pay/hit the new high/low or fade every dopey move. It was a very productive conversation over a few Brooklyn Lagers that will make me and them better traders.

GMan also offered an excellent example of how talking to a developing trader can help a developing trader. He blogged:

A new trader will find that a well-executed play by a peer in their class is easily remembered compared to hearing about it from an experienced guy. Seriously, imagine watching a guy who just started with you explain how they chopped it up in a trade talking in detail what they saw. An explanation of their play can be much simpler than that of an experienced trader. The experienced guy may just have way too many if-then statements. I have tried to explain to a new trader how I buy into a pullback and I can just see their confused faces. But I have seen a new trader explain to another one what an unusual hold looks like and they remember this stuff.

A few of our traders had an excellent Monday, Tuesday, and Wednesday recently. They blew off our VRS (video review session) on Wednesday. These are guys doing very well whose progress I am proud of. But I cannot stand stuff like this. So we had a meeting behind closed doors with some of the culprits. One guy claimed he had a doctor's appointment, another said he had some paperwork to handle, another said he wasn't feeling well, and another said he was tired. At this stage of the book, you may be able to anticipate my response. I was not overjoyed.

So we met and talked. I calmly offered reasons why attending the Tradecasts were in their best interest. My best argument centered around the importance of trading ideas. I argued they were not acting in their self-interest by skipping the VRS. I could have just yelled and ordered, "Don't miss another Tradecast." But almost always I prefer to offer a convincing case why missing the Tradecast was harmful to their trading.

I explained that the core ought to teach the new traders. Doing so will make our desk stronger. The core will be rewarded. Mentoring a new trader, attending the Tradecast and offering suggestions to the new trader, will help our newbies. These newbies will in return offer more trading opportunities to the core. It's called reciprocity, All it takes is one great trading idea to make your week. We had all crushed WFC the day before. Steve called out the 25.25 level and we all rode the strong upmove into the Close. But next time, that idea may come from a newbie.

As for being too tired to attend, I asked them to "10-10-10" it as developed by Suzy Welch. What would be the consequences of them missing this

VRS in 10 minutes, 10 months, and 10 years? In 10 minutes, they would be free of the office. In 10 months, they would be sitting on a weaker desk, which was not in their self-interest. And in 10 years, they would want to be on a strong desk, with a free flow of valuable trading ideas, with fully developed trading skills. So after 10-10-10, the decision that was best was for them to suck it up and attend the VRS.

They all shook their heads. Their eyes told me they understood.

Scorsese

Let's wrap up this topic from some thoughts from one of my favorite traders, Scorsese:

Cue the camera.

We open on Mark, who, with his quiet intensity, is riding a stock up (or down) and making a quick killing. Some exhalation of success will occur, indicating that a trade is working. One thing is for sure: When things aren't working, Mark will not gesticulate. He will not scream (unless he's just had his spleen forcibly removed from him). No, when things are down he just quietly sucks it up and accepts the bad day. When things are good, there's some whooping and hollering. Who can blame him? He's one of the best traders on the desk and things usually go his way. What does a new trader learn from Mark? He learns what it's like to be a momentum trader. He learns to Read the Tape, but in an extremely quick fashion. For example, Mark will plow through an offer again and again if he sees the bid stepping up in a rapid, quick-fire way.

Camera pans to Zi, who trades like a quiet and meditative philosopher. He's hands are crabbed on the upper right of the keyboard (due to his unique keyboard setup). He waits. He waits some more. The offer decrements, he gets in last with 500 shares, the stock shoots up 20 cents—and he's out. And then he is silent as he mulls over a new opportunity that someone has just mentioned over the headset. Zi is like a dedicated hunter, quietly bagging his game. But Zi demonstrates severe discipline as well. If he thinks he has a good position on, but it goes against him just by a few cents, he's out. Done. Finito. No regrets. He admits that he was wrong and does nothing more than shrug. Good. Yelling and slamming things will get you nowhere. You were wrong, accept it, move on to the next stock—or stay with the same stock and wait for a similar setup. What does a new trader learn from Zi? He learns the value of being extremely patient. He learns from Zi what it means to respect levels and to be sure that the necessary volume is there to make the move significant.

Andrew. This is a trader who likes things slow. No scalping for this guy. Uh-uh. Someone calls out that GS is tearing through a resistance level? Andrew doesn't give a crap. He's not interested. Because he's in his short right now. He noticed the WWW popped nicely at the Open and appears to be topping out. This could be a real winner on the day, he thinks. Looking at the long-term chart, I could get a buck out of this move, at least 50 cents. And so he begins his position. Puts in a bit. Waits. Likes what he sees. Adds a bit more as the thing slowly sells off (slow because Andrew doesn't like high-volume stocks; too volatile). Unlike Zi, who's in and out within seconds, Andrew will hold this stock for 45 minutes—and make $430 on the trade. Nice. But Andrew can be hot-tempered. If you are busy with a trade and then suddenly hear what sounds like a rain of plastic, you can be sure it was Andrew who has just hit his keyboard, which sends his keys up into the air and then back to earth, like a fast, momentary drizzle of artificial precipitation. But if Zi is patient, Andrew is über-patient. Andrew's style is really only for those who have an intraday swing-day mentality. If scalping's your thing, you're wasting your time talking to Andrew.

Playmaker. Here's an all-or nothing guy. He likes the big moves with big size. Yesterday there was blood on the floor, but today he's back in the saddle. He saw that Boeing had great earnings. He wants this one at the Open. He wants it bad. The bell goes off; BA quivers. It hems and haws. It looks ready to explode to the upside. Little Mike sees the bids stepping up with size. This thing is going to fly. Screw it, he thinks. I'm in. He puts in a thousand shares. He reels for a moment. Getting that sick feeling because it looks as though the bids are stepping down. No, wait. They're stepping down but holding at a new level. ARCA's holding. It's holding. Boom, someone takes out the offer and sends it into the stratosphere. He makes a quick and cool $600 on the trade and he's out.

Steve. This guy, one of the partners, is Mr. Focus. He's relentless. No jumping around from stock to stock for him. He knows commitment, and when something has worked, he'll stay with it. Yesterday, he killed it with AAPL. This morning, he's back in it. Why should I move to a different stock? The earnings were great yesterday, it only got stronger near the end of the day, and I'm back in it this morning because the futures are still strong and AAPL is now out of its tight range. I expect to be "In Play" again today. And so it is. Awesome trader—and this is why it behooves any new trader to seek him out, to watch him trade, to listen to his tapes, and to hear him explain why certain levels were meaningful. What does a trader learn from Steve? First and foremost, he learns the rewards of understanding the recent past. Sure, volume is important (and something like AAPL will always have the required volume) but he's keen and meticulous when it comes to keeping track of significant levels from recent days and thereby recognizing opportunities for significant breakouts.

New traders will come in with a "pre-set" temperament, and the exposure to various styles can be very significant. Thing is, a new trader really has no idea who he is when he starts out. Hardly a clue—and the only clue is the kind of person he is when he walks in. But once certain skills are acquired, that person can change. You've seen this many times in your career. And so while a new trader at the end of the day has no choice but to trade and get started and to discover who he is as his career commences, it behooves him to see and watch and talk to others all the time, to see what's it's like to be a momentum trader, to see what it's like to trade only slow stocks and so on.

AND YES, WE DO HAVE DEEPER POCKETS

A few years ago, Steve and I did something really smart: we dramatically improved the payout of our traders. Our payout structure is a bit complicated. But essentially, we offered our traders a better deal, hoping this would lower our costs as a firm. (I'll explain . . .) We were not in the position to offer this much better payout. But we bet on our traders. And it worked.

As such, the cost of us doing business dropped by about 10 percent for all of our transactions. As active traders, this left the firm in a much stronger financial position. I remember this decision like it was a few minutes ago. We were not going to make money unless our traders stepped up significantly. And they did.

Despite what I might have babbled on about for the last 100 pages, a proprietary firm is not a video game you pick up at Best Buy. It involves setting up real infrastructure (office space, desks, chairs, computers, high-speed Internet access, cabling, and so on) and a fair amount of cash to boot. A prop firm must negotiate a deal with a clearing firm or piggyback off of a larger firm that does so. If an individual trader were to approach a clearing firm for a deal, he would not get as good a deal as going through a prop firm. He would not have access to mentoring, trading ideas, cutting-edge technology, as much capital, and other successful traders. This is a win/win for the trader and the firm.

The basic idea is that the better our firm does, the more generous we can be with our payout. As a young firm, as we have done better, we have passed along this success to the payout of our traders.

By definition, and I certainly hope in practice, a proprietary firm has deeper pockets than the individual retail trader. Very few retail traders have the resources to fund an account of hundreds of thousands of dollars. If you trade retail, you can only receive 4-to-1 margin. For a prop firm, this is not an issue. A proprietary firm negotiates with a clearing firm to gain intraday buying power. The firm then doles out this buying power based upon its judgment. When you have a desk full of consistently profitable traders, your costs are lowered significantly. A firm with a core of successful traders can obtain almost unlimited intraday buying power.

New traders often ask how much money they can trade with when they start. This is not a good question. We can offer as much buying power as you need . . . within reason. The issue is not our deeper pockets. The issue is whether you can handle the extra buying power. You cannot ask us for a reasonable amount of buying power that we cannot provide. We have never had a trader who needed more buying power than we could offer. And we never will.

Thankfully, being part of a prop firm allows new traders to learn on a cushion of cash (or in this case, mine and Steve's cash). We can withstand much bigger losses than you can as an individual trader. (Unless you inherit some type of eight-figure trust fund.) It is often not a big deal for us to lose $25k-plus on a trader when he starts. Two guys on our desk who will probably become excellent traders started down over $50k. If it doesn't happen for these guys, it is not a big deal to SMB. They are a good bet. If we are going to lose money, we have no problem doing so on these talented developing traders.

But how many individual traders can withstand a loss greater than this when they begin? On a prop desk, your losses are usually offset from the profits of other traders. And if the firm is negative for the month, then it uses its reserves that it has built up from its profitable months. And these are considerable. It is almost impossible for our firm to be negative for the trading day. We make sure of it. We spread out our risk amongst many profitable traders, leaving our collective risk at almost nil.

Not everyone who is negative when he begins is offered the opportunity to continue. As I said previously, if a trader is not working hard, then he is asked to leave. But if you are working hard every day, it is not significant to the firm that you are in a hole of tens of thousands of dollars. It's hardly a blip on our radar screen. Just don't bleed us for multiple years please and then leave.

We had one trader (call him Leech, for slowly sucking us dry over the period he traded with us) who lost a few thousand dollars every month he traded with us. Other traders were doing well, and the firm as a whole was doing well. Leech was not losing enough each month for us to worry. But he was not getting better. So we had to let Leech go. When we tabulated his results after he left he was down almost $70k (including health insurance). We had not even noticed.

ENFORCING TRADING RULES

Sometimes the most important thing a prop firm leader can do for a developing trader is to say, "No."

No, you cannot leave early.
No, I will not raise your loss limit since you are stopped out and your mother feels bad for you.
No, you cannot trade with more size yet.
No, you cannot blow off the AM meeting.

One day, our desk was down big during the Midday. Our traders were doing well on the Open, but gave back too much of their gains between 11 AM and 3 PM. This had to stop. I called a firm meeting to discuss this issue. I calmly explained our problem. I asked our traders to come up with some rules that we as leadership would enforce to solve this issue. And then I left.

I heard during this meeting that there were a few youngsters complaining about developing rules. They didn't want any rules! The Peter Pan world of the American elite university clearly had not prepared them for a world with, dare I say, "rules?" JToma commented, "If you don't want any rules then go somewhere else and trade your own money. Whose money do you think you are trading?" The traders respect JToma and understood his valid point. We strive to be as non-bureaucratic as possible at SMB, not creating useless and unenforceable rules like at a humongous corporation. But there was a problem. It was losing the firm money and leading to lighter paychecks for our traders. We needed to fix this . . . fast.

So we created a bunch of reasonable Midday rules with the traders consent, one being that traders are not allowed to lose more than 30 percent of what they have made on the Open. (Hedge funds set similar internal stop-losses on a month-to-month basis if the fund is up a certain amount over the course of a calendar year.) If they lose more than the allotted 30 percent, then their tier size is lowered on the Open, starting the next day. If traders are penalized for their mistakes, most are less likely to make these mistakes going forward.

Like any rule, there is always the first violator. This Rule-Tester was sent an e-mail when he ripped up his day after the Open and needless to say, he was not happy, but a rule is a rule, no? And likewise, what would a rule be if someone doesn't try to circumvent it on a technicality? This is what I would have been paid to do as a lawyer, after all. Rule-Tester tried to do this. He sent us an e-mail before the Open the following day to explain an emergency that he needed to take care of. Emergency? On a beautiful sunny Friday in the summer? This was clearly a "summer sick day."

The following Monday he came back to work, and true to form, we lowered his tier size at the Open. Rule-Tester did not seem to understand. He thought that the lowering of his tier size was related to the previous Friday. Our Floor Manager said that it was, but you missed that day, so we were enforcing the rule today. Sorry R-T, the rule carries over, even if you skip a day.

Many traders trade independently with their own money from their house. They have their own rules but when they break them there are no consequences. For example, an independent trader will create the rule that if he exceeds his intraday loss limit, then he will shut down his trading for the day. Let's say that that intraday loss limit is $1,500. The independent trader will be down $2k, recognize that he has exceeded his intraday loss limit, and continue trading. The independent trader will offer excuses to himself. That rule was not meant for a day like today. I just got screwed today, the rule does not apply. And then this trader will proceed to rip up another $1k. Does this sound familiar?

It is the job of a proprietary desk to ensure that you are following your own (and the collective) rules. If, for example, you must be prepared before the Open, but come in late, then you cannot trade the Open. We do not make exceptions. You must be prepared to trade on the Open, and if you arrive late, then you are not prepared. If you are not prepared, then it is not in your self-interest (or mine) to trade the Open. Instead, you trade on the demo until 11 AM. Traders will often ask for an exception to be made. My answer is, "No."

Shrinkage: Enforcing A Loss Limit

One of our better developing traders, Shrinkage, continually complained about the intraday loss limits that Steve imposed on him. Shrinkage was a pretty good swing trader. He preferred trading AAPL and RIMM intraday. He felt most comfortable trading the same group of stocks regularly. He had a few good months but then started to struggle, and was consistently losing money. We lowered his loss limits so that he would slow things down, get back to basics, and make only the trades that work best for him and with smaller size. It was important for Shrinkage to limit his trades to his best setups, improve his confidence, and get back on track.

Then, he would hit his loss limit. He would ask to have it raised and Steve would say, "No." When a trader is stopped out, they must sit and watch stocks trade all day and learn. He is not permitted to go home. Shrinkage went home. When he came in the next day, Steve placed him on the demo and Shrinkage whined like an infant. Steve explained that the demo is your punishment for leaving early. Shrinkage questioned why he needed to stay and watch stocks trade. Steve explained that doing so would help him gather information. Staying and watching stocks trade would help Shrinkage find levels that he could exploit the next trading day. After all, we didn't pay him to go home.

A few days later, Shrinkage hit his loss limit again. Three days later, he did it again. The next week, he got stopped out twice. A few weeks later, he hit his loss limits three times. In the course of a month, he was stopped out on 10 trading days. This new trader was not happy with our loss limits and asked to talk with Steve.

Now Steve, like me, is extremely busy. He has only so much time in the day. If you have a legitimate question, he will stay and answer it. If you need to watch tape with him, then you just have to ask. If you want to watch some tape with Steve on the weekend, he is always available. But he doesn't like to waste his time.

So Shrinkage questioned the need for these stop-losses. He felt that they were hurting his trading. Steve calmly explained why these rules were in Shrinkage's best interests. Privately, Steve complained to me, "I have saved him $40k over the past two months. If he were smart, he would thank me." And Steve was correct.

I later sat down with Shrinkage so he understood that our actions were in his best interest after Steve had told him "No." I was reminded of Rick Pitino's heart-to-heart with Edgar Sosa, his struggling point guard from the Bronx. Sosa was unhappy with his playing time. Coach Pitino suggested Sosa transfer to a school where he wasn't required to play defense. Ouch! Sosa declined and picked up his D after being motivated by Pitino's challenge. Being the trading coach that I am, I wanted to tell this newbie to go and find a desk that would allow him to be undisciplined, not cap his losses, and let him blow up. But I am not Coach Pitino, so I pivoted. "You are not in a huge hole. Clean up your Midday losses and your results will improve dramatically." But the coach in me wishes I could have tried that Pitino tactic.

We had saved this trader tens of thousands of dollars. We did so by just saying, "No."

And this is not the only type of beneficial communication on a prop desk.

THE BANTER ON THE PROP DESK

A good prop trading desk shares its best ideas. You can see only so much while you are trading. Sixty pairs of eyes are better than one. We have trained our desk how to communicate valuable trading information. The airwaves on our desk are like an emergency broadcasting network. Only that which can make us money should be heard. We speak a specific language.

Also, trading on a desk is just fun. It is more enjoyable trading on a prop desk than at home and pretending to figure things out yourself. You can drive yourself crazy just being with yourself all day long (I have done this and didn't care for the lack of interaction and how easy it was Midday to "need a nap"). Funny banter keeps the trading day more interesting.

Let's bring in a few of our guys to give you some color on how communication helps them. Let's start with our friend, Uncle B, older than most on our desk but as personable as your favorite uncle.

In a world with 5,000-plus stocks, you can't be aware of everything. Filters can help, but it's the willful sharing of good ideas that makes everyone a better trader. For example, I remember many occasions when I would call out certain stocks to Zi because I came to understand the kind of setups he liked, but only I knew about what he liked (and worked) because of his prior call-outs to the rest of the desk. And so it goes with everyone else. MMC's experience influences Franchise, who influences GDI, who influences DP, who ... you get the picture. It's a funny, paradoxical thing: we're all doing this for our own personal gain, but when people are trading together, everybody wins.

One trader who desires to be like Franchise provides us with an excellent example.

Today, after bribing Franchise with an orange, he told me of the play in QDEL. After coming off from 12 all the way to 9.7, there was a long period of tight consolidation around the 10 level. He told me that they dropped it out once and that he was long 800 shares from 10. I typed up the stock and watched it for myself. The 10 bid would buy several thousand shares, and then drops, but the offer would never be 10.

Also, there were a ton of white prints around 10–10.01 and no one would hit more than 100 shares at 9.99. I got long myself at 10.01 and set a stop at 9.98. The stock eventually went to 10.40 at a point in time. Now, without bribing and then talking with Franchise, I would have never found out about this stress-free trade that made me money.

The environment of a prop desk is probably the furthest thing from a typical, dull corporate environment as glorified in the cult classic "Office Space."

- Speech is unfiltered. If a real stickler HR professional spent one day in our office, he or she would probably want to fire us all.
- A dress code is non-existent, save game jerseys and sandals. Come in jeans if you want.
- There are no annual subjective performance reviews that determine politically motivated promotions. As I've explained already, at a prop firm, performance is judged daily with a huge scoreboard (your P&L), and reviewed often. (Though very much like corporate America, if someone is underperforming, a layoff is most certainly in the offing.)
- And there is certainly no "sensitivity training."

Let ALJ's story be the example of what I'm talking about. ALJ is as white as a piece of paper, Catholic, conservative, who brings butter from home to spread on his bagel. Recently, when our water filter clogged, he started bringing in water as well. One day, ALJ twittered for @smbcapital a possible FCX trade. When the trade was presented, he shorted a small position and I implored him to be more aggressive. Like I said, ALJ is conservative.

ALJ presents the persona of a trader who would never say anything negative about anyone else on the desk. I suppose this fits in along with his conservative nature. Right around the time that JToma was being considered for a spot on CNBC's *Fast Money*, ALJ muttered under his breath, and doing his best Seinfeld imitation, "JToma has a face for radio." This comment was not intended to be heard by anyone else and certainly was just a joke. I reminded JToma of what ALJ had said about him loudly about 20 times over the next week. JToma then labeled ALJ "Mr. Negative."

I was trading a stock poorly one morning, buying a breakout, instead of buying into the pullback. I would buy and then hit the bids lower, buy and then hit the bids lower. It was frustrating. One play I announced that I hit the bids, while ALJ contemporaneously announced that he was getting long. ALJ continued, mocking me, "I get short when you get long, and long when you get flat." Here's how it went:

JK:	"ALJ is taking the other sides of all your trades, Bella."
Bella (to ALJ):	"Did you just tell me my trading was no good?"
ALJ:	"Bella, you keep complaining about buying and hitting. So I am shorting and covering."
Bella:	"So let me get this straight, ALJ. First you say that JToma has a face for radio and then you claim the partner of this firm can't trade? JK, ALJ is trouble. He is a bad apple. There is always a guy on a desk like this."
JK:	"That ALJ is indeed trouble. But at least he's keeping the firm flat while you rip it up!"

Fast forward a few days and JK was trading a different stock and struggling.

ALJ:	"JK, my stock is better."
Bella:	"ALJ, so first you say that JToma has a face for radio, then I can't trade, and now JK, who used to run his own prop firm, can't pick the right stock? You are always causing trouble."
ALJ (laughing coyly):	"No, that's not what I mean."

(At least he knows to defer to my power sometimes.)

On a trading desk, there is banter back and forth all day long. Friendships are forged. Feelings are not spared. The most interesting person is always whoever is making the most money. Anything funny goes.

JToma will say while frustrated with a tough stock, "That stock is a$$ banging me."

"I am not sure you have to use language like that," will be my response.

Dr. Momentum will chirp some news about a stock he is trading.

"Oh, Dr. Momentum, so young, and so much to learn," will come from my mouth (playfully with all the double entendre).

JToma was getting on Franchise the other day about not holding a stock. I offered, "JToma, are you jealous? Franchise is dating a former UVA Dance Team member. You'll be changing diapers later tonight."

Someone will offer an opinion about the direction of a stock and Steve will respond, "Chirp." Meaning stop giving your opinion and just watch the way the stock trades.

One night Playmaker invited our desk to a bar where his sister was guest bartending. Playmaker is 6'3" and 300 pounds, hence his nickname. Playmaker had one request of those attending. Under no circumstances was anyone permitted to hit on his sister. GMan got bombed and closed the bar down. GMan hit on Playmaker's sister. Not a week went by after the event when we did not point this out to Playmaker.

JToma ended up landing a regular spot on CNBC's *Fast Money Half-time Report*. He was terrific the first two appearances without much practice. He rehearsed for his next appearance with vigor. JToma prepared for two questions that had been fed to him by the show's producer. And he had them down cold. ALJ's desk prepared him some more. Before JToma walked from our offices on 5th Ave to NASDAQ where the show is shot, ALJ said, "JToma's answers are so good he will dazzle them."

And then the show starts and the question that JToma is expecting is not asked. Well, it is, but JToma can't hear the first part of the question. What he hears does not make sense to him. And he is caught off guard. And he is on national TV. He quickly recovers and does very well. But the desk razzed him for his initial hesitation for a whole week.

First GMan played a scene from *Billy Madison* on our shared monitor. The one where the principal says, "Mr. Madison, what you've just said is one of the most insanely idiotic things I have ever heard. At no point in your rambling, incoherent response were you even close to anything that could be considered a rational thought. Everyone in this room is now dumber for having listened to it. I award you no points, and may God have mercy on your soul."

Then ALJ had GMan play a video of a guest who appeared on Fox offering commentary and actually fainted on air.

"JToma, you were not as bad as that guy," ALJ offered.

And it still wasn't over. One of our new traders, a former college baseball player used to jock-like give and take, chimed in. This from a guy who was two live trading days into his career. Gutsy.

This new trader imitated JToma on *Fast Money* pleading to now former co-host Jeff Macke, "Macke, I am about to faint. I am about to faint. Help me!" This was met with thunderous laughter.

JToma responded. "Ok, I'll remember this, guys. Bella, should a guy who's been here two days be allowed to talk on the desk?"

Unfortunately, not all traders enjoy the company of those on their desk. As a prop firm grows, you can control only so much for corporate culture and recruiting the best fit.

One of the unwritten rules on a desk is that you do not profit off of another trader on the desk. I guess it's no longer unwritten now, huh? In fact, if someone has a big long position and he announces that he is selling, the unwritten rule is that you do not undercut this trader's position or front run his efforts. You wait until he gets a sale and then you attempt to sell. Back in the day, one trader boasted about how he was shorting a stock that almost the entire desk was long. This prop trader had a history of doing stuff like this: shorting while the others were still long. The stock went against most of the desk and yet this trader yapped boastfully about his chop. The leader of the prop desk, furious, leaped over the desk and punched this trader in the face. He just flat out popped the guy with a right cross. Well, he deserved it!

I walked in the other day four points in the money for an STT position. I hit the bids on 400 shares for a cool $1,600 to start the day (remember, we do not take out overnights often). AL J, wise-ass that he is, comments, "Imagine if you had the full $1k."

I said smirking, "You can't just sit there and offer congratulations or encouragement. You have to focus on the negative."

One of our guys got a hold of head shots of a few traders on our desk. Maybe he did this from Facebook shots? Maybe some other way, I'm not sure. He then found this video program where you can place photos of people and combine them with preset videos. There was a video of a Chippendales' spoof. The pictures of our guys were placed on Chippendales dancers. And the program ran. Bare chested men with head shots of our guys were grinding and striking sexy poses on the dance floor. It was hysterical.

If good times cannot persuade you to prop trade, how about superior statistical analysis?

COMPILING TRADER STATISTICS

Every successful prop trader knows his best setups. There are some traders who just know a great setup when they see it. But when you begin, it is important to measure your trading. We do so with our SMB Chop Tracker and our review process. Developing prop traders must know their win rate for their different trading setups. Ask yourself, if you made this trade one thousand times, how many instances would you profit? To reiterate, we search for setups where our win rate is 60 percent or higher, with a downside of 1 and an upside of 5.

For example, do you trade momentum setups better than buying into a pullback? If so, then you should spend more time trading momentum plays. One of our traders is an excellent momentum trader, but he trades gold too often. He feels most comfortable trading gold stocks. He has traded these stocks very well when they are In Play but only when they are In Play! It is not really that he trades gold stocks well, because if you look at the entire body of work, this is not accurate.

So recently I have made a point of complimenting him when he jumps into another momentum play that is not a gold stock. I have sent him numerous e-mails suggesting that he trade to his strengths and find more momentum trades. While trading, if I am in a momentum stock, I will talk with him. I try to get him into these stocks.

GMan has an engineering background. He loves to quantify everything that he does as a trader, so he created the SMB Chop Tracker for us. It records what stocks you trade best, your most profitable time of the day, your profit per trade, and more. Every day, you get a snapshot of your trading day with trading statistics and can make the appropriate adjustments armed with this data.

This is important. For example, we have learned that most of our desk trade poorly during the Midday. As a firm, we made adjustments. If you are killing it on the Open but then giving back your Open during the Midday then this is data that can revolutionize your results, such as trade with more size on the Open and with a lower tier size during the Midday, playing defense and holding your gains.

One of our most talented traders has a checkered history of jumping into anything that moves during the Midday. He loves our filters, which Trade-Ideas has helped us implement. Filters used properly offer more profitable trading opportunities. But filters used improperly by an over-aggressive trader during the Midday can be a disaster. And this talented trader would make $1,500 on the Open. And then he would try to turn $1,500 into $3k, which is great but not at this time of the day and in these stocks, with these setups. And then he would rip it up.

He came into my office to talk with me. This trader needs a lot of attention. Some traders you plop down on a desk and let them go. They listen. You say things once and they get it. They are low maintenance. This trader was the Mariah Carey of trading. This was just one of many talks. Maybe he just liked the way I talked. I don't know but I can remember many talks with this Diva trader. I actually liked him a lot so he got away with his neediness. He was dejected. And I said, "Your numbers are fine. You just have to make adjustments Midday." His trading skills were there, he just was mixing his results with trading plays that were not statistically profitable. When he learned to cut out these trades, then his numbers would more accurately reflect his ability.

We gave him a game plan for a lower tier size during the Midday, created rules that forbade him from giving back more than 25 percent during the Midday, and worked on highlighting the setups that worked best during the Midday. If he follows these rules, his results will be excellent.

For me, I make the most money statistically right on the Open. There are momentum trades that I trade best. One of them I have blogged about in the past and will share below. The importance is not necessarily to learn this trade but it is to understand what works best for you. I raise my tier size, and hold these trades longer.

V Right on the Open: Where I Want to Be

On April 30, 2009, we saw it again.* We had seen this in QCOM, MSFT, and now V. Right on the Open, V traded straight up (see Figure 10.1). If I told you I had a three-point trade in less than 15 minutes that reoccurs, would you be interested? As an intraday trader, this is a trade you must add to your quiver. Let's discuss.

I hear it all the time.

"Bella, that stock was too scary."

"Bella, that stock was too steep."

"I missed that move because I was trading PG."

"Bella, I do not like to trade on the Open."

"Bella, I like to wait fifteen minutes until the market settles."

- These are all excuses to miss a great upmove right on the Open in QCOM, MSFT, and on this day, V. This is like a golfer who can't hit his 3 iron. This is not a scary trade. I was aggressive right on the Open with V today because it was very strong into the Close yesterday. It never

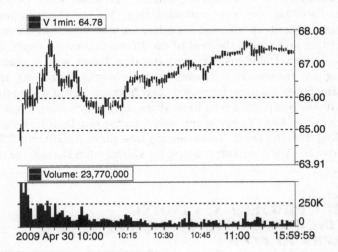

FIGURE 10.1   V Open 4/30/2009

---

*This section was adapted from a April 30, 2009, posting at Bella's Blogs (www.smbtraining.com/blog).

traded below 61.80 after the Fed and held nicely near 63.50 into the Close.
- The first ticks were up above 64.
- The first tested bid held.
- The next resistance was not for miles, 67.
- V has a history of being explosive.
- V is a Tier 1 stock that hedge funds and institutions buy. Think best of breed.
- The SPYs are above 87.
- Strong stocks have made strong moves after solid earnings.
- The bids kept stepping up and holding. This is the key. When I see this, I think "game on." Now I am aggressive.
- The bids never dropped from 64 to most of 67.50.

I do not care where V closes. This was a momentum trade to be made on the Open. Later, the market rolled over, so V plummeted. I care about a pattern that I see time after time, which most developing traders miss. This is easy money.

Well, there it is. A trade that you should master, place in your quiver, and utilize every week. For those who say, "Bella, the stock is too scary," that is garbage. Your job is to become a well-rounded trader. The market does not care that you are anxious during such a trade. This is a trade that works. Learn it. Get over your trepidation. And make some easy money.

One Saturday, we were watching tape. We are three hours into our Tradecast, with Steve offering his critiques and me sitting on our trading floor writing and eating the rest of the Bravo thin-crust, fresh mozzarella pizza delivered. Delicious! To start the day, I met with a trader who is breaking out. He should. He deserves it. He works his tail off. He used to sit out the Open because he would take frequent rips and be stopped out before 10 AM. Not a great way to start the day. I have worked on plays like the above with him. Today in my office during our huddle, he said, "I am just killing it on the Open. Those are my best plays statistically." This is the stuff I love to hear from our traders. He knows what butters his bread.

SECRET PROJECT X: FINDING CUTTING-EDGE WAYS TO TRAIN TRADERS BETTER

One day I was sitting around pretending to watch TV when I thought of a great idea. As a former competitive athlete, I think often of the importance practice had on my game days. The more I practiced, the better I played.

How can we find ways for our traders to practice? And I thought of Secret Project X.

Secret Project X took a long time to develop, a great deal of money, and was fraught with technical difficulties. GMan spearheaded this project and found a way to get it done. It has become a revolutionary training tool.

Why the name Secret Project X? Because this is a game changer and I didn't want anyone copying my idea. I recognized just how brilliant this idea was (with humility, of course).

Secret Project X allows our traders to practice. We record live data during the trading day of the Stocks In Play. We separate the trading data by specific trading patterns that we often trade. Then we offer our traders the opportunity to trade on a simulator practicing these specific trading patterns. How can this help? At one point, our new traders were killing it trading FAZ. A trader must learn how FAZ moves, how to use IYF and XLF to gain an edge, and become comfortable trading it. Now, some traders can just jump into FAZ and learn it. But at first they will lose money. Better to practice this ETF first and then trade it live.

I shared a V trade in the Trader Statistics section. A few of our traders were not comfortable jumping into V right away. ("Bella, I don't want to trade V. It's too scary," as they fled like a frightened son to his father's arms in a tent at Boy Scout camp.) So now we can record V on the Open, and sit these traders down and let them practice, while offering our commentary.

If you want to be great at anything, you must practice. And the genius of Secret Project X is that it allows you to engage in deep practice. Prop firms find inventive ways to help their traders succeed.

To Dapper Don, who approached me after the Traders Expo, I hope this chapter helps you understand the benefits of working for a prop trading firm and the education they can provide. We will make sure you are in the right stocks, help you sidestep potential land mines, offer adjustments you must make when the market changes, include the advantage of our deeper pockets, share our best trading ideas with you, allow learning from others on our desk, review video of your trading, make sure you can crunch your trading statistics, provide a few laughs at work, demand you follow your trading rules, motivate you to get better, and show you how to be professional. So really, my question to you, Dapper Don, is this: Why are you trading alone? Every good one has superstar teachers and a dynamite education program that develops the firm's next superstar traders. That could be you.

CHAPTER 11

The Best Teacher

> "I am not bound to win, but I am bound to be true.
> I am not bound to succeed, but I am bound to live by
> the light that I have."
>
> —Abraham Lincoln

New traders frequently think that learning from the most talented traders is the best way to learn. On the contrary, new traders should seek the *best* teacher. There is a difference. I don't believe in the old mantra "those who can't do, teach," because in trading many do both. But sometimes the best trader has no personality, or poor people skills, while a consistently profitable, but not top 10 trader, can emerge as a premier lecturer, one-on-one communicator, and mentor.

During one interview, a potential candidate boasted, "I plan on being your best trader. Do I get a chance to watch your best trader?" With his engine of ambition, this Ivy League–educated candidate believed that learning from the most talented traders was the best way to learn. Just like a lot of platitudes one would assume to be intuitively obvious, such as "learn from the best," this is not one of them. New traders need to find the best teacher. But I liked the young man's confidence nonetheless.

My philosophy echoes throughout the prop trading world. A friend of mine in the business who leads his prop firm's training efforts was quick to share with me that he was not the best trader on his desk. This is not exactly a slight since his firm is loaded with excellent traders, almost all of whom he personally trained. His firm is certainly not of the "League of Lesser Firms" I mentioned in Chapter 3.

As much as we preach the importance of the process, our guys are more interested in my mentorship when my results top our leaderboard. This is not to say that they do not listen when I am not on top of our leaderboard, but certainly they listen much more carefully when I am. But just like in all of human nature, we chase what's hot. When Steve or GMan or JToma leads the pack, people swarm to them. When I first started trading, it was almost hysterical watching traders swarm like bees to honey to the desk of a hot trader whose name they hardly knew.

Some traders obsessively monitor the leaderboard. We have one trader who lurks near our leaderboard, just staring at it. To this trader, our leaderboard is as mesmerizing as Scarlett Johansson is to the rest of the male population. I once asked him, "Do you think we are gonna quiz you on those results?"

One of our former traders spent so much time near the leaderboard I don't know how he had any time to trade. Perhaps if he spent more time learning how to trade than staring at the leaderboard he'd still be with us. We have a detailed, state-of-the-art clearing site that keeps track of the numbers for all of our traders. With this guy, who needed a clearing site? He was like that friend in elementary school who walked around like he was the Baseball Encyclopedia, "out-stating" friends and soon-to-be non-friends. It is just human nature to be interested in how others are doing, especially compared to you. But this mentality is not in the new trader's best interest.

"Mike, doesn't it make sense that you ought to learn from the best?" people ask me. "Don't I need to learn from the best to become the best?" they continue.

No.

If this were the case, then Steve and I would be sitting next to our friends, some of whom are the best traders on the Street. It just doesn't work like that.

Think about it. Who are some of the best professional coaches? Were they preeminent players? Let's take a look at a few professional coaches:

- Phil Jackson: A 10-time NBA champion as a head coach, but was a fan favorite role player when he played for the Knicks.
- Bill Belichick: A 3-time Super Bowl champion as a coach, yet never played a down of pro football, and played his college ball at Division III Wesleyan University (a school better known for its poets, artists, and writers).
- Pat Riley: A 5-time NBA champion as a head coach, but like Jackson, was a role player in the NBA. He averaged just over seven points a game as a pro.

- Isiah Thomas: Zeek was a 2-time NBA champion as a player, Hall-of-Famer, and member of the 50 greatest NBA players. He was also a three-time destroyer of franchises as a coach or executive. Things fell so far for Isiah that when he was introduced as the head coach of Florida International University in the spring of 2009, the athletic director called him "Isiah Thompson." That hurts.

The same applies at the collegiate ranks.

- Rick Pitino: One NCAA title and five Final Fours (with three different teams) as a college coach. While he has sent many players to the NBA, he never played there himself.
- Gino Auriemma: Has led the UConn Women's Basketball program to seven NCAA titles, but had no distinguished accomplishments as a player at small West Chester University.
- And my favorite, Coach K: 4 NCAA titles as a coach, but never played professionally after graduating from West Point.

The trend continues.

Joe Torre seems to be one of the few exceptions of great players (he was a nine-time All-Star and borderline Hall of Fame player), turned certain Hall of Fame manager. My dad and I spent many summer evenings in our season seats at the old stadium appreciating his steady, classy leadership during the Yankee dynasty of the late 1990s. As the "Big Aristotle," Shaq tweeted about his former coach Phil Jackson, "When the general doesn't panic, the troops don't panic." How many prodigious former players have the patience of Mr. Torre?

If the top coaches were not the best players, then why do new traders look to the best traders for mentorship?

I posed this dilemma to the best trading teacher I know, Dr. Brett Steenbarger. He responded, "Many of the great coaches were competent players in their own right, but not all-stars. They knew the game, but their passion was for teaching and developing players. They worked on their coaching game as hard as the all-stars worked on their playing game. It's all about knowing what makes you tick, and what you're really good at." Spot-on commentary from the trading coach of all trading coaches.

The skills necessary to become a great trader are different from those required to be an effective trading coach. Being a star trader requires superior pattern recognition and discipline. On the other hand, superstar trading coaches are often:

- Obsessed with finding better ways to teach
- Highly motivated

- Communicate clearly
- Consider a trader's unique style
- Patient
- Know when to get tough
- Unselfish
- Set firm values
- Believe in the student

This chapter explores why finding the best coach and looking inward at your trading breeds the most improvement for your trading.

NEVER SATISFIED

Before every new training class at SMB, I scrub our training program that Steve and I spent two years developing. I identify all of our weaknesses. I make a list of what we can do better. Before one class, we added SMB Webinars, which is now our best teaching tool. Before another class, we added videos of statistically profitable trading plays with audio commentary. As I write this book, we plan on adding Secret Project X to the course. We never stop improving our training program. We never will.

A great trader constantly thinks about how to become better. They scour charts to find the next big trade and diligently reassess risk management. A great teacher thinks about better ways to instruct. Creating our webinars, videos, morning meeting agendas, trading plays, and the rest of our training program took years of work and many after-hours alone in my office saturated in grunt work.

I was once asked by a trader, "Bella, what are you most competitive about?"

I act a little laid back around our traders. Joe Torre was always so calm around the Yankees during their great run. No matter what the situation, when the camera found him in the dugout he always wore a calm exterior. This made an impression on me as a teacher. Part of my job is to be calm and reassuring while teaching. But this should not be mistaken for a lack of competitiveness. I am most competitive with developing our training. I am most interested in offering the very best equity intraday training program on the Street and building our firm. This is most challenging to me and the best use of my talents. It is just not interesting to me to be the best trader on the Street anymore. That dream is now for those I teach to pursue.

The Enforcer, our Floor Manager, an expert on the best cheeseburgers in NYC (he says JG Melon), and one of the most disciplined traders I have ever trained, likes to kid that our training program is much better than when he began a few years ago. Of course it is, burger boy. And in two years, it will be even better than today. Our newest tool, Secret Project X, has cost us a great deal of money and time to develop.And this was my idea. Call it an obsession, but I think about this stuff constantly. It costs a great deal of time and money for a firm to ensure its traders are mentored in the right way.

HIGHLY MOTIVATED

A great trader may lack the incentive to create the best training program. They are making millions trading, so why bother teaching a new trader? If SMB builds a desk of 150 profitable traders, then the personal and monetary rewards will be substantial. So needless to say, I am motivated. One day, perhaps Steve and I will be thought of as the Julian Robertson of intraday equities traders. (Robertson, chairman of Tiger Management, has seeded directly or indirectly over 50 hedge fund managers in the last two decades. His protégés are aptly called Tiger Cubs.)

My business partner, Steve, is recognized as one of the top intraday traders in our community. When I first approached Steve about starting a firm, his response, mixed with laughter, was "Why would I want to do that?" Steve immediately calculated the potential loss from mentoring. His lack of interest was crystal clear.

For myself, I was just looking for a different challenge. I believed my skills could be better utilized running a firm. Trading just was not enough for me anymore.

But then Steve started thinking, and I started offering a clear vision of a prop firm that we could create. (I really just ignored his initial response. My best friend from grade school wasn't going to get a pass that easily. What if Vincent Chase didn't have Eric Murphy as his manager in HBO's *Entourage*? He was going to be a part of this new firm whether he agreed to it or not.) I just started working, and I kept involving him in the process. He really never had time to object once he immersed himself in it with me (I know Steve wants to kill me some weekends when we are buried in work no trader would ever want to do). And along the way, after further reflection, we both recognized that if we developed an excellent training program, our sacrifices would be rewarded.

COMMUNICATE CLEARLY

A great teacher communicates exceptionally well. A great trader can be incoherent. When I first started, I approached the best trader at our firm. This English-challenged former Russian chess champ, though very nice, was unintelligible. Many great traders are just the same; they can't explain their methodology coherently. (Nor do they wish to for fear of eroding their "edge.")

SMB had an interest in opening up an office in India and set up a meeting with some entrepreneurs; the plan was to find one good trader, have him trained in our system, and leverage our training program to develop a desk. I rose from my seat in our former conference room, which could act as a sauna in the after-hours if necessary, stepped toward our white board and wrote this:

- Successful Trader
- SMB System
- Teacher
- Mentor
- Manager
- Recruiter
- Growth

I explained to those in the room that these were all separate jobs, and that they would need all for a successful trading office in India. I continued that first it would be very difficult to find a successful trader, and then it would be even harder to find one who would agree to learn and follow our system. And even then, it would be a 1 in 50 chance that this successful trader would also happen to be a good teacher. We suggested a different business proposal, where SMB played a bigger role in teaching and mentoring, to improve the chances of success. These sharp businessmen quickly grasped the importance of restructuring their business plan. And we were off.

I recently had dinner with a great trader. This trader is a superstar prop trader with excellent communication skills. We were discussing momentum trading. This well-known prop trader mentioned he found it difficult to teach momentum trading. He asked me how I teach it. Now the gap between his trading ability and mine is so wide I am not sure we are playing the same sport. Yet this star trader wondered if I could teach momentum trading better. Teaching momentum trading is very difficult. But a good teacher can sit down and figure it out. And I did.

Chip and Dan Heath argue in their book *Made to Stick* that for a message to stick, it must be:

- Simple
- Unexpected
- Concrete

- Credible
- Emotional
- Filled with stories

As coaches, we must teach our important points with the preceding criteria. Like a great trader who can point out the most important technical levels, a great teacher communicates each important teaching lesson with these principles. Does a great trader have the discipline and knowledge to do so?

BUILDS ON A FIRM FOUNDATION

An outstanding trader may have developed a trading system above your skill level. His system may just be too complicated or difficult for you to execute at this stage of your trading career. You may not be able to recognize when exactly to short 70,000 SKF when he can. You may not have the skills to manage that position if it initially trades against you. When you begin, 300 SKF may be all that you can handle.

Consistently profitable traders constantly evaluate their trading system. They make adjustments every month, every day, and even intraday. I have substantially changed my trading system six times since I began. I have traded through the Asian Financial Crisis, tech boom, Internet Boom, bursting of the Internet bubble, 9/11, a range-bound market, and now the near collapse of the banking system. Every day is new. There is no "system" to learn. It is about developing trading skills and then making adjustments continually.

A new trader must start by learning the basics. Architecture students do not start by designing skyscrapers. New traders must focus on developing trading skills, discipline, and controlling their emotions. They must develop a foundation from which they can build. They should start with straightforward trading setups. Simply, they should first learn how to trade.

RIMM: Learn How to Trade

One of the most helpful and funniest traders on our desk one day complained about getting stopped out in a RIMM trade. During our morning meeting, we identified 82 as a level. Steve shared that he would look to short near this level. We even tweeted RIMM as our best morning idea. (Before each Open, SMB tweets its best morning idea for the Twitter and StockTwits communities.)

This trader showed me his executions and explained how he shorted at 82, and got stopped out above 82.32. RIMM immediately traded down to 79 afterward. Some stop-hunting market maker cleared this trader off his book at an intraday high! And then he went back to doing what he was doing to help the firm, without more comment. He seemed content with thinking that he got screwed.

My response? "You are not kidding, are you?" Did I really teach this guy? I think maybe he may have missed a few lectures. There is nothing in our training that suggests that trading is as easy as getting short in front of resistance and watching a stock melt. Sometimes this happens. And these are great trades. But you must also know how to trade. And what I mean by that is that you must also be able to trade this very simple fake breakout that RIMM offered.

Bear with me on this one . . . the following rundown of this failed RIMM trade and how to improve it gets very technical in a hurry, so brush up on your terminology.

82 is a level. There are trades where this level will hold and the stock will melt. On the Open, when the volatility is the highest, makes it less likely that the stock will just hold this resistance level. It is very possible that RIMM will quickly trade above 82, shaking out weak-hand shorts.

Of course, you short RIMM near 82. But on the Open, you piece in to the trade. You short some near 82 and wait to see if the 82 level holds. If it quickly trades above 82, then you short some more above, perhaps 82.17 since 82.25 is a level. When RIMM trades above 82.25 you watch to see if it holds above this level or just immediately cover. If you cover and the stock does not hold a bid above 82.25, then you whack the bids again. Now you actually have a better short than you originally had since there are more short-term players long above 82 that now have to hit the bids caught short.

But you must be able to trade this level with more than one simple result, a held offer at 82. And there are going to be more subsets of this resistance level trade on the Open. And you must learn how to trade each of these subsets. The big picture is still the same. You have points of downside and minimal risk that RIMM will trade higher as of yet. Crush this trading opportunity.

With a trading foundation you can trade all the different ways RIMM may trade around or a little above 82 on the Open and crush this trade. With the mindset that all you must do is follow prescribed levels, then you are going to get stopped out, complain, and lose money. The market demands more. The market does not reward the trader seeking lazy trades, buy here and sell here.

When I attended the 2009 Trader Expo, where I also gave a speech to the trading masses, there was some absurd trading system being sold that tells people where to buy when their screen becomes green and sell when their screen turns red. They had about one thousand more visitors than we did over the course of a weekend. Anyone who thinks that trading is that simple deserves the consequences that are about to follow—trading losses and lots of them.

The market is always changing. Setups that worked yesterday may not work tomorrow. It is paramount to develop trading skills so traders can adjust to market changes.

YOU SAY TOMATO, I SAY TOMAHTO

One of our better traders once shared with me his frustration that he could not trade like Steve, who can watch eight open positions simultaneously like some kind of supercomputer. Moreover, I know of numerous examples, at multiple prop firms, where the positions of superstar traders initially visible by firm members were taken down. These firms were suffering losses as weaker traders tried to copy the superstar. Without fully developed trading skills, novice traders were unable to execute these advanced setups.

A superstar teacher, however, will teach you comprehensive trading skills so that you gravitate toward a style that is best for you. The importance of the principle was highlighted by Los Angeles Lakers guard Derek Fisher commenting on his coach, the aforementioned Phil Jackson, "He doesn't try to control you. He empowers you to be who you are."

In an anecdote I found while doing research for this book, Boris Stein of Stein Management, LLC, a program trader, shared his lowest moment as a trader occurred "after trying to trade the mechanical systems of several famous traders and losing much money."

In an interview with *Trader's World* magazine, Mr. Stein replayed a painful learning experience:

> *One of my first trades was in 1996, and I wanted to apply some lessons from a book about placing stop orders. I placed a stop order to buy the S&P above the current price, and after getting filled, I placed a protective stop-loss order below the current price. Both stop orders were placed at the levels recommended in the book, and I was not going to move my stops no matter what, because it was described as the biggest trader sin. Right after my buy order was filled, the S&P went straight down, and my stop-loss was hit. After stopping me out, the price went straight up. I lost $5,000 in 25 minutes. My buy price was the exact high of the day, and my sell price was the exact low of the day. To this day, I still cannot believe it.*

Now it's quite possible some savvy shark market maker saw this newbie chump's orders and separated him from his $5,000 with relative ease. But Stein quickly recognized that he couldn't trade out of a book like these stars without first learning the basics. He needed to develop his own system.

We trade an active short-term style at SMB. There have been traders on our desk whom I have recommended trade elsewhere because our style is not best for them. Ed Seykota of *Market Wizards* fame offered on this topic: "There is no best system, any more than there is a best car. There might, however, be a best car for you." These traders were better suited for a slower, longer-term trading style perhaps accompanied by some analysis that an investment banker would use on a balance sheet. They could not process all the indicators that we watch and make millisecond decisions or this was just not their trading niche.

Chart Climber

One of these traders was one of my favorite people we have trained. Chart Climber (named for his affection for all things charts) was intellectually curious. He would e-mail me articles from *The New Yorker* or *The Onion* that I had missed. During the 2008 election, he was one whose thoughts I most enjoyed concerning Pakistan, the Bailout, and tax increases.

This former prop trader was linked to numerous chat rooms, and other traders via IM. He had worked for too many years in one of those jobs that no one could possibly enjoy after a few years and loved trading with us. At the first firm in which SMB was housed, where space allocated to SMB was limited, we were asked to cut this trader from our desk. I refused.

In fact, this was partially the reason why we ended up finding a new home. Traders make a firm, not some non-trader in a back office keeping the books. Steve and I, traders, knew best who should stay and who should be cut. During a group meeting explaining our move, I spoke from my heart, "Traders are the most important part of any firm. Traders decide the future of a firm. This firm will always be run by traders for traders. And we will not be forced to cut any of our hard-working traders, even if they are our weakest, if they are working hard, adding value, and making progress." Chart Climber was the most optimistic trader we have ever trained. He would make a chop into the Close and this was the only trade he remembered for the month. He was like a hacker golfer who made an 80-foot par on the 18th hole and all he could remember during drinks in the clubhouse was that miracle bomb he drained.

But after a substantial time, he just wasn't making money with us (the landlord who wanted us to cut Chart Climber was correct in the end, but at the wrong time and most important, for the wrong reasons). It was not fair for us to let him believe we were the best firm for him going forward. We were not losing much money on him but he wasn't in the right place for himself. And we let him go.

For those interested, he does still send me interesting articles, which I always appreciate. He stills drops by the office to say hi. And this trader has found a home as a futures trader.

LOOKS INWARD

Developing traders who wish to make more ought to look inward. Most new traders need to become better at the setups that are working for them, make more of them, and learn to add size in these trades incrementally. They also need to eliminate their mental weaknesses. Contemporaneously but slowly, they should add new setups to their quiver. This is the path to improving profits.

As traders, we can learn from Abraham Lincoln again, who said we must be disciplined "by the better angels of our nature." Poor traders blame their trading platform. They blame those who sit next to them. They complain about the A/C. They harp on things out of their control such as SEC taxes, ECN charges, and data fees. There is always something or someone to blame.

Yet often, these are the same traders who miss easy setups, never conquer their psychological demons, and wouldn't think of keeping a detailed trading journal. And their mind wanders, "If only I were taught by the best trader on the Street, then I would be doing better." I don't think so.

For example, one trader I know who needs to improve holds his trades for too short a time. For him there are not enough Trades2Hold in his quiver. Almost every trade is just a move to move trade. This trader was recently moved to sit near some guys who understand the big picture better. This developing trader needs to identify the trades that are best for him to hold. Then this youngster needs to work on actually holding these trades and not exiting so quickly as he almost always does. We could sit this young trader next to Steve Cohen and this would still be his issue for him to improve (of course, Mr. Cohen might just tell him to hold or be fired).

PRACTICES PATIENCE

A great trader may not be patient enough to work with a new trader. Perhaps it is a lack of desire to be a mentor, or frustrated when the protégé doesn't "get it" as easily as the master.

At times, I have these thoughts. For example, one of our talented young traders was not a fan of our loss limit rules. But when he started, he just could not keep his profits from the Open. As we discussed, we have a rule on our desk that you cannot give back more than 30 percent of your profits from the Open during the Midday. And if you violate this rule, then we reduce your tier size the next day.

At one point early on, this young trader ripped it up during the Midday, when all our stats show traders do the worst. (In fact, this loss limit rule was put in place because of traders like him.) Steve sent him an e-mail informing him that he would be enforcing the rules, much to the chagrin of this newbie. This likable young trader responded angrily via e-mail that this is not fair, kind of like a fifth grader. Now this is not the first time this has happened. And the rule was implemented for his benefit.

A great trader may not have the patience to respond to this trader. A great trader may just tell the newbie, "Shut the (expletive deleted) up already and stop losing money Midday." I cringe relaying this particular anecdote. While trading on a prop desk in the middle of my career, I watched a promising young trader get bounced by an excellent trader with only, "You are through. Get the hell off of our desk. Go lose money for someone else."

Back when I started with Steve, our mentors thought cutting edge instruction was 100 pushups for every mistake we made trading (speaking of acting like a fifth grader). But research shows that only about 20 percent of children and adults are able to handle put-downs without emotional pain or psychological damage. (Bobby Knight might take exception to this data.) It takes four positive comments to make the impact of one negative comment to most. Mark Twain said, "I can live for two months on a good compliment." I have found that every trader is different. Some, if you raise your voice, become very uncomfortable, almost causing a traumatic experience for them. Others, if you are not screaming at the top of your lungs, do not pay attention. Coaches need to think carefully before they speak, so they are providing targeted, individual messages and feedback to their students, which is best for their development.

I was on a long overdue summer vacation to the pristine Outer Banks. A call with one of our remote traders who had been struggling had been set up for me. This trader had taken a special master's program in Switzerland to learn more about the markets. He was previously a professional pop musician. This trader, let's call him Pop Trader, wanted to talk. He had been trading so poorly that Steve cut off his buying power. Now as much as this trader was technically fired there was still the possibility for us to continue our relationship.

On Sundays, he sent me detailed analysis of his trading progress. He was also just about the nicest person you could ever meet. Pop Trader calmly and respectfully relayed that in his opinion he had been cut off too quickly. He mentioned that we teach improving every day and this was his focus and now it was unfair that he was just dismissed. This set me off. Offer whatever critique you want about the firm that I have built but do not label anything we do as unfair.

Our desk had outperformed the Street in August 2009 and he lost money. Our traders were in the Stocks In Play and he was in mostly non-moving garbage stocks day after day. Our desk had mastered momentum trading and he was fearful to jump into them. Pop Star continually failed to hit stocks that traded against him.

I felt Pop Star was using our mantra, improve every day, as an excuse. He clearly was not doing everything possible to improve every day. He was in the wrong stocks, unable to conquer a common psychological hurdle, and resisted trading the Stocks In Play. I pointed out his underperformance and lack of improvement heatedly.

Pop Star listened. Eventually after exhausting any frustration one could muster while looking directly out at the ocean, I asked him to write me an e-mail about some issues he needed to improve. He agreed. And I hung up the phone.

Talk about being a horrible teacher. What a mistake by me. I did not listen. Pop Star was not one to respond to loud confrontation. I put my desire to go back to whatever I was doing on vacation before his progress. I was disrespectful. I did not teach him as much as I could during our conversation. I hung up the phone singed with embarrassment. In fairness to myself I was not mentally prepared to field this call since I was on a much needed vacation. I never got the e-mail I wanted from Pop Star.

John Wooden wrote in *Wooden on Leadership*, "Many leaders don't fully appreciate the fact that by telling someone what to do you must teach him how to do it. And this process requires patience." As a trading teacher, you must explain why a rule is in a trader's best interest. You ought to get the new trader to buy into the importance of this rule or any rule. The great speech writer and *Wall Street Journal* contributor Peggy Noonan in "On Speaking Well" counseled that "the most moving part of a speech is always the logic." Great teachers use solid reasoning to make their teaching points. Being the boss is not a good enough reason to enforce a rule. Well, it may be, but it is not good teaching.

GETS TOUGH

It is also the job of a mentor to challenge their students. I empathize with the new trader. Trading is difficult. If a trader is working hard but not yet getting it then they deserve patience. But standards must be set. And when traders are violating core market principles, their feelings should not be spared.

Sometimes you must get a trader's attention by raising your voice. Sometimes the desk struggles or a trader is underperforming. Coach K said on Charlie Rose after his Gold Medal coaching performance that "you have to talk strong in weaker times." And we spend thousands of hours with our traders. Every so often you must communicate in a louder, more passionate voice so they understand the importance of a particular point.

In February 2009, I was disappointed with a few traders on our desk, and I called a meeting. I growled, "Your mental preparation is unacceptable. This is your opportunity to do something great. You will not realize your potential until you improve your preparation." This was all premeditated, and like a great actor I seemed pissed. Regardless of what I did, mainly I was leading them to set a higher standard for themselves. The desk subsequently went on a trading tear.

A good teacher is most concerned with the improvement of their students and not being the most popular guy on the desk. As part of getting tough, sometimes a trader needs to be called out. When some of our developing traders first starting getting good, they still lacked Trades2Hold for their playbook. And we ripped into them when they missed easy opportunities for Trades2Hold. GMan would challenge, "Why aren't you still holding that (Tickster)?" Steve would call out, "(Dr. Momentum), that is a play you must be in."

At first, our traders who were starting to do well did not like being called out. Some asked to speak with me in private. "Why is GMan always on my case?" And "Steve is so hard on me." I sat there, listened, and then had a flash-back. I thought back to how guys were disciplined back in the day. A trader was sat in the middle of the trading floor forced to wear a dunce cap for the entire day. This is certainly not a technique I would ever use. Then I spoke, "If we make you so uncomfortable for missing a trade, you will eventually become so disgusted with being called out that you will stop missing the trade."

And I had a few sit-downs with some core traders unhappy with being called out. I explained that it was our job to make sure we did everything we could to motivate them to develop their Trades2Hold. We would continue to point out Trades2Hold after the Close, so they knew which of these trades were most opportunistic. We lauded those who made successful Trades2Hold and spoke with traders who missed opportunities. And our guys improved.

Today, some of those traders who spoke with me behind closed doors now are armed with Trades2Hold. And this is all that is important.

SACRIFICES

Great teachers must be unselfish. They must sacrifice a considerable amount of their trading profits as they improve their teaching. There are talks you must have when you are tired and want to head home. There are days you have to work when you want to rest.

I talk through my trades with our newest traders in real time, which diminishes my focus and manifests missed trades. We have a training call to which our new traders are connected. I explain why I am buying, why I am selling, and what I am thinking. Together, our new traders and I trade a stock.

But during this instruction, I miss trades explaining what I am thinking. Sometimes I am considering how to make a point more clearly and I just miss a trading opportunity as my mind is focused on my explanation. I quickly finish my point and add, "I should have bought there instead of talking." And I choose stocks that are easiest for new traders to follow. This affects my overall profits.

Here is a scene repeated frequently on our prop desk. Steve returns from his office after a discussion with a developing trader. Steve sits. Steve scans the markets. And then it comes. Steve almost without fail cries, "Oh, I cannot believe I missed that!"

One of the things I loved about being just a trader were the weekends off. Oh, do I miss the trips I took, the people I met, the fun I had. Those days are gone. Saturday is a work day. Sunday is a work day. There are conversations to rehearse to help our traders. There are new lectures to write. There are new trading patterns to discover and explain for our traders to exploit. There are better ways to teach that must be discovered. Even near the end of mass on Sunday my mind starts to make a list of things to accomplish. I shake hands with Father O'Connor, thank him for his sermon, leave mass, and head back to work.

SET FIRM VALUES

A good teacher sets values. How should prop traders spend their day? What will their work ethic be? How will they judge their trading days? All this starts at the top. It begins with the teacher.

Our traders are taught the value of hard work on my desk. I preach that fully developed trading skills is the answer to their trading consistency. I am an exceptionally hard worker. I stay late, work weekends, and work consistently. This is not lost on any trader on my desk. Our training program starts with a five-week program where every minute for 10 hours a day is mapped out for them. And this is just the very first part of our training program; next comes Trader Development. This allows me the legitimacy to preach hard work. And this rubs off on my desk.

SMB recently spent a few days trading at another firm because of a tech emergency. The head trader of that firm asked, "How do you get your traders to sit in their seats so long? We can't get our guys to stay still for more than an hour." And these words came from an excellent prop trainer at an outstanding prop firm. I was very proud of our guys. In a new environment, with plenty of change to complain about, they sat, focused, and traded. The answer is because my partner Steve Spencer sits in his seat all day long and never misses a tick.

Next I'll share one of my favorite blogs that I wrote. Nothing can explain my teaching philosophy more than below. Not my trading setups, or when I sweep or offer, not when I load up. These are my values.

10x Equals X

Maybe I am starting to get a little old.* Maybe the half a generation removed from most of our traders is the difference. But I see a disturbing trend with a few developing traders and some potential new traders whom we interview. I want to emphasize that I see this with only a few. These new traders believe that if their work output is x, then their reward must be x. If only that were the case. When you begin as a trader, your work output must be 10x to make x. Let's discuss.

I do not want you to be in that group of a few. And I have seen this with a few former talented individuals on our desk who consequently were asked to leave. And I see this with a few of our present traders who have all been talked to. And some of these above were the most talented people we have ever trained. But that is never enough for the market. Potential absent sustained effort is not rewarded by the market.

What I see from my seat as a mentor on a trading desk is crystal clear. The developing traders who love trading and work at it do the best. Our most improved trader this month has done everything a developing trader is supposed to do and more. Much, much, more. Today as he reviews his numbers for the month, there will be a huge smile on his face.

Little things can make all the difference. Do you watch the markets trade during the Midday and search for important levels into the Close? Or do you take a two-hour lunch? After the Close, do you obsessively

---

*This section was adapted from a May 2, 2009, posting at Bella's Blogs (www.smbtraining.com/blog).

replay your trading day in your head and feed your mind with your best setups? Or are you immersed in Fantasy Baseball? Do you take all the time that is necessary to ensure that you are in the best trading stocks for your style before the Open? Or do you settle on the first stock that could work? Do you work on your mental weaknesses by performing visualization exercises? Or do you just assume you don't need to do stuff like that?

From my seat, most developing traders struggle when they first start. This is all part of the process. And then they have a choice. They can increase their work output to 10x. Or like all traders who fail, they can do 1/2 x. After they start doing 1/2 x then their results are inevitably -3x. Traders who decide to do 10x then see x (good thing I am the product of an excellent public school district to get that math above correct).

With trading experience and a constant work product of 10x, developing traders see 2x, and then 3x. Then, with this experience, their work product can decrease to 9x and see a gain up to 5x, and then 8x for a gain of 6x, and then 7x for a gain of 7x. Only after years of a work product that is not proportionally rewarded can they then see a work product that is properly rewarded.

Last night I was at a Hall of Fame (HOF) dinner for a friend in upstate NY. One of the HOF recipients had passed. His wife spoke in his honor. Her speech was moving. This woman's accomplished husband had passed and she was still so young. What was there really to gain from this speech? The people in the room respected her husband, which was why he was being inducted. Most of the people were her friends, so she didn't need to impress them. She was retired so it's not like this was going to help her career. There was little for her to gain.

And yet this woman inspired the room. With the care she had taken with the preparation of her words she shouted to everyone in the room, "If you are asked to do something, then you do it well. Do it with love." She never uttered these words. But it was in every line as she reflected on her husband's life. She had scoured his old yearbook, called up old friends for anecdotes, and asked her children what was most important about their father. She had worked on this 5-minute speech for days, with almost no reward to herself. In a room filled with mostly retired jocks, she left many in joyful tears, remembering the life of her HOF husband.

We can all learn from this remarkable speech. If you want to be a HOF trader, then embrace the value of doing something well for the sake of doing something well. If you are asked to do something, then do it as well as you can. There really is nothing else that is as satisfying. For the developing trader, 10x equals x.

The new trader who values hard work just may very well become a superstar trader.

BELIEVE IN THE STUDENT

A good teacher believes in every one of their students. Let me share an anecdote where my belief may have helped a future star trader.

Tickster did not excel when he first started. I saw his talent, his unordinary ability to process information, his lavish passion for the markets. After about a year, he was doing Ok but still not as well as I perceived he could. I had a talk with him. We talked about trading adjustments. And then I finished with "you will be the next great trader on our desk." He improved dramatically but still not as good as I knew he could be. I had another talk with him. Again I looked him squarely in the eyes, paused, and finished with "you are going to be the next great trader on our desk." He improved some more.

There is another trader on our desk, JLA, almost ready for this talk. But I am not quite ready for it yet. You cannot give these talks until you really believe them. I believed that Tickster was ready. He needed to believe. It was my job to plant this thought in his head and repeat it.

There are traders who just need to be told they are ready. They are like great thoroughbreds that just need a whip from their jockey. "It's time." They can do it, they just need to be led with a teacher's personal belief in them.

THERE'S ALWAYS MORE TO LEARN

It is an excellent idea for all of us to reach out to great traders. I do and I learn from them. Some are also effective teachers. I am interested in what they are trading and why. I love to hear the stories of their great trades. But I know that I trade differently. When I play pickup basketball, I do not attempt a 360 reverse jam on a breakaway. I can barely touch the rim these days as it is.

Walter Peters in his article, "What I learned From the Best Trader I Have Ever Known," shares what he learned from his "Millionaire Trader Friend." Particularly interesting is Mr. Peters learned from his Millionaire Trader Friend that you do not have to reinvent the wheel. Mr. Peters learned that you must find a system from existing systems that makes sense to you. That you can let trades come to you. And, you should continually learn.

John Netto of NetBlack Capital made the point in an interview that what we can learn from a great trader is one's trading is just a mirror of one's life. To be a disciplined trader, you must first in fact be disciplined in *your* life. We saw the importance of this with Mad Max earlier. What good does it do to teach a new trader to trade with discipline if he is not disciplined in his own life?

Here is what I learned from a good friend of SMB and respected trading educator, Brian Shannon.

Ten Things I Learned from a Professional Trader (Brian Shannon)

Brian Shannon of www.alphatrends.net and @alphatrends was our special guest speaker yesterday. During a busy week of trading, the NYC Trader Expo, and meetings, SMB was grateful that our good friend found some time to talk with our desk. It was a lecture not to be missed. Thank you, Brian!

Here are 10 things that I learned from Brian's lecture:

1. Brian does more preparation than 98 percent of all the traders with whom I have traded or trained.

2. Brian knows exactly how he makes money as a trader and which setups are best FOR HIM.

3. Brian accepts that the trading patterns that are best for him often may not work.

4. Brian reduces his risk in trades that are not working for him quickly.

5. Brian trades Stocks In Play just like SMB, but he goes about his search distinctly. He carries around a list of 200 stocks he most wants to watch during a given period and then hammers down from these options daily.

6. Brian readily admits two weaknesses in his trading, which are also mine: selling too early and not having size for the entire move. There is no destination for a trader. There is nothing to get. There is only continually working to improve every day.

7. Brian knows more about technical analysis than almost all traders but seeks confirmation from the order flow.

8. Brian shares that a setup may not work the first or second time. But he has the confidence and persistence to stay with his best setups and make that third trade, which may lead to a winner.

9. Brian left me an autographed copy of his book, *Technical Analysis Using Multiple Timeframes*, as a gift and could use some help with his handwriting. But seriously, what an awesome gift!

10. Brian loves drinking with GMan. Hard to meet a better person and trader to learn from than Brian Shannon of alphatrends.net.

I have been trading for 12 years. I have traded multiple financial and geopolitical crises as well as dull markets. I had a run before very recently where I had been positive every single month for five years, save one. I have read hundreds of books on coaching and trading. I have a law degree. And I run a trading firm that is recognized for its exceptional training program.

But when I need advice, I contact the best trading teacher that I know. We are all perpetual developing traders, and I recognize there is always more to learn.

If you are a new trader or an experienced trader who needs some advice, then find the best teacher.

Let's end our discussion with an idea that separates the experienced trader from the novice, the winning trader from the underperformer, the consistently profitable trader from the up and down. It's a skill all great traders possess. It is the ability to adapt.

CHAPTER 12

Adapt to the Markets

T here is nothing to "get" as a trader. What works one month may not the next. Trading setups you crush one year may be extinct the next. As prop traders, our job is to recognize present patterns and exploit them. But we also must have the humility to accept that these patterns might change at any moment. And when they do we must find new patterns. We must adapt. But before I delve into the details of how I have had to adapt my trading style throughout the years, I can't help but tell the story of my first interview.

During the spring of 1997, I attended an interview in New York City with an upstart prop trading firm. As if I were still in high school and applying for a lifeguarding job at the local country club, my mother drove me. It wasn't around the corner either. My mom drove me all the way from our house in Port Jefferson, over an hour away from Manhattan. I changed into my Wall Street power dealmaker uniform in the parking lot of the Omni hotel. I wore a blue pinstripe Hugo Boss suit, a red Armani power tie, and Ferragamo shoes. I was a mix of a high profile basketball coach and Gordon Gekko, minus the suspenders. I looked good. Damn good. But my GQ wardrobe was unnecessary, if not irrelevant. I was a friend of a friend and as long as I did not show up drunk I was getting this job.

My first question from the head of the firm's HR department was naturally, "Why do you want to be a trader?"

True to the lines I had been rehearsing in the car ride over, I confidently replied, "Trading is a meritocracy. I want to earn a salary commensurate with my production. I enjoy the fast pace of the trading environment, and I thrive on daily challenges."

Using that word meritocracy was code for "I have a friend who prepped me on exactly what you want to hear. So you can save some time and move on to your next candidate because I have all the correct answers ready to go." Again, I was getting a job offer. (The business hadn't quite evolved to the recruiting matrixes that Steve and I would design years later.)

Even though I had the job in hand, I took the Connecticut bar exam anyway in the summer of 1997. I am not sure why. Perhaps I wanted something to fall back on in case I did not succeed as a trader. I passed. Phew! Then I signed up for the Series 7, which, by the way for those who have heard otherwise, is not a difficult exam. This was my summer and fall of noteworthy exams.

So I had options. What I did not know nor could have ever imagined was what was about to happen next.

I am not one of those people who dreamed of being a trader since childhood. Actually, I wanted to pitch for the Yankees, but at UConn I learned like many college athletes that that was not going to happen. What I knew about my new job was that I was likely to make $180k in my first year. I could wear pretty much whatever I wanted. I could make even more when I traded my own account. I might get to travel via helicopter to Newport, Rhode Island, on the weekends like some of the firm's traders. *And*, I got to do something fun. Why exactly did I go to law school, again?

During the economic recession of 2008–2009, the media sometimes acts as if the indulgent life is over. They all have short memories. My "generation" of traders I started with got a taste of cold reality during the Asian Financial Crisis. That was the first time we all realized that trading was not quite the money-for-nothing-and-chicks-for-free life it was purported to be. Many on the desk were struggling. For the first time in this firm's history, people were fired, with whispers that more were coming. Many were in a hole for the year. I was not making money during the first half of my "rookie" year. Many on our desk were nervous that we could make money going forward. But at the end of year, the market improved, and through grit and patience we made it through. This was just a bad time that we needed to survive.

Once the fear subsided, my first great month happened. I got a check for $30k! I did not know anyone else who made $30k in a month. I'm sure if I ask my parents now, they'll probably tell me when they were first married that they didn't make that amount in a year . . . combined! I was essentially playing an awesome video game all day while my law school peers were writing some obscure briefs on—insert the most boring legal topic you could possibly think of here. And I had just made $30k.

THE ASIAN FINANCIAL CRISIS

The popular strategy that enabled me to show off my nouveau riches was a subset of swing trading. We traded Relative Strength Plays (we bought stocks that indicated they were stronger than the market on a given day). We traded high-beta NASDAQ stocks exclusively. Our bread-and-butter stocks were CSCO, DELL, MSFT, INTC, the semi-conductors of AMAT, KLAC, and NVLS. At the time, we did not have access to NYSE stocks, but we didn't care. I'll take $30k a month over NYSE access, or so I thought.

Our day included watching the NASDAQ futures and extrapolating how strong or weak the stocks above were. So if we were watching tech stocks, the NASDAQ futures went up 5 points, and CSCO went up half a point, MSFT did not move, and INTC went up a point, then we would focus on loading up in INTC. Keep in mind this was before stock prices became decimalized. The movements came in quarters (25 cents) and halves (50 cents) of a dollar. As a result, swings were rapid, and we moved our money around to those that were stronger than the market.

At 3 PM, we found the strongest stocks and loaded up. "Three O'clock Lighting" we called it. And we would hold our best positions till the closing bell.

Our superior trading platform also provided us a huge advantage over others on the Street. Our platform would show prints executed on ISLD, which is now NASD. Sometimes market makers would pay through 25 to 50 cents for a stock, and we knew first. Let me explain.

We would be trading MSFT, and would see a print through on ISLD for 25 to 50 cents, bought by Goldman. Yet we could still buy the stock on the offer at the inside market. We would pick off the offer at 25c and put our stock up for 50c and instantly get filled. Out platform could offer us information that a Goldman or Morgan was willing to pay through the offer. So we would buy and assume there was more to be bought by an institutional player. We could easily make 50c on a few thousand shares in less than five seconds. Now that really was money for nothing!

We made a lot of money in bounce plays as well. When INTC, CSCO, MSFT would open down considerably we would get long to catch a bounce on the Open. When they held higher, we would get longer. I still use this "old school" bounce play. Rule number one, do not be the first to buy. Let the market stop going down, and then dip your toes into the water and buy a little. Let the stocks hold higher and then when they do, this is when you load up. You only take on huge positions after the market has stopped going down *and* the stocks and market has held higher. Don't be a hero and try to be the first one to catch the bottom. There is more money in loading up after the stocks hold higher.

I have seen prop traders make over $400k in a bounce. They did not load up at the bottom. I have seen Steve make over $100k twice in bounces. He did not buy the bottom.

THE INTERNET BOOM

As if picking off market makers and riding bounces off the Open weren't enough, then came the dot-coms. AOL, YHOO, EBAY, AMZN, KTEL (yes this is not a typo, KTEL), LCOS, EXCITE, BRCM, VRSN, JDSU (Just Don't Sell Us . . . oops), JNPR, QCOM. We went from swing traders to momentum traders. Just as we gutted out the Asia crisis, we had to adapt.

I always find it funny when people think that trading back in those days was easy. If anything, it was a lot more nerve-wracking. Try buying 5k shares of a stock that could drop 10 points in five seconds. And our mindset as traders before this whole Internet thing was to be deliberate swing traders. We bought into pullbacks. We bought at great prices. And now we had to pay the offer a point above the last print in a stock that had no revenues and that had gone up 100 percent in two days. If the stock didn't move, we would lose a point just because that was the spread. If we were wrong, we would lose three points. And we traded multiple 1,000-share lots. I never started a position with less than 3k shares back in the day. So basically, if we paid the offer in a stock and it did not lift and trade higher we could lose $9k in less than a few seconds. This was NOT money for nothing and chicks for free. This was the market mistress taking our money and the chicks fleeing in droves.

Most of the better traders then were trading their own money, not from a proprietary partnership pool. So while a good day for me could be $10–25k on an average day, I could also lose $10k by losing my focus for just a few moments. But really, the biggest adjustment was our mindset. We were defensive traders now turned offensive. We were like defensive fighters now being mandated to let our hands go. If we didn't, then we would not make money.

Our floor was packed. The ceilings were eight feet high like a traditional New York apartment. Traders had room for a chair and a few inches on each side and that was it.

We had no supporting analysts to help us crunch the proper valuation of any of these stocks we were buying. There were no charts. We had one computer screen, a dinosaur CRT monitor. Our trading platform—as innovative as it was—could go down at any minute, and for hours. And when it did, you were just stuck with your positions. There was no help desk to call to sell you out. There was just hope, the hope that you wouldn't get killed until the platform worked again (and this was the best equities platform on the Street at this time).

I remember losing $18k the day KTEL (now delisted) announced they might start selling music over the Internet. My mentor pulled me aside and noted that I had shown an ability to put up explosive numbers but needed to control my implosions. From this day on, I worked on my consistency. I passed on upside in favor of trades that were best for me. I was like many new traders, thinking trading is about making money instead of One Good Trade at a time. My check at the end of month was profits minus losses (not just the gains). I started to concentrate on putting together smaller positive days. To this day, I embrace this philosophy.

On the positive side, there was a day when I was up $75k in EBAY and YHOO. There was a long streak (about 18 months) of mostly five-figure days. I laugh thinking back at it now, and I remember receiving a credit card bill for 15k and writing a check like I was paying for coffee from a street cart vendor. Reality set in a few months later, though. I had landed in Savannah, Georgia, for a week of golf in Hilton Head and answered a call from my accountant. He told me how much I would owe in taxes. I would repeat the number but it was so obscene I can't even write it. Clearly, I also needed a new accountant.

During the Internet Boom we were Relative Strength traders turned Momentum traders. We traded exclusively from the long side, and only traded NASDAQ securities. But as much opportunity as this Internet boom offered, it was our ability to adapt to this new market that booked our outlandish profits.

In early 2000, George Soros famously warned, "The market today is dominated by much younger people who have not experienced a bear market." Hard times were about to visit.

THE BOUNCES OF 2001

While the Internet bubble was bursting, our daily profits plummeted. We did not short. We were not even allowed to short. We did not know how to short. If anything, our psychology was to wait for a pullback and load up. And this is what we did from the long side as the bubble started to burst.

Even though stocks were trading lower, we were still able to make some money. We had superior trading skills. We kept our stops tight. We focused on the quality Internet stocks. If AMZN went down 3 points, up a point, then down three, then we were in that one point upmove. Our win rate decreased but we adjusted quickly. We waited for better long opportunities. We learned technical analysis for this new market very quickly, finding the safest places to start our long positions. But we were not making as much money as we had. Five-figure days had gone the way of vinyl records, as now you really could download music over the Internet.

During 2001, I made a living playing two historic bounces on the NASDAQ, and grinding it out. On January 3, 2001, the Fed unexpectedly cut rates 50 basis points. When this news broke, I immediately bought 8,000 shares of BRCM. That was a memorable trade and a fortunate one. BRCM first ticked down after I bought. A possible 20k plus rip was staring at me. That will give you an instant shot of adrenaline.

Here's the exchange between Steve and me at that moment:

Bella: Oh! That is not good.

Spencer: No, just give it a few seconds.

Bella: Ok.

A few seconds pass . . .

Bella: I just got taken on the offer in BRCM 8 points higher!

Soon enough, BRCM popped up immediately, and I was selling on the offer and reloading 5 points lower (see Figure 12.1). I made more than $100k in less than an hour. Many guys in our firm made much more in this bounce. And this was just the first few ticks in that historic bounce.

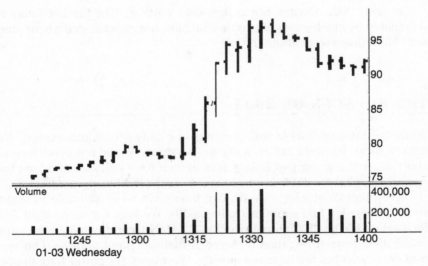

FIGURE 12.1 BRCM 1/3/2001

NASDAQ bounced 14 percent intraday. That is two years of movement in a few hours.

On April 18, 2001, the Fed again surprisingly cut rates 50 basis points intraday. The NASDAQ exploded 8.1% to the upside. This was another huge day. In 2001, there were 11 rate cuts by the Fed as the market collapsed toward new lows not seen in years. Despite the end of the consecutive streaks of five-figure days, this was our year.

How to Play a Market Bounce

As an intraday trader, I have learned information gained from watching my stocks print and trade was superior to the charts. I ripped through some charts after one Close in 1/09 to prepare for the next trading session. It was hard not to notice that everything traded down this day. And most of everything finished near its lows. GS, WFC, RIMM, AAPL, IBM. All the bigger stocks were sold.

And now from a technical standpoint I knew that SPY 88.50 was important. *Technically, we should bounce off of SPY 88.50*, I thought. SPY traded between 88.50 and 88.93 for a while before finally breaking out. We should have specially bounced off of this level the first time.

But I recognized that I must do more than just get ready to play a bounce off of 88.50. 1) Will the bounce start above 88.50? If so, what will I look for to enter this trade? 2) Is there some selling in the market that should cause me pause to play the 88.50 SPY bounce? I need to talk with the guys on our desk that have seen the selling to make a better determination. 3) What stocks will I play for a bounce? IMB, GS, RIMM, AAPL, FCX, WFC seem the most obvious, but I must look through my charts to find the best stocks for me. 4) We are still a distance from 88.50. How can I make money on the short side down to 88.50? 5) What happens if we break 88.50 SPY? What is my trade then?

Remember, if you are playing for a bounce of 88.50 SPY, have a list of stocks ready to go with great prices. Near 88.50 buy just a taste of the stocks you wish to trade. Wait for SPY to hold higher. See which of the stocks that you bought a taste of are trading the strongest. Buy more of these stocks. Below 88.50 SPY, you must exit your stocks. Set plans to exit your stocks if they trade in your favor.

Fundamentally, this is how you trade the 88.50 SPY level. That is how you play a market bounce. But what about a bounce in just one stock?

A Single Stock Bounce

ROH tanked on the Open. Fading it on the long side was like trying to catch a falling knife. And many of you have heard the Street expression "Don't catch a falling knife." These tank jobs in ROH happen every day. As we discussed during our SMB morning meeting, it is a mistake for a new trader to try to catch the bottom. Let's discuss.

It is human nature for some traders to try to catch the bottom of the market or a stock. Some wish to be that one trader who was correct while others on the Street were wrong. Some desire to be that guy on the desk who calls the bottom and receives the adulation from other traders. But this is just ego. And trading to stroke your ego will manifest a short trading career. The object is to make money consistently. Not try to prove you are smarter than others.

You will make the most money in a bounce after the market or a stock has stabilized and held higher. Trying to get long at 47.50 yesterday, though the bottom in ROH yesterday, is bad trading for new and most experienced traders. Traders will often comment that a stock feels like the bottom. And that may be the case. But with a stock falling quickly, your feel must be confirmed by the price action.

But what is most interesting about these patterns is that there is no money trying to catch the bottom for a new trader and most experienced traders. 1) You will be wrong sometimes and take huge rips when the stock is not at the bottom. 2) Even if you catch the bottom you will be unsure whether it is the bottom. This will cause you to sell too quickly too often. A stock often looks the worst at the bottom. There will be signs of weakness near the bottom. The sellers are still concerned with dumping their shares. And buyers are still cautious to take a big position. And when you see this weakness, you will most likely sell too early into the beginning of the bounce and thus miss the huge upmove.

The money trading a bounce is in waiting for the stock to bottom, seeing the stock hold higher, and then getting long. Also, if the stock is going to bounce, let the stock breathe when it first starts to trade higher. ROH traded up $2\frac{1}{2}$ points, found some support at 50, and then traded 4 points higher. You want to be in the move from 50–54. This is where the easy money is. This is where your win rate is 60–70 percent with an upside of at least 5 and a downside of 1. This is a play where you will consistently make money.

Now, there are some experienced traders who pick bottoms. And they play these stocks for retracements. This is for experienced traders. And this is a very difficult trading technique. Even for an experienced trader, I would suggest following trends. There is more money to be made. And your results will be more consistent trading with the trend of Stocks In Play.

You will see chart patterns like ROH again. Let the stock stabilize and hold higher. Then, and only then, should the new trader get long. And then let the stock run. Do not sell at the first sign of weakness. Play for a bigger chop than normal.

After these historic bounces, everything was about to change. Everything. And for all of us.

9/11

I lost $36k trading CMRC in the late spring of 2001. I was studying technical analysis at the time and using my new knowledge to buy into technical support levels. Boy, was this an expensive lesson. Support levels from the Internet boom turned out to be no levels at all as the bubble was bursting. This is a common mistake developing technicians make. There might be a support level on a chart, but the would-be technical traders fail to consider the overall psychology during the period when this support level was created, and if this psychology is still intact. If not, forget about that support level holding up.

Despite the CMRC losses and some other rips I had taken, I decided it was time for me to take a break. I had given back close to $75k for the year just before that summer, and that was real money to me. I was still flush from capturing the benefits of one of history's greatest trading eras, so I decided, along with Steve, to hit the road. I still did not have shorting skills, but I was exhausted from the Internet bubble. It was time for me to get away and work on my golf game.

Steve and I traveled and played tons of golf. We went wherever we wanted (Vegas, Palm Springs, Santa Monica, Portland). We stayed wherever we wanted (The Venetian, Mondrian Hotel, La Quinta). We ate where we wanted (Nobu, Asia de Cuba, Sparks, Fore Street). We did whatever we wanted (probably best if I leave out all of those details). And yet we still had plenty of money. My grand goal for that summer was to break 90, and I did that at PGA West in Palm Springs just before we headed home.

I decided I would head back to work on 9/11/01. The fun ended real quickly. I got off the subway downtown that morning and there was all this commotion. I looked up at one of the World Trade Center, buildings, and it was in flames.

I started to walk toward the World Trade Center as this was on the way to our trading office on Broad Street. Within moments, I saw a huge plane crash into one of the towers (come to find out this was the second of two planes to crash into the towers that day). I turned and sprinted toward the South Street Seaport. My sunglasses flew off my head, lost to the ground, as I turned and ran as fast as I could. I did not need anyone to tell me what was happening.

A few clear thoughts hit me as I sprinted away from the carnage and dust. Do not use the subway. Stay away from the Empire State Building.

Stay off your cell phone so the phone lines are not overflooded. Get uptown!

I soon found Broadway and followed it all the way up to the Upper West Side, about a 5-mile journey. I received a call from a friend and quickly stated that I was Ok and got off the line. Once I got to the neighborhood, I calmly walked up to Sarabeth's on Amsterdam near West 81st Street. I sat down and ate an egg-white, goat cheese, and spinach omelet with fresh-brewed ice tea and lime. (In seminal world-changing moments such as this, you remember every detail, even if you have a generally poor memory.) I really didn't know what else to do. I was just trying to stay out of the way.

The markets did not reopen until the next week, Monday, September 17th, a near miracle spearheaded by the tireless efforts of then-NYSE chairman Dick Grasso. All while Grasso and his minions and peers worked sleepless nights to get the market machines up and running, there was talk of future attacks. There were concerns about the air quality downtown. *Should we go back to work?* we thought.

Now if you have not gleaned by now, I am analytical. If you send me to buy a loaf of bread, it might take me five minutes to find the right loaf. But the decision to go back received zero contemplation from me. Most on the Street felt like I did. "F*^% them!" was the general sentiment among all of my peers. I am going back to work. I am not a fireman or a cop who ran into one of those burning buildings, and I never served in the military. The least I could do was go back to work and prove to the perpetrators of this most hateful act that they were not going to win this battle.

For the first few weeks, we wore mask filters on the walk to work because the air downtown was contaminated. There were checkpoints near the NYSE, which I needed to pass to get to Broad Street. You needed to present your license and a letter of employment to the military guards. The guy checking my identification had an M16 strapped to his shoulder. Bomb detecting dogs patrolled the area. This was a new Wall Street.

The markets were still weak. I ground it out each day, reinvigorated by my time away and the recent events. I scalped the crap out of the market, unsure what direction it would turn next.

Focusing on the Next 50c Trade, Sometimes Scalping

We were in the office watching tape one Saturday when an interesting trading topic emerged: when to forgo a scalp.

There is this notion that day traders just scalp. Wrong. Actually, we rarely scalp these days. But there is also this elitist belief that scalping is somehow beneath some traders. Not me. When I take my check to the bank at the end of the month they do not ask, "Hey, did any of that money come from scalping?" They cash my check.

As a trader I ask, "Can I find a trade that offers me an edge?" And sometimes a scalp offers me an edge. So I scalp.

However, as day traders we can fall victim to over-scalping. Scalping should just be one trade of many in our quiver. And scalping should not be our focus, especially in this market. If GMan catches you doing this on the desk, he will call you out. I can hear him lecturing, "Stop trading like a piker day trader. That is not what we do here."

Most importantly, we cannot let a scalp trade interfere with our main objective. And that is to find the next 50c trade. If a scalp will alter our focus such that we can make a quick 7c, but miss the next 50c trade, then this is a poor trade.

Also, scalping against the trend with really strong or weak stocks is not advisable. Scalps are for stocks that are not clearly directional. When a stock is really trending, we want to focus on where to load up with the direction of the trend. We want to focus on a big trade. Wasting mental energy on 7c is not a good use of our time with a clearly trending stock.

But as we poke around with a stock sometimes, especially on the Open, a scalp can be the proper trade. Sometimes we must scalp a stock on the Open on the short side and long side to get a feel for the stock. This scalping often helps us identify the stock's important intraday levels. Often by trading in and out, we spot the next excellent 50c trade.

During our review session, we were watching GES. Our trader made a scalp trade at 52c to 64c. I barked, "Stop the tape." I was concerned that this trader was not focusing on the big picture, the next 50c trade. He was. My bad. He recognized that the short at 64c was the trade that offered the most likely next 50c trade. So he got short. He scalped the 52c to 64c trade and then had the mental agility to start a short position.

This is excellent trading. But not everyone has this superior mental agility. And if you don't, then you can't make that 52c–64c scalp trade. All you can do is make the short at 64c trade. Because you should be focusing on that next 50c–$1 trade. This is the trade that you can't miss.

In October 2001, my dad and I watched from our season seats at Yankees Stadium as President Bush threw out the ceremonial pitch for Game 3 of the World Series. We were all just trying to do the things we had normally done like going to a ball game. The president threw a strike wearing a FDNY jacket, as F16 fighter jets buzzed the stadium. This was all new for the nation. White House spokesman Ari Fleischer stated the president was "helping to do what all Americans are doing now, which is keeping the country doing what it typically does at this time of year."

But as a trader, I knew I had to get better. The market demanded that I develop. The Internet bubble had burst, the bounces were over, and a very difficult market was here to stay for a while, not to make any significant moves for years. The market has ebbs and flows. And this ebb was a long, difficult, slog. It was time to either get better or go home.

A BEARISH CYCLE IN THE EARLY 2000S

Many traders claim that you improve more during a difficult market than one ripe with opportunity like I saw my first few years. I totally agree. During the bearish cycles of 2002 and 2003, I didn't make a ton of money, but I became a much better trader and started developing the trading system that I preach today. It was then that I began concentrating on the "Stocks In Play" concept. I learned how to make money even when the headlines were not flooded with breaking news. I was ultra consistent, making money in 17 out of 20 trading days per month. Every day, I found one stock with fresh news and made decent profits. I soon learned that these In Play stocks were easier to trade than the JDSUs and AMZNs of yesteryear, and that their technical levels were cleaner.

From 2003–2006, the market had stabilized and we traded in a range. In the process, I taught myself how to fade stocks. I would find a Stock In Play and short it when it was too strong and buy it when it was too weak. The trades weren't nearly as exciting or sexy as the late 1990s, but I had adapted accordingly and was still able to grind out daily profits. Some of my peers never made the mental leap, lost lots of money, lost their overleveraged homes, and left the business, or at least blew up enough backers to be forced into switching to the sell-side.

Thanks to my humility and ability to reinvent myself as a trader, I never had to do that. By concentrating on fading a stock, I became an absolute expert in reading the tape. I wanted to fade my stocks at the tops and bottoms of the moves, and eliminate almost all of my risk. And to catch the bottom and top of the moves in order to fade takes extreme concentration and absorption of a stock's prints.

Adapting by Cutting out Negative Influences

During the bearish cycle of the early 2000s, I sat next to a good friend, Josh Florsheim, who traded OIH, an ETF tracking oil service companies, every day. Many traders will relate to his story. At the time, he was in a horrendous romantic relationship. In short, the girl he was dating was insane. At 9:31 AM, right after the bell had rung, and after a night of fighting, she would call to pick a fight.

Josh: Honey, I'm trading right now. I'll call you later. (Click.)

At 9:35 AM, the phone we shared would ring again as our eyes were glued to the screen at the most volatile time of the day. Josh would still pick up the phone.

> **Josh:** Honey, I'm sorry. I really can't talk now. I will call you later. (Click, but quieter this time.)
>
> Of course she would call back a few minutes later.
>
> **Bella:** Will you please stop calling? We are trading. (SLAM!)
>
> Obviously, there was no way for poor Josh (or me, or our entire desk) to concentrate on trading. Often, when I made assessments to improve my trading and cut out distractions, it dealt with cutting down on drinking or learning how to read charts or the tape better. I never thought that dumping my friend's girlfriend would be one of them. So I took matters into my own hands.
>
> During some downtime, I was looking at some pictures of a night out with my sister and her friends. When I showed them to Josh, he quickly asked, "Who is that?" referring to one of my sister's friends. BINGO! Our problem would soon be solved. I told Josh I could set him up with this young lady if he wanted. Thankfully, he was in.
>
> Fortunately for all parties involved, the first date went very well. My matchmaking skills were so elite that Josh and my sister's friend are now happily married with a child. Soon enough, we all went back to making money.
>
> Conclusion: bad relationships can ruin your trading results. In this case, adapting did not mean learning a new style to trade, but rather cutting out negative personal influences. While I'm no Dr. Phil, if the dynamics of a romantic relationship turn sour, so too can your P/L.

My tape-reading skills on the market improved every day during this difficult 2003–2006 period. It got to the point where someone could show me a stock I had never seen or heard of, not know a thing about, and I could still make money. All I needed was to watch it trade for 20 minutes, all because I spent day after day learning a skill, Reading the Tape, that had been forgotten for decades.

During these range-bound years, we were reinventing ourselves. Critics might say that our fast-living peers got their comeuppance in the early 2000s, but the reality was, we went to work every day like everyone else and tried to make a consistent living. Call it blue-collar trading, and it felt like that. Instead of building the proverbial skyscraper in a day, we were building houses brick by brick for several years, waiting for better times to come and improving our trading skills. So what happened to those opportunities from the late 1990s? Ok, maybe we won't see them again, but there has to be better trading than 2001 to 2002. And better trading came. Only because I reinvented myself during these lean markets of 2003 to 2006, by learning the new trading technique of fading and grinding out profits, could I enjoy the swing and momentum markets that returned in 2007 to 2008. To offer more perspective on this time in the markets, here is a blog I wrote titled "A Fade Trade."

A Fade Trade

During our video review session today we watched some tape of TGT. One of our experienced traders, NYU, faded TGT into its second upmove on the Open at 33.75. There was a struggle at 33 and the buyers won, sending TGT quickly to 33.80 (see Figure 12.2). NYU thought the move was overdone and got short. This was a poor fade trade. One that I see new traders make too often and shouldn't. Let's discuss.

First, some advice before I begin. We do not let new traders fade when they first begin trading with SMB. If you are a new trader, learn this trade after you have established yourself as a profitable trader in today's momentum market. These are difficult trades. Most scouts preach that it takes 1,500 at bats in the minors to develop into a major league hitter. This is kind of how I feel about fading. You need a ton of experience first. Stick with support and resistance plays first.

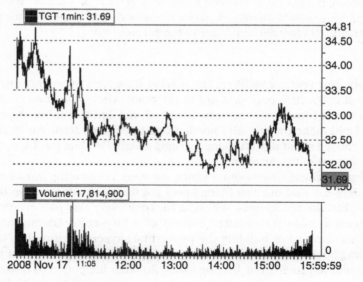

FIGURE 12.2   TGT 11/17/08

Things I did not like about this fade:

- The win rate was too low.
- The risk/reward was poor.
- There was no way to tell where the top would be at this moment.
- I only fade a stock that is at least two standard deviations from its correct temporary price. And it was way too early to determine this.
- It was just early to fade without historical knowledge and TGT was still in an uptrend.
- BBY rallied after its earnings and now here was another retailer bouncing on the Open.
- It was just wrong. To be a great fade trader you must make thousands of fade trades. And that one was just not right. As much as I have conceptualized my reasons above, the trade just didn't look right on the tape.

When you fade, your upside must be 5 with a downside of 1. With this trade, NYU's downside was probably 1.23c with an upside of maybe 40c. TGT showed no signs of a top. In fact, it was in the middle of only its second move. The potential intraday top of TGT at this moment was much higher, possibly 35. This is not the ratio we are looking for. Further, his win rate for this trade was probably 40 percent. The tape did not offer any evidence that TGT was about to trade lower. I do not fade unless I conclude my win rate is 80 percent.

I only fade when I have determined a stock is at least two moves away from its correct temporary price (this is based upon my experience as a trader and examination of the stock intraday). But to determine this I must either have watched it trade the past few days, which NYU had not done, or get a feel for TGT on this trading day. And it was way too early to have a feel for TGT at that moment. So we could not determine that TGT was at least two moves from its correct temporary price at this moment.

We could discuss fade trading for hundreds of blogs. Hey, maybe we will. I survived 2004 and 2005 by fading. I really learned how to fade during these years. Some were forced out of trading because they could not adapt. But check out the charts from 2004 and 2005 and compare them to today's. You do not want to focus on fading today. This is a momentum trader's market. There are fading opportunities, and I make my share of fade trades in this market, but again, this should not be your focus. And as a new trader, you should not be focusing on one of the harder trades with a market where it is wiser to follow the momentum.

This is a great trade to master. You are going to need this trade at times. But not when you are a new trader. And not with this market.

Always Save Money

I learned another valuable lesson during these difficult trading years. SAVE! Whenever you have a great stretch as a trader, SAVE! Save for the difficult times. The markets of the late 1990s did not last. The fall of 2008 was not going to last. I think back to those $15k credit card bills and I learned a valuable lesson. When the VIX was above 60 during the financial meltdown we knew these days could not continue. Today, I have a very modest budget. I do not spend more than $3k a month, ever, which is no easy task in New York City region. No matter how bad the market gets, I know I can make enough to cover my bills. And if I need something, I must have a ridiculous month before I buy this new thing. During the huge days of 2008, I bought an HDTV after a great month, a new mattress after a big month, a new coach after a gigantic month. And that was it. The rest went into my bank account. And it sits there for a rainy day, so to speak.

THE SPREAD OF THE PENNY

As the active trading world has evolved every year or two in my career, a lot of my peers dropped off the radar, unable to make each transition in lockstep. Some were weeded out after the Asian crisis. Some blew up after the dot-coms. Some couldn't learn how to fade the ranges. One more challenge that Steve and I had to overcome was the narrowing of spreads and a switch from a manual market making system to a hybrid one.

When I first started, stocks were quoted in quarters of a dollar, dating back to a quotation system as old as America itself. (The NYSE was founded in 1792.) As such, bid-ask spreads tended to be in quarters and halves. One popular stock from the 1990s, INTC, usually traded with a 50-cent spread. So if I made the spread in INTC with 2k shares, I made a quick thousand bucks. Though soon after I started in 1998 through 1999, quotes kept getting halved, and spreads got narrower. Eighths became sixteenths, also called "teenies," or 6.25 cents. Then came thirty-seconds, 3.125 cents. Once we got to sixty-fourths, or 1.5625 cents, it became nonsensical. Pennies were inevitable. So much for making a quick thousand bucks. With spreads winnowing down to around three cents, making the spread on those 2k shares meant a quick sixty dollars and change. After commissions, maybe I could go buy a nice dinner that night. I certainly couldn't buy a new pair of Ferragamos as I did in the past.

To undercut another trader on our desk by a sixty-fourth was called chiseling. We quickly figured out the traders who would do this, and naturally called these cheap bastards "chiselers." There was an unwritten rule that you didn't chisel someone on your own desk for a sixty-fourth. As always though, some didn't get the inherent memo.

I'll never forget the day someone on our desk tried to pull this stunt, and chiseled our head trader. There was no hiding, as we could see who was doing this on our proprietary trading platform. His initials came across on the trade as the perpetrator. Head traders generally have a sizable ego and are not comfortable being ignored.

Our head trader quickly walked over to The Chisel Man's workstation, told him to turn off his computer, and exploded, "Get the f*^$ off of this trading floor. Come back when you are ready to become a real trader, you f*&$%&* chiseler." That weasel trader most certainly deserved it. It was as if he showed up the prom king at homecoming. You just don't cut the line like that.

So it is with this context that I find it hard to believe that then one day came pennies. And it is just getting worse. Every day, I see some market player selling stock, hidden, at a half a penny above the bid. This is not chiseling. This is just called being a jackass. My message: learn how to trade, Chiseler.

When pennies appeared in 2001, many were displaced as traders. Market makers used to making an eighth on every trade folded up their operations, as their monthly costs exceeded spread revenue. Many said this was the end of intraday trading. Reading the tape was over. This was an exaggeration, if not a flat-out lie. Every big action always has unintended consequences, and going to pennies was no different. As spreads narrowed, the volatility in stocks actually increased. Greg Ghodsi of Raymond James explained at the time, "Less profit leads to less capital and less capital leads to less liquidity." When trading moved to pennies, costs actually increased by about 7 percent on each trade, according to the General Accounting Office. One part of me says, "Can we please go back to trading in eighths?"

But the good traders adapted. You have to find a way. And for us, this meant trading more actively, heightened setup selectivity, and learning new patterns that worked best for this new market. Hey, you had a choice. You could have become a whiny ex-trader ("Pennies make it impossible to make money"), or adapted and conquered this new market.

THEN CAME HYBRID

The bursting of the Internet bubble washed out the lesser traders, pennies sent some more packing, and then NYSE adopted Hybrid. This washed out scores of mediocre intraday prop traders. Steve and I traded NASDAQ stocks exclusively until around 2004, before dabbling with NYSE or "listed" stocks. As a NASDAQ trader, I didn't like how the NYSE specialist could hold my order for almost a minute before he had to execute. The system allowed for the specialist to manipulate the spread in his favor and front run my order. (In 2004, a handful of specialist firms settled with the SEC for $250 million after being accused of stepping in front of customer orders for years.) My advantage as an intraday trader is speed, and with this delay my edge was removed. But nonetheless, we started wading into the waters of "listed" names.

When NYSE went to a Hybrid system, where ECNs could compete with the specialist for better prices, we traded NYSE much more. In the first three months of 2007, 82 percent of NYSE volume was executed, automatically compared to 19 percent pre-Hybrid. Hybrid effectively turned the specialist into just another ECN, marginalizing the specialist and opening up more opportunities for someone like myself with electronic trading skills. That is the way it should be. Competition for stocks should be open and fair. Traders with the most advanced trading skills should be most rewarded, not a trader who knows how to manipulate a specialist's order book.

When the order flow left the specialist's book, some day traders had trouble adjusting. They were used to trading off of the order flow they could spot from the specialist. Over the years, they had learned how to trade with the different specialists for different stocks, eventually manipulating them. Many day traders could not make the adjustment. Their bread-and-butter plays were eliminated as ECNs made it harder for them to Read the Tape. For us, it was an ocean of new opportunity. Heck, it was oceans. Now the NYSE stocks traded more like their NASDAQ counterparts. For an experienced NASDAQ trader, trading NYSE with Hybrid was a layup. I kept asking, "How is this difficult?" Now specialists couldn't hold my orders, and I could get stock when I needed it. The Hybrid system would reward superior tape-reading skills.

While traders like me benefited from this evolution, I still find it hard to talk about this period without also recognizing the many who lost their jobs. We certainly felt for those who lost-high paying jobs through the new technology that had swept the NYSE. I can't imagine what it was like for those traders and specialists with families used to living a certain lifestyle whose skills no longer had a market. Specialist firms closed up shop by the dozens. The floor lost thousands of participants. High-earning middle-aged men, some of whom were running third- or fourth-generation family businesses, had to learn how to reinvent themselves in the latter half of their careers. When CNBC shows camera shots of the floor now, it's more like a museum than an active bustling center of capitalism. To those in the trading community, a lot of this was very sad. But at the same time, the market should be open and fair. Traders should not rely on market flow as their main source of income. A trader's income should be determined by their own proprietary buy-and-sell systems and decisions—eating what they kill, so to speak.

One-Trick Pony

I encounter too many traders who just live off of one play. Commonly, this play is as follows: a trader sees a big bid and steps in front or sees a big offer and steps in front. This is my definition of scalping, which as we saw, was rampant post-9/11. This is a play that ought to be in your playbook. But it should not be your entire playbook.

I met with an ambitious developing trader recently unhappy with his firm. He reached out to one of our traders and somehow figured out how to parlay that into a meeting with me. His records are solid for a new trader. Bright, good background, realistic learning curve, nice young man. We all liked him.

This developing trader is one year into his career and his entire playbook consists of searching for big bids and offers. Obviously, he is very good at this. But this is all he was taught by his first firm. I am hesitant to ever criticize another firm. In fact, I am not even sure this is a criticism so much as I am just making an observation. This is not trading.

It is important to find easy plays for new traders to make when they first start. We have a bunch. A quick history lesson for our readers. This technique used by the developing trader above is one of the last trades remaining from before Hybrid. Traders would search for big NYSE bids and offers and step in front. There was good money finding these plays. But then came Hybrid, like an infectious disease for the One-Trick Pony traders.

And then there were so many fewer of these plays. When I first started trading, there was the old High Bid Join party. Whenever a market player went high bid and was then joined by another bidder, this was a signal to buy. And this play worked for a few years. Then there was high bid ARCA and higher bid ARCA play that worked for a few years. Of course, my favorite was the MSCO high bid, without dropping, for 50 straight points in YHOO play. These plays eventually become obsolete like the steel shaft driver (think graphite). One play is not enough. You cannot be a One-Trick Pony.

It's funny because I was talking to GMan about getting some new filters for big bids and offers for one of our traders, Z$ or Mush. He is such the master at this play, remember, that we actually name the trade after him. We say to Mush the play. And GMan gave me a look that said this to me, "Bella, what the hell are you talking about? This is a trading desk. We don't want to expend any energy finding dopey plays like this. We want to find strong stocks and get long and weak stocks and get short. Go back to writing your dopey book and leave stuff like that to me, please." Anyway, this is what his look said to me. And I got the point.

I understand that this trade works. I understand that there is money with this trade. And I on occasion make such a trade. But you cannot make a career off of one trade. Another market was about to premiere. A new trading play would star. A setup that I had not mastered but needed to.

THE UPTRENDING MARKET

During the middle of 2006, the market started an uptrend. Finally! At the start of this period, I continued to fade. Stocks I thought were overbought kept trading higher. I struggled at the inception of this new, uptrending market. Fading was not working as well. During my end of the month review, this was undeniable. And the patterns were consistent. Strong stocks were finishing near their highs. The market was screaming, "Bella, you need to adapt!"

These upmoves were not like those during the late 1990s. So this was at first a little confusing to me. These stocks were not exploding, so naturally I would conclude that they were not that strong and fade them. Mistake. Instead of moving up 20 points as they had in the dot-com days, they simply trickled higher. Strong stocks moved higher intraday and finished at their highs, though in a subtle manner. And for a guy who remembered the Internet bubble, slow is generous. These upmoves were snail-like.

I would find a strong stock, watch it, and yell, "Go up, already!" That made me feel better but somehow my encouragement would not make it go up any faster. Again, I had to accept that we were in another different market. We were in an uptrending market, but a painstakingly methodical one. Our job was to find strong stocks, buy into pullbacks, and be patient. The market is not concerned with how you would like stocks to trade. Your job is to adapt to what the market is offering.

After watching strong stocks sell off for years, it was hard to buy a stock into a pullback. For the previous three years, this would have generated losses. But these were the patterns of this market. The range-bound 2003 to 2006 era was over and we were left with the bulls running out of the gate in slow motion. It was nice to see stocks go up again. We had not seen this since the late 1990s.

Believe it or not, this was one of my weaker trading periods. When a stock is strong, I have a bias for it to go up. Who doesn't? I personally prefer a trading strategy with a higher win rate than simply uptrending stocks. It is hard for me to be wrong so many times as a trader. Naturally, I am better at trading plays where my win rate is 70 percent than 40 percent. This trade to me is like sitting on the runway for hours waiting for clearance to take off. I know we are going to take off. But I just hate sitting in that cramped plane getting ready in anticipation. Can we take off already? But I had to overcome this and master these trades.

This is the most difficult intraday trade. It requires patience, guts, a belief in your system, the ability to be wrong often, and the backbone to hold the stock for its entire move. On our desk, I get the most questions about how to trade this play. And if you can't do this, then the math doesn't work.

AGA was a great uptrending trader, with the patience of a saint. During this time period, he was the best trader on our desk. He could hold these winners. He liked them moving slowly in his favor. I guess this was best suited for his personality. AGA was passed by lesser traders during momentum periods. But for this year-plus time period, he was the man on our desk. And this is when GMan joined us, and was not a great time period for his personality; not enough fast action.

This market was different from the upmove from the semi's and tech stocks I saw as a swing trader in the late 1990s. Those stocks were all in clear uptrends. They moved up at the end of day with bigger spreads and more definable moves. Honestly, these up trending stocks of 2006 to 2007 were no fun. They moved at all different times, often Midday, when I was most interested in eating my lunch (didn't they know I was eating my lunch?). But we adapted. And we added the excellent trading play Buying into Pullbacks to our quiver.

Buying on Pullbacks

Buying on pullbacks can be difficult to do.* But this is a skill that every trader needs to learn to take his game to a new level. Like any other skill, the more you do it, the better you get at it. Below are a few guidelines that have helped me find good entry points as a stock pulls back from a recent upmove. I will use the current market we are in for examples of what I am looking for. I will be explaining pullbacks from the long side. I also use the same guidelines to short stocks in a weak market.

- *It helps to be in a trending market (i.e., Market is a bull or bear).*
- *Know what sectors are leading the market's trend.*
- *I like buying market leaders and leaders in the sectors that are leading the market trend (i.e., GS, AAPL, FCX, TGT).*

---

*This section was adapted from a May 12, 2009, posting at JToma's Blogs (www.smbtraining.com/blog).

- *This point is key: I like to see these stocks pull back to support levels on LOWER VOLUME. Sometimes the pullback is pretty intense, especially in higher-priced stocks. But as long as the volume is average, or better yet, below average, I stay the course. If this occurs, I am pretty confident that this is still a pullback and not a reversal.*
- *I want these leading stocks to pull back to support or key levels. This can mean different things to different traders, depending on their time frame and risk tolerance. To figure out what those levels might be, I like to use the following:*
  - *Past resistance as support.*
  - *Price action at certain levels. This can happen anywhere, but it means some kind of unusual held bid or a fight that occurred between buyers and sellers where the buyers won.*
  - *The stock pulls back to a moving average. I like to use the 14-day, 20-day, 50-day, and 200-day simple moving averages, depending on my time frame.*
- *Another key point: After entering into the trade, I like to see the stock go up on VOLUME. LOW VOLUME ON THE PULLBACK, HIGH VOLUME AS THE STOCK ADVANCES HIGHER. This is a sign of strength.*
- *Lastly, and this goes without saying: WHEN I AM WRONG, I GET OUT OF MY POSITION!! NO IFs, ANDs, BUTs, or MAYBEs ABOUT IT. I am not in the business of averaging down. There is a difference between averaging down and buying in to a pullback. One makes you money and the other ends careers.*

These are guidelines to follow, but keep in mind not much in the world of trading is black and white. Be aware that pullbacks can be messy and uncomfortable, especially for newer traders. But your ability to recognize good entry points for strong stocks pulling back in an upward trending market will make you more money and help you become a consistent trader.

Good Luck. —JToma

THE HOUSING CRISIS

I had learned everything, right? I had lasted through the Asian Financial Crisis, crushed the Internet Boom, survived 9/11, remade myself during the lean years, and developed a full quiver of trading plays. What else was there to learn? What else could possibly happen? Ha ha. I was about to trade through the worst economic crisis since the Great Depression.

CFC? MBI? ABK? I can honestly write that I had never traded a share in any of these stocks until the summer of 2007. We were in that ponderous uptrending market since the middle of 2006 and then there was this news about CFC (see Figure 12.3). And it wasn't good.

I had learned to trade momentum during the late 1990s, but I had never concentrated on playing the momentum in a stock on the short side. And then came CFC, MBI, ABK. I had to become an expert . . . and fast.

I am not an expert in real estate, though I have learned much about residential and commercial property from watching my father's investments. It did strike me as odd that home prices had risen so dramatically compared to the cost of building materials. Many of my non-trading friends had solid jobs and could only afford a mediocre house in Nassau County. That didn't make sense to me. But it is not as if I noticed stuff like this and started shorting the homebuilders and the subprime players. John Paulson, I am not.

But I did notice CFC gapping down one day.

GMan: Steve, do you see this CFC?

Steve: Yeah what the hell?

GMan: Bad news.

Steve: You think?

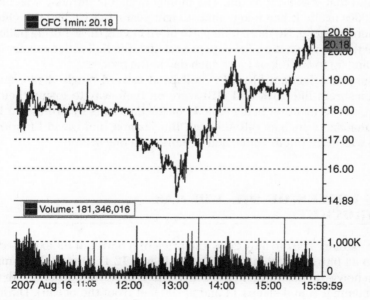

FIGURE 12.3 CFC 8/16/07

GMan: What do you think?

Steve: I don't know. I am just going to trade it.

GMan: Bella?

Bella: Watch for the bounce, if not, then I am going short the crap out of it.

And CFC was not bouncing. Sellers held offers and stepped lower. I was not entirely sure exactly why or what was going on yet but as a trader I knew what to do. I got short. And I traded these securities on the short side as long as the intraday momentum was down.

This was the first period that reminded me of the late 1990s. And it was the first time the traders that we trained on our upstart prop desk started to make serious money. I remember the huge smile on GMan's face after trading CFC when this news first hit. GMan's smile said to me, "Oh, so this is what this trading thing is all about. You guys weren't kidding about the money we could make. This is pretty freakin' cool!" But GMan had been honing his skills during more difficult markets. He was ready. If we were pitching this movie, it might go something like this: Trader who struggles for a year, but develops his craft, meets a beautiful new market, falls in love with it, and has the time of his young life in NYC. GMan started talking about buying a Ferrari. Given my earlier plea about saving, I had to step in there and nix that idea.

And that was a lot of fun. The money available intraday was like the late 1990s again. It had taken almost eight years, but we had our chances. No more slogging. No more fading. No more buying these boring pullbacks. It was time to sit on the edge of your seat and ride that roller coaster down, grabbing up to $5–10k or more each day in the process.

Subprime lenders like CFC collapsed toward single digits, and the bond insurers like ABK and MBI were on their way to losing their AAA rating, not to mention being called out for their sins by prominent hedge fund managers such as Bill Ackman, Jim Chanos, and David Einhorn. But there was more fun to come, and in more than one sector.

THE PRICES OF OIL AND GAS SKYROCKET

From January 2007 to July 2008, the price of a barrel of oil exploded from $50 to an intraday high of $147.11 (see Figure 12.4). During the summer, I rent a house on the ocean in the Outer Banks of North Carolina with GMan (our summer rental sleeps 14 and is 200 feet from the ocean). During the

FIGURE 12.4 Oil Prices 1999–2009

summer of 2008, the weekly rent for our house fell from $8,000 to $2,200 partly because vacationers could not afford the gas in their car for this remote location. Americans were spending a larger share of their income on energy than at any other time since 1986. I had only infrequently traded oil or gas until this phenomenon. I didn't care for the way that oil stocks ticked intraday. It just didn't fit my eye as a professional golfer might say about a particular tour stop. Oil stocks tended to break levels and then reverse. This is my kryptonite. Moves like this just leave me frustrated. Almost always, there are better stocks for me to trade.

But oil and gas were impossible to ignore during these years. And I had to just get over my animus for these stocks and the way they traded. But they moved differently during these particular months. They moved more like stocks that I preferred. They trended. They respected trading levels. Orders were real. I preferred HK, CHK, VLO as staples during this period. I followed the momentum and I scalped the crap out of them when they were most In Play.

Sometimes, stocks that are not kind to you become easier to trade. When a stock is really In Play, they respect levels and trend better. If a sector or a stock is In Play, then I will trade it no matter how poorly it fits my eye during normal trading times.

Our trading Super Bowl was about to visit. A market that one might see once a century. The near collapse of our banking system was to arrive, ripping the Street apart and contemporaneously offering opportunity to nimble equity traders. It was the year of the intraday trader.

THE NEAR COLLAPSE OF THE U.S. FINANCIAL INDUSTRY

During the near collapse of the financial industry, reams of fresh news were available to digest. And I was often not sure how the market would respond. So I just traded. LEH, BSC, JPM, WFC, MER, GS were most profitable playing the momentum from the short side. If I noticed that the market did not trust a financial company's reassurances, then I traded that stock with a short bias. The trading gods were awoken, offering a market we will all tell our grandchildren about.

Instead of discussing some more about the collapse of legendary institutions and how we crushed them on the short side, let's discuss how even the leading financial company plummeted. GS was clearly the best financial company, based upon its initial price action. GS had little exposure to the CDO mess (or at least eliminated their exposure ahead of time). When Warren Buffett invested $5 billion into GS via a purchase of preferred stock to stabilize its downmove and provide the bank with liquidity, GS traded higher initially. Buffett also gained the right to purchase shares of GS at $115 any time over the next five years. As such, $115 was support for a while after this deal.

Naturally, we traded GS on the long side while this support held. But when the Street started to question the business model of an investment bank that could leverage itself so heavily with low-interest overnight loans to increase its return on equity for shareholders, GS started to trade below $115. This is when we got short. Once GS broke the Buffett support, it was in deep trouble (see Figure 12.5). GS was able to fall just about anywhere until the shorts were forced to cover. We were not sure of the impact of the news but we understood our trading levels and followed the downward momentum of the stock. It was one of the simpler rules to follow in my entire career: above $115, we were long, assuming the intraday trend was up. Below $115, we went short and heavy.

During the near collapse of our banking system, we strictly played the momentum of the financials. We often did not know if they would fall lower. Was this the end of our banking system? Or was this all exaggerated and we were about to put in a bottom? Unsure of what would happen next, and before Congress passed their historic bank bailout on October 3, 2008,

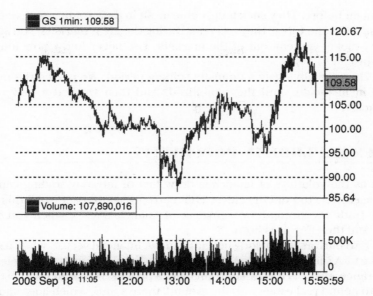

FIGURE 12.5　GS 9/18/08

we exited when stocks slowed in the direction of their last move. If stocks were ticking down, we whacked the bids, and when these stocks slowed, we covered. If these stocks broke their intraday downtrends, then we got long.

The intraday chart in Figure 12.5 ought to make you laugh. That was an intraday move in GS, the very best financial stock. And this after history's best investor sunk $5 billion into the company. GS was still removing the CDOs off its balance sheet. In fact, they had shorted them during the downmove. Even GS was not immune to the crisis at hand.

GS touched 47.41 during its deep dive. Imagine sitting on a trading desk making serious money and thinking, "please make this stop." The first part of the downmove was interesting, if not fun, but when things go ugly, I wondered what the heck the markets would look like in the future. Would there be markets? Would anyone place his money in securities after this disaster? How much worse could things get?

You never know when the market is going to offer one of those historic days. During the Internet bubble, there were two memorable days the day after Thanksgiving, which I showed up for. They were obscenely profitable days that would have been irresponsible to miss. You must sit in your seat as much as possible. Professional traders show up for work every day, just like rest of the world. They do not miss days because of overly fun activities the night before. They suck it up, come in, sit in their trading seat, and grind it out. After the Close, they can rest. During the great markets, you squeeze every nickel you can out of the markets. You never know how long they will last.

This was obviously a fantastic trading period. We played the momentum in financials until they stabilized. And then we had a new market to tackle.

ETFS EXPLODE IN POPULARITY

Just as the volatility of financials drew lots of intraday trading capital to the sector, so too did the clever ETF entrepreneurs react to fill this niche. Why trade the strength or weakness of financials at 1x when you can do 3x? And thus FAS was born.

FAS mirrors 3x the long potential of the financial sector, while its counterpart FAZ leverages 3x on the short side. For those with slightly less risk tolerance, there is the 2x short financials play of SKF. And for those wishing to pound real estate into the ground, there's SRS, which goes short that sector 2x. And do not confuse that with SDS, which shorts the S&P 500 with a 2x weighting.

During the end of 2008 and the start of 2009, these ETFs exploded in popularity. Some on our desk struggled during these months and needed a way to get back on track. In February, I noticed that some had. What were they trading? FAS, FAZ, and all of their leveraged synthetic friends.

First, these ETFs are their own animals. They are not companies. They don't have earnings per share, or a management team. They are basically tracking stocks that move with more zip. For about four months, these traders scalped the crap out of the FAZ, FAS, SKF, SDS, and SRS. They put up some impressive numbers. Many argued that ETFs were a substantial contributor to the market volatility of 2008 to 2009. Some thought it was irresponsible to offer investment vehicles that were leveraged up three times, like FAZ and FAS. Isn't this what caused the near collapse of our banking system? As intraday traders, we believe this is a philosophical debate for others. We are not SEC policy makers, central bankers, or economics professors. Let them write a book about that.

It is our job to spot patterns, and during this stretch these ETFs were offering the best trading opportunities. So we traded them. Was it scalping? That was not the issue to me.

Our guys were in a slump, and many on the Street were struggling. Our guys found a way out, and scalping the ETFs was their solution. I applauded them for digging their way out of a hole and making significant profits after a slump, while most could not make a dime.

TRADES2HOLD

In late 2009 and 2010, we refocused our trading strategies again. Now its Trades2Hold, longer-term intraday trades, which we developed for another distinct market. The market is uptrending, though, with serious economic concerns about the national debt, unemployment, higher taxes, housing foreclosures, a new wave of bad loans, China, a tight credit market, the bailout in Greece, and on and on and on. But every dip is bought. Bad news is shrugged off and the market and stocks head higher. Many individual stocks that gap down, bounce and finish positive. Whenever the bears announce the next downleg, or the start of a "double dip recession," in come the bulls pushing the market higher like thugs stealing a weaker kid's meal money.

So we spot inflection points, intraday levels, and find ways to take positions following the trend of stocks. We hold for bigger intraday moves. Our traders are concentrating on bear and bull flags, consolidation plays, and longer-term support and resistance trades. One of our best traders said recently, "I am exclusively concentrating on Trades2Hold." We are leaning on technical analysis a touch more, which works well in a trending market. We have recently started holding overnight positions again; let's call them 3daytrades.

We have become less active as traders. We build positions and trade around them. GMan is like a mini PM as I write, with 30 open positions. Steve is talking more these days like a hedge fund manager: "RIMM is the weakest of all the tech and a potential short candidate." Now it's all finding the trading patterns for Trades2Hold that work best. That is, until the next market. It's called trading!

To last in this business you must reinvent yourself, tweak your profitable setups, and embrace the mindset of change. If you do this, your reward will be improved trading skills, and a larger bank ready to risk on the best of markets.

CHAPTER 13

The Successful Trader

S o after all of the ups and downs in the markets, I have been continually developing the trading system that we teach at SMB Capital. We trade the Stocks In Play. We trade off of levels that we spot intraday, prices where sellers and buyers exchange the most stock. We search for epic battles between the bulls and bears. We want to see a lot of volume done at a price. Once it is, then we have a level. We are long above this level and short below.

When the market is quiet, I recommend scalping the crap out of it. During earnings season and active trading periods, we emphasize finding important intraday levels and building positions around them. We hold these positions until the stock's trend is broken intraday. These are our Trades2Hold. But I stand ready to change the focus of our system tomorrow. It's called trading!

This is certainly a great time to be an intraday trader. Bill Cara's recent comments on his blog Cara Community (http://caracommunity.com/) fascinate me as an intraday prop trader, "Although we don't like to use or hear the word *never*, it could be that 'buy and hold' trading is never coming back. There is a possibility that globalization, electronic communications, real-time trade execution systems, and the like have combined to cause permanent change in the way we trade." If this is the case, then my electronic trading skills are positioned to grow even further in value.

With the interconnectedness of the world, the improvement in transmitting data, particularly trading data, why can't a U.S. equities electronic trader trade the Hang Sang, Shanghai, or the Nikkei using intraday strategies? We are working on providing these opportunities for our traders right now! What a chop it would have been to trade Asia after the Dubai World mess. Think of all the new trading opportunities we will have.

There are times when I am discouraged with my trading. I have written e-mails to Steve about how this might be it for me. I struggle for five to seven days in a row. Nothing works. And I let my mind wonder if this is the end. Is it time for me to hang it up? I have had these thoughts on and off for 12 years. And I suspect that if I trade for another 10 years that I will have these feelings again. While I successfully navigated many trading periods, I stand humbled by the market.

I suppose I should not have these feelings during difficult stretches. But my personality, like most successful traders, is to be really hard on myself at first. After a few hours, I get tired of being so depressed, and I start finding a solution to my slump.

I received this poignant tweet about experienced traders struggling at the end of 2009:

Omarm784@smbcapital: Many traders at my desk have recently quit after trading for many yrs, claiming trading has become too difficult. Do you agree?

I don't agree. Let me remind you of that old school trading anecdote by JToma. A person in his trading class walked into the Managing Partner's office to quit and proclaim, "There is no more opportunity in this market. We cannot make money how we trade." This trader quit in September of 1998. He quit right before the start of the Internet Boom. JToma went on to make 1-plus million that year while his classmate was working for his father's plastic business.

For me, the way out is always the same. I lower my tier size. I stick to my best trading setups. And I just try to put up a number. I focus on the trading patterns that are working best for me for that market. I do this for a few days. And after the second positive trading day, I have regained my confidence. After that, I forget the e-mails I have sent to Steve announcing my retirement. And then the next day I try to make just a little more. And then the next a little more. Before I know it, I have run three weeks in a row of profitable days, with a touch of overconfidence that I must censor.

I adapt. I focus on the trades that are working for me at this present time. I make a list of these setups and trade just them. I control my risk and let the winners naturally manifest. I obsess about the thousand little things that have everything to do with making money and that you will never hear anyone on a major financial network talk about. I regain my confidence. I rebuild. This is why I am a professional trader and have been one for 12 years.

During all of these times, I have reinvented myself, mostly out of necessity. I started as a relative strength trader, then became a momentum trader with a long bias, then mastered bounce trades, then fading, then uptrending plays, then momentum trading from the short side. I overcame pennies, embraced hybrid, mixed in NYSE trading, and learned to short. I did not curse the market that my swing trading did not work during the Internet bubble. Instead, I learned how to momentum trade. I did not wallow in self-pity when the Internet bubble burst. I saved a year by playing a few historical bounces. Scalping was not beneath me during the lean years as I used a fading technique to profit and improve as a trader. When momentum trading was not rewarded in 2009, I simply created our Trades2Hold.

There is always a solution to your recent struggles. But that solution mandates that you look in the mirror and determine what is not working and find the trading patterns that are. Even after becoming a consistently profitable trader, you will have to tweak your system. You will have to adjust your trading plays weekly, daily, and even intraday. This is the life of a trader.

Instead of longing for eighths or tech stocks that move 25 percent from Open to Close, thank the market for changing. Every different market will make you a better trader. What doesn't blow up your account will make you better.

Trading is about skill development and discipline as we learned from studying those who failed and *These Guys are Good*. Today, modern training gives new traders the opportunity to speed up their learning curve, as we discussed in Trader Education, and find out just how good they can be as traders. I hope I have shared how important listening to Mother Market is, following her rules, and how unimportant bold predictions are for the short-term trader. Like great athletes, successful traders obsess about solid fundamentals, like One Good Trade. Those who last do the thousand little things each day, like in Pyramid of Success, which make the difference between consistent profits and being eliminated by the markets.

As I sit here today and write, I have traded through so many different markets. Some have been very difficult. I have gone through some periods when I did not make money for an uncomfortable period of time. Somehow, I fought to live another day. The reward for all of this is today I am a well-rounded trader. I am not the best trader on the Street—far from it. But I have developed the skills to trade any market that is thrown at me. And that is a significant life achievement. I wish you that type of trading success.

Bibliography

Bartiromo, Maria. "Against the Odds: He was just another dropout—until he got the measles and a goal." Reader's Digest. September 30, 2009. www.rd.com/your-america-inspiring-people-and-stories/maria-bartiromos-money-makers-the-road-to-universal-studios/article26397.html.

Bellamy, Ralph, Ameche, Don. *Trading Places*. DVD. Directed by John Landis. Los Angeles, CA: Paramount, 1983.

Bernstein, James. "Wall Street Panic." *Southcoast Today*. April 15, 2000.

Bespoke Investment Group. "Triple Leveraged ETFs On Fire." *Seeking Alpha*. November 26, 2008.

Bradley, Jeff. "Failure Fuels Me." *ESPN*. March 26, 2007.

Brenson, Alex. "The Markets: Market Place; Distracted, Wall St. Ignores Signs of an Economic Bottom." *The New York Times*. August 22, 2001.

Brick, Michael. "The Markets: Stocks & Bonds; Blue Chips Manage Modest Gains After Fed Cuts Rates." *The New York Times*. February 1, 2001.

Brick, Michael. "The Markets: Stocks & Bonds; Shares Fall Hard as Fed Rate Cut Disappoints Investors." *The New York Times*. March 21, 2001.

Brooks, David. "Genius: The Modern View." *The New York Times*. Op-ed, April 30, 2009.

Buffett, Warren. *The 2007 Berkshire Hathaway Annual Meeting*. Conference. Berkshire Hathaway. Colorado Springs, CO. March 28, 2008.

Buster, Olney. "Moyer's Pearls of Wisdom." *ESPN Insider*. March 19, 2009.

"Cal Ripken Jr." www.nationalsportsagency.com/cripken.html.

Cambers, Simon. "Classic Wimbledon Final Shows Revitalized Andy Roddick's Resilience." *Guardian*. July 06, 2009.

Cara, Bill. "Market Environment." *DailyMarkets*. May 22, 2009. http://Dailymarkets.com.

"Carlin Financial Group Launches Online Trading System for Experienced Investors." *PRNewswire*. February 17, 2009.

Chan, Lawrence. "Basic Tape Reading—The Importance of Sub-minute Charts." *Neoticker*. May 15, 2006.

Chapman, Peter. "Unshackled." *Traders Magazine*. August 2008.

Rose, Charlie. "Coach K on Coaching the U.S. Basketball Team," April 20, 2009. www.charlierose.com/view/clip/10245.

Rose, Charlie. "A Conversation with Pete Peterson." April 2, 2008.

Colvin, Geoff. *Outliers: Talent is Overrated: What Really Separates World-Class Performers from Everybody Else.* New York: Penguin Group, 2008.

"Consumers Face Tough Choices as Gas Prices Rise." *PBS.* May 23, 2008.

Cosby, Chip. "Pitino Asked Sosa to Transfer, Glad he Didn't." *KentuckySports. com.* January 5, 2009. www.kentucky.com/kentuckysports/latest/story/646643.html.

Crampton, Thomas. "Half-Point Move Comes Too Late for Asian Stocks After a Volatile Session: Fed Cuts Rates in a Bid to Bolster Confidence." *New York Times.* September 18, 2001.

Blair, David. "The Kirk Report: The Crosshairs Trader Interview with Founder Charles Kirk." *Crosshairs Psychology.* June 15, 2009.

Davis, Ann. "Blue Flameout: How Giant Bets on Natural Gas Sank Brash Hedge-Fund Trader." *The Wall Street Journal.* September 19, 2006. Page A1.

Day, Sherri. "The Markets: Stocks & Bonds; Modest Rally Fizzles After Merck's Warning on Earnings." *New York Times.* December 12, 2001.

Denninger, Karl. "HFT: The High Frequency Trading Scam." *Seeking Alpha.* July 24, 2009.

"Do Poker Players Make Good Day Traders?" *Chartshark.* July 21, 2009. http://chartshark.com/183/poker-players-day-traders/.

Douglas, Mark. *The Disciplined Trader: Developing Winning Attitudes.* New York: Prentice-Hall, 1990.

Durden, Tyler. "JP Morgan: High Frequency Trading a Form of Parasitic Market Making." *Seeking Alpha.* July 12, 2009.

"Echoes, Emotional Architecture, & Performance Patterns." *TraderPsyches.com.* July 2, 2009.

Elder, Alexander. *Trading for a Living: Psychology, Trading Tactics, Money Management.* Toronto, Canada: John Wiley & Sons, 1993.

Farley, Alan. "Tale of the Tape." *Trading Day.* July 7, 2009.

Finkelstein, Ben. *The Politics of Public Fund Investing: How to Modify Wall Street to Fit Main Street.* New York: Simon & Schuster Touchstone, 2006.

Frank, Chuck. "Boris Stein Interview." *Traders World* magazine. 4943 (43), 2007.

French, Kirsten. "Today's Market: Stocks Slide Lower as Market Awaits a New President." *The Street.* November 7, 2000.

Fuerbringer, Jonathan. "The Markets: Market Place; The Fed Cut Rates, and Wall Street Yawned." *The New York Times.* May 16, 2001.

Gladwell, Malcom. *Outliers: The Story of Success.* New York: Little, Brown and Company, 2008.

―――. "How David Beats Goliath: When Underdogs Break The Rules." *The New Yorker.* May 11, 2009.

————. "Cocksure: Banks, Battles, and The Psychology of Overconfidence." *The New Yorker*. July 27, 2009.

Goldstein, Matthew. "So You Wanna Be a Day Trader?" *SmartMoney*. July 23, 2009.

Guglielmo, Connie. "Steve Jobs Says Hormone Imbalance Caused Weight Loss." *Bloomberg*. January 5, 2009.

————. "Jobs's Health Still Concerns Some Apple Shareholders." *Bloomberg*. January 6, 2009.

Guglielmo, Connie, Garner, Rochelle, and Gale, Jason. "Steve Jobs May Have Pancreas Removed After Cancer." *Bloomberg*. January 15, 2009.

Guglielmo, Connie, Lauerman, John, and Bass, Dina. "Apple's Jobs Said to Be Considering Liver Transplant." *Bloomberg*. January 16, 2009.

Guren, Adam. Interview by Damien Hoffman. *Wall St. Cheat Sheet*. Wall St. Cheat Sheet 2009. Web. July 15, 2009.

Hack, Damon. "FOOTBALL; Patriots Once Again Bring the Mountain to Peyton Manning." *The New York Times*. January 15, 2005.

Hagan, Joe. "Stock-Surfing the Tsunami." *The New York Times*. January 25, 2009.

Halpern, Sue M. "Making It." *The New York Review of Books*. May 28, 2009.

Hamilton, Walter. "Warren Buffett's Investment Bucks Up Goldman Sachs." *The Los Angeles Times*. September 24, 2008.

Hassett, Kevin. "Harvard Narcissists With MBAs Killed Wall Street." *Bloomberg News*. February 17, 2009.

Heath, Chip, and Heath, Dan. *Made to Stick: Why Some Ideas Survive and Others Die*. New York: Random House, 2007.

Henneman, Jim. "Cal Ripken, Jr.: The Everyday Player for The Ages." *HOFN.com*. January 9, 2007. www.hofmag.com/content/view/527/60.

Hoffman, Damien. "Q&A Series: Professional Trader: Adam Guren." *Wall Street Cheat Sheet*. May 2009. http://wallstcheatsheet.com.

————. "Q&A Series: Entrepreneur: Howard Lindzon." *Wall Street Cheat Sheet*. June 2009. http://wallstcheatsheet.com.

————. "Exclusive Interview: Macro-Strategist Barry Ritholtz." *Wall Street Cheat Sheet*. July 1, 2009. http://wallstcheatsheet.com/knowledge/interview-knowledge/exclusive-interview-macro-strategist-barry-ritholtz/?p=736/.

————. "Exclusive Interview: CEO of Minyanville Todd Harrison." *Wall Street Cheat Sheet*. July 27, 2009. http://wallstcheatsheet.com/knowledge/interview-knowledge/exclusive-interview-ceo-of-minyanville-todd-harrison/?p=1029/.

————. "Q&A Series: Macro-Strategist: Barry Ritholtz." *Wall Street Cheat Sheet*. July 30, 2009. http://wallstcheatsheet.com.

Holbrook, Hal. *Wall Street*. DVD. Directed by Oliver Stone. Los Angeles, CA: 20th Century Fox, 1987.

Hovanesian, Mara Der. "The Rabbi of Day Trading." *Businessweek*. December 4, 2000.

Immelt, Jeff. "Innovation Can Give America Back Its Greatness." *Financial Times*. July 8, 2009.

Isana, Ron. "High-Frequency Distraction." *Zerohedge*. July 27, 2009.

"Jillian Michaels Offers Career Advice." *MyFox National Reports*. June 7, 2009.

Jackson, Samuel L. *Pulp Fiction*. DVD. Directed by Quentin Tarantino. New York, NY: Miramax, 1994.

Kiev, Ari. *Trading to Win: The Psychology of Mastering the Markets*. Toronto, Canada: John Wiley & Sons, 1998.

Kirk, Charles. "Avoid Confirmation Bias." *The Kirk Report*. February 11, 2005.

Kuepper, Justin. "Introduction To Level II Quotes." *Investopedia.com*. August 8, 2009. http://investopedia.com/printable.asp?a=/articles/trading/06/level2Quotes.asp.

Ladendorf, Kirk. "Kershner Trading finds profits in market volatility." *Statesman*, April 19, 2009. www.statesman.com/business/content/business/stories/other/04/19/0419kershner.html.

"Lance Armstrong." *Sports Injury Bulletin*. www.sportsinjurybulletin.com/archive/lance-armstrong.html.

Lauerman, John. "Surgery May Have Spurred Steve Jobs's Weight Loss." *Bloomberg*. January 5, 2009.

Leblanc, Tom. "Inside Eli Manning's Automated Condo: A Creston Home Control System Helps The Super Bowl MVP Manage All Aspects of His Home Entertainment System." *Electronichouse*. October 7, 2008. www.electronichouse.com/article/inside_eli_mannings_automated_condo/D3.

Lefevre, Edwin. *Reminiscences of a Stock Operator*. New York: George H. Doran Company, 1923.

Lefton, Brad. "Doctor: 'Ichiro Has A Very Fine Prefrontal Cortex'." *The Seattle Times*. March 19, 2008.

Lewis, Michael. *Liar's Poker*. New York: Penguin, 1990.

———. *Moneyball: The Art of Winning an Unfair Game*. New York: W. W. Norton & Company, 2003.

———. "The No-Stats All-Star." *The New York Times*. February 15, 2009.

Lindlaw, Scott. "Bush Throws Out First Pitch Before Game 3." *USA Today*. October 31, 2001. www.usatoday.com/sports/baseball/01play/2001-10-30-bush.htm.

Louderback, Jeff. "Jon Papelbon." *Sox and Pinstripes*. August 8, 2007.

Lucchetti, Aaron. "Wall Street's B-List Firms Trade on Bigger Rivals' Woes." *The Wall Street Journal*. August 11, 2009.

MacDonald, Dan, and Hutchings, Ted. "Effective Communication for Coaches." www.tradingmarkets.com/.site/stocks/how_to/articles/What-I-Learned-From-the-Best-Trader-I-Have-Ever-Kn-80930.cfm.

Martin, Mitchell. "Surprise Rate Cut Spurs U.S. Stocks." *The New York Times*. January 4, 2001.

Matthews, Chris. *Life's a Campaign: What Politics has Taught Me About Friendship, Rivalry, Reputation, and Success.* New York: Random House, 2007.

Megna, Steve. "How To Make Money Day Trading In the Open." EzineArticles.

Mostel, Josh. *Billy Madison.* DVD. Directed by Tamra Davis. Los Angeles, CA: Universal Studios, 1995.

"Michael Phelps On Making Olympic History." *CBS.* May 31, 2001. www.cbsnews.com/stories/2008/11/25/60minutes/main4633123.shtml?tag=contentMain;content Body.

Netto, John. "10 Attributes of a Great Trader." *TradingMarkets.* www.tradingmarkets.com/.site/stocks/how_to/articles/10-Attributes-of-a-Great-Trader-79932.cfm. January 29, 2009.

Newport, John Paul. "Mastery, Just 10,000 Hours Away: Forget All the Talk of Natural Prodigies—Being the Best Really Takes Hard, Hard, Hard, Work." *The Wall Street Journal.* March 14, 2009.

Noonan, Peggy. "The Case for Getting Off Base: How Republicans Got Cast As The Part of 'Angry White Males'." *The Wall Street Journal.* June 15, 2009.

———. "A Farewell to Harms." *The Wall Street Journal.* July 11, 2009.

———. *On Speaking Well.* New York: HarperCollins Publishers, 1999.

Norris, Floyd. "The Markets: Market Place; 10th Fed Rate Cut This Year Raises Hopes for a Recovery." *The New York Times.* November 7, 2001.

O'Neil, Danny. "Ichiro Is Just So Consistently Consistent." *The Seattle Times.* June 5, 2009.

———. "Notebook | UW Softballers Honored at Safeco Field." *TheSeattleTimes.com.* June 13, 2009. Accessed on

Ortega, Edgar, and Martin, Eric. "High-Frequency Trading Faces Challenge From Schumer." *Bloomberg.* July 27, 2009.

Ortega, Edgar, Martin, Eric, and Kearns, Jeff. "High-Frequency Traders Say Speed Works For Everyone." *Bloomberg.* July 28, 2009.

Peters, Walter. "What I Learned From the Best Trader I Have Ever Known." *TradingMarkets.com.* www.tradingmarkets.com/.site/stocks/how_to/articles/What-I-Learned-From-the-Best-Trader-I-Have-Ever-Kn-80930.cfm.

Petroff, Eric. "Who Is to Blame For the Subprime Crisis?" *Investopedia.com.* June 26, 2009.

Phung, Albert. "Behavioral Finance: Key Concepts, Confirmation and Hindsight Bias." *Investopedia.com.* June 24, 2009.

Pesci, Joe. *My Cousin Vinny.* DVD. Directed by Jonathan Lynn. Los Angeles, CA: 20th Century Fox, 1992.

Pilon, Mary. "The Big Bored: NYSE Traders Look For Diversions as Life Slows on Floor." *The Wall Street Journal.* May 4, 2009.

Raschke, Linda B. "Tape Reading." *Traders Log.* July 29, 2009.

Red Belt. Dir. David Mamet. Perf. Chiwetel Ejiofor, Max Martini. Sony Pictures. 2008. DVD.

Riper, Tom Van. "Most Expensive Private High Schools." *Forbes.* December 11, 2006.

"Rocket Booster: Clemens, Rivera Pitch Yankees Back Into Series." *CNNSI.* October 31, 2001. http://sportsillustrated.cnn.com/baseball/mlb/2001/worldseries/news/2001/10/30/game_three_ap/.

Rosenberg, Hilary. "Investing With: Mayer Offman; Carlin Equities Group." *The New York Times.* May 28, 2000.

Rosenbloom, Corey. "Another Powerful Trend Day Befalls Us." *Afraid To Trade.* May 4, 2009.

Rossignol, Carol. "Effective Communication." *Professional Skater.* July 2008.

———. "Advice from a Pro: Effective Communication for Coaches." *lifeskate.com.* Sept. 5, 2008.

"Run Your Own Race." *Babypips.com.* January 4, 2009.

"S3 Analysis Shows High-Frequency Trading Has No Impact on Retail Equity Pricing." *Earthtimes.* July 7, 2009.

Sacco, Christopher. "You Know How Much Ted Danson Makes?" *The Seinfeld Encyclopedia Blog.* February 26, 2007.

Salas, Caroline. "Eat-What-You-Kill Bond Traders Rise From Wall Street Wreckage." *Bloomberg News.* March 24, 2009.

Saluzzi, J. "High Frequency Trading Roundtable." *Themistrading.* June 17, 2009.

Scherer, Ron. "The Rising Impact Of High Oil Prices." *The Christian Science Monitor.* April 18, 2008.

Schiffman, Betsy. "Sandisk Shares Drop on Intel-Micron Deal." *AP.* November 21, 2005. www.uic.edu/classes/actg/actg516rtr/Notes/05-SanDisk-Shares-Drop.htm.

Schwartz, Allison Abell. "Connecticut's 'Rodeo Drive' Abandoned as Hedge Funds Collapse." *Bloomberg News.* March 20, 2009.

Schwager, Jack D. *The New Market Wizards: Conversations with America's Top Traders.* New York: HarperCollins, 1992.

Serchuk, David. "Decimalization and Its Discontents." March 10, 2009.

Shell, Adam. "Technology Squeezes Out Real, Live Traders." *USA Today.* July 11, 2007.

Sherman, Joel. "All For One: Rotation Close As Fire Yanks-keteers." *The New York Post.* March 16. 2009.

Sorkin, Aaron. *The West Wing.* New York, NY: National Broadcasting Company, 1999.

Smith, Gary B. *How I Trade for a Living.* Toronto, Canada: John Wiley & Sons, Inc, 2000.

Soshnick, Scott. "NFL's Talent Gurus Look Past Model Draft Pick." *Bloomberg News*. April 21, 2009.

———. "Michael Jordan, Shaq Excuse Doesn't Fly Anymore." *Bloomberg News*. June 15, 2009.

Stalter, Anthony. "Peyton Manning." September 30, 2009. http://74.125.47.132/search?q=cache:p10ci3b4f0gj:www.legends.com/69/peyton-manning/+peyton+manning+watches+game+film&cd=2&hl=en&ct=clnk&gl=us.

Steenbarger, Brett. "Reading the Market: More on What Every Short-Term Trader Should Know." *TraderFeed Blog*. August 02, 2006. http://traderfeed.blogspot.com/2006/08/reading-market-more-on-what-every.html.

———. Kershner Trading Group. Austin, Texas. June 23, 2007. Guest Lecture.

———. "Overconfidence and Underconfidence in Trading: Biases in Processing Emotions." *TraderFeed Blog*. July 5, 2007. http://traderfeed.blogspot.com/2007/07/overconfidence-and-underconfidence-in.html.

———. "Stress and Performance in Trading." *TraderFeed Blog*. November 18, 2008. http://traderfeed.blogspot.com/2008/11/stress-and-performance-in-trading.html.

———. "Two Days Down, Ten Day Low: What Next?" *TraderFeed Blog*. June 17, 2009. http://traderfeed.blogspot.com/2009/06/two-days-down-ten-day-low-what-next.html.

———. "Interview With Henry Carstens of Vertical Solutions." *TraderFeed Blog*. June 23, 2009. http://traderfeed.blogspot.com/2009/06/interview-with-henry-carstens-of.html.

———. "Why Daytrading Stocks in the U.S. is an Increasingly Limited Proposition." *TraderFeed Blog*. July 12, 2009. http://traderfeed.blogspot.com/2009/08/why-daytrading-stocks-in-us-is.html.

———. "Trading Order Flow: Lost Skill, Important Art." *TraderFeed Blog*. July 20, 2009. http://traderfeed.blogspot.com/2009/07/trading-order-flow-lost-skill-important.html.

———. "Market Context: The Importance of Non-Confirmations." *TraderFeed Blog*. July 24, 2009. http://traderfeed.blogspot.com/2009/07/market-context-importance-of-non.html.

———. "The Challenging Economics of Trading for a Living." *TraderFeed Blog*. August 1, 2009. http://traderfeed.blogspot.com/search?q=the+challenging+economics

Stein, Boris. Interviews by Chuck Frank. *Traders World* magazine. 2007. Web. March 15, 2008.

Stevenson, Richard W. "The Rate Cut: The Overview; Fed, In a Surprise, Cuts Rates Again, Spurring Markets." *The New York Times*. April 19, 2001.

———. "Fed Lowers Rates by Quarter-point in 6th Cut of Year." *The New York Times*. June 28, 2001.

———. "Fed Cuts Its Benchmark Rate To 2.5%, Hitting 39-Year Low." *The New York Times*. October 3, 2001.

————. "Fed Cuts Key Rate by One-half Point in Aggressive Move." *The New York Times*. November 7, 2002.

Suddath, Claire. "Holy Craps! How a Gambling Grandma Broke the Record." *Time*. May 29, 2009. www.time.com/time/nation/article/0,8599,1901663,00.html.

Taibbi, Matt. "On Giving Goldman a Chance." *Taibblog*. June 30, 2009.

The Federal Reserve Board. "Open Market Operations." June 24, 2009.

Tilsner, Julie. "NYSE Traders: Going The Way of The (Electronic) Dodo." *Blogging-stocks*. February 16, 2007.

Torre, Joe, and Verducci, Tom. *The Yankee Years*. New York: Random House, 2009. Print.

Turner, Nick, and Guglielmo, Connie. "Apple CEO Jobs's Health Reports Since 2003: Timeline." *Bloomberg*. January 14, 2009.

Turner, Toni. *A Beginner's Guide to Day Trading Online*. Avon, MA: Adams Media Corporation, 2000.

"U.S. in 'grip of a bear market'." *The Journal Record* (Oklahoma City). FindArticles. com. September 30, 2009. http://findarticles.com/p/articles/mi_qn4182/is_20000505/ai_n10137348/.

"We Fear What We Don't Understand." *Kid Dynamite's World*. July 26, 2009. http://fridayinvegas.blogspot.com/2009/07/we-fear-what-we-dont-understand.html.

Welch, Jack, and Suzy. "Why We Tweet: We're Now Big Fans of Twitter. To Those With Eyebrows Aloft, Here's How It Happened." *BusinessWeek*. June 2, 2009.

Welch, Suzy. "The Rule of 10-10-10." *Oprah*, May 8, 2009. www.oprah.com.

Brackney, Carson. "What's Confirmation Bias?" *GreenPandaTreeHouse*. June 2009.

Whitmer, Michael. "Rankings Go By The Numbers: Mickelson Could Overtake Woods." *The Boston Globe*. March 26, 2009.

"Why are oil prices so high?" *BBC News*. September 28, 2004.

Wooden, John. *Wooden on Leadership: How to Create a Winning Organization*. New York: McGraw-Hill, 2005.

Wyckoff, Jim. "Kaufman Uses Multiple Trading Methods, Cites Market 'Noise'." *Traders Log*. June 15, 2009. www.traderslog.com/Kaufman-Interview.htm.

Zuckerman, Mortimer. "Nine Reasons the Economy is Not Getting Better: Jobs Data Paint A Discouraging Picture Of More Pain To Come." *U.S. News*. July 13, 2009.

About the Author

M ike Bellafiore is a co-founder of SMB Capital, a proprietary trading firm in New York City. He is a regular contributor to thestreet.com's RealMoney. He has written numerous articles for *SFO* magazine. His trading strategies have been featured in Brett Steenbarger's book, *The Daily Trading Coach*. He is a regular contributor to the SMB Blog, which provides market stories and trading advice. He hosts SMB University on StockTwits TV. He is a graduate of the University of Connecticut School of Law and a former member of the University of Connecticut Board of Trustees. He currently resides in New York City.

Index